Different Times

~~ A View ~~

Narrated by

William Kenneth Jones

Bright Pen

Visit us online at www.authorsonline.co.uk

A Bright Pen Book

Copyright © Authors OnLine Ltd 2006

Text Copyright © William Kenneth Jones 2006

Cover design by William Kenneth Jones ©

All rights reserved. No part of this publication may be reproduced, stored in a retrieval system, or transmitted in any form or by any means, electronic, mechanical, photocopy, recording or otherwise, without prior written permission of the copyright owner. Nor can it be circulated in any form of binding or cover other than that in which it is published and without similar condition including this condition being imposed on a subsequent purchaser.

ISBN 0 7552 0210 4

Authors OnLine Ltd
19 The Cinques
Gamlingay, Sandy
Bedfordshire SG19 3NU
England

This book is also available in e-book format, details of which are available at
www.authorsonline.co.uk

A Dedication

This collection of narratives is dedicated to the memory of my mother who nourished and watched over her children, and her mother who, in her time, did the same.

An Appreciation

I wish to express a particular thanks to my sister, Ellen, for contributing some of the scenes and for assiduously researching the needed historical details. Also for supplementing my earliest recollections by giving dates to events that my childhood memories - arising as they did from the timeless time of childhood - could not give.

In addition, I wish to express gratitude to Aidan O'Rourke www.aidan.co.uk for encouraging the completion of these narratives and for giving advice and technical assistance regarding cover design.

Finally, I wish to express my appreciation to those who read these narratives. In doing so, they will share with me the memories of a time once known; and, by this, resurrect the spirit I believe that time possessed.

A Regret

Many people involved in the various incidents portrayed in these narratives are no longer with us, so permission to use names cannot be obtained.

However, where names are used, they are, I believe, in a context that does credit to the persons mentioned.

Contents

1.	Prologue	1
2.	A Glance at the Setting	5
3.	A Normal Part of Life	7
4.	As a Matter of Interest: Charter Street	23
5.	No Time for Childhood	27
6.	As a Matter of Interest: Churchill and Charter Street	40
7.	Making Do	46
8.	Work Is Where You Find It	53
9.	High Spirits - Low Expectations	61
10.	Through a Child's Eyes	67
11.	The House	69
12.	As a Matter of Interest: Wirelesses and Crystal Sets	85
13.	The District	92
14.	Earning a Crust	107
15.	Astonished Eyes and Ears	117
16.	As a Matter of Interest: The Airship R100	125
17.	A Walk Around the Shops	130
18.	And Even More Shops	151
19.	A Matter of Life and Death	172
20.	Kettle, Coal and Soft Gaslight	184
21.	Gasworks and Games	196
22.	As a Matter of Interest: Coal, Gas and Steam	205
23.	The River Irk	211
24.	The Dark Arch	220
25.	Child's Play Isn't…	227
26.	Swings, Steps, Slides and Skipping Ropes	238
27.	As a Matter of Interest: Ring and Pretend Games	262
28.	All the Street's a Stage	268
29.	The Jubilee and Cake for Tea	279
30.	As a Matter of Interest: King George V	292
31.	What Would the Neighbours Think?	297
32.	In Tune with the Times	320
33.	A Question of Coal in the Backyard	328
34.	The End of a Time?	350
35.	No Step to Sit On	366
36.	Epilogue	373
37.	To Complete the Picture	376

1
Prologue

In the last five years of my mother's life (she died in the October of 1991) I arranged to spend more time with her. By then, she'd found her favourite pastime of reading increasingly difficult and, from time to time, seemed to find it beneficial to reminisce about certain events with someone willing to share her memories.

During our conversations, various recollections emerged with a clarity I found quite startling. These revealed aspects of her childhood I hadn't previously known; and portrayed a time so remarkably different from the one we know now it seemed incredible that the world she knew as a child and the one she experienced during her later years could exist in the space of one lifetime.

In the midst of our discussions, I came across an article written by an American historian - Alan Brinkley - that echoed aspects of this change by stating:

Where once society organised itself around a cluster of powerful and widely shared values, many of them emphasising restraint, self-discipline and personal responsibility, it is now dominated by a new and more permissive ethos that emphasises personal fulfilment, desire and identity.

It may be that many people would dispute his implied sharp discontinuity between a particular period and the one immediately following - and, with this, the emergence of completely opposite values. Also, his evaluation centred on American society and it might be possible he'd offer a different assessment regarding other places? Nevertheless, it seemed to me the change he inferred has parallels in Western societies in general.

This suggestion of discontinuity seemed to permeate my mother's recollections. Not in any way intended to make judgements but more in the form of explanatory remarks related to happenings she thought might not "fit in" with present-day thinking, when she'd say:

"Of course, we thought about things differently in those days."

Such were the extent of the changes revealed in our conversations that this comment emerged quite often; and sometimes with a touch of sadness - particularly when she spoke about an incident concerning her friend, Nancy, who we'll meet as these narratives progress.

However, to get back to our conversations in general; and why I tended to delve especially into the economic conditions and social attitudes prevailing during the time of her childhood.

Before giving her my long overdue attention, I happened to see a report published in 1901 by the researcher Seebohm Rowntree. This referred to social circumstances existing in the year preceding my mother's birth - stating no less than twenty-eight per cent of the population lived at a level barely satisfying physical needs.

Remembering this, and knowing that she was born in an area we would now deem massively deprived, I deliberately turned the conversations towards her earlier experiences and how they might relate to Rowntree's findings. This seemed all the more compelling because the conditions of that long-ago report still "lived" within the memory of a person I'd taken so much for granted.

As our talks progressed, I also recalled an article mentioning a Tea-lady reputed to have made a comment to Winston Churchill on his visit to the blitzed East End of London, during World War Two. She remarked it was just as well her house had been bombed that day - before she started doing up her parlour.

This called to mind that she and my mother were of the same generation and - considering their birthplaces - born under similar circumstances. They also, it seemed, shared the same capacity to express the most tragic events in a spirit of light-hearted humour, which appeared to be a typical trait of that generation. In addition, the Churchill incident became all the more relevant since he entered into one of my mother's earliest - although brief - recollections.

Numerous illustrations of this light-heartedness emerged during our conversations: one of these being my mother's tale of "lentils for tea" - which you'll come to know if you care to read through the narratives. When she told me of this event, it wasn't so much the conditions implied by Rowntree's Report being a constant experience for many in those times, which came out in her telling, but more the joy of knowing there was, that day, some lentil soup to anticipate. The recaptured joy that came to her voice when relating this incident told me more about the resilience people in such circumstances can develop than anything else ever could.

It seemed to me this resilience - personified by the Tea-lady's words and the experiences of the generation to which she and my mother belonged - was what made Churchill's "fighting on the beaches, in the streets and never surrendering" much more than mere rhetoric. If the words hadn't expression the real nature of the people of that time, they would've gone down in history as a falsity and not for the true spirit later events showed they actually represented.

In the greater scheme of things, my mother would be considered as "ordinary". Yet the success of most endeavours and therefore the direction of history depend on the qualities of all such ordinary people - whose lives, in the main, hardly receive a mention. Because of this, I felt it might prove worthwhile and even represent an obligation to portray some of the conditions in which these "unremarkable" people once lived and how their qualities may've been generated.

As one of the ordinary folk, my mother would also, perhaps, be perceived as a person without distinction. Nevertheless, she was a perfect representation of her class, generation, circumstances and time. And this, I believe, is her distinction.

But returning to that remarkably different world implied by my mother's recollections: it seems the period in which Churchill and the Tea-lady played their part marks the great divide between the two worlds my mother's lifetime encompassed. This divide appeared even more startling because, as inferred, many of the attitudes, values and beliefs of the second half of the century in which she died seemed directly opposite to those of the first half in which she was born.

Her recollections revealed these changes with such dramatic force that those small but enormously insisting words - "how?" and "why?" - constantly fretted in the back of my mind. I therefore felt compelled to explore whatever reasons and explanations seemed appropriate. These I've presumed to offer in the latter part of the narratives.

Yet - if you progress through all of the narratives - you'll see the pre 1939-45 world was not only that of the deprivations implied by the Rowntree Report, but also one possessing the less reported richness of neighbourly communities and the relationship of people within those communities. And since there's so much concern about the communities we now try to construct, going back to a time when they "lived" in a very different way from those of the present may help cast some light on present-day concerns.

Moreover, we've experienced the period of transition from one century to its next, which seems all the more important because it coincides with the end of a millennium. And to look back over the full years of the millennium's final century, whilst the memories of those allowing us to do so are still accessible, seems all the more compelling - especially when the two halves of that one hundred years appear so distinct, they might have been centuries apart.

We must also bear in mind that the direction each period takes is one set by its previous. Therefore, to know about whatever aspects of this preceding time we are able to know might, perhaps, indicate how and why our present society is set on the path it seems to be following.

The experiences of a child in any particular period might be thought to have very little contribution to make. However, any pair of eyes can offer a viewpoint that may, in their own special way of seeing, present their own distinct insights. Therefore, and in addition to my mother's recollections, I've included the period applicable to myself as a boy in the nineteen-thirties - the decade leading up to the events bringing about the century's great divide.

To begin: we'll start in the first years of the nineteen-hundreds in a district near the centre of Manchester. Although set in that particular place, we'll soon recognise it represents all such places where people similar to and possessing the same resilient spirit of the mentioned Tea-lady may've been found.

It seems to me that all the possibilities of human nature are present in every age. Yet certain periods have their own particular demands - which, I believe, bring out the qualities necessary to face even the most adverse of circumstances. To see how this may be so is, I believe, all the justification we need to re-live such a time; through the memories of those who knew that time...

~~~~~~~~~~~~~~~~~~~~~~~~~~~~~~~~~~~~

Below is a quick and - to her unexpected photo I took of my mother during the mentioned conversations.

She had a high capacity to face adversity and a laugh to gladden your heart.

2
A Glance at the Setting

~~~~~~~~~~~~~~~~~~~~~~~~~~~~~~~~~~~~

An undulating plain, or rather a collection of little hills. Below the hills a narrow river - the Irwell - flows slowly to the Irish Sea. Two streams, the Medlock and the Irk, wind through the uneven ground and after a thousand bends, flow into the river... the fetid, muddy waters stained with a thousand colours by the factories they pass...

A sort of black smoke covers the city. The sun seen through it is a disc without rays... the crunching wheels of machinery, the shriek of steam from boilers, the regular beat of looms, the heavy rumble of carts, those are the noises from which you can never escape in the sombre half-light...

The above is a description of Manchester's industrial centre as seen by the French philosopher and aristocrat, Alexis de Tocqueville, during a visit he made to the city in 1835.

He saw with obvious trepidation an explosion of industry whose magnitude had never before been witnessed. What he did not know - but we in retrospect can know - is what he viewed could be described as the labour of the modern world's birth.

The nature of its energy is indicated by the fact that in 1814 - just over twenty years before his arrival - power looms did not exist in Manchester, but by the time of his visit their presence had exceeded 30,000. Also at that time, Lancashire possessed more power-driven machinery than the rest of the world put together - and most of this concentrated in and immediately around Manchester. These facts combined with Tocqueville's description had, to me, such imaginative force I tried to encapsulate its imagery in verse - a media capable of expressing a multitude of feelings in a minimum of words.

What emerged is a million miles away from being "Wordsworthian" - and, perhaps, amusing in its attempt. Nevertheless, it expresses my first deep felt emotion upon coming across Tocqueville's view of a place in which my antecedents and I were born. In this context, my attempt is offered as nothing more than an indication of that emotion:

> *Tocqueville said, all he could see*
> *Was awful, striving, industry.*
> *He wondered on the fate of folk*
> *Who stoked its fire*

And breathed its smoke.
He wondered how such folk could live?
Yet, nevertheless, they did...

In the following narratives, we'll find out how many of them did live.

The verse and Tocqueville's view are offered because they focus on an area we in turn shall view, some sixty-five years later than the time when he made his observation; and where we'll see a continuation of the industry in which people still strived in an atmosphere almost unchanged. Also, many of the streets of our particular visit existed at the time of his arrival, so the scene will be, in many ways, much the same as the one he saw.

The place of our proposed visit is portrayed in the photos you'll see if you choose to read on. As these photos indicate, the area is now in a state of dilapidation and neglect - representing a last silent witness of the nineteenth-century impelled "crunching wheels of machinery and the shriek of steam from boilers".

However, let's experience the area when industry's wheels and the steam from boilers were incessantly heard.

There's no convenient time-machine for us to step into, so we'll need to go back by way of a link constructed by the memory of a person who knew the place when it retained much of what Tocqueville saw.

If you're ready to read on, we can go there now...

3
A Normal Part of Life

~~~~~~~~~~~~~~~~~~~~~~~~~~~~~~~~~~~~~~~

My mother (Elizabeth) was born in September 1902 - sixty-seven years after Tocqueville's visit. No relevance, of course, except that the district in which her life began still contained many features described by that visitor.

She came into the world in a small terraced house in a street called Hargreaves Street - this no doubt named after James Hargreaves who invented, in 1764, a device he called the 'Spinning Jenny' which allowed a number of threads to be spun simultaneously by one person. This principle of enabling a single operator to perform many identical tasks became - it seems - a crucial factor in generating the industrial world into which she was born.

The street was (and still is at the time of writing) situated about half a mile from the city centre in an area known to those who lived there as "Red Bank". Its name was, it seems, derived from a prominent slope of red clay or sandstone once forming the bank of the River Irk in that place, which may have existed at the time of Tocqueville's visit - but this is speculation on my part.

I sketched a map of the Hargreaves Street area based on my mother's remembrance, which I offer below.

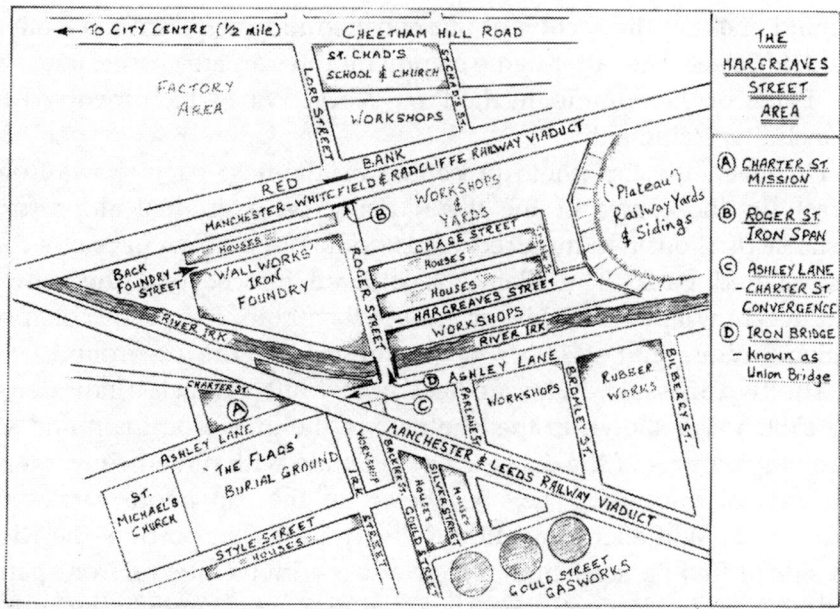

At the time of my asking about the features of the district, her recollections had to span a gap of almost eighty years and many of the aspects she would've known in her childhood had long since disappeared.

The photos you'll find on the following pages supplement the sketch. They were taken in the early 1990s during the extensive demolition of the area; but the main features as they were at the time my mother knew the place still existed. So, with the aid of sketch and the offered photographs, I hope a "clear picture" of the district she would've known in her early childhood will emerge as we progress; and give an "impression" of the sort of view Tocqueville experienced.

I subsequently checked the offered sketch against a map published in the early 1920s, which I found some time after completing my drawing. This shows the area as it was near the time when she lived in the district and indicated that her memory had a workable accuracy. For this reason, and because my drawing depicts her actual remembrance, I've left it as originally produced.

From the sketch, you'll notice that Hargreaves Street (portrayed near the centre of the sketch) forms a right angle with Roger Street - then the main street of the district. Also, the lower end of the last mentioned street had a short length of bridge spanning the River Irk. This used to be known as Union Bridge; possibly because of it being built to join Roger Street to what was known, in the time we'll be visiting, as Ashley Lane.

In later times, Ashley Lane - for some reason - became known as Aspin Lane and the section of our consideration acquired the name of Dantzic Street. The latter name commemorates an area associated with the Battle of the Somme, in the First World War, which involved the Manchester Regiment.

However, the top photo presented on the next page shows Roger Street (in the centre of the view) rising on a gradual slope for a distance of about two hundred yards, to then meet the curve of a road named Red Bank. The "Bank" is situated just beyond the railway viaduct shown in the middle ground of the photo. The partly collapsed Union Bridge - shut off by a row of railings - is in the foreground.

The two massive, many arched, brick-built viaducts (indicated in the sketch and shown in the photos) are the most dominant and still standing features of the district. They contain within their convergence the area of our visit. The one shown in the top photo carries the Manchester-Whitefield-Radcliffe Railway Line that borders the River Irk side of Red Bank's length. This viaduct with its integral iron span is at the top end of Roger Street. The other viaduct - shown in the bottom photo - carries its section of the Manchester-Leeds Railway Line. This is situated beyond Union Bridge from Hargreaves Street and therefore on the far side of Ashley Lane. Both these lines merge at the city centre under the massive roof of Victoria Station.

The next photo is a view along Hargreaves Street. It presents what you'd see if looking down the street's length whilst standing on the patch of cobbles revealed by the worn tarmac in the photo above.

The dilapidated Union Bridge (once known, locally, as the "Iron Bridge") and the viaduct of the Manchester-Leeds Railway Line would be on our right-hand side.

When my mother first became aware of the district, the viaducts cut their way through and above a conglomeration of factories; foundries; factory-yards; storage-sheds; blacksmiths forges; workshops and clusters of small terraced houses - the latter compressed into whatever space the dominating industry had rejected.

To gain an insight into this first awareness let's, by way of our imagination, go back to the time of her early childhood, to experience the district as it was in the first decade of the nineteen-hundreds, long before its final dereliction shown in the photos. Let's begin by standing at the corner formed by Hargreaves Street and Roger Street.

Looking along the length of Hargreaves Street we'd see - on our right - a huddle of workshops crowding along the River Irk's bank; and, facing these, a row of terraced houses containing the one in which my mother was born.

A feature dominating the street is the high wall at its end, holding back a steeply rising earth embankment some hundred and fifty yards or so from where we stand. This forms a plateau built level with the height of the viaduct, and thereby being thirty or so feet above the street's cobbles. A railway siding occupies its height and a collection of engines and carriages loom precariously along the edge. To our left, and towards the end of the street, a cluster of factory-yards thrust against the embankment's wall.

However, let's turn away from Hargreaves Street and shift our attention to the other side of Roger Street.

Across this street is the long, dark-brick frontage of an iron foundry, locally known as The Wallworks. This stretches to our right and left. It contains a series of soot-grimed windows and - about half way along its extent - a large wooden gate. Its frontage occupies the length of Roger Street from the bank of the River Irk up to the narrow width of Back Foundry Street - a street contained between the end of the foundry and the high arches of the viaduct.

The start of this street is on the left-hand side of Roger Street and a hundred yards or so up its slope from where we're standing. The viaduct's brick archways appear to loom large above the slate roofs of the row of terraced houses we see on the street's far side. We'd know they were squeezed into the narrow space at the base of the viaduct, during the decade of 1850, to accommodate foundry workers moving into the district - not long after the erection of the structure that towers above the houses they'd occupy.

The iron span - some twenty or so feet above the cobbles of Roger Street and to the right of the row's end - links the line of archways behind Back Foundry Street to their continuation on the right-hand side of the span. A short stay in the district would soon reveal how its metal construction amplifies the already fearsome noise of the trains as they rumble along that part of the viaduct.

Beyond this span, we can just make out the upper half of the tall watchtower belonging to Strangeways Prison. Moving to our left a few steps or so from the corner of Hargreaves Street allows us to see - to the right of the span - the upper part of the tower belonging to Saint Chad's Church. Both these buildings stand on the much higher ground of Cheetham Hill Road and - although not a great distance away - their outlines are constantly dimmed by the smoke-haze induced by the railways and factories all around.

A little way up the slope of Roger Street and on the side of the street where we're standing we see the opening of Chase Street. It's about the same length as Hargreaves Street and ends at the factory yards crowding the base of the railway embankment. The nearest side of this street contains a row of terraced houses crowded into the limited space available. These are identical to those in Hargreaves Street and share the same rear alleyway.

Just beyond Chase Street, a tight conglomeration of yards and workshops take up the remaining length of Roger Street to crowd against the railway viaduct.

But the main thing constantly thrusting itself into our awareness amidst this confusion of brick, slate, iron and steel, is the continual noise of industry and the passage of trains swirling their smoke down from the height of the viaducts - this to mix with the constant seepage from the factories and workshops. Thus, on that first day of September 1902, when my mother's life began, this was the air she first breathed and the noises she first heard and the sights she would soon begin to know.

At the time of her birth, her mother (my Granny Corrigan) was about twenty-eight years of age. She already had three young children - Willy, Jim and John - who'd escaped the more serious health hazards of early childhood. But one child who did not, she nursed through the long hours of a winter's night until the baby's condition began to worsen.

Swaddling the infant in a blanket to keep out the chilled early morning mist creeping up from the River Irk, and with her shawl wrapping the infant tightly to her, she took the gas-lit walk up the mist-dampened cobbles of Roger Street; then to pass under the its iron span. Crossing the cobbles of Red Bank, she climbed the steeper slope of Lord Street to turn right into Cheetham Hill Road. On admittance into the Infirmary along that road, she was told:

"The child has died. Take it home".

And so she did - to arrange for the child's burial.

But the shadow of death was no stranger to the infant's cot. In that time and circumstances, one child in every five died before reaching its first year. None of the provisions later periods would take for granted, which protects and insulates against life's indifferences, existed. To those of her situation, what happened had to be endured as a normal part of life. Grief there would be, yet a grief not uncommon to those around her.

But let's digress, for a while, to travel further back in time to the earlier years of the person whose walk we've just followed.

The main part of her childhood she spent in Silver Street - shown in the lower middle part of the offered sketch. This consisted of a narrow alleyway of back-to-back dwellings built between two streets then known as Parker Street and Back Irk Street, in a district called Irk Town. The area would appear essentially the same as when Tocqueville made his visit but with the addition of the Manchester-to-Leeds railway viaduct that came to loom large above the tallest of workshops. The route this line follows is the one surveyed in 1839 by George Stephenson, of 'Rocket' fame, in co-operation with his son, Robert. Its construction - involving the viaducts spanning the Irk valley - began in the decade immediately after that survey. However, the area for our particular attention we'll find on the other side of this viaduct away from Hargreaves Street, but in actual distance not much more than a stone's throw from that street.

During her time in Silver Street, certain members of the family (chiefly her elder brother, William - who lost an arm in an accident when a young boy) earned a living by soldering squares of tinned metal on to wire skewers to make price tags for the local shops and markets. This they did in the house they occupied - using the heat from the household fire. Her father earned a living by painting signs for the various businesses in the district.

Her mother, Mary (my mother's grandmother and therefore my great-grandmother - whom, it seems, had an aptitude for pacifying even the most restless of horses) acquired a few extra shillings as a horse minder at various nearby stables and at Shude Hill Market. This she continued to do up to the time she died at the age of seventy - when she had, by then, moved to Heelis Street (a street we'll visit in a later period). Before the Old Age Pension brought its first tentative relief to those of her circumstances, work had to be done until it could be done no more.

But let's return to Silver Street as we'd find it in the latter part of the eighteen-hundreds. A glance along its short length shows it being little more than a narrow passageway, starting at a cluster of small workshops squeezed against the side of the Manchester-Leeds viaduct. Although the street is situated outside the convergence formed by the two viaducts - and is thereby away from the large iron foundry and the River Irk's impurities - its position allows no escape from industrial domination. Looking along the street away from its viaduct reveals three massive gasometers forming part of a chaotic sprawl taking up a large area of what is known as Gould Street.

These structures occupy the top of a steep slope rising from behind a high wall, similar to the one we saw at the end of Hargreaves Street. This wall borders the far side of what is no more than a narrow passageway, known, then, as Charlotte Street (probably named after the wife of George III) which forms a 'T' junction with the top end of Silver Street.

Thus, the bulk of the tall gasometers - commanding as they do the high ground immediately beyond the end of Silver Street - block out much of the sky in a confine already gloomed by the viaduct. The street of our visit is, therefore, in many ways less favourably situated than Hargreaves Street and similarly subjected to the constant noise and smoke from factories and trains.

In an effort to escape these conditions, the family moved to Style Street - near the defunct burial ground belonging to Saint Michael's Church. Its space became locally known as Saint Michael's Flags, because flagstones eventually covered most of its area.

A short time before making their move, this rare piece of open space had been part-landscaped to produce, around its edges, what was, for that district, unusual greenery. This represented an effort to create a playground for the local children along with provisions for adults to sit - despite the sad and grim reminders of the district's many cholera epidemics that the once extensively used burial area presented in some of its remaining gravestones.

The photo - taken in the early 1990s and offered on the next page - shows a section of the flags' area with the disturbed remnants of some of its stones.

One of the nearest contains this inscription:

Esther Daughter of James & Catherine Morris died May 25th 1795 1 year & 6 Months

However, to continue with our main theme. Although the gasometers and viaduct could still be seen from their new location, the street's position and its elevation above the viaduct's height (conferred by the rising slope of the district) did, at least, provide some escape from the total domination of both structures.

In addition, the move offered that rare commodity previously mentioned: an open space made all the more unusual because of its greenery.

But this advantage was relinquished by the person we followed on that early morning walk when she married my grandfather, John Corrigan, whose family came from Ireland to settled along Cheetham Hill Road, near Saint Chad's Church. This move took her to Hargreaves Street, which - as we know - offered no real improvement on the conditions experienced in Silver Street (except, perhaps, the housing was marginally better).

So, our meandering has returned us to Hargreaves Street and the period we left prior to making a diversion into an earlier time. Our return offers an opportunity to examine another feature of the area - one which the local people call 'The Boneyard' - located by the bank of the River Irk and not far beyond the railway embankment we saw at the end of Hargreaves Street.

In the period of our visit, various versions of the boneyard existed in and around almost all the industrial districts of most towns and cities. These represented an age when the lack of widespread and efficient refrigeration necessitated animals being brought into the urban areas to be butchered where immediately needed, in what were then called Slaughter-houses. Also, the multitude of work-horses employed at that time were - after serving their "useful life" - similarly dealt with in what went by the name of Knacker Yards, also found at various locations within industrial cities. The particular boneyard of our interest existed as a part of this general process; its main purpose being to store and clean the accumulation of bones it then supplied to industries finding them useful.

Before the ubiquitous plastic became the material for virtually everything, bones were extensively used for making cutlery handles; buttons; hairbrushes; corset-stays; collar studs; carved ornamentation and numerous other artefacts. Those suitable for such usage were prepared and supplied by the yards with the rejected remainders being ground up - in situ - for fertiliser or for making bone-glue.

An unintended by-product of this storage (as no doubt it was for all similar places during the hot weather) happened to be the accumulation of maggots amongst the piles of bones waiting to be cleaned - a happening not discouraged because it "helped" with the "cleaning" process. As a consequence of this, a person the children of the district named "The Maggot Man" regularly called during the summer months. This he did with an open cart containing buckets to collect the proliferation, which my mother believed he sold for fish-bait. That impulsive curiosity possessed by all children at all times and in all places invariably overcomes any sensibilities they tend to learn later; and the Maggot Man became another subject for that almost insatiable urge. His comings and goings were always watched by a gathering of wide-eyed children.

But, for most times, the children of that district had little time for what seemed idle curiosity. One aspect of my mother's childhood involved joining the gangs of children following the carts from Gould Street Gasworks as they carried their loads of coke down the slope to the local iron foundries. She and her brother, Jim, would scramble amongst the many kids gathered to pick up any coke that happened to fall off the horse-drawn carts jolting down the cobbled incline.

Some of the coke fresh from the retorts could give an uncomfortable burn. As a precaution against this, the children developed the habit of spitting on their fingers before picking up the hot pieces - a practice done with little time to test its efficacy; for if these pieces were left lying around, even for a second, more daring fingers claimed possession. Those with a quick hand and a tolerance for discomfort could fill a bucket from these "fall-offs", caused by the carts bumping over the rough cobbles. This represented a valuable supplement to the sometimes-scarce fuel for the home fire.

Besides this early schooling in the art of survival in the streets around her, the formal aspect of my mother's education took place at Saint Chad's School. This, as we previously saw, is situated above Red Bank and at the corner of Saint Chad's Street and Cheetham Hill Road. Its strict regime focused on the spiritual welfare of the individual rather than their worldly needs - a focus deemed proper for that time.

However, another centre existed to address the more mundane essentials of its attendees by providing nourishment - such as a cup of cocoa and a slice of buttered bread - to ease the many stomachs not frequently filled in that district. This much valued and constantly attended place (officially named "Charter Street Ragged School", but known to the local people as "Charter Street" or simply as "the Mission") was, and still is - but with a change of purpose - situated almost opposite the old burial ground of Saint Michael's Flags, where a section of the Manchester-Leeds viaduct spans the convergence of what used to be known as Charter Street and Ashley Lane.

As matter of interest: Ashley Lane derived its name from Ashley Field; a once verdant area on the other side of the Irk from the later built Roger Street. This witness to a pastoral past finally disappeared under the industrial encroachment, beginning in 1820.

At the time of taking the next group of photos (the early 1990s) the Mission happened to be in the process of having its industrial grime of many years removed, revealing the original impressiveness shown in the first photo.

An ornamented plaque high on the wall to the left-hand side of the corner entrance commemorates the construction of its particular section of the building. The plaque declares:

The Rt. Hon. the 7th Earl of Shaftesbury laid this stone on the day of the 6th October 1866.

This new construction provided a front-extension to the original Bricklayers Hall in Nelson Street (the street alongside the Mission that connects Charter Street to Ashley Lane). It seems the Hall - first used by the Mission in 1860 - proved inadequate to meet growing demands.

Behind the plaque is a cache containing newspapers produced on the day mentioned, along with coins minted that year. The total cost of the extension at that time came to £2,030 - which, as near as I can ascertain, would be something like £850,000 in present-day value.

The Earl became responsible for much of the legislation alleviating the consequences of the Industrial Revolution as it affected those suffering from its worse indifferences. Other endeavour emerged in his forty-year role as chairman of the 'Ragged Schools Union'; a position instrumental in building the Mission of our interest, whose function during our visit is the same as when it was first constructed.

Before becoming the 7th Earl, in 1851, he held the title of Lord Ashley; under which he helped fund the Mission from its first concept. He also assisted Florence Nightingale in her efforts to enhance soldiers' welfare and sponsored various Acts restricting child labour.

Returning to the plaque - shown in the photo below: the stone embossment beneath the plaque's ornamental frame records the date of the building's construction. It reads: OCTOBER 6th 1866

Let's image it's a Sunday evening, some time during the year 1910. And with the aid of the photos and the details you've just read, Let's imagine we're now in Hargreaves Street and will accompany my mother as an eight-year-old on a visit to Charter Street Mission. We'll make this visit along with other children coming from Chase Street and also from Back Foundry Street.

Leaving her house, we turn left into Roger Street and then cross the short length of iron bridge spanning the River Irk. The black-brick wall of the iron foundry we know as the Wallworks looms high on our right where its buildings extend over the Irk. Just ahead of us (at the Ashley Lane and Charter Street convergence) tower the tile-clad walls supporting the viaduct's massive girdered section spanning both passageways - either of which we could use to reach the Mission.

The white but smoke-stained tiles, cladding the walls up to the underside of the metal structure they support, are intended to relieve the gloom cast by the heavy span. Nevertheless, they fail to realise this intention: the contrast between the white tiles and the span's blackened iron and steel seem to make its girders hang more threateningly above our heads. As we approach its bulk, we become mindful of the trains that constantly shake its structure and pour their smoke down to the cobbles where we're about to walk.

As if fearful of the continual intimidation the structure represents, the cluster of small shops and work-places to our left along Ashley Lane seem to huddle together for mutual protection against the thundering threat of iron and steam passing constantly above their roofs.

To give this threat a reality, a train rushes along the girdered span - whereupon the whole latticework of iron and steel echoes and vibrates from the weight and noise of its passage. We instinctively swerve away from the cloud of acrid smoke swirling down from the span to hurriedly take the left-hand passageway, where the smoke has not yet reached.

To our left and just beyond the span is the curved length of a high brick wall. This forms the left-hand side of the Ashley Lane continuation we've now entered. The wall contains a narrow opening about half way along its length, which gives access to a well-worn flight of stone steps built against the wall to the right of the opening. These lead up to what was once the burial ground belonging to Saint Michael's Church. However, the space has become know as Saint Michael's Flags - this because of it being covered with flagstone to provide a place where children can play in a district that provides little space for their enjoyment.

It's also the place where we saw the sparse greenery that seemed an odd intrusion in a world where its presence had long since been banished.

The Flags' steps are known to the people of the district as "Angel Steps"; a name given because it is said that local folk saw visions of angels at the top of the steps - as if guarding the spirits of the children buried beneath the Flags.

Just ahead of us and to our right, and immediately beyond the high bulk of the viaduct, is the place we've come to see: the tall, four-storey building known as Charter Street Mission. It stands thrust against the viaduct as if to rival its height; as if asserting its charitable intentions in defiance of the trains' noise and smoke and their constant shaking of the iron span slanting alongside its rear wall.

Yet the Mission's apparent defiance has not been able to prevented the blackening of its once bright-brick exterior, and thereby bearing the mark of industrial supremacy in the greater scheme of things all around. But the children we're with seem happy, as indicated by their chatter as we walked along beside them; for - within the walls of the place we've come to visit - charity still prevails; and this is what we want, so much, to see.

The route we used to avoid the smoke gave access to the Mission's Ashley Lane entrance. We could've gone by way of Charter Street if the smoke had allowed, and saw the commemorative plaque high on the Mission's wall. Also, we could've seen the carved stone embellishment above the corner door with its title "Working Girls Home" - telling the building originally provided a place of refuge for homeless young girls.

But the smoke has now cleared, and the children from beyond Irk Street (the street which meets Ashley Lane on the other side of the viaduct away from the mission) are only just beginning to make their way under the girdered span.

We'll be in the mission before them. And - if we're quick - we'll get a seat by the table where the lady serves the bread and cocoa...

~~~~~~~~~~~~~~~~~~~~~~~~~~~~~~~~~~~~~~

The next illustration presents a copy of a map showing the Rochdale Road area and its vicinity as it was in 1922, and virtually as it was in 1900. It shows a section of Manchester containing the districts of our interest.

The lower rectangle frames the area we've just visited and the one to its right delineates an area we'll visit later.

The rest of the map indicates other places we'll need to visit from time to time as we progress through the narratives.

4
As a Matter of Interest:
Charter Street

~~~~~~~~~~~~~~~~~~~~~~~~~~~~~~~~~~

We've walked around a district typical of the many found in the industrial inner cities in the first decades of the nineteen-hundreds. In this, we visited an institution representing what, in the Rowntree Report world, would be the main and sometimes the only means many people in such areas had of gaining any amelioration.

To add some depth to our understanding of the district's economic plight, it's worth quoting the contents of a Christmas Appeal sent out by Charter Street Mission in the year preceding my mother's birth and - by coincidence - in the year when the mentioned Report was first published.

A person we'll come to know in more detail when we make our next visit produced this appeal. It's worth presenting in full in order to gain some appreciation of the effort this type of establishment and the people serving within it made to relieve the conditions indicated by the Rowntree findings.

Christmas Appeal, 1901.
Charter Street Ragged School and Working Girl's Home,
Angel Meadow,
And Manchester Medical Mission, Red Bank

I beg to enlist your help and sympathy, during the coming winter, on behalf of the work carried on in the institutions.

I think the nature and extent of our labours during the last forty-seven years in this, the poorest and most neglected part of the city, is pretty well known to our subscribers and friends.

Each winter, thousands of poor, helpless children are provided with food, clogs and clothing; and every Sunday morning during the season, hundreds of destitute men and women (most of whom are without a friend in the world) are served with breakfast; and we try, by God's help and the bestowal of a word of comfort and cheer, to arouse in them a feeling of hope which may lead them to a higher and noble life.

The children, however, always have our first consideration in all branches of our work (over four thousand of whom pass through the schools each week during the winter) and it is for them that I would especially plead. Their childhood is a hard and bitter one, with a bleak outlook for the future. One never meets or looks upon a poor ragged child without thinking of Him who commanded to us, if we would remember Him, to think of these little ones: "for inasmuch as ye do it unto the least of these, ye do it unto Me."

Our own Christmas will be happier in the knowledge that we have contributed some measure of comfort and pleasure to these children, whose circumstances at the very outset of life are such as tells against their future. By making the coming Christmas a memorable one, and giving them a helping hand through the dreary winter months, we, at any rate, do something to lighten their burdens and make their lives a little more tolerable. They never forget a kindly deed done unto them, and to their childish imaginations, we ourselves represent to some extent the deep sympathy and brotherhood of Him who keepeth and loveth all.

Last year, over 60,000 partook of breakfast or supper; over 300 had clogs and stockings put on their bare feet; many were partly or wholly clothed, and at Christmas and New Year nearly 3,000 were made happy by the distribution amongst them of dolls, drums, trumpets, toys, etc.

Again this year, with your aid, I, together with co-workers, should like to bring a gleam of brightness into the lives of the hidden-away little souls of the Charter Street district, and I feel sure you will give us a helping hand in this endeavour to alleviate their sufferings and implant in their hearts a feeling of affinity with Him who gave us Christmas.

I may here say, and you will be pleased to learn, that we have completed our new building extension, the final additions to which were opened by the Duchess of Sutherland, last year. At the present time we have thirty-seven girls residing in the Home. We took up this sphere of action as one of the noblest that could be engaged in - to help young women, in their hard battle of life, to preserve their character and womanhood.

The Medical Mission, under the charge of Dr. R.M. Fenn, is doing a grand work amongst the poor suffering humanity, over 10,000 visits being paid to it last year. We hope to enlarge its scope of usefulness by erecting premises more suited to its needs, where we may more successfully than ever carry on the operations of a Medical Mission.

For the maintenance of the School and Home for the ensuing year we shall need at least £600 - not a large sum to ask for in a great city like this. I feel sure that I shall not appeal in vain, but that you will come to our assistance as readily as you have done in the past, to enable us to continue our ministrations amongst the poor and unfortunate of this district.

I should be pleased to send on a Report of the Schools and Medical Mission to any subscriber or friend.

Parcels of clothing, dolls, toys, and subscriptions may be forwarded to the Schools; to the Treasurer, Mr. George Harker, Nicholas Street, Mosley Street, City; or to

> *yours sincerely,*
> *Thomas Johnson.*

Apart from its religious style and content - which would be fully accepted and appreciated at that time - the appeal indicates with a direct and compassionate impact the immensely human concern felt by its writer.

The appeal also refers to the opening of an extension by the Duchess of Sutherland. The following photo (a copy of one taken in the year 1900) shows a gathering awaiting her arrival. They're congregating opposite the Mission in that part of Ashley Lane just beyond the railway span that you saw in a previous photo.

The wall, on which some children are climbing to obtain a better view, contains on its far side the area we know as Saint Michael's Flags.

Incidentally, some of the children's appearance indicates their desperate need; this giving substance to the quoted appeal and the conditions the Rowntree Report implicitly highlighted.

These children would have come from the Mission's immediate area and especially from a district known as Angel Meadow. This lay over the other side of Ashley Lane from the Mission and just beyond Saint Michael's Flags.

The Meadow - as it was locally known - occupied a slope rising from Style Street (a street we came to know in our last visit) to end where Rochdale Road (a thoroughfare we'll come to know later) runs along the top of that slope. Gould Street and its Gasworks (an area we saw in our previous visit) bordered the Meadow on its left-hand side - as seen looking up the incline towards Rochdale Road. Angel Street - some 400 yards away across the slope from Gould Street - formed the Meadow's border on that side, with its row of houses and factories.

This area thus contained consisted of a conglomeration of narrow, mainly residential, streets with - here and there and rising above the other dwellings like isolated reminders of a bygone age - a number of substantial Georgian edifices used as lodging houses.

At the time of Mr Johnson's appeal, the district had an enormously high population density. The Reverend J.R. Mercer (who presided over Saint Michael's Church in the period around 1897) indicated its extent in a talk he presented to the Manchester Statistical Society on the 28th April of that year, in which he offered these details:

It [Angel Meadow] contains about thirty-three acres, which supports seven thousand people. The density of the whole area is three hundred people to the acre and is on a par with the metropolitan slums of St. Anne's ward of Soho, Whitechapel and Bethnal Green.

He went on to say that the average mortality rate in the whole of England, per annum, was less than 19 per thousand of population but in Angel Meadow the corresponding figure was just over 50 per annum. He nostalgically, and regretfully, also went on to say:

This, then, is Angel Meadow: Once a wealthy district, with Georgian Houses and Porticoes, nestling amidst beautiful scenery of undulating landscape views and trout streams.

Of course, his regret had in mind a district as it was years before the Frenchman, Alexis de Tocqueville, paid his visit to that area in 1835 - at the time when industry's rapid encroachment began to drastically change the landscape.

It certainly did not, in any way, related to the district in which Mr Thomas Johnson issued his appeal - as we've seen...

5
No Time for Childhood

Now that we've come to know Charter Street, let's delve more deeply into the wider economic and social background of its period.

The photo we saw in the previous narrative, showing a group of children awaiting the Duchess of Sutherland's visit to the Mission, presented a graphic indication of the Rowntree Report's estimation that nearly twenty-eight percent of the population lived at a level barely satisfying basic physical needs.

This condition wasn't helped by the lack of sickness and unemployment protection - tentatively introduced under the National Insurance Act of 1911. Before this marginal amelioration to the lot of many working-class people, the principle generally applying was: no work, no pay. This regime prevailed during the time of my mother's childhood when her father's health became uncertain, and therefore family income became correspondingly uncertain.

In a world that seemed largely "resigned" to such plights, people had to seek whatever help they could. In this setting, places such as Charter Street became a valuable source of practical compassion. As we've already seen: Charter Street not only preached the message of a caring world to come but also cared enough - in the immediacy - to offer material comfort to those whose earthly circumstances could not ensure its regular provision.

When providing what relief it could, religious affiliations were often ignored. For instance, some of the Jewish children living along Cheetham Hill Road and in streets adjacent to Red Bank (whose plight could be just as acute as those in the areas immediate to Charter Street) were also offered whatever welfare the Mission could manage to give. Mugs of cocoa or tea along with a "butty" (a slice of bread with a suitable spread applied: such as jam or butter) were often provided. And - on special days - there was cake.

For many children, what Charter Street had to offer wasn't just a treat but more than likely the main meal of the day. They obtained this valuable contribution to their inconsistent diet by way of attendance at the evening service - consisting mainly of bible stories and hymn singing. My mother enjoyed both the stories and the singing, although - she told me - not as much as the food to follow.

Adults were sometimes invited to the children's sessions and she attended these along with her mother, whose favourite hymn was 'Fight the Good Fight'. However, the one my mother particularly liked started with the words: "There is a Happy Land, far, far, away..."

I later tried to find its full verse in the book of 'Hymns, Ancient and Modern', but it seemed not to be included. Yet, during the course of my questioning about those early years, I'd formed a trustful respect for her memory and since she seemed adamant the hymn was sung, it seemed best to stay with her conviction. (Perhaps it happened to be a Charter Street composition?)

Its first line held her attention to the exclusion of all else. This because she felt the "Happy Land" the hymn proclaimed with such certainty must exist somewhere. Also, knowing that the word "land" could be used in actual place-names (such as England and Scotland) furthered her conviction.

After the first line, her attention invariably strayed to wondering what that Happy Land was like and where it could be found. She imagined lots of smiling people who always said "Hello" and lived in nice houses with white-lace curtains; and had cake for tea every day, served on plates with gold rims and pictures of flowers around the edges. She felt convinced that if she discovered where the place was, and saved enough pennies for the tram-fare, she could go to see it.

However, such is the simple versatility of a child's mind it can turn any appealing abstraction into a reality - in which to dwell for a while. But even if this imagined reality was - in reality - far, far, away, nevertheless the uplifting tunes along with the staunch words many of the hymns offered probably gave courage to those who sorely needed such. In this respect, Charter Street - in addition to its more worldly role of providing a warm place and the welcomed something to eat on a winter's evening - also served the essential function of raising the spirits of those who found few causes for elation. And the communal singing, in itself, must have provided entertainment for those whose circumstances allowed hardly any.

At a more subtle and possibly unforeseen level, Charter Street may've played its part in a remarkable process started in the latter half of the Victorian era, when, from the period 1860 to 1900, the general rate of crime throughout the country fell by over fifty percent. Obviously, this happening had many causes and complexities. However, it requires no great stretch of the imagination to assume the "moral messages" constantly evoked by such charitable centres throughout the country may have been absorbed by the willing attendees, along with the jam butties and the mugs of cocoa. After all, various researches into criminal behaviour appear to indicate that it's not so much a consequence of economic deprivation but more an attitude of mind.

From my notes, here's my mother portrayal of Charter Street and its activities:

"The entrance we usually used was the one in Ashley Lane. This had a large wooden door leading into a big assembly hall with bare wooden floorboards and many rows of long benches (like church benches) on either side of a central aisle.

"The end of the hall, away from the railway viaduct, had a raised stage with curtains, and, on most evenings, they'd place a row of tables along the front for serving slices of bread along with tea or cocoa - this after the hymn singing. Sometimes, the smell of cocoa and fresh bread being prepared in the nearby room made you feel so hungry, you'd forget to sing the hymns.

"Other times, shows and concerts were held on the stage; done by various local groups or Church or Factory Bands. All these events were free and always had a long queue of children waiting to get in. If you turned up late and the hall became full, you'd be turned away.

"On occasions, children in real need received clogs and clothing when these were available.

"Christmas Day was a special session and you'd only be admitted with a ticket. You'd get a stocking containing an orange, a new penny, some toffee and a toy or a doll. The toys and dolls were mostly second-hand but always in good condition.

"To get a ticket, you needed to attend the services without break for some weeks before Christmas. You'd be marked in a register and then given the ticket just before the special day. Adults were sometimes allowed to attend these sessions along with their children; and, on Christmas Day, they'd receive foodstuffs such as mince pies, a Christmas pudding and a packet of tea."

Thus, my mother's description of Charter Street.

In the world of the Rowntree Report, it requires very little reflection to realise it must've been the absolute heart and soul of the district for most children. This especially on Christmas Day when the gifts given were, in all probability, the only ones the children would receive. Also and as previously mentioned: the children of Jewish families in the area were offered similar benefits but, out of respect for their sensibilities, on the New Year's Day session. In these ways, the blessed place my mother knew as Charter Street extended its charity as far as it could.

However, since so many children in the immediate and adjacent areas needed relief it became almost an impossibility to meet its full demand. So much so that on one occasion my mother overheard a man she knew as Mr Johnson (the Supervisor whose appeal we read and whose kindly manner she particularly remembered) saying nearly two thousand children had to be accommodated, best they could, over the Christmas period.

At such times of almost overwhelming demand, it became a pressing necessity to assess each attendee to ensure those in desperate need were given top priority. My mother told me of one such instance involving her cousin, Louise, who had a rather dark complexion and hair to match. The person with the unenviable task of being a scrutiniser, amidst the confusion of so many children, applied his assessing too restrictively and said to her:

"I'm sorry, Love. You'll have to come back on New Year's Day. That's when Jewish children attend."

There were quite a few children in the Cheetham Hill area with parents of Eastern European origin; and it seems the tickets omitted any reference to affiliation or related session, since the attendees were expected to know the day allocated and would turn up on that day. However, Louise felt too taken aback and was also too retiring to insist on her rightful eligibility. Moreover, she hadn't the nerve to attend the New Year's session for fear her true affiliation might be recognised - and, again, be faced with the charge of wrongful attendance.

This left Louise with a disappointing Christmas, but friends rallied around to give and share whatever they could. And since Louise could hardly change her complexion, she decided to carry a note from her mother to explain her "true position" if it ever became necessary.

As this incident illustrates, the demand on resources must, at times, have been so great it impose a very painful burden on those whose nature was instinctively charitable. Also as we've seen: the number of children waiting at the door for each session could often exceed the capacity of the hall to accommodate. In these instances, children had to stand in the space to the rear of the seats and in the aisles - and even then, many had to be turned away.

In such circumstances, and as the hall approached a capacity strained to the limits of safety, those making assessment were forced to include all sorts of "details and particulars" that might indicate who amongst the children seemed most deserving of admittance. In one such instance it became my mother's turn to experience mistaken status - but in this case, due to wearing a certain garment.

A month or so after Louise's unfortunate Christmas experience, she had the (compensating?) good fortune of obtaining a smart and very warm new coat. On a particularly cold night shortly after this happy acquisition, my mother borrowed the garment to join what she knew would be the long line waiting for the evening session. The same person involved in the Louise incident again had the confusing and unenviable task of assessing the "condition" that the children crowding to gain admittance might imply by their appearance.

"Sorry, Love," he said, when she reached the door. "This evening is for really poor children."

When telling me about this event, my mother remarked with a grin:

"Although missing out on an anticipated treat, I did, at least, have the compensation of being thought well-to-do. But this elevation to the ranks of the rich didn't quite compensate for my loss of a treacle butty and a mug of cocoa."

However, the lesson was well learnt; and to avoid any further tragedies concerning mistaken status, she and Louise waited until the coat looked suitably worn before using it for future attendance.

Although these stories may contain an element of humour, and were characteristically related to me in that spirit, being turned away could have been - indeed - a real tragedy. Virtually all of the attendees were in varying degrees of need (as those having to make assessments no doubt fully realised) and the very fact that a charitable institution had to turn children away - against all its deeper instincts - shows how pressingly widespread this need happened to be.

It also shows how deeply distressing it must have been for those having to decide, by whatever indications they felt appropriate, which child seemed in the most desperate circumstances. In such a world - wherein even the charity of Charter Street was sorely stretched to the point of distress - many families had to fall back on their own efforts in whatever way they could.

At one stage, when my mother's father became unable to work, her mother had to search for any menial tasks she could manage at home. However, the pay from such work hardly provided enough to sustain the family even in the most basic of necessities. During these times, real and painful hunger wasn't a rare experience. My mother told me of a day when that experience was particularly felt.

On being met after school, she asked:

"Mam? Have we anything for tea?"

"We've got some lentil soup," her mother replied.

Never - my mother told me - had she felt such a surge of happiness as in that moment. She said her joy was so intense, she felt like skipping all the way down Lord Street.

Some years ago - when going through one of my all too frequent and self-indulgent grey patches in life - she said to me:

"Always have something to look forward to - even if it's only your tea."

This simple recipe for maintaining a hopeful disposition no doubt had its roots in the lentil soup incident.

The incident has to be understood in the context of Rowntree's observations, which our more auspicious period may find difficult to believe. Those subjected to its uncertainties lived in a world centring on simple expectations (such as a hopeful anticipation of a meal). They had to hope and trust that far better times would eventually arrive and appreciate whatever small mercies came along in the meantime. Thus, the generosities of anyone disposed to be generous were always received with great gratitude. And, it seems, kindness, and therefore cause for gratitude, were always to be found by those willing to appreciate even the smallest of favours.

During one particularly difficult period, when a day without regular meals became almost an expectation, my mother and her brother, Jim, happened to see the workmen from the mills and factories along Ashley Lane having their lunches. At that time, most workplaces provided no proper facilities wherein employees could eat their mid-day meal; therefore, they usually sat on the steps or pavements outside the factories during their short break.

Seeing the men eating made it seem a long time since breakfast and a long and hungry wait to the next, by no means certain, meal. This anxiety promoted them to impulsively ask for any food the workmen might be able to spare.

"Please? Have you anything to spare from your lunch?" my mother and her brother asked the assembled men.

Workmen in those times had hardly enough for themselves; but, from what my mother told me, they showed an amazing generosity with whatever they happened to have. Since they were only little children, their plight (one probably all too familiar to the workmen, living as they were against the background of the Rowntree Report) quickly moved the men to give anything they could.

One of the workmen took it upon himself to encourage and then collect whatever his workmates felt able to donate. And - to her and her brother's great joy - they were given a rare treat: half a packet of cream cracker biscuits. They could hardly believe their good fortune. This, they were able to share with the other children in the family.

During that period - which my mother said, with her usual capacity for understatement, happened to be "especially difficult" - her mother needed to take every available work-opportunity. Some of its demands forced her to leave the more able children very much under their own supervision during the school-hours periods. She therefore arranged for her children to have what she thought was a really filling breakfast of porridge-oats, and hoped this would see them through until the end of school's afternoon session.

In those days and districts, it wasn't at all unusual for people to go quite some time between meals. They either got used to this or learnt to accept it. The "filling" breakfast was given on that basis. However, as my mother remarked when telling me about the workmen incident:

"A child's appetite doesn't understand having to wait."

Her mother was completely unaware of the initiative the two children impulsively took to relieve the situation. Some years had to pass before national awareness offered amelioration more certain than that of the limited provisions places such as Charter Street were able to provide and the chance generosity of people like the workmen could afford. Although the idea of providing school meals had its introduction in 1906, this became heavily dependent on the family's capacity to pay; or, if they couldn't pay, on charitable funds. Therefore, and for most areas such as the one of our concern, a less payment-demanding condition had to wait many years.

In the 1910-20 period, hardly two per cent of the school population had full coverage. Also, the valuable nourishment provided by a daily, free, half-pint of milk in schools had to await the legislation of 1934.

But let's return to the immediate problems. Her mother also took any work she could manage to do in the evenings, such as hand-stitching the turn-up seams on trouser-legs (which the existing machines couldn't properly do) for clothing manufacturers located in the city centre. She'd receive a halfpenny per completed pair of trousers with no allowance for collecting and returning the items. It took a considerable amount of time to meet the demands of neatly stitching and carefully ironing a complete pair of trousers, so the return for even the most dedicated efforts hardly contributed towards luxurious living.

Nevertheless, the extra earnings - although small - could and did go a long way when spent in the right places. Various sources of cheap nourishment existed in and around the district and could offer a substantial return for just a few pennies; and if those few coins became regular, the hoped for "better times" would seem to have made their long overdue, but nevertheless welcome, arrival.

One such opportunity existed in the form of a small warehouse, called Curry's, situated on Shude Hill (a place near the city centre and at the end of Rochdale Road) which specialised in egg packaging and distribution. My mother and her constant companion - brother, Jim - would, with unremitting hope, take a dish to this place towards the end of the working day. If an accident occurred during the day's loading or stacking, the warehouse sold off the damaged items just before closing time - so even a penny could fill a dish with something like a half-dozen cracked but nevertheless still wholesome eggs. However, those responsible for undue breakages had to make up the deficiency from their wages and the workmen became extremely careful to avoid its penalty.

Yet accidents are bound to happen even in the most careful of circumstances, and hope lives eternally in the hearts of those wherein hope is mostly all they have. My mother and her brother would stand at the packing-yard's gate - in hope. She was hardly much more than eight years of age at the time and her brother no more than two years older. They waited, holding their dish and with faces showing hopeful expectation and their eyes following every movement of the men completing the last of their packing.

Their wait and hopeful expectation must've disturbed the workmen - or, more than likely, the generosity typical amongst their type at that time came to the fore. When no breakages occurred, the workmen would surreptitiously (with possible risk of a deletion from their pay or even loss of job) give each of the children an egg. These they'd carry home carefully - watching every step against tripping or stumbling. An egg not cracked represented a very special treat.

To people with experiences confined to the present period, the idea of young children going to the places mentioned, unaccompanied by an adult, would be considered dangerous neglect and would "raise eyebrows". But the expectation people had of children in those times extended to almost adult capabilities; and people would still be alive who'd remember children starting work as young as eight years of age.

Therefore, in the circumstances of that time, my mother, her mother or anyone else in those days wouldn't think it at all unusual for children to do the things described. Children in the period of our interest had far more freedom of movement and parents much less anxiety about their safety than - unfortunately - we know now. This relaxed supervision, that we would now think represented irresponsibility, elicited that previously mentioned remark my mother often made during our conversations:

"People thought about things differently in those days".

If you progress through the rest of these narratives, you'll realise that playing in the street and beyond its immediate confines for long and unsupervised periods was the normality for children of that time. Also, what used to be called "running errands" required constantly going to shops and various places around their district without adult accompaniment. In our present period, people feel more comfortable if children are kept "safely in sight". In the period of our interest, denying children the opportunities for extensive outdoor activities would be thought "unreasonable" - a reversal of attitude indicative of the astonishing differences between then and now.

But getting back to the business of living. Another opportunity for a few well-placed pennies existed at a group of warehouses in a place called Factory Yard - this situated between Angel Street and Miller Street, just beyond Angel Meadow. One warehouse received cartloads of fresh herrings for preparing and then preserving by smoking. From there, a good-size fish - still wholesome but damaged enough to make it unfit for processing - could sometimes be obtained for a penny.

To add to this fortuitousness, the workmen, with the same instinctive generosity displayed by the egg-men and those we met outside the factories when having their lunch, would include a small but tasty fish along with the damaged one (if they could get away with this without being seen by the Gaffer). This they'd quickly wrap up in a sheet of newspaper - as an extra - along with the one purchased.

Another hope focused on the bacon-smoking sheds located near the Cathedral at the centre of the city, where Hanging Ditch met the bottom of Shude Hill. Here, a goodly portion of bacon scrap-ends rejected as unsuitable for processing could be obtained for a halfpenny. After exploring this possibility, my mother and her brother, Jim, sometimes did a detour - making their way home by way of the market at the top of Shude Hill. If they arrived there at the right time, the end-of-the-day's fruit and vegetables too old or too damaged to sell were sometimes given away by the various stalls.

But opportunities such as these were, as we've seen, a matter of luck - and luck only favoured those constantly alert to where luck's chances happen to fall. Many children in and around the district sought the same opportunities and it became part of my mother's life to be aware of these chances, whenever and wherever they appeared. Growing up had to be done very quickly.

As I remarked at the beginning of these narratives: the focus of conversation with my mother centred mainly on hardship, because I wanted to know how people coped with a degree almost unknown in present times. When I asked how this coping was done, without severe damage to hope and morale, she replied in her typically matter-of-fact and cheerful way:

"You either did what you could for yourself or face the Poorhouse. And being able to avoid that raised your spirits."

She also said she felt her circumstances and what these dictated weren't in any way unusual. Nearly all the children she knew were in a similar position; and, in some cases, situations even more acute - especially when ill health became almost the normality in some families. An indication of how prevalent this "normality" became is shown by the army recruitment figures for around that time.

During the Boer War and the first decade of the nineteen-hundreds, nearly forty percent of applicants for army services met with rejection on medical grounds. These rejections involved young men who should've been in their physical prime. They occurred on tests based on medical criteria that modern standards would judge as extremely relaxed. This caused so much national concern it impelled reforms such as those related to school meals and the amelioration represented by the later unemployment and sickness insurance - instituted in 1911.

Before legislation had its full and much delayed affect, debilitating ill health held terrifying consequence. The strict and somewhat unsympathetic Poor Laws of the Victorian era still largely influenced the thinking of those with power to decide on the fortunes of the less fortunate. For those whom, for most times, were only one uncertain week's pay away from poverty, the initiatives taken by families and individuals to make ends meet - and the support of charities like Charter Street, and the generosities of people such as those previously described - were virtually the only means available for escaping the felt shame of submitting to the Poor Law's administration.

The most frightening of all consequence was the loss of a breadwinner. The families thus affected were invariably forced to vacate their house and seek shelter with relatives already sorely pressed. Vacancies often occurred as a result of such circumstances and - although resulting from the misfortune of others - sometimes provided opportunities for those in less congenial areas to move to what appeared to be a better street.

My mother's family became constantly alert to such opportunities. The area in which they lived was, as we've seen, situated along the banks of the River Irk in an area known locally as "down in the dip". Under certain winter conditions, this area could suffer a chilling, damp, industrial fog that sometimes persisted all day, whereas the higher ground along Rochdale Road enjoyed a much better ambience. My mother and her brothers often looked around the more favoured areas for vacant houses being offered for rent - even though the rents in these "better streets" were invariably higher.

Such houses usually indicated their availability by a large card in the window with the brief message: "House for Rent. Apply to..."

On seeing one of these, she'd run home to announce excitedly:

"Mam! I've seen an empty house in a nice street! Can we go and have a look at it?"

By one such chance - when my mother was about ten years of age and when improved family circumstances happened to allow a higher rent - they eventually managed a move to Limer Street. This stood on the much higher ground along Rochdale Road and thereby offered some relief from the river's impositions. It also represented an escape from the almost-on-the-doorstep domination of the more polluting industries.

Although the street contained a number of small yards and warehouses, these were mainly for storage rather than manufacturing. Also, an important attraction centred on the railway being far less dominating in the new location - having left the viaduct to approach a cutting hidden by a high wall at the lower end of the street from Rochdale Road.

Another factor in the move's favour lay in its manageable distance from Hargreaves Street. Whatever limited possessions people had would be transported by the people themselves, usually using a borrowed or cheaply rented handcart - this to avoid the expense of a removal service. Therefore, in making a move, short distance became a major consideration.

A further desirability in any relocation lay in it offering proximity to other members of the family, for the ready and mutual support this could provide. As it happened, a recently married younger sister of my mother's mother (named Elizabeth) had recently set up home in Limer Street - thus making this location even more attractive. Also, Elizabeth was only a few months away from an expected birth; therefore - in a time when the main and sometimes only help had to be provided by neighbours and/or family members - to have a sister close by was, for her, a comforting prospect.

My mother told how she sat on the front steps of a newly found playmate's house, not many weeks after the move. Whilst sitting there, awaiting her mother's return from being urgently called to her sister's house, two women neighbours walked by. My mother heard one of them say to the other:

"Elizabeth died. And the child..."

Soon afterwards, the husband of hardly a year went to live with his sister in another district. Thus, another house became vacant.

To be deprived of what we now take to be the comfortable expectations of life was a continual possibility for those dwelling in such circumstances. Those who lived in the centres of large industrial cities had long endured a further dispossession: that of fresh air to breath and green fields in which to walk. What meagre patches of soil had escaped the sprawl of tightly huddled together factories, railways and row upon row of cramped housing had become so oil and sulphur soaked by decades of pollutants to be almost sterile. Only the most hardy and tenacious of weeds could draw from the soil whatever sustenance was left in its near sterility.

The people in this environment, had, unlike their country or their suburban counterparts, no gardens or plots of land on which they could cultivate additional nourishment. They lived where no grass grew and had to become as hardy and as tenacious as the weeds to survive. But some found themselves unable to cling. The struggle to live had sapped what little strength they had left.

Again a grief, but again a grief from circumstances not uncommon at that time. The affects of Childbed Fever (Puerperal Fever) prevalent in the Victorian Era, to the extent of affecting one in every four births, was not unusual in the time and districts such as the one we're visiting - even though, by then, medical science knew much about its cause. It had to await the Midwife Act of 1936 for the first and effective recognition to emerge. But whatever the cause of this tragedy, the loss of Elizabeth along with her baby deeply affected my Granny who had a particular affection for her younger sister, and had named my mother after her.

Shortly afterwards, my Grandmother lost her youngest child, aged eighteen months. Perhaps all these losses caused the family to leave Limer Street and the sadness it represented. Although the new street they found (Heelis Street) was again hardly a great move in distance, at least it was solely residential. The industrial activities all around were not directly seen or unduly heard from the street and its immediate vicinity. And for the first time, they could look up and down and across the street where they lived and see only houses.

Not long afterwards, my Grandfather Corrigan's health again started to deteriorate. He'd been on relief work (temporary work provided for the unemployed). This involved joining the workforce excavating the site that eventually formed the boating lake in Boggart Hole Clough Park. It required arduous pick-and-shovel work done in all weathers, for which a major portion of the limited amount of pay took the form of a voucher exchanged for a food allowance.

On Monday evenings, after their schooling at Saint Chad's, my mother and her constant companion, brother Jim, took a clean white pillow-case along with the previous week's food-voucher to the old Workhouse situated in the centre of the City. This required a walk down Cheetham Hill Road to the massive glass, iron and brick structure of Victoria Station; and then a short way beyond its extent to reach New Bridge Street where they'd join the long line waiting for the Relief Centre's doors to opened.

Here's my notes taken from my mother's description of the scene she found inside the Workhouse:

"The surrender of the voucher allowed entrance. Only those holding vouchers were permitted inside. Women were allowed to take their babe-in-arms into the building if they had no-one to mind the infant.

"Its large hall had a line of wooden tables placed down the centre of its bare, wooden floor.

"People silently filed past the tables: old men and women; young men; young mothers with children in a long line whose only sound was the shuffling of feet. Everyone silent. Even the children silent.

"Each in the line held open their pillow cases as they reached the tables: first to be given a loaf of dark bread; then a bag of oatmeal; a bar of soap; a packet of tea; a bag of sugar; and, lastly, a tin of black treacle."

On obtaining their allocation, the two children made their way home in the darkening hours of the evening; taking turns to carry the pillow case past Charter Street Mission and under the great girdered span of the railway viaduct; then to walk along Ashley Lane's extension to reach the slope of Dalton Street - and, finally, their home in Heelis Street.

In this way and in the ways previously described, the two young children spent their days.

There was no time left for childhood...

6
As a Matter of Interest:
Churchill and Charter Street

~~~~~~~~~~~~~~~~~~~~~~~~~~~~~~~~~~~

Before leaving Charter Street and its efforts in that small part of the world to give whatever relief it could, I'd like to tell you about a casual remark my mother made during our conversations.

Whilst discussing Charter Street and its related happenings, she mentioned Winston Churchill visited the area some time during her childhood. In contrast to the many events she described quite vividly, she seemed somewhat uncertain about the date and details. Because of this, I though, perhaps, her recollections about the incident might be confused - or even mistaken.

Yet, having come to respect her memory's accuracy, I pursued the point further by asking how old she was at the time and why she remembered this particular event. She paused as if searching her memory for a moment, then said:

"I must have been very young, but I remember hearing people mentioning him. The nearby Saint Chad's school looked like a church on a hill from where we lived. That's why I became interested in the name."

To associate a name with a feature prominent in a child's life would be a likely thing for a child to do. I therefore thought it may've been possible that Churchill came near, or, perhaps, was mentioned as being in the vicinity for some electoral purpose: this because I knew he happened to stand for a Parliamentary Constituency in the north-west of Manchester in the early nineteen-hundreds. But since she couldn't supply any further details than the chance remark, I pushed what she told me into one of those remote filing cabinets I have scattered somewhere in the back of my mind - which eventually becomes impossible to find and its contents therefore lost.

However, and as mentioned previously: my sister, Nellie, gave valuable assistance by providing dates and details to support certain events mentioned in these writings. When I asked her to help with some background information about the history of Charter Street Mission, she - with her usual careful persistence - came across an account of Winston Churchill having made a visit: thus validating my mother's comment.

In the weeks before the election prompting this visit, it seems Churchill raised considerable interest on the part of the Press - especially the Daily Mail and Manchester Guardian. The latter appeared particularly inclined to champion his cause and gave him and his campaigning activities widespread and attentive publicity.

Churchill had already gained attention for his exploits as a War Correspondent when acting for the London based Morning Post during the Boer War - and particularly for being captured by and escaping from the Boers in the December of 1899. His arrival in any district would therefore carry associations regarding those exploits and gain him greater public interest than he would, perhaps, otherwise receive.

To give you a feel for the type of publicity he attracted at that time, I can do no better than quote a small extract from the Daily Mail's edition of Friday, January 12th 1906:

He glories in the crowd and the cheering, and the frank, unaffected, beaming manifestation of his delight in it all redoubles the interest and exuberance of the crowd... The harder he works, the fresher and keener and brighter he grows.

So this was the Winston Churchill who could draw the crowds, no doubt because he delighted in the crowds (as the Daily Mail observed) and, it seems, a crowd feels pleased with those who feel pleased with the crowd.

The Manchester Guardian implied this in its issue of Friday, January 5th 1906, when, soon after his arrival in the city, it stated:

There is no question about it, the public interest of Manchester in the general election is centred and focused on the personality of Mr. Winston Churchill... He is wearing a new old-fashioned hat, a flat-topped sort of felt hat, and already the hatters are having enquiries for articles of that pattern.

The same paper also reported:

He was billed to speak in the Manchester Coal Exchange at three o'clock yesterday [Thursday 11th Jan]. At half past two, the hall was packed with a struggling crowd; a second crowd was struggling on the staircase leading to the hall; and a third crowd jostling for standing room on the pavement in the street.

All the attention he received explains why my mother - although in the very early years of childhood - became aware of his visit. No doubt her parents and others around her would've been mindful of his presence and the impression he was making.

But let's find out what his immediate presence in my mother's district entailed. To do this, we can fortunately turn to another report in the Manchester Guardian for an event that took place in Charter Street Mission - a place we now know well enough to imagine the proceedings. His visit took place on January 7th - the Sunday preceding the election that brought him to the city - and I quote directly from the newspaper's report:

The school is outside the Northwest Manchester Division, and not even his strongest political opponents could accuse him of wishing to make capital out of his visit, which was in no sense political... No member of a British Government has ever been before within its doors. It was the usual Sunday morning gathering; over 400 children received breakfast; and in another room over 400 men, the flotsam and jetsam of humanity, were also given a meal; nearly 100 waiting outside in the street were given some food. The Manchester Sacred song Association were present, and contributed some excellent music...

Mr. Churchill, before rising to speak, asked for the 'Glory' song to be sung, and it was joined in most heartily. He then said that he had been very deeply touched by the singing. It made one feel very far removed from the ordinary, outside world, especially from the, at times, brutal details of politics and elections. He was quite disinclined to speech-making there, because he did not wish to be thought that he was taking advantage of that occasion to push himself forward on matters in which he was greatly interested. Let them look at some of the larger courses in which life lay, and which perhaps, led us to the consideration of life beyond.

He quite agreed with Mr. Johnson (the Honorary Superintendent who had introduced him) in what had been said of the terrible sufferings and perplexities of life in these great cities of the present day. There had never been such great cities before where poverty and wealth and suffering jostled each other as they did today. The increased education had enabled people to appreciate the evils by which they were surrounded and to see the pleasures which dangle just beyond their reach. They saw on every hand evidence of great luxury, and, he feared, of waste also.

It was a grave and sad reflection that with all our advance and science and skill and wealth we did not seem nearer to solving the old unhappiness of the human heart - physical suffering - than we were hundreds of years ago. It was helpful work Mr Johnson and his friends were doing. Humanity could only be helped under the Providence of God by human beings. No Bill in Parliament, no code or system, could alone help them, although these would contribute in making conditions in which the world might grow brighter and happier.

Thus was reported Winston Churchill's visit to Charter Street.

However, what of the election that took place on Saturday, January 13th; the results of which were announced that day, at half past nine in the evening?

Votes: Churchill 5,639; Joynson-Hicks 4,398

Therefore, the visitor to Charter Street held his seat in Parliament as a member of the Liberal Party, by a substantial majority. Not long afterwards, in the Parliamentary time-scale of getting things done, and in the year of 1911, Churchill sponsored the major part of the Liberal Government's National Insurance Bill. This introduced protection against sickness and unemployment that marked the eroding away of the old repressive Poor Law System, in force since 1834, along with its Victorian Workhouse associations.

In Churchill's writings to the then Prime Minister (Lloyd George) in which he pressed for the Bill and the Prime Minister's support for its acceptance, Churchill (who had previously visited Germany in 1907 and 1908 to assess its system of unemployment and sickness insurance) stated:

The Minister who will apply to this country the successful experience of Germany may or may not be supported at the polls, but he will at least have left a memorial which time will not deface of his administration...

As history tells: the Bill was successfully passed; and as we now know, this marked the beginning in the following years of a series of enactments leading to what we now call the Welfare State. It would therefore be nice to believe that what Churchill saw and heard at Charter Street that Sunday morning in 1906 shaped his thinking in sponsoring the 1911 Bill - and thus the results to accrue.

Moreover, perhaps all this legislation arose from the belief expressed in the pertaining words of his speech in Charter Street - as reported in the Manchester Guardian:

...these [Bills in Parliament] would contribute in making conditions in which the world might grow brighter and happier.

After the 1939-45 war, it seems the returning service men and women - whose efforts Churchill had encouraged so effectively during the war - became suspicious that the additional social reforms they expected as a return for their war effort would not be realised under his Government. In view of this, Churchill Administration failed to get the support of the country.

However, it seems Churchill's difficulty with accepting the reform centred more on a number of controversial details the Beveridge plan incorporated and, it seems, with its author's rather uncompromising personality when presenting various stages of the plan, rather than with the general principle of the reform itself.

Churchill's main anxieties focused on the expected cost and the possible American attitude to its commitment - as expressed by his advisor, Lord Cherwell, who, on seeing an advanced copy of the Beveridge Report, gave warning in a memo to Churchill:

If it were accepted, it might prove difficult to obtain an extension of Lend-Lease after the war, as Americans may think they were being asked to pay for social services in the U.K. far in advance of their own.

Another warning arrived by way of Churchill's financial advisor, Sir Kinglsey Wood, in a Treasury Paper he issued entitled 'Financial Aspects of the Social Security Plan'. In this he laid stress on other major charges likely to fall on the Exchequer at the same time, such as the cost of maintaining armaments in a dangerous post-war world.

Churchill envisaged this possibility of an expensive "cold-war" in what became known in the immediate post-war period as the "Red Menace": a perceived danger emphatically expressed in his 'Iron Curtain Speech' presented at Westminster College, Fulton, Missouri, on March 5th 1946, in which he said:

Nobody knows what Soviet Russia and its Communist international organisations intend to do in the near future, or what are the limits, if any, to their expansive and proselytising tendencies... From Stettin in the Baltic to Trieste in the Adriatic, an iron curtain has descended across the continent...

So Churchill's worries, it seems, consisted of the need to maintain two things: America's continual support for and alliance with what would appear to be a financially prudent Britain; and a financially solvent Britain being sufficiently armed, through its own finances, to play its part in what might be a dangerous post-war world. In this, it seems Churchill still had his mind on the war; seeing it as not yet finished but taking another form.

It therefore appears he didn't have his mind on the type of peace those returning from the war believed they had won and the expected benefits they thought their efforts deserved.

However, I suspect his memory of the Charter Street visit hadn't fully faded, nor had the desire he'd voiced in that place. The social reforms he first instigated in order to express that desire he no doubt envisaged as a process he'd like to have seen continuing in "better times". Therefore, the immediate post-war years represented, to him, uncertain times and the proposed reforms had to await future betterment.

But what about that hardly known person - Mr Thomas Johnson - whom we met through his appeal in the Christmas of 1901 and Churchill met during his visit?

Although not writ large on the world scene as was the great figure of Winston Churchill - and his name is therefore known only to a few -

Thomas Johnson nevertheless implied he worked for a far greater ordinance than that given by any worldly authority. In this, it seems humility was part of that ordinance.

Angel Meadow was his place of birth where, as a young boy, he became an orphan. He sold newspapers to earn a precarious living in the streets around the city centre. Eventually, the proprietor of the Manchester Courier (one of the newspapers he sold) noticed him selling that paper whilst standing on the corner of Mosley Street. He particularly noticed what he called "his industry combined with a wretched appearance" and would now and again treat Tommy (as he liked to be known) to a good meal. This no doubt acted as a valuable supplement to any nourishment he obtained from sources such as Charter Street.

He subsequently acquired a full time job on the Manchester Courier and even progressed to the position of being listed on the roll of City Magistrates. However, during those years, he never lost contact with Charter Street Mission and its work. He eventually became head of its organisation and constantly attended its evening sessions during the time when my mother, as a child, noticed his kindly disposition.

Although having a position allowing reimbursement from the Mission's finances, for any personal expenses his position imposed, he nevertheless maintained his full time job in order to contribute towards and not draw upon its funds.

He must have found the work extremely demanding because the Mission no doubt took up most of his free hours, during which he probably penned the Appeal for the Christmas of 1901. His commitment also ensured his presence on that January Sunday morning in 1906 and therefore his meeting with Churchill.

Yet as previously implied: to the world in general he is hardly known. But in writing this narrative - and thereby hoping to mention Tommy Johnson as being part of the greater picture in which Churchill appeared - I remembered the opening words presented in a book called 'The Cloister and the Hearth', written by the Victorian author, Charles Reade, which stated:

Not a day passes over the earth, but men and women of no note do great deeds, speak great words, and suffer noble sorrows. Of these obscure heroes, philosophers, and martyrs, the greater part will never be known...

I suspect these words could aptly apply to Tommy Johnson - and people like him...

7
Making Do

~~~~~~~~~~~~~~~~~~~~~~~~~~~~~~~~~~~

By the beginning of 1912, shortly after my mother's family moved into number fourteen Heelis Street, the children of the family were, in order of age: John (who, by then, had joined the Scottish Border Regiment) William, Jim, Elizabeth (my mother to be), Mary, Joseph and Edward.

Also, my mother's maternal grandmother, Mary Clynes, moved into the street to occupy number ten. I believe she must've been about sixty-three years of age at the time, but still maintaining her independence by doing odd jobs; amongst which was her regular stand-by: minding horses at the local stable-yards and markets.

Just across the street (at number seven) lived the Jones family. They had, I believe, recently moved from Angel Meadow (the district we saw near Charter Street).

History claims Angel Meadow was once a grassy expanse covered with a profusion of wild flowers. It offered a "Garden of Eden" view of a vale containing the pure waters of the River Irk, alive with eels and trout and meandering through fields and blossom-filled woodlands. It could readily be assumed, therefore, that the origin of the prefix "Angel" came from the view the Meadow once provided. However, this was before Tocqueville made his visit and before industry fashioned the area somewhat differently.

I once heard a verse associated with the district, obviously related to a time after the Garden of Eden view became no more:

> *I climbed the steps of St. Michael's place,*
> *And near Angel Meadow, I came face to face,*
> *With ghosts from its graveyard -*
> *They gave me a scare -*
> *To go back again, I never would dare.*

It's easy to imagine this verse arose from the grim reminders of the cholera epidemics carved in the stone of Saint Michael's Flags and therefore was, in all probability, a local composition.

After the severe epidemic of 1849, a legend had it that angels were seen in the skies holding out their arms to raise the dead children from their earthly resting-place. This, associated with the once "heavenly view" must've added its contribution to the name 'Angel Meadow'. It's also likely that some people in the district could remember traces of its rural aspect from their childhood, before the rapid industrial advance beginning in 1820. Previous to this, accounts described the Angel Meadow area as:

Grounds from which one of the most beautiful view of vale and river, hills and woodland could be had.

The area's lingering attractiveness is testified by the development of what, in 1797, became known as Vauxhall Gardens. This verdant place of Coffee Houses and Tea Gardens, situated by the bank of the Irk, no more than half a mile upstream from the then recently built Saint Michael's Church, became eulogised as "the finest place in the nation".

Yet another support for this heavenly view the area once possessed came by way of my mother. She habitually made use of the district's library wherever she lived, and her main borrowings centred on all things history.

At one time, one of the books she happened to borrow gave an account of Bonnie Prince Charlie's Jacobite Army arriving in Manchester and then camping by the River Irk - whose gently sloping, wooded bank he decided to rest upon, for a while, before continuing his march to London.

He selected one particular area because of its pleasantly sheltered scene and the opportunity to catch trout from the fresh, clear-flowing waters of the river. His sojourn is just an incidental in history. Yet the fact that the place contained enough attraction to entice him to linger is echoed by the name of a short stretch along that particular bank of the Irk, not far from Hargreaves Street. This bears the simple title of 'Scotland'.

So here we have another incident of history indicating that the area once offered a view heavenly enough to delight a person who believed he was a rightful contender to the throne. It appears he thought that particular place was, so to speak, "fit for a king" - or, at least, one hoping to gain that status.

You'll obtain a forceful insight into the enormous transformation that the "power of industry" imposed upon this particular area if you read through to the narrative with the title 'The Dark Arch' - a feature situated at one end of the place called 'Scotland'. The before and after implications of this is, I believe, why Alexis de Tocqueville viewed the "progress" of industrialisation with such trepidation.

He would also observed - here and there amongst the spreading mills and factories - patches of landscape retaining some of its original attractiveness. He obviously saw the last indications of how it was when under the care of nature as being subjected to a seemingly unstoppable man-made forces - one that could transform the sun into (to use his words) "a disc without rays".

But back to our immediate concern: on the same side of Heelis Street as that of my mother also lived the Griffith family - related to the Jones family - who'd moved from Wales in search of employment and subsequently occupied number twenty. This coming together of closely related families - some eventually achieving the relationship by a future marriage - should've created a happy situation. However, a year or so after moving to the street, my mother lost her father when in his late forties.

The still persisting Poor Law system demanded that a widow should work to keep her and any dependent children - if physically able to do so. The tentative implementation of a meagre, strictly conditional, widow's pension had to await 1925 for its introduction. Before this, and like many other women in her circumstances, the bereaved had to maintain the family in accordance with the prevailing situation.

Again like many women in her circumstances, only acute desperation would force seeking any temporary assistance from what was then called The Poor Law Board of Guardians (an institution we met briefly in our previous visits). To avoid this dependency and its more than likely consequences of her children being placed in care under the local Authorities, she found work as a part-time cleaner at Crumpsall Hospital at a wage of ten shillings per week (twenty shillings to the pound in those days). This she supplemented with whatever evening work she could find. Her ability to do neat hand-stitching, which we saw she'd acquired during one of our previous visits, became useful for these possibilities.

My mother must've been twelve years of age by that time. This permitted leaving school if domestic circumstances dictated. The main dictate proved to be the inadequacy of her mother's ten shillings wage and therefore the need for her to take full-time employment in the hospital. So - because the three younger children needed care and attention during the day - my mother's schooling (basic as it was in those days) had to be curtailed to allow the more demanding education of looking after the household and its younger members. Thus, with whatever help relations living in the street could provide, she took on the role of a mother whilst still but a child herself.

Not long afterwards came the outbreak of the First World War and, as we've seen, the first-born, John, had already become a member of a regiment. William (known to the family as Willy) went into the army a year or so after the outbreak of that war, to be followed in its closing years by Jim (who must have been well under age - not much more than sixteen). However, such was the desperate search for more "young blood" to fill the trenches, the question of age was, by then, not treated with any great interest: sufficient the candidate appeared suitable.

Mr Jones from across the street (eventually to be my grandfather) happened to be first amongst those in the immediate area to go to War. He subsequently received news of his later enlisting sons (Willy and Joey) being included in the fatalities for the battle-area in which the three of them were simultaneously engaged.

But let me offer a comment concerning an incident I chanced upon nearly two decades after the war, to show how its consequences can persist long after its supposed ending.

My Granny Jones seemed prone to weeping, from time to time, when she though nobody would be there to witness her distress. This I stumbled upon when calling, uninvited, at her home - as I was wont to do whenever I could. The reason for the quiet tears confused my unsophisticated and still self-centred mind and I thought it might be due to an exuberant mischievousness I tended towards, at times.

I discovered much later that the distress arose from the framed photographs of her two sons she kept on the wall, which she wouldn't take down, despite the sadness they evoked, because she said they were her only contact. They (uncles I never knew) were both buried in France and funds were not available to allow a visit.

But back to the events surrounding such losses. It seems my grandfather experienced warfare as a youth in the Boer War (1899-1902). This no doubt because military needs offered a living otherwise denied or insufficiently catered for at home (as many working-class lad of that time who happened to be able-bodied found out). After his service in that conflict, he then remained on a contractual reserve for future hostilities.

The enormity of the 1914-18 war brought floods of work - as wars seem to do. And as the men went off to battle, the women and girls filled the factories. Thus, at the age of fourteen, my mother started work at Wilson's Gas-mask Factory, Carruthers Street, Ancoats, where she received twelve shillings and sixpence per week for a six day week. This, in those days, was an astonishing amount for a fourteen-year-old girl to earn.

Yet and as we've already seen: the war exacted its price for any affluence it created. It bled Heelis Street and the adjacent streets of many able men and even some of its boys. Its blind capriciousness took my mother's brother, John, to Gallipoli where he spent dusk until dawn in the water and under constant fire from the shore after the sinking of the troopship carrying him to the battle area.

He survived this ordeal to be taken to France where he died in the early hours of Easter Monday - the 9th of April 1917 - in an attack on the town of Arras, whilst a late flurry of snow swirled around the advancing men.

Willy also became subjected to the Western Front's campaigns. However, chance ordained his survival - as it did the later joining and under-age Jim.

The somewhat faded photograph of my grandmother was taken some time between 1916 and early 1917. She'd been asked by her three sons (Willy, Jim and John - then serving in France) to send each of them a photo. In her right-hand is one of the letters they'd written.

When, during our conversations, my mother showed me this particular copy (which is one either Willy or Jim brought home after the war) she said it indicated the deep anxiety felt by her mother at the time of its taking - this on knowing where the photos had to be sent.

However, when the conflict came to its end, the wage-affluence its four years duration had created also came to an end, and the economic situations similar to those known before returned. This forced Jim to emigrate to Australia where he again experienced warfare in World War Two as a member of the Australian Forces in New Guinea. He died in Australia not long after the war from the delayed affects of wounds received in the New Guinea campaign.

But to return to Heelis Street: in 1920, when my mother reached the age of eighteen, her grandmother, Mary Clynes, came to the end of life in her seventieth year. With the instinct of her kind to be independent and therefore a burden to no-one, she worked to within a few months of her death.

To fulfil the duty-bound commitment of providing a proper "resting place" for Granny Clynes meant supplementing the sale of the few possessions she'd acquired during her life (mainly some items of furniture) with what other members of the family could afford to contribute.

A great fear in those days was not being able to provide a proper and respectable burial for family members. I suppose this fear lingered from the Victorian's deep compulsions to honour and respect the dead, arising from the powerful religious feelings associated with death. Also, the Anatomy Act of 1832, which extended its influence into the early part of the nineteen-hundreds, authorised for medical "use" any deceased seen as "not properly claimed" by next of kin.

So the idea of a "pauper's grave" and the possibility of medical intervention filled people with dread. The certain safeguard against any chance of this happening lay in arranging a properly conducted and conventional burial along with its religious service. People were therefore willing to subject themselves to a great deal of sacrifice in order to emphasise that their deceased appeared suitably respected.

However, life, it seems, in its peculiar twists, can often mix misfortune with opportunity (as we've previously witnessed). A short time before her grandmother died, my mother had married Edward, of the Jones family - who was to become my father. The newly weds were seeking a place to live - preferably in the immediate surrounds to be near both families - and the death of her grandmother offered the opportunity to rent the now empty number ten.

But as we've just seen, no inheritance of furniture came with the rented house, so the method used by most newly-weds in that time and place had to be implemented. They bought discarded wooden packing-crates, at threepence per crate, from the Premier Works in Dantzic Street. With some hard and inventive work, applications of paint and varnish, pieces of cloth and further ingenuity, these large and roughly made boxes could be converted into acceptable seats, tables, cupboards and storage chests.

My father, being a reasonable "handyman", no doubt did a presentable job.

Carpets were considered a luxury beyond even a brief consideration, so "It was one less item to worry about," my mother humorously remarked. Floor coverings (where such was used - particularly to cover the front room's bare wooden floorboards that could be immediately seen from the street) consisted of a piece of linoleum, known as Lino. This, they felt bound to obtain. "We had to look respectable," my mother said with a smile.

Thus - by making-do - the house became furnished. If they'd waited for better days to provide better things, they would've waited for a very long time.

And so my mother's married life began, and for the majority of people who shared her situation in the world she knew, it began in circumstances little different from those they'd always known. War production had ceased and that brief burst of wage-prosperity it created had collapsed. Post-war unemployment rose alarmingly. Those surviving the trenches entered the labour market to swell the ranks of work-seekers. Income for most working-class people lucky enough to be in work reverted to what it had always been: low in its amount and uncertain in its continuation.

As in all times of adversity, the greater burden fell upon the women of the family who sought whatever jobs they could, whilst at the same time looking after their family's day to day needs. My mother was not one to see her hands left idle - nor, like most of her kind, could she afford to leave them that way. Thus, and in accordance with her upbringing, she sought to employ them in whatever way the circumstances of that time would allow.

One place for possible employment seemed to be the large Jewish community occupying the area in and around Cheetham Hill Road. The war and its previous disruptions had caused the usual flight of refugees from mainland Europe. Those in textiles and its allied activities sought Manchester and especially the Cheetham Hill area - where, it seems, situations existed to re-establish their trades. Many clothing and textile workshops were thus added to those already existing in that district.

Besides offering the usual long hours of work in the factories, the area also offered those in my mother's situation a chance for casual employment - especially in the various households in the residential parts, for reasons we'll see later.

My mother told me about her first search for work not long after her marriage (a time when she said, with one of her characteristic understatements: "Money was somewhat short"). Since her only viable skills lay in housework, the mentioned residential area appeared to be the best place to look.

If you care to join me in our next visit, we'll follow her search.

However, brace yourself - it involves a long walk on a cold morning...

8
Work Is Where You Find It

~~~~~~~~~~~~~~~~~~~~~~~~~~~~~~~~~~

Let's imagine it's some time in the early nineteen-twenties. Let's also imagine it's a Saturday - the Jewish Sabbath.

On this day, households in the Cheetham Hill area will be looking for those willing to do casual housework - this to allow observance of their special day's demands. It's also the day we'll follow my mother's search for work, soon after the birth of her first child. The cost of transport is out of the question and walking will be the only means of reaching the place where work might be found.

She rises early to do whatever is needed to maintain the household during her absence. This is followed by a hurried breakfast of tea and buttered toast. She then wraps her infant in a warm blanket and - quietly closing the door behind her - takes the child to a neighbouring relative who'd offered to mind the child during hours already agreed.

Heelis Street is quiet. A few households are only just beginning to stir. Smoke from their first-lit fires drifts fitfully across the night-dampened slates of the rooftops. The slight breeze of the early April morning chills the air; and although the sun has risen above roof height, the haze from the previous day's outpourings of the city's smoke still clings to the higher part of the atmosphere, to subdue its light. As she emerges from the house where her child will be minded, we can see she's dressed in the fashion most Lancashire women of her background and time adopt, as indicated in the offered photo.

She draws her shawl tightly around her to keep out the morning chill. She has in mind the route you'll see outlined in the sketch presented on the next page.

Her intention is to reach the area around Faraday Avenue (the place marked 'B' at the top left of the sketch).

The start is Heelis Street (marked 'A ' - lower right). She'll then follow the part of Collyhurst Road where she can then veer left into Smedley Road, to follow its direction until reaching Queen's Road intersection. At the end of this road is the area in which work might be found.

But let's return to the start of her walk. On reaching the end of Heelis Street, she turns right to take the short downward-sloping length of Davy Street - locally known as "the bruw".

She then crosses the cobbles of the street running across the end of that slope to enter a narrow passageway breaking the line of houses directly opposite the incline she's just descended.

The flight of well-worn stone steps the opening contains takes her down to the short length of path leading to Collyhurst Road. Following this, she then crosses the road's cobbles to reach the pavement bordering the River Irk.

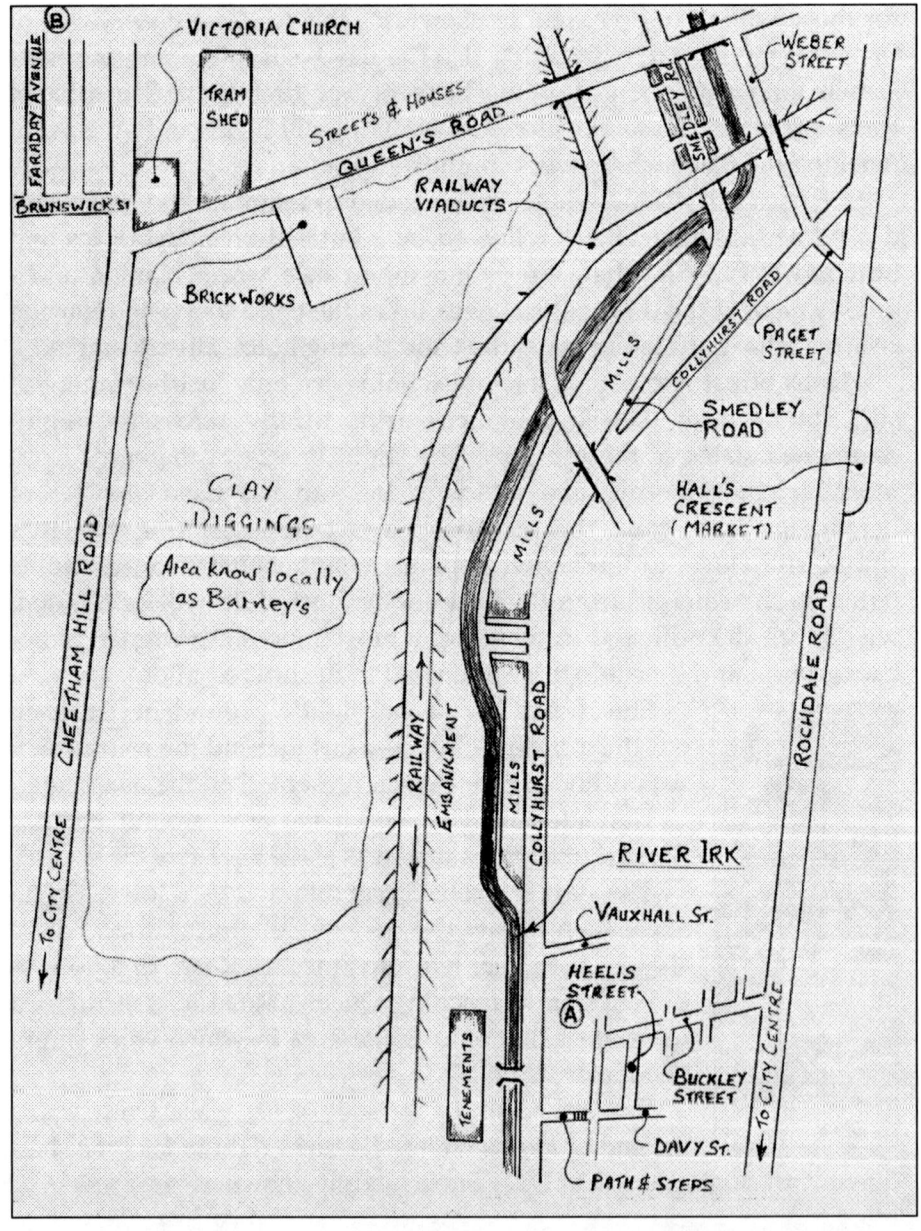

A quick glance to her left through the iron railings along the edge of the pavement shows the Irk's waters contained between its eroded brick-lined banks and swirling five feet or so below the level on which she walks. Its waters look mud-stained and as chilled as the morning air: it must have rained heavily, somewhere upstream, during the night. Drawing the shawl more tightly around her shoulders, she continues her hurried walk along the road's pavement.

A few hundred yards further on takes her to where the river begins to curve away from the road. Here, the cotton processing-mills, occupying the space between river and road, tower their dark-brick frontages above the pavement. On her left, she passes two narrow streets compressed between the mills' bulks. These run at right angle to the road's length and end at the river's bank.

The houses are similar to the ones in Heelis Street and, as in that street, smoke from the first-lit fires drift fitfully from a few chimneys along the terrace rows. It seems the people employed in the nearby mills have only just risen for their Saturday work.

Another hundred yards or so beyond the streets brings her to where Collyhurst Road deviates to her right, just ahead of her, to then obliquely climb the steep slope forming that part of the Irk's valley. Again the houses lining each side of the road's rise appear much the same as the ones in Heelis Street; and again the chimneys clustering along their night-dampened slates show signs of only a few fires lit. This again tells that the morning is not too far advanced and she's making good progress.

Just before reaching the road's deviation, she passes beneath the girdered bridge spanning the cobbles some thirty feet or so above her head. She becomes wary of the smoke drifting down to her part of the pavement as a train pulling its assortment of wagons rumbles across its short length. It reminds her of the Charter Street span she knew as a child. However, beyond this feature no charitable mission exists: only a route she must take to where work might be found.

Constantly in her mind is the thought of being late in the area she needs to reach, and how this will diminish her opportunities. Her anxiety forces an increased pace whilst continuing on the left-hand pavement, that veers at a slight angle away from Collyhurst Road. The sign high upon the wall of its first building tells she's now entered Smedley Road, whose left-hand side contains a line of mills similar to those of the previous half-mile she'd just walked - these again occupying the space between road and river.

A further two hundred yards or so along this route brings her to a sharp left turn where the road bridges the River Irk. She glances over the low parapet to see again the swirling, mud-stained waters now rushing past the eroded stone walls forming the rear of the mills she'd just passed. But her glance is only brief. Her attention is drawn immediately ahead to the high, red-brick viaduct spanning the road just beyond the bridge - whose archways stretch in a long line across the Irk's valley, to her right and left. This, she knows, is a continuation of the railway line dominating the area of her childhood; and, like the viaduct she knew then, a slope rises immediately beyond its archways.

However, this rise appears far longer and steeper than the one she'd climb each morning to reach Saint Chad's school; and no formal schooling exists at the top of its slope. Instead, there's the urgent need to learn from her own efforts how to find work in a world seemingly indifferent to its provision.

She passes beneath the viaduct's archway to give a hurried glance along the rows of terraced houses lining each side of the long climb ahead. These, unlike the houses she knew as a child and those belonging to the street where she now lives, have the advantage of a low wall and a small patch of garden between house and pavement.

This indicates the fringe of a more prosperous district and tells she's now reached a distance nearly half way to the area where work might be found. The smoke issuing from an increasing number of chimneys shows the morning's advance and this again impels a sense of urgency: others will be seeking the same work she hopes to be offered. She quickens her pace - managing to sustain this to the top of the steep incline where the long, level stretch of Queen's Road forms a right angle to its end. She feels a sense of relief: no more long climbs.

Double-decker tramcars now filling with workers are beginning to rattle and whine along the lines set in the centre of the road's cobbles. She awaits a gap in the traffic and hurriedly crosses to reach the pavement on the far side, then to take its left-hand direction. The continuing sense of urgency quickens her pace as she passes the numerous streets and rows of houses now on her right - these similar to the ones in Smedley Road. Again, the signs of many more fires having been lit indicate the increasing advance of the morning.

Ten minutes or so of hurrying brings her to the enormous, redbrick bulk of the Tramways Car Shed, where double-decker trams - having sheltered overnight beneath the shed's long roof - make their exit from its high-arched doorway. They jolt and rattle as they make their sharp left-hand turn into Queen's Road. Others lurch sharply to the right, taking the opposite direction towards Cheetham Hill Road - a hundred yards or so ahead of her.

The ever-increasing numbers of Saturday workers beginning to board the trams at the various stops intensifies her already acute awareness of passing time. She's also aware that the early rise and the urgently paced three-mile walk could make her appear weary and not completely composed - thus lessening the chance of employment.

A low wall in front of Victoria Church, just beyond the tram-shed, invites rest; but again the pressing sense of urgency makes this brief. She quickly rises to her feet and then adjusts her shawl as neatly as she can around her shoulders. She also smoothes her hair with her hands in the hope that it looks tidy, then crosses the cobbles of Cheetham Hill Road - dodging the traffic rumbling along its increasingly busy length.

Immediately before her is the entrance to Brunswick Street. This and the various avenues in its vicinity contain the large, prosperous looking, three-storey houses built a decade or so before the turn of the century. Their occupants are, by then, just finishing breakfast and - from talks with others having made a similar quest - she knows this to be the opportune hour to find the employment she needs. She feels pleased about having reached the area in good time and glad the night's rain hadn't continued. Her shawl gives little protection from the wet; and appearing bedraggled would diminish her work-chances.

But let's digress for a while from this hopeful search for work, to consider the informal rules governing its activity. Also, let's consider certain aspects of this search not explicitly stated in talks she may've had with those knowing this method of finding work, since such details are so much a part of the ordinary life they'd hardly need mentioning. You might, for instance, ask how the inhabitants of the area would recognise those seeking employment?

The answer is this: seeking work in the way we're now witnessing is not at all unusual. The formal institutions administering the availability of work are felt by many working-class people to be inflexible and repressive, since they carry the stigma of the old Poor Law from which they arose. Moreover, the applicant is forced to take whatever job might exist, regardless of preference. Because of this, many people seek work of their own choosing under their own initiative - especially for casual work.

Also in the time we're witnessing, there's a much greater and more marked difference in the dress of the various classes than we see in the time from whence we came. As we've already noticed: my mother is dressed in the way of a working-class Lancashire woman. In particular, she wears no coat. Instead, she wears a much cheaper woollen shawl - which is, in all probability, home knitted. Thus, by her dress she will be known and her social position thereby declared. And even by a quick glance, the inhabitants of the houses she's reached will recognise her as a person who - if in that area on that day and at that particular time - seeks casual employment. Those with work to offer will be on the lookout from their windows and respond accordingly.

On this day, my mother has - partly by chance and partly by expectation - walked to Faraday Avenue (the second avenue on the right down Brunswick Street). A woman we'll come to know later as Mrs Gottlieb is looking out of her window. She's extremely anxious for someone to do housework; for, besides being their Sabbath, it is also a time nearing her son's bar-mitzvah, when help in preparing the house for this important event will be especially welcome.

We see her leave the window and come to the front door of her house to approach the person she recognises as a possible candidate. So, by chance, my mother's search for work ends and her work begins.

However, let's withdraw from witnessing the brief negotiations leading up to her acceptance and look in advance to what happens from then on. She finds the Gottlieb's house large and - after working at its cleaning for a hour or so - realises that meeting the householder's requirements demands more hours than she'd planned. She becomes anxious about her child's care and begs an hour or so leave in order to arrange extra time for her infant's minding.

In the period before making her request, she'd established a favourable rapport with the person giving employment. Based on this, she obtains permission for the requested work-break and an assurance that the job would be held if she makes a quick return. Having no other means of communication, she hurries back to Heelis Street to arrange the additional hours of child minding. Then, with the same sense of urgency, returns to continue the task until mid afternoon.

For the hours actually worked, she receives two shillings and sixpence (roughly twelve and a half pence in present-day currency) plus a snack at midday. This amount of money may seem derisory to our present-day economic sense of proportion; since that amount would hardly entice anyone to do five minutes work - even with a snack "thrown in". However, in the time we're visiting, it isn't a trivial amount. A packet of tea can be got for a penny; a pound of sugar for twopence; a pound of lamb-chops for fourpence, and a bag of coal (about 120 pounds weight) for sixpence. A lot can be done with two shillings and sixpence - and even sixpence can keep the household fire burning for quite some time.

But let's witness the events after the work is completed. My mother's efforts seemed to please Mrs Gottlieb, for she suggested a return the next Saturday. Having got used to the requirements and the facilities available, the next session proved somewhat easier. She found Mrs Gottlieb's instincts leaned strictly towards business-like expectation for money paid out, but it also dictated a firm sense of fairness. Although the second Saturday's work took far less time, my mother received the same amount.

In addition, Mrs Gottlieb's satisfaction for what she considered work well done led, soon afterwards, to an opportunity for additional employment on Saturday afternoons. She recommended my mother to her sister, Becky, who owned a fish and chip shop in Stocks Street - a street just over the other side of Cheetham Hill Road from Faraday Avenue. This involved a few hours of chores offering the usual two shillings and sixpence and - what is more - generous helpings of fish and chips to be taken home to be warmed up in the fire-side oven for the family's evening meal. The day's work was now showing a return of five shillings - plus fish and chips.

Again returning to the question of fair pay. A female shop assistant would earn something like two pounds and two shillings per week (twenty shillings to the pound, twelve pence to the shilling) for a forty-five hour week - which, in the currency related to the period of our visit, works out at about eleven pence per hour. So, two shillings and sixpence would represent just over two and a half to three hours work - which is near enough the hours my mother eventually provided for the money received, when familiarity made her able to meet the requirements in that time. In addition, she received a bonus of a meal in the first job and take-away fish and chips in the second.

Moreover, the timing of the final pay-out happened to be fortuitous. Lack of widespread refrigeration made it necessary for shops to clear surplus perishables before closing for any length of time - a practice particularly applicable to late Saturday evening. On completion of her last job, my mother hurried to a large butcher's shop situated along Rochdale Road, where cheap sell-offs might be on offer.

Again, it was a case of "first there, first gets". She'd hurry the three-quarter mile or so along Queen's Road, passing the top end of Smedley Road on her right, to reach the not-far-beyond entrance to Weber Street; then to follow its length to Paget Street where it meets Rochdale Road. Crossing that road, she'd turn right to pass Hall's Crescent on her left, where - in the advancing gloom of the evening - she'd see the market traders preparing to close their stalls by the light of acetylene lamps. But she'd quickly pass this activity - having a more pressing mission on her mind than chance bargains around the market stalls.

Just a few hundred yards or so along the road will take her to Smith's shop; and if she arrived in time, her effort could be well rewarded. Amongst the sell-offs might be a leg of pork for little more than a shilling; or a shoulder of lamb for the same amount; or a couple of pound-weight of stewing steak for less than sixpence. Part of her Saturday work would be immediately converted into nourishment to bless the Sunday table - and, possibly, some of the day's tables beyond.

However, to return to Mrs Gottlieb: she proved to be a helpful and generous woman to those she considered "conscientious". Although she couldn't, herself, provide work beyond the usual Saturday morning - and although my mother's circumstances meant she had to attend to her own family's needs, and therefore limit her commitments - nevertheless, Mrs Gottlieb was the source of many convenient filling-in recommendations, such as the previously mentioned introduction to her sister. She also found an occasional few hours for my father's ability to do household repair jobs.

Another recommendation in the Cheetham Hill area was a Mrs Lee - living in Honey Street, situated at the end of North Street and about half a mile distance from the Gottlieb's house. This street could be easily accessed from Cheetham Hill Road. Here, my mother's reputation for fast and efficient work again earned further recommendations; so much so that on one Saturday she actually did the basic requirements for five houses in and around that street - all in one day. This earned the magnificent sum of twelve shillings and sixpence, constituting almost a fortune for those of her circumstances in that time.

The work began early in the morning, well before breakfast, with the lighting of fires for all five houses. Then going to each house - again in turn - to clean up after the family breakfasts; then moving from house to house in a rotating schedule of work until the final task was finished in the very late afternoon; making a day of labour not easily repeated.

On relating this event, my mother commented that she felt so rich - having twelve shillings and sixpence in her hand, all at once - and in one day - she almost believed she could buy a Stately Home.

However, she went to the butcher's shop instead...

9
High Spirits - Low Expectations

~~~~~~~~~~~~~~~~~~~~~~~~~~~~~~~~~~

When my mother's regular sources were unable to offer work, she would - by way of the various introductions mentioned earlier or by searching under her own initiative - find other opportunities.

This could sometimes be done without too much difficulty because the Cheetham Hill community had numerous households wanting the domestic services my mother could provide. These households represented families of astounding variety, coming from virtually every corner of Europe. A particular example was Mrs Bodkin who came from Russia to finally settle in Cheetham Street - a street which, I believe, no longer exists, but then ran off the opposite end of North Street from Cheetham Hill Road.

Mrs Bodkin shared a characteristic possessed by many in the recently formed community in which she now lived: that of having been previously accustomed to "more advantageous" circumstances. Thus, she became reluctant to do any work considered demeaning by the dictates of her background and therefore became appreciative of anyone willing to relieve her of that embarrassment.

This situation caused my mother a great deal of amusement, mixed with astonishment - which she, of course, kept hidden from the lady in question. Mrs Bodkin seemed well able to do housework herself; and although the family found themselves, for most times, in difficult financial circumstances, she still showed an extreme aversion to putting her hand to what appeared to my mother as the most undemanding of chores.

In all fairness to Mrs Bodkin, it seems her reluctance stemmed mainly from her husband's attitude. Although needing almost every penny he possessed to maintain his tailoring business (recently set up in a little shop somewhere near the city centre) he nevertheless insisted that the "position due to his wife" should be honoured and respected. This meant Mrs Bodkin being forbidden to do any housework other than that involving the smallest, unavoidable, task.

And so it was. Such is the power of background and custom it can impose itself upon any behaviour - even to the extent of financial discomfort. But this background and custom had a somewhat different aspect from that of my mother's, wherein the prevailing custom was: if you needed anything doing, you got on and did it yourself - since little chance existed of anyone else doing it for you.

However, Mrs Bodkin was, in essence, a kindly soul and despite the perplexity created by what appeared to my mother as the strange customs Mrs Bodkin had been committed to follow, she got on very well with her. Because of this, the work expected from my mother, if not lessened, became, at least, companionable. They both shared the same midday meal of rye bread, steamed fish and horse-radish sauce (which, I assume, was a typical Russian fare) whilst Mrs Bodkin, in her uncertain English, told stories of "Old Russia".

During the telling, my mother helped with the English for what proved to be a series of fascinating tales - an experience producing the previously mentioned taste for reading history, persisting well into her old age.

But returning to the household chores: Mrs Bodkin paid the usual two shillings and sixpence for every two and a half hours work completed; and although her husband's business hadn't reached the happy state of providing a cash surplus, the due amount never failed to be ready and available.

However, there were some whose financial position couldn't properly meet the expectations their previous background decreed. For instance, a Mrs Sugermann of the same street found even two shillings and sixpence difficult to raise and offered piano lessons in exchange for work provided.

My sister, Nellie, happened to be about seven or eight years of age at the time, and although my mother's priorities were directed towards earning much needed cash, she nevertheless thought the offered lessons could present an opportunity to develop any latent talent her daughter might possess. Although plenty of willingness existed, not enough talent seemed to go with it; thus the lessons, along with the housework, had to be discontinued.

Unfortunately, not everyone displayed the virtue of fair-mindedness. Some were readily prepared to take every advantage of those they thought desperate for work - this especially when the economic depression of the late nineteen-twenties made finding such jobs even more difficult.

But as previously implied, the belief that - for status or religious reasons - or for both - certain tasks were not "fitting", persisted even when those involved couldn't really afford this indulgence, either in cash, kind, or consideration.

Rather than offering comments of my own, an event my mother described is far more telling.

One particular experience involved a family living not far from Mrs Gottlieb. The lady of the house made employment conditional on my mother arriving for the stipulated jobs before 8 a.m. on the Saturday morning, whilst the family were at prayer. The family consisted of father, mother, four sons and a young daughter. For two shillings and sixpence and a meagre morsel at mid-day, their large house had to be cleaned from top to bottom - sufficient to last until the following Saturday with only the minimum of attention in the meantime. This included the polishing of many brass candelabra and various items of silverware. In addition, my mother had to do the laundering for the whole family.

In those days, to do a week's wash in a very limited time for a family of that size - without the assistance of the aids we now take for granted - required the stamina of a marathon runner, let alone doing housework on top of its demands. There were no: set the automatic program; pour in the biological soap powder and fragrantly scented rinse-liquid; then lean back in a comfortable chair and have a nice, relaxing, cup of tea type of machine.

Instead, the wash was a scrubbing board using; rock-hard soap scraping; boiling and pummelling test of endurance until both hands were nearly red-raw. All this labour demanded starting well before breakfast and sometimes continuing way into the late afternoon - depending on the pile of washing.

After a couple of gruelling weeks, my mother told the lady of the house she'd have to pay at least five shillings for the work expected. The lady paid the "at least" amount; but then proceeded to surreptitiously add some of her relations' washing to the already substantial pile; whereupon my mother was forced to withdraw her services - much as she needed the money - for the sake of her self-respect and physical survival.

When telling me of this incident she said, with a grin:

"Even a donkey refuses to go on when the load's piled too high; and I considered I'd as much sense as a donkey!"

However, in spite of this attempt to pile it high, many decent folks did, in their own way, correct what could've been a totally bad experience. The Gottlieb family, for instance, proved to be a source of fair earnings enhanced with much kindness, right up to the time the family emigrated to Australia in the late Twenties - a period producing the October 1929 Wall Street Crash and its consequential economic depression.

But even before this severe downturn, the years weren't ones of great prosperity for those in similar circumstances to my mother's. They were as they'd always been: a day to day struggle to make ends meet, even for those in regular employment. This condition became far more austere in the years after 1929 because the scarcity of work provided scope for employers to reduce wage-rates.

In this milieu, most working people of my mother's background were constantly one week's pay away from poverty. Amounts generally earned each week allowed very little margins for providing cover against the proverbial rainy day. And, for many, the rainy day could easily turn into a downpour.

Those experiencing such circumstances could find themselves forced to turn to the Board of Guardians (the administration that allocated financial relief) as a final act of desperation. This Board represented the old nineteenth-century Poor Law system with certain revisions to bring it up to date.

Some of these changes were made in an attempt to soften the interrogative and punitive method of determining whom amongst its applicants were "deserving" or "undeserving", and making provision (or non-provision) on that basis - as the old Poor Law tended to do.

Also, the Board of Guardians' administration became under the direct control of Local Authorities, to give (it was thought) a greater sensitivity and a proper understanding of local peoples' needs and conditions - and thereby allowing more "acceptable" judgements. But as we've seen in the case of background and customs: old habits die hard and the old Poor Law ethos was likewise hard to kill off. The original principle of assessing the worthiness of those subjected to its judgements constantly surfaced - intentionally or unintentionally - amongst those schooled in the old order.

My mother related an example of this process concerning a friend know from her schooldays - named Nancy.

When Nancy was about eighteen years of age, she gave birth to what the Poor Law would describe as a "child conceived outside of wedlock" and therefore deemed illegitimate. This situation forced her to live in one of the worse areas occupied by those whose life's circumstances allowed little choice of accommodation: the meagrely furnished lodging-rooms of the Ludgate Hill part of Angel Meadow, not far from Gould Street Gasworks.

Her "case" was submitted to the Board of Guardians. It decided that the birth of the child was the result of her own lapse; and she'd thereby excluded herself from financial assistance. The Guardians directed her to seek support from charities that provided for people in her situation. This she had to do and in doing so became dependent on the type of charities we saw in our previous visit, along with any help that friends she had left were able to give. My mother visited her whenever she could and gave whatever assistance she could - which, at that time, had to be limited.

However, another friend of Nancy's - also from schooldays - happened to be a man living in Sand Street, by the Municipal Tip, not far from the 'Umpteen Steps' (an area we'll come to know in a later visit). He happened to be the successor to the Maggot Man we met in my mother's childhood and earned his living by the same occupation. Although not the father of the child, he eventually married Nancy and thereby made any further appeals to the Board of Guardians unnecessary. This, at least, was a change to better circumstances for someone whose situation may have remained "difficult".

But even for those able to help themselves, the end of the nineteen-twenties and its following decade presented little change in the difficulties they always had to face.

As we witnessed in a previous narrative, my mother's mother had acquired a full-time cleaning job at Crumpsall Hospital. This necessitated rising around four o' clock every morning to light the household fire and prepare breakfast for all the family; after which she'd take the three mile walk to her work, irrespective of weather. Then the long hours until the walk home, where more tasks waited before she could seek her bed.

In the July of 1931, she took ill whilst scrubbing the hospital floors and had to be taken home. Within a week or so, she died of heart failure caused by a chronic kidney condition. It seems, at the age of fifty-nine, the years of effort had finally taken their toll. Her condition must've been worsening for a number of years and its pain progressively becoming almost unbearable.

She was, however, a person with all the desperate independence possessed by a women of her generation and circumstances; driven by the anxiety of not being able to provide for herself or family; and, in her sickness, having the fear of imposing a burden on those already burdened. No doubt because of this she made no complaints, even under circumstances that must've been awful to bear. Therefore, nobody around her knew how ill she really was.

Yet, although my grandmother's and my mother's experiences had their own particular circumstances, they were in many respects representative of virtually all the people in their district and similar districts in the inner cities of that time. From their very beginnings, their lives were spent in areas not noted for affluence and scenic beauty - and where hardship would be another word for "life".

These circumstances produced a people with an astounding capacity to tolerate discomfort. This they acquired from having to endure sorrows and circumstances hardly imaginable by present day standards.

Even the conditions of Heelis Street and its surrounding area - with what our present time would deem its chronic overcrowding and minimal comforts - represented a vast improvement for many in that street compared with what they'd known before. Their expectations were low, but their spirits were high. They knew from past experience that they could endure whatever life sent for them to face.

Just before my Granny died, she bought for me a pram from Yaffee's second-hand shop on Rochdale Road - a place we'll visit later. It cost three shillings and sixpence, which represented a large proportion out of the not many shillings she received per week as a cleaner. My first views of the wider world must have been from that pram.

And so my view of life began with the period called "The Hungry Decade" which also saw the beginning of "The Means Test".

Yet, the people of my mother's kind were - as we've seen - well schooled to cope with its adversities. They'd learnt the strength of family and that they could rely on the mutual help and support the neighbourly community in which they lived would offer.

But most of all, they'd learnt the art of self-reliance. By turning their hands to whatever they could, they'd manage to survive.

Let's look at the nineteen-thirties. But this time, mainly through the eyes of a child...

10
Through the Eyes of a Child

The path we've followed now takes us to the beginning of the nineteen-thirties, whose decade we'll see mainly through the suggested eyes of a child.

This becomes necessary because the memories I tended to prompt during the conversations with my mother centred on the periods up to the time I was born - chiefly because I wasn't there to know anything about those earlier times. Although we did, now an again, speak of the nineteen-thirties, it wasn't to the same degree and depth as the discussions concerning the preceding decades.

Yet, over the years, I'd picked up various pieces of information about her experiences during the Thirties, and therefore thought what I already knew would suffice until she felt more inclined to accept further questioning. Unfortunately, circumstances did not allow this to happen. Therefore, the final decade leading up to the time when the immense changes splitting the century apart occurred needs to be seen mainly through the perspective of the child I was then.

Nevertheless, this perspective can offer the benefit of seeing things from a different angle, so to speak; more especially since one of the most startling transformations the century's second half engendered concerns attitudes towards childhood and its conditions.

However, when trying to relate the experiences of the child I once was, I found it presented many problems. These centred on the fact that a child's perspective is somewhat "at odds" with that of an adult's. We realise this when returning to a place we knew as a child, and find - to our astonishment - the high wall we remembered towering above our head is no more than shoulder high and that tremendously long street is no more than a short walk.

This astonishment usually turns to amusement when we immediately "see" our childhood perspective was obviously "incorrect" and the wall and the walk are - in actuality - the way our adult visit reveals them to be. But when we make this "correction", it becomes almost impossible to view the wall as we once did or pace the distance in our mind with the child's legs we once had. What we were as a child is lost in the adult we've now become and we find it increasingly difficult to feel, or even understand, the experiences of the child we've left behind.

Because of this, many of our earlier memories just won't "fit" our later perspectives and we either distorted them - to make them fit - or find their complete lack of compatibility with the way we've come to see things inhibits their full awakening. (Perhaps this is why much of our childhood becomes "forgotten"?)

I then decided: if the childhood world of our proposed visit is to be recreated - in all its "reality" - the memories must be allowed to rise from their original source in whatever way they would and in the form they first occurred. A large part of what follows is, therefore, expressed from that point of view: using a child's eyes, a child's voice, and a child's perspective. This I ask you to accept wherever it appears; for - as previously inferred - a more conventional mode of expression would, I believe, take away the reality of the childhood I'm trying to convey.

In allowing the chosen perspective to find its own "tongue" - so to speak - I found many of the images came encapsulated in verse and rhyme; this no doubt because that long-ago world from whence the images arose was one essentially of play, wherein verse and rhyme seemed to be its main "language". Because of this, you'll find the sketches offered at various stages throughout the following narratives portraying scenes shaped by a child's viewpoint. Also, the offered verses and rhymes used to "explain" the scenes will reflect the simplicity of a child's expressions.

However, and where appropriate, many of the passages are expressed by way of a more conventional viewpoint, containing details derived from formal sources, supplemented by the comments of people you've yet to meet. But even in this, a child's voice may now and again drift through; since it was a child's eyes and a child's understanding that perceived a world of childhood which the last half of the twentieth-century and the period we've now entered seems mainly to have lost.

Yet, I believe the essence of that child's world is important for us to understand; for every period is a product of its people; and the nature of its people is a product of their childhood...

11
The House

~~~~~~~~~~~~~~~~~~~~~~~~~~~~~~~~

Our travels along the path of time took us from a street we knew as Hargreaves Street, as it was in the September of 1902, to a street we now know as Heelis Street. To further our understanding of how and in what way people of those times lived, we'll spend a little while looking around the last named street as it was in the nineteen-thirties.

I've drawn a sketch of the area where the street belonged. This again is based on memory and although memory is never complete what remains in the mind are those aspects of a place assuming importance to the person remembering. In this respect, it can represent an actual record of what appeared to that person as most significant.

On returning to the time when Heelis Street lived, we'll first make a visit to our house. This is depicted in the representation you'll find on the next page. Later on, we'll take a walk around the area. We'll do this by following a proposed route indicated thus ------> in the sketch presented below.

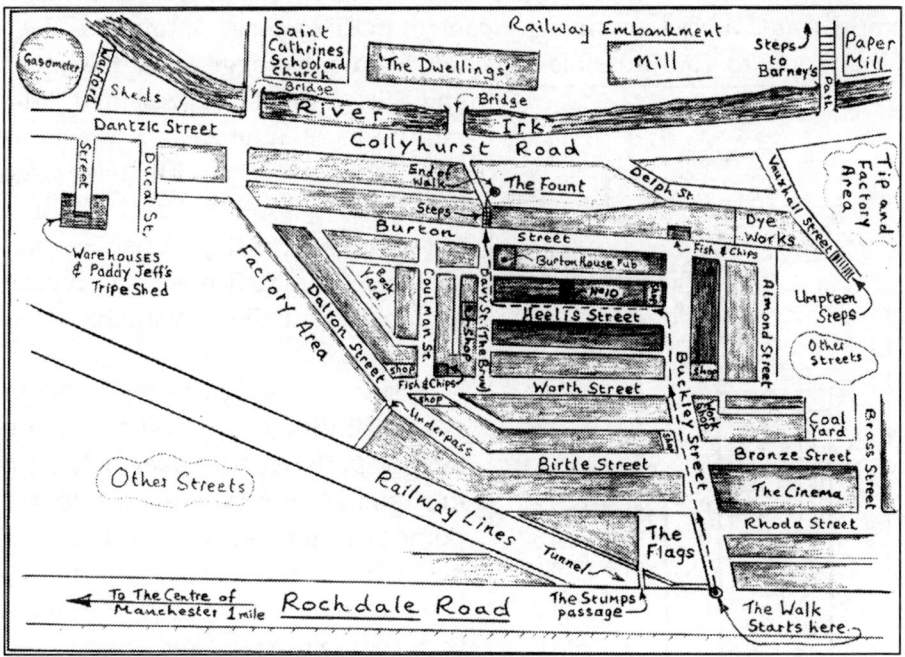

But let's delay our intended walk, for a while, to get to know the house and gain a brief introduction to its street.

Immediately before the 1939-45 war, the whole area of our interest became subjected to a series of planning regulations intending extensive demolition and reconstruction. Our house was finally demolished towards the end of that process, so the memories I have of the house and its district are those belonging to a child. Nevertheless, I believe the recollections I can offer possess their own validity; this especially when related to the way of life and its associated features that a child's - sometimes acute - observations are capable of making.

Moreover, this way of observing is particularly useful when independent sources can provide verifications. Therefore, in order to recreate what did exist before its final destruction, it'll be necessary for the child I was then to take you around and describe what that child felt as important.

As previously requested: I hope you'll readily accept this mode of viewing because it's essentially the way we all perceived that part of the world of our first experience.

However, you might now rightly be asking: "Why bother visiting a small, nondescript house and street of such little consequence that records of them ever existing are difficult to find; and, if found, would represented a brief and insignificant jot in the passage of time?"

In reply to your possible objection, I can only suggest that the house and its street represented the multitude of houses and streets as they once were in all our large industrial towns and cities. Therefore, recording a direct and intimate experience of a typical example is, I believe, valuable in its own right.

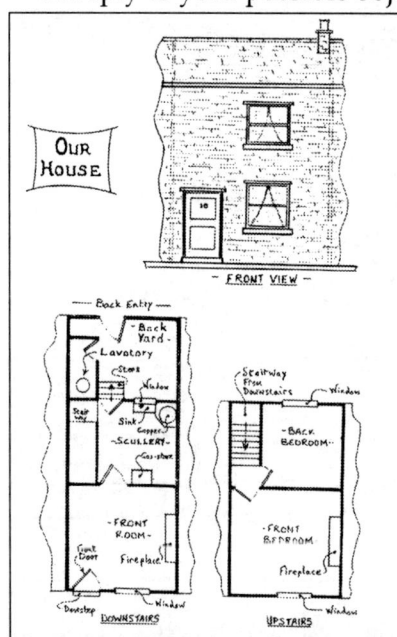

Also, if you care to immerse yourself in their time and place, you might, perhaps, discover what on first sight appears ordinary to the point of insignificance could take on qualities you may feel as extraordinary - compared with what we've come to know and expect.

In returning to that time and place, we'll visit one of the small terraced houses situated in Heelis Street in the nineteen-thirties. This house is essentially the same as the thousands upon thousands of houses in the numerous districts clustering around the centre of industrialised Manchester and its similar northern towns and cities, in the decades before the 1939-45 war. It comprises two rooms up, two rooms down and a flagstone yard at the rear. By the time of my birth, it was already occupied by my father (Edward) mother (Elizabeth) sister (Ellen - aged 9) and brother (Edward - aged 6).

During our visit, you'll notice a prominent feature of its district is the line upon line of identical backyards built upon the rear of rows upon rows of identical houses. These backyards are about the size of a small room and represent the only - what might be called - private open space each household has. Virtually all of them display the practice of having their bare-brick walls coated with lime-wash (known generally as "whitewash") to which some "dolly-blue" has been added.

This mixture - widely used at that time - is no longer necessary in the present age of ready-made preparations and the absence of backyards needing whitewashing. So, in case you don't know what dolly-blue is - and why it was used - here's a quick explanation.

It's a mild dye produced in powder form and contained in a small linen bag purchased from the local shops. The most popular version has the name 'Reckitt's Blue Bag'. Its real purpose is for adding to the water used for washing white linens and cottons. This gives the washed articles an extra brightness by imparting a barely perceptible tinge of blue to the white. Folks found it performs the same trick when used in whitewash, therefore, and in this case, giving extra brightness to the yard's small confines.

But let's have a look at our yard. It's typical of all the other backyards and has a tiny brick-built shed with a roof consisting of a large slab of flat stone - on which our cat sleeps when the sun is warm. The shed (known locally as the closet) is built against the rear wall of the house and on the left-hand side as you face into the yard. It has a wooden door with a latch and contains the lavatory - this being flushed by a cast-iron cistern fixed to the wall above the bowl and operated by a chain with a wooden handle.

The cistern is prone to freeze during the winter if care isn't taken; and to stop this happening, our Dad leaves an oil-lamp burning which he hangs on a hook he's screwed into the wall immediately below the cistern. He always does this when it looks as if there could be a cold spell during the night. It provides just enough heat to stop a freeze-up.

The inside of the closet is also whitewashed - which our Dad does at the same time as he does the yard.

Stood against the opposite wall to the closet you'll see a large mangle whose wooden rollers are worn by the many squeezing of household washing. Our Dad painted its iron frame with black paint to stop it rusting. To me, it appears gigantic; and I fear my fingers could get caught in its gears and rollers; but our Mam says it's all right as long as I keep them well away when the handle's being turned.

By now you've probably noticed that the backyard wall is topped by lengths of flat stone and has a gap to provide for a wooden door giving access to a narrow alleyway. We call this the "back-entry" (or just "the entry"). A similar brick wall separates the yards of each adjacent house - but without a door, of course.

The entry runs between and therefore separates the yards of the row containing our house and those belonging to the row in the next street. You'll find the same back-to-back arrangement in nearly all the streets in our district.

Every Monday morning, the Corporation workmen use the entry to get the dustbins (locally known as "midden-bins") from the yards, for emptying into a cart waiting in the street. Although the entry's width isn't much more than that of a man's outstretched arms, they seem to manage all right - even when carrying heavy bins filled mostly with ashes from the household fires. These they carry by gripping one of the handles fix near the top of the bin, and then twisting and heaving the bin on to their back. The bin-men must be strong, because I can hardly move the bin even when it's no more than half-full of ashes from our fire. They wear a jacket whose rear panel is made of padded leather to stop the load from feeling too uncomfortable.

To empty the bin, they heave it up to one of the openings along the side of the dustcart. This usually makes a cloud of powdery ash that sometimes drifts in the air. When they use the horse-drawn cart, this can make the horse a bit restless. However, each opening has a sliding cover that the bin-men are supposed to quickly pull down, to stop too much dust floating around.

We keep our midden-bin against the wall to the right of the backyard door, as viewed from the house. The bin-men open the door themselves to collect the bin and bring it back. They're able to do this because the door has only a latch and is therefore never locked. Nobody thinks of locking their backyard door, and we've never found any need to lock ours (even if we had a lock to lock, that is).

You might want to know the number of our house? It's number ten and occupies about the middle position of the row comprising twelve houses. These all have even numbers and are faced by a row of identical houses - all with odd numbers. The frontage of each house consists of a door opening directly onto the street and two small, wooden framed, sash windows with stone sills: one up, one down (as shown in the sketch I've offered). The windows are to the right of the door when facing from the street. The lower one belongs to the downstairs living room and the upper to the front one of the two bedrooms.

The houses across the street have an opposite arrangement so that their windows are to the left of the front door. I don't know why this is - except, perhaps, to makes the rows seem a bit different?

However, back to our house: the front door allows immediate access to the downstairs front room directly from the street - as is the case for all the houses. The first thing you'll notice as we go in is the fire burning in its fireplace built into the centre of the wall to our right. The fireplace also has a small, brightly polished, cast-iron oven positioned on the left-hand side of the fire's grate, and has our large iron kettle simmering in its recess on top of the oven.

You might think it's a bit strange to have a fire burning on such a warm sunny day, but we need to do this because the fire is our main means for cooking food and heating water. Also, our Dad likes a "brew-up" when he gets home - which is the reason why the kettle's kept simmering. He usually has two large mugs of tea when he gets in before he does anything else.

Positioned at the centre of the wooden mantelpiece is a chiming clock set in an oak case with a few porcelain ornaments on either side of it. But what you'll notice straight away is the picture on the wall above the clock. It's called 'Monarch of the Glen'. The giant stag has massive antlers and is standing in a misty landscape with its head turned sideways. You feel as if it's about to turn its head, to look straight at you, when you enter the room.

Another thing you've probably notice is the shiny fender around the hearth. On first glance you mightn't realise it's really made of wood. This is because it's covered with thin brass sheeting embossed with an ornamental pattern. Our Mam gives it a good polish with Brasso to make it gleam from the fire's glow, even in daylight - as you can see. She says a bright fender make a fireplace look cheerful and there's nothing like a cheerful fireplace for brightening up a house. She does the same to the brass rack holding its poker along with its brush and small shovel that's standing on the hearthstone, just inside the fender.

We need the fender to guard against burning coal or hot cinders accidentally falling out of the fire-grate and damaging the linoleum covering the floor - which can happen when the fire's being poked. You might notice the lino has recently been laid and has a light-brown pattern resembling wooden blocks. It's what some people call "parquet".

When our Dad laid it down, he first covered the bare floorboards with sheets of thick cardboard (I watched him do this) which he got from the paper-mill near the River Irk. He said this stops the sharp edges of the boards marking the lino and then wearing through. Nevertheless, it still needs replacing now and again. It seems to wear out more quickly around the front door. Our Dad says it's because our Mam scrubs it too hard; but she says she wouldn't have to do this if people wiped their feet properly when they came in.

The room's wallpaper also needs a change every so often because it gets shabby around the fireplace. This mainly happens because smoke sometimes gets into the room when the fire's lit first thing in the morning - especially if there's been a chilly night. Cold air becomes trapped in the chimney and prevents the newly lit fire from drawing up properly.

Most people have a thin metal sheet - called a fire-drawer - for covering the fire's opening as soon as the fire's lit. We keep ours just inside the closet in the backyard. To use it, you block the fire's opening with the metal sheet and leave just the lower area of the grate uncovered. This forces a draught through the small gap. The firewood and coal soon blazes as the draught drives the cold air upwards and out of the chimney. You need to be very careful when doing this, because the metal gets very hot if left up too long.

Our Dad screwed two hooks on the underside of the wooden mantelpiece and suspends the metal sheet by wires threaded through holes at each of its top corners. This holds it in position whilst the fire's drawing up. Then - when there's a good blaze - it can be taken down by holding the wires, which stay cool. However, you need to be careful about using the fire-drawer longer than necessary. It'll make the fire blaze too fiercely and can set the chimney alight - that's if there's an excess of soot accumulated in its flue. Because of this, it's a good idea to have the chimney swept regularly by a good Chimney-sweep. Otherwise, you'll find not only your wallpaper gets ruined.

You'll see our wallpaper with its yellow and pink floral pattern looks quite bright. That's because it hasn't been up long. You'll also notice our Dad finished it off with a matching border where it joins the ceiling. He said this costs a little extra but it makes the job look neater. He uses flour and water for the wallpaper paste. I helped him mix it.

The large photo on the wall at the rear of the room and facing the front window is one of my mother's mother, taken a few years before she died. She was, of course, my Granny Corrigan who I told you about during a previous visit.

But you're probably wondering what the long rack suspended from the ceiling above the fireplace is used for. It's called an airing-rack. You'll find one of these in most houses. The four equally spaced wooden bars, fitted to their crescent-shaped wooden ends, are for draping the washing over if it needs a final airing after being out, on the line, in the yard. Although it's very useful, it can be a bit of a nuisance when full; especially for grown-ups who have to duck their head when passing beneath it. The ceiling isn't high enough for even a short person to avoid the dangling clothes - even when the rack's fully raised - so our Mam mostly uses it during the day when we're all out.

You can raise and lower the rack by the cords you'll see passing over each of the two pulleys screwed into the ceiling and then tied to each eye-screw fixed to the top-centre of the rack's wooden ends. The cords are tied together at their loose ends so that they can be pulled as one. To hold the rack in whatever position is needed, you loop the cord's end over the clinch-hook you'll find fixed to the wall around the left-hand side of the chimney-breast.

Anyway, you've probably noticed that the room's small enough as it is, even without the rack; and it isn't really big enough to hold very much furniture - even if we could afford more than we've got. The table with its four chairs positioned in the centre of the room and a spare chair near the fire takes up most of the space. Then there's our wireless standing on top of its small cupboard, in the chimney-breast bay nearest the window.

You might be interested in this (the wireless, I mean, not the cupboard). It's a Philco - made by the Philco Radio Corporation. It's advertised as the 'People's Set' because it's supposed to be cheap enough for everyone to afford. But most people in our district wouldn't think it's all that cheap. It cost five guineas (five pounds and five shillings) which is nearly two weeks wages; and that's a large amount to pay in one go. So if anyone gets really desperate to have a wireless, they'll get one the way we did: seven-an'-six (that's seven shillings and sixpence) for the first payment, then one-an'-eight (that's one shilling and eight pence) each week for eighteen months. This finally pays it off.

You've probably realised that amount is a bit more than the wireless would cost if paid for all in one go, but the extra charge is for the payments being spread. You must keep up all the payments without a break, otherwise the shop takes the wireless back.

Ours has an accumulator (that's a type of battery). We keep it in the cupboard on a shelf just below the wireless. It smells a bit acidy when the wireless is turned on for any length of time; but our Dad said we needn't worry about this because it's normal for it to smell that way. However, he warned it could be dangerous if the glass case got broke and the acid spilled out - so we have to be careful about bumping into the cupboard. Anyway, we've no electricity; and that's why we use an accumulator.

You can get batteries that don't smell. These are less dangerous, but cost a lot more than an accumulator. Also, they can't be recharge.

An advantage of a set running from a battery or accumulator is it costs a guinea (one pound and one shilling) less than a set working directly from electricity. Some people are lucky enough to have electricity supplied directly to their house, for lighting and working things such as a wireless, but there's no houses like that in our district. Also, in the total cost of buying and running a wireless, you need to take into account the expense of renting the accumulator from the wireless-shop along Rochdale Road; also the bother of taking it back to the shop when it needs recharging. Another cost you need to consider is the ten shillings a year for the licence - but that applies to any wireless, whatever the type.

We like our wireless. Its shiny, domed-shape, dark-brown Bakelite casing and its matching light-brown baize behind the speaker's grille looks quite decorative. The rectangular dial you see below the grille has a knob at its centre for tuning in the various stations. The Long Wave stations (long distance and overseas) are indicated on the left of the dial, and the Medium Wave (our country and those nearby) on the right. The right-hand knob of the two below the dial allows you to switch waves. The other is for switching the wireless on and off and also for controlling the volume. It takes a minute or two for the valves to warm up before you can hear any sound; but there's a bulb behind the dial, and this lights up straight away so you'll know the wireless is switched on and getting electricity. The light also makes it easier to read the stations.

You'll notice the dial shows quite a lot of stations - even some as far away as America - and if the accumulator is fully charged and the weather's right, you can tune in to nearly all those shown - although some might sound a bit faint and crackly.

One time, our Dad stayed up all night to hear Tommy Farr, the Welsh boxer, fight Joe Louis. That was in 1937. The broadcast came all the way from America. He said it came through very faint and sometimes faded out entirely for a moment or two, but he could make out most of the commentary. He said Tommy Farr nearly won. He said the more expensive model (the one with four valves and working directly from electricity) would give better reception, but we've found ours good enough for what we want - most times.

We had a wind-up gramophone (an HMV) before we got the Philco. Its cabinet used to be where the cupboard is now; but our Dad sold it to help him with the payments on the wireless. Anyway, we're glad we've got the wireless because we can hear all the latest music. We needn't wait until Woolworths gets new records - as we had to do previously. Records cost sixpence each and are easily scratched or broken. Also, we don't have to make do with just the few records we can afford.

With the wireless, you just switch on to hear the very latest tunes such as: 'On the good ship, Lollipop', played by Ambrose and his orchestra. Also 'When the red, red robin goes bob-bob-bobbing along', sung by Layton and Johnstone. And, of course, 'Little man you've had a busy day', played by Jack Payne and his band.

I like the last song. The first part goes like this: "Little man your crying, I know why you're blue, someone took your kiddie-cart away. Better go to sleep now. Little man, you've had a busy day. Johnny won your marbles; I'll tell you what we'll do: Dad'll get you new ones, right away. Time to go to sleep, now. Little man, you've had a busy day..."

You can learn all the words from song-sheets obtained from Woolworths (they cost a penny a sheet) but the words can be learned just as well by listening to the wireless - as I did with the song just mentioned. Also, you can hear lots of plays. One night, just before Christmas, we sat by the fire with the gaslight turned off and with only the fire's glow lighting the room, and listened to 'A Christmas Carol' by Charles Dickens (that's the one with Scrooge and Marley's ghost). The voice of the ghost gave us all the creeps. Afterwards, I didn't want to go to bed. Anyway, it's easy to get scared in the dark - especially when the candle makes lurching shadows on the walls when you carry it upstairs. But I tried to look as if I wasn't scared.

However, back to the furniture: the last piece we have is the treadle sewing machine positioned beneath the window overlooking the street. This and the other items just about fill the room. If we've visitors, it's almost as our Dad says: "Standing room only". But we've a couple of wooden stools in the front bedroom and a chair in the back bedroom we can bring down, if needed.

Now that you've seen the front room, we can have a look at the one at the back. It's called the scullery. Its doorway is the one just to the left of the picture of my Gran. As we go in, you'll notice it has a part wooden, part flagstone floor and also a little window overlooking the backyard - similar to that of the rear bedroom directly above. It also contains the staircase built against the wall to the left of the doorway from the front room, with its bottom stair at the rear of the scullery.

The way the staircase is built allows the back bedroom to have a recess over the stairs, as in all the other houses in our street. Everyone calls this recess "the bunk". It's used mostly for storage space - usually to hang clothes - but folks sometimes use it as a place to put a small cot for an infant to sleep.

Anyway, let's go upstairs to have a look at the two bedrooms. Both of these you can see from the small landing at the top of the stairs. You might think they look a bit small, but that's probably because beds take up lots of space. In the rear one, there's a bed in the centre of the room with its headboard against the wall away from the window, and also a chair and a cupboard against the wall opposite the doorway. In the front one (that's the largest) you'll see a couple of stools and two beds - one to the left of the doorway against the wall and the other immediately in front of us, against the wall to the right of the window. I supposed there's hardly anything worth noting about both bedrooms - except, perhaps, the front one has a fireplace and its window overlooks the street.

I like the front bedroom because I use it for having a quiet read on a rainy day; and I can look out of the window to see if it's stopped raining, and if any games are being played in the street.

But let's go downstairs and into the scullery again. Here you'll see the only tap in the house. It's fitted just below the window overlooking the backyard. It flows with cold water straight from the mains by way of a pipe made of lead rising from the wooden part of the scullery floor. The pipe is fixed against the wall with a few metal clamps. It burst one freezing night and made a mess. Our Dad had to do a repair using lead-solder and a blowlamp he borrowed. You can see the shiny bulge on the pipe where he fixed it.

The tap flows into a rectangular sink made of stone - known, locally, as the "slopstone". It's supported at each end by what could be called little brick walls. These form a handy recess for storing the two buckets and scrubbing brushes you can see in there now. The slopstone drains through a lead pipe passing through the wall and then into a grid in the backyard. This grid is known, locally, as the "suff" - a name used in our district for a backyard drain. You may think this a bit odd, because we call the street-drains "grids". However, at school, I happened to discover that there's a Latin word "suffusus" which means "to pour into". How the shortened version of this word (if that's what it is) came to be used in our district, for a drain in the backyard, is a bit of a mystery?

But back to the slopstone: the door immediately to its left and between it and the stairway allows access down into the backyard by way of two stone steps. But you've got to be careful when opening this door because it has a bar for hanging towels; and if you swing the door open too hard, the rail bangs against the slopstone and it can break (as I found out).

Anyway, what you might find more interesting than me getting into trouble for breaking the towel rail is the bricked-in "copper" built in the corner of the scullery to the right of the slopstone. We call it the copper but it's really made of cast-iron. It's used for boiling our washing but it can also be used for heating water when you need to have a good bath. I'll show you where we keep our bath, later.

Every Monday washday, our Mam lights the fire underneath the copper very early in the morning and cuts slabs of hard Sunlight Soap into flakes so that it dissolves quickly as the water heats - this before putting in whatever washing needs boiling, such as work-overalls and the like. If you go into the backyard and look upward at the rear of the house, you'll see the fire's small chimney-pot near the edge of the roof.

During a stormy night, next door's main chimney-pot crashed down into our backyard and broke some slates as it fell. We were all in bed at the time but it woke us up. Afterwards, we noticed our copper's chimney-pot seemed to be leaning over a bit, so our Dad borrowed a ladder and straightened it up, using some mortar to hold it firm. He also replaced some of the slates. He said its quicker to do things himself rather than waiting for the landlord to put things right - which our Dad said he's not always eager to do.

However, that's offered as a bit of interest (if you think it's interesting - that is?) so let's get back to the washing. This takes most of the day; involving a constant stirring and pummelling of the boiling washing with a device that looks like a small, three legged, wooden stool fitted to the end of a long pole with its legs pointing away from the pole. Some people call it a "wash-dolly", but most people in our street call it a "pummeller". You can see it standing in the space between the copper and the slopstone.

Our scrubbing board (that's the hard, thick, rectangle of ribbed glass held in a wooden frame you can see hung on the wall just above the copper) is used with a well-soaped scrubbing brush to remove stubborn stains from work-overalls and suchlike, before putting them in the copper for a good boil. Its bottom edge is placed in the slopstone so that the scrubbing can be done on its ribbed surface.

After boiling for a half-hour or so, the washing is lifted from the copper using that short piece of broom handle you see lying on the top of the wooden lid we use to cover the copper. It's then dropped into the large white enamelled bucket we keep under the slopstone. But you've got to be careful that you don't slosh water over the scullery floor - or even get a bad scald if you don't take sufficient care.

Each steaming bucket-full of washing is then emptied into the slopstone and rinsed under the tap. The rinsed articles are then put back into the bucket to be taken into the backyard, where the excess water is squeezed out by passing the items through the mangle.

It's far easier to do the mangling if two pairs of hands are available, especially for heavier articles: one to feed the items through the rollers and the other to turn the handle operating the rollers. These are turned by way of the gears fitted inside the mangle's frame. If you glance out of the scullery window, you'll notice the biggest gear is fixed to the handle. The smaller ones are attached to the end of their roller and mesh with the larger one so that they turn the rollers in opposite directions.

The screw positioned upright in the centre of the mangle's iron frame has a small iron wheel fixed horizontally at its top. If you turn the screw by this wheel, it operates on what looks like a cart-spring positioned just above the top roller. Winding the screw up or down varies the roller tension to suit the thickness of the items you need to put through the mangle.

When I became old enough, I helped our Mam by turning the handle; but always made sure my fingers were kept well away from the gears and rollers.

Having now been warned about fingers, let's get back to the washing. After it's done, the hot soapy water remaining in the copper is emptied by using the small bucket kept inside the larger one stored under the slopstone. Each bucket-full is then used for washing down the yard and the closet's stone floor whilst the water is still hot. The remainder is used for washing down the pavement immediately outside the house - as most people do in our district, every Monday washday. By the end of that day, our Mam's hands look somewhat sore; but I've never heard her complain about this. I suppose she considers it silly even to comment on what she'd think was the result of doing an ordinary day's washing.

There's a much better way of doing washing than causing all the inconvenience of filling the scullery with steam for most of the day - this especially when the window has to be kept wide open, even when the weather's really cold. The better way is to use the local Washhouse. We might be able to see this and where it is - on another day, if funds allow.

Anyway, I promised to show you our bath. It's the large, zinc-plated one you'll see hung by one of its handles on a hook fixed to the wall in the backyard. If you go outside, you'll see it's just to the left of the scullery window. We bring it into the front room and place it before the fire for our bedtime wash-down. Our Mam says we need this because we get as grubby as little piggies when we've been out playing. But I think she's a bit fussy.

The hot water for our wash-down is got from the large iron kettle you saw simmering in the recess on top of the fire's oven when you first came into the front room. The kettle's put directly on the fire for the wash so that it rests on the burning coals where it boils very quickly. However, and as mentioned before: if you want a really hot bath, you'll need to heat enough water in the copper and then have your bath in the scullery. You might think this could be a bit uncomfortable, but the scullery gets quite warm when the copper's fire is lit.

Returning to what's in the scullery: on first entering, you probably noticed the stairway allows space for a small cupboard beneath its stairs. We and most of the houses in the district use this space for storing coal (avoiding the need to go out into the backyard on a cold, dark night) and, for obvious reasons, it's known as the coal-hole. It's too small to hold very much coal, so the main lot is kept in the yard in the space between the rear of the closet shed and the back-entry wall - that's the space to the left of the backyard door, when looking from the house.

Also, you probably noticed there's a gas-stove in the scullery, fitted against the wall just to the right as we entered from the front room and against the same wall as the cupboard we use for storing plates and food. The stove's used for cooking and heating any water that the fire in the front room can't accommodate. But when we do this, the gas-meter fitted in the front room, in the chimney-breast recess to the left of the fire, seems to gobbles up pennies as fast as we can be put them in, so we use the fire as much as possible. Because of this, the gas is only needed mainly for the front room's gaslight. This is the only gaslight in the house and doesn't burn much gas. We use candles or an oil-lamp to light the other rooms.

The landlord empties the meter when he calls for the rent every Saturday morning. He sometimes asks why we don't use the gas more often than we do. Our Mam told him we would, if it didn't cost so much. But he didn't do anything about that. Anyway, our Dad said that's the way landlords are; so let's go back to the front room where you'll see the gaslight.

It's located in the centre of the ceiling and has a tap fitted in the exposed part of the pipe for turning the gas on and off. This is done by using the lever fixed to the tap - whose ends have a little chain with a ring on its end to make it easier to hold and pull. Pulling on one chain turns the gas on and pulling the other turns it off.

Due to the gaslight being directly over the front room table, our Mam needs to stand on a chair to reach the chain. She lights the gas with a wax taper lit from the fire. The mantle covering the jet then glows a brilliant-white and lights the room quite well. Otherwise - without a mantle - there's just a yellow-blue flame giving hardly any light at all.

To make the room appear much brighter, our Dad whitewashes the ceiling with the same mixture he uses for the yard. He also cuts a piece of bright wallpaper into a shape like a small sun with rays, and sticks this to the ceiling around the gas-pipe - using wallpaper paste. This makes the protruding pipe seem less unsightly. Also, the gaslight has a shade made of glass that has a pattern of coloured flowers around its surface. These look quite bright when the gas is lit.

Now that we've seen all there is to see in our house, let's take a look outside. You'll notice the street's cobbles are small, rectangular blocks of hard stones with rounded upper surface, known as cobble-sets, and the pavements in front of both rows of houses are three flagstones wide - as they are in most streets in our district.

Another thing you'll probably notice is that all the houses in our street are built of the same brownish brick and the roofs are clad with the same grey slates. Also, the street has two gaslights: one on the right-hand corner and on the other side of the street from our house - as seen if looking out of our front door.

You can see that the four-sided glass housing fixed to the top of its iron post contains twin gas-mantles and a gas-tap. The maintenance man rests his ladder on the crossbar just below the housing when he needs to change these mantles or do any repairs.

The other streetlight is mounted on the wall of our row and positioned between numbers twelve and fourteen (that's about the middle of the row and to the left as you look out from our front door). It has the same glass housing as the gaslight on the corner, but instead of having a post it's supported by a scrolled iron bracket fixed to the wall - about level with the upstairs windows. Looking to the left from the front door, you'll see another gaslight at the end of the street. It's positioned just across the cobbles of Buckley Street that runs at right angle to the top of our street. It's really for lighting its own part of Buckley Street but it helps light that end of ours.

Another thing you might've noticed is our street has a slight incline across its width. It's because it's built across the main slope of the district that starts at Rochdale Road and ends at Collyhurst Road, where it runs parallel to the River Irk. Because our row faces up the slope, our house, along with the others in its row, has no front doorstep - only a threshold - whereas the houses facing down the slope and therefore on the opposite side of the street have two steps.

If you happen to stay in our area for a while, you'll notice most houses leave their front door partly open during hot weather, because of needing to keep a fire going for cooking and maintaining a supply of hot water - as you saw in our house.

When the door's left that way, having two front steps in a district where the street is almost a continuation of the houses, itself, is like having extra furniture. You could almost call the steps "street chairs", as most people do - this because they're much used by the kids of the street as a place to sit and have a chat; or to rest with their playmates after hectic games; or to discuss the next game to be played. (Any loud disputes get a good telling off.)

One time, when I complained about our house having no front steps, our Mam said this made her glad because "there's none to clean and less noise to put up with from you kids sitting on them". But I think she didn't mean it, really, because I saw her having a secret smile straight after she said it.

Anyway, when it's really hot and sunny some of the grown-ups bring chairs out on to the pavement to sit and have a chat with their neighbours and also watch the kids playing games. This shows grown-ups like a place to sit outside in the street as much as we do.

However, playing is a story we can hear about later. For now, let's take our promised walk around the district...

12
As a Matter of Interest:
Wirelesses and Crystal Sets

~~~~~~~~~~~~~~~~~~~~~~~~~~~~~~~~~~~~

Before taking the intended walk, I'd like to tell you a bit more about wirelesses.

The visit we made to our house showed how the wireless's tuning-dial could select many stations, transmitting broadcasts from places home and overseas. We also saw how this new and entertaining addition to the household quickly became a central feature in almost every home in the land in the 1930s.

Of course, it wasn't always like that. Little more than a decade previously, broadcasting hardly existed; but when it did come, its magic completely astonished those who heard its first sounds - as we'll find out in a later visit.

Before these sounds "without wires" came through the air, people had long been accustomed to transmission over long distances - this being done by direct connections through wires carrying telegraph signals by way of devices invented by Cooke and Wheatstone in 1837. The method of signalling was later refined, in 1851, by Samuel Morse who contrived the familiar telegraph code bearing his name.

Then, in 1876, came voice transmission along wires using the telephone system invented by Alexander Graham Bell and later improved by Thomas Edison. But sound coming mysteriously from "out of the air" was another matter. In order to appreciate the feelings of that time it seems appropriate to offer, at this stage, a brief "hearing" (if you haven't heard it before) about how these sounds came "out of the blue", so to speak.

The first broadcast in this country happened in 1921, when the Marconi Company obtained permission from the Post Office to send signals from a small hut at Writtle (near Chelmsford). At first, these consisted of calibrated signals for wireless enthusiasts who possessed the equipment able to receive such transmissions. So, at that stage, it was little more than an experimental endeavour, mainly to test the possibility of signals being sent and then received over wider areas.

From these developments, the Marconi Company finally persuaded the regulating and controlling Post Office to allow them to extend the scope of transmissions. This they then did from the same hut and for a half-hour period each week. During this time, they played records, sang songs, gave news and chatted to an unseen and uncharted audience, done mainly by a person named Mr Peter Eckersley. It could therefore be claimed that Peter Eckersley became the first "disc jockey" in this country; and, from all accounts, he did the job very well.

By the summer of 1922, the broadcasts from the hut at Writtle had been supplemented by a station using code-name 2LO. This gradually expanded its range to become the best know broadcaster of that time. Two other stations soon appeared under the auspices of an Anglo-American consortium - one of which became known as the Manchester Metrovic Station, transmitting under code-name 2ZY.

The air "began to hum", so to speak, and other interested consortium - now beginning to see the lucrative and expanding possibilities of broadcasting - put in numerous complaints to the Post Office. These consisted of "worrying" about the main outputs being entirely in the hands of foreign interests and that British Companies with similar capabilities weren't getting a "fair share of the air".

The disgruntled complainers maintained they, also, were capable of broadcasting a public service in the form of weather reports, news and music, but were denied permission to do so. However, the Post Office - having complete control over those who could and could not broadcast - needed, in its controlling position, to be constantly mindful about "overcrowding the airwaves", since wireless had, by then, become extensively used for shipping and aircraft signals.

As an interesting flash-back: Queen Victoria had a special experimental receiving-set installed by Marconi at Osborne House, on the Isle of Wight, in 1897. This she did in order to pick up bulletins transmitted in code-signals about the progress of her injured son (The Prince of Wales - later Edward VII) whilst he convalesced aboard the Royal Yacht, fitted with transmitting equipped and moored at Cowes a few miles away. So the old Queen at the age of seventy-seven was - to use modern parlance - "with it" and eager to make use of "all the latest".

Four years later, in 1901, the first message crossed the Atlantic from Poldhu, in Cornwall, to reach a receiver in Newfoundland. The receiving station had a long aerial attached to a kite and a faint letter "S" in the form of Morse Code was caught by the aerial to enter the waiting ears of Marconi and his assistant. This generated a great debate because it wasn't thought possible for signals to travel that "immense" distance. Many sceptics therefore claimed that Marconi and his assistant had only imagined they heard the letter's coding.

But further and unarguable sensations to confound the doubters were on their way: this time, a rescue at sea. On a very foggy night in the January of 1908, a collision occurred between the steamship Florida and one called the Republic - both sailing off the East Coast of America. A receiving station in the Massachusetts area picked up a distress signal - again sent by Morse Code - transmitted in the form of the then agreed distress call of "CQD". (What was thought to be the crisper signal of "SOS" became popular some time later.)

An Englishman by the name of John R. Binns happened to be the person making that transmission, and a receiving operator along the nearby coast notified several other ships in the area by way of Morse Code, allowing for a successful rescue. This became a sensational "first" and therefore one of the wonders of what was claimed to be the modern age. However, another sensation followed - again at sea. This came on the 14th of April 1912 in the form of the wireless-transmitted distress signal sent from the Titanic when, on its first voyage, it struck an iceberg off the coast of Newfoundland. Unfortunately, its distress message had a slower response because the sinking occurred on the wider ocean.

Every newspaper editor knows it's in the nature of people to be constantly interested in dangers and disasters, so these two shipping incidents had a wide, but appalled, and yet excited, readership. Again every newspaper editor knows that it is also in the nature of people to be constantly interested in evil doings. So, adding to the sensation of the mentioned two disasters, a dramatic event of that "attraction" occurred in between. It came in the form of Doctor Hawley Harvey Crippen (an American living in England) who murdered his wife and then boarded a liner - the SS Montrose - hoping to escape justice by making a hurried trip back to America along with his mistress, Ethel le Neve.

By that time (1910, and two years before the sinking of the Titanic) Marconi had arranged to install transmitting and receiving equipment in many ships - the Montrose being one. It seems Crippen was wanted for questioning and his description appeared in newspapers at that time. It also seems the ship's captain, Mr Kendall - believing he recognised Crippen as the involved man - sent a signal back to London to that effect. This resulted in information being transmitted to the port authorities just before the ship reached Quebec on the 31st of July 1910. Imagine the sensation, dramatically expressed in a Sunday Special Edition of the newspaper named 'The Weekly Dispatch' whose "arresting" headlines read:

CRIPPEN'S LIFE AT SEA DESCRIBED BY WIRELESS.

It went on to tell how the details of Crippen's "daily doings" were transmitted to the police authorities and how he'd booked his passage under the name of Robinson, but on occasions failed to answer to that name - thus adding to the captain's suspicions. Also, the newspaper related the dramatic story of the police waiting to arrest the completely taken-by-surprise Crippen at the port of disembarkation, on the basis of the signals sent.

All these sensational events and their expanding possibilities were the reason for the Post Office's felt need to "control the airwaves" - keeping them free for important signals.

But let's get back to the arrival on the air of entertaining broadcasts.

The Government's attitude was one of avoiding the direct involvement of providing a service through public subscription, but was, nevertheless, willing to allow various companies to broadcast on the basis of "self earned revenue". It seems negotiations based on this principle went on for several months, but within confusions being caused by the Post Office constantly changing its controlling Postmaster General.

Finally, six companies were left in the race; but these were unable to decide amongst themselves who should construct the transmitting station. This they resolved by forming a consortium under the name of the British Broadcasting Company Limited, whose main aim was to bring together the top British radio manufactures and thereby encourage the purchase of wireless sets (made by them) by sending out "entertaining and useful broadcasts". On this basis, emerged a public service - but one which, at the same time, received financial returns by the mentioned purchasing incentives. Thereby, on the 14th of November 1922, the BBC (British Broadcasting Corporation - as it later became known) started its first broadcast.

As a turn of chance, this happened to be the day of the General Election which ended the Coalition Government of David Lloyd George, in whose administration Winston Churchill served during the time we met him when we visited Charter Street. The BBC had the capacity to readily broadcast the election results and, at the same time, a news bulletin stating the Postmaster General (Mr Kellaway, who gave permission for the licensing of the BBC) had lost his seat in Parliament. On being "freed" from his parliamentary position, he appeared to be the ideal candidate for the role of the BBC's General Manager. However, he declined this job and joined the Marconi Company instead.

I do not know whether or not Mr Kellaway declined the position in a fit of pique because the BBC had announced his electoral defeat to the world? But whatever the reason, the job became filled by a person known as John Reith (then a thirty-four year old ex-engineer without particular fame or title) who eventually became well known as Lord Reith. He progressively shaped the BBC into his own image and saw it through to the time it became - fully - a Public Corporation, in 1927.

The emerging BBC also justified itself in preparing the way for that public role during the General Strike of 1926 when all the newspapers were unable to publish. John Reith, himself, announced the beginning of the strike over the "air" and also happened to be on duty to inform the country of its ending nine days later. During the strike - and against all government pressures - the BBC gave out what appeared to be impartial news bulletins every hour. This "unbiased service" no doubt accelerated its move towards its final and dominating position in broadcasting, along with a reputation for impartiality.

So we're now in the 1920s when the wireless had reached a position of almost indispensability for homes able to afford one. However and as mentioned previously: at that time, the average household of the economic status we saw in Heelis Street found a wireless set not easily affordable, since, in its early developments, it could cost nearly four or five times that of a weekly wage. This remained so until the advent of the reasonably low cost "People's Set" made by Philco (an example of which we saw in our house) and similar sets produced in the early 1930s. Before that, those able to do so constructed what became generally known as a "cat's-whisker-and-crystal-set" - or, as it came to be less wordily known: a "crystal set".

As previously promised: we'll be present at a first hearing of those magical sounds through the air, by way of such a device, in one of our later visits; but, for now - and in case you might be interested - here's a brief description of how a crystal set is constructed.

During the course of radio experiments, certain crystals were found to be sensitive to radio waves. The most easily obtainable of these were known as Ganela Crystals found in the slagheaps of lead mines. So the basis of the mentioned set was a crystal picking up the signal energy received by a long length of insulated wire acting as an aerial - the received signal being converted into sounds made intelligible to the listener by way of a set of earphones.

An essential component in all of this consisted of a special piece of wire made of gold or silver and drawn out to be almost as fine as a "cat's whisker". This needed to be positioned to touch the most sensitive part of the polished crystal. Also, the set required a "tuning coil" made of bare copper wire on which a movable wire connected to the free end of the cat's whisker could be carefully slid along the coil's length - this in order to find the right "tuning in" position to receive the transmitted signals.

Finally, what the wireless-trade then called a "variable condenser" had to be inserted between the crystal and the mentioned earphones to stabilise the current. All these components were fitted to a suitable - usually plywood - base in their appropriate connecting positions.

So, what we have in order to receive the transmitted signals is the erection of an aerial, about 75 feet long. This would've emerged from our scullery window and taken up the rear wall of our house to be fixed to its guttering. From there, it would stretch above and across the backyard for its end to be attached to a tall pole erected near the backyard door. The scullery end of this thin, flexible and insulated aerial-wire would then be made bare for connecting to the terminal of the previously mentioned tuning coil mounted on its plywood base.

The "energy" of the radio waves received by the aerial went through this coil and into the crystal by way of the connecting cat's whisker and then into the earphones fixed to the other side of the crystal by way of the variable condenser. The total assembly completed the "radio circuit" by being earthed on the earphone's other side to a convenient point in the house - which, in our house, would have been the water pipe in the scullery. This device needed no external power source (such as a battery) because all the energy to activate the crystal is supplied from that received by the aerial.

But what is most needed is the operating skill to tune the set to pick up audible signals. This, as previously implied, requires an extremely careful positioning of one end of the cat's whisker to connect with the crystal at its most sensitive part, then to adjust its other end along the tuning coil to pick up the "wave-length" pertaining to a convenient transmission. Such a set would only be capable of picking up signals from transmitters no more than ten miles or so away - depending on the efficiency of the aerial and the user's skill. It's more than likely that the first sounds received in our house were those transmitted by Station 2ZY, located in the centre of Manchester.

So there you have it. And if you happen to be transported by a time-machine back to the early 1920's, you'll know how to make a crystal set - to hear the latest news.

But what we'll be doing in our own particular time machine (one built by various recollections) is making a return to the district wherein many backyards may've seen the erection of an aerial such as the one described. This to bring into each house the wonders of sounds transmitted from one place to another - without wires.

In other words: the sounds came "wireless".

Anyway, let's now take that promised walk...

13
The District

~~~~~~~~~~~~~~~~~~~~~~~~~~~~~~~~~~~~~~

One of the most marked contrasts between the first and second half of the century we're considering and also pertaining to the century we've now entered is the change in what we could call "street life". In this context, we need to pay particular attention to the various activities taking place during our proposed walk around the district, and to recognise how certain geographical features influence life in the streets and the form it tends to take.

As a reminder: the route of our intended tour is indicated in the sketch, offered below, like this ----- >

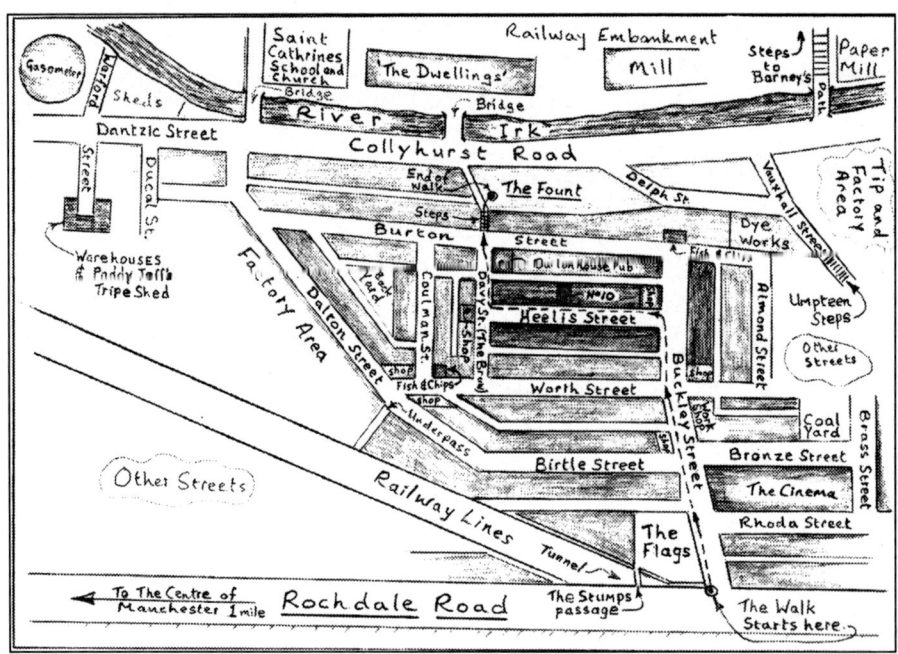

The publication 'The Victorian City' (Routledge and Kegan Paul - 1973) offered this observation:

In back-streets of a certain formation or social composition, lived little communities that knew themselves so well, that shared their common identity with such jealous pride, that for all ordinary purposes of life they comprised a village of a sort that was not basically distinguishable from those surrounded by fields. The old face-to-face relationships more readily associated with the traditional village were implanted in the heart of the Victorian city...

Obviously, not all conditions would allow such "villages" to form. Nevertheless, many did - and in the way our visit will show.

Professor Geoffrey Gorer in his 'Exploring English Character' (published in 1955) implicitly supports the street and housing arrangement as an essential ingredient in the creation of these communities, when he stated on page fifty-one of his survey:

It is chiefly in the middle-size towns, above all in the Northern regions, that the English people find friends amongst their neighbours. This is especially true of people who live in terraced or semi-detached houses...

As our walk progresses, we'll experience one of these "neighbourly villages" along with the social ingredients that made it that way. We'll also notice how certain geographical features create a distinct enclave enclosing a cluster of what the first-mentioned quote describes as "back-streets of a certain formation".

The main demarcation of the enclave we're about to see consists of a railway line (an extension of the line we saw at Charter Street) and the district's main road (Rochdale Road). In addition, we'll see other features combining to complete the demarcation.

Although their boundary-forming function obviously occurred by chance, they nonetheless act together to form a typical example of the suggested "little communities".

During our walk, it will again become necessary to see things through the eyes of the child who knew the district in the way only a child can. However, and as pointed out previously: this can offer certain advantages.

We can start our tour from the corner formed by Buckley Street and Rochdale Road, near where the railway runs through a cutting spanned by that road. The usual access to this position from Heelis Street and its immediate surrounds is by way of Buckley Street. This street forms a gradual downward slope starting at Rochdale Road to then end at Burton Street - which we'll come to know as we progress.

In addition, there's access from Rochdale Road to the Heelis Street area by way of a short length of pedestrian pathway contained between high, black-brick walls situated near the top end of Buckley Street. Here, the pathway runs along the edge of the railway cutting and is known, locally, as "The Stumps" because of the three cast-iron (stumpy) bollards set at each of its ends, to prevent its length being used by handcarts or similar conveyances.

At this stage, the main thing we should note is that the pathway leads from Rochdale Road directly onto a paved area known, locally, as "The Flags".

It's a place much used by the kids of the districts, mostly for playing whip-and-top games - an activity we might see later. So, let's now begin our walk; starting on an early, sunny, Saturday afternoon in the middle of the nineteen-thirties.

From where our walk begins, we can see - stretching to our right - the length of Rochdale Road leading to City's centre, about a mile or so away. To our left is the road's longer length leading to Harpurhey and then to Blackley and finally through the town of Middleton - to then reach the Rochdale of cotton mills, canals and the birthplace of its famous singer, Gracie Fields. You'll notice the twin rows of tramlines set in the middle of the road's cobbles are brightly polished by the flanged iron wheels of the many trams passing to and from the city centre. Although the sun is somewhat subdued by the usual industrial haze, they nevertheless gleam in the afternoon's light.

Approaching from our right is a noisy double-decker tram; rattling and whining towards where we stand; drawing its power from a cable supported high above our heads by the tall, iron posts positioned on each side of the road and along the pavement's edge. The tram's pick-up trolley slanting upwards from its roof makes a tiny shower of sparks as its contact-end slides over the cable's joints.

You'll notice the driver stands just in front of the access door and the wooden stairway opposite that door, which winds up to the top deck. His upright stance allows seeing the road ahead more clearly; but he's provided with a tall stool to give support against the tram's jolts.

Intending passengers have to go almost to the centre of the road to board the tram and therefore need to be alert when doing so. For instance, those three horse-drawn carts jolting along in a line between the tram and our part of the pavement deserve careful watching. However, the clatter of hooves and the rumble of the carts' wooden wheels with their iron-hoop tyres make a clamour on the cobbles loud enough to alert a stone statue.

The lettering you see on the carters' caps indicate their convoy has come from the LMS Railway Yard, in Thompson Street, near the city centre. They're loaded high with cotton bales and are making their way to the local mills to deliver materials for Monday morning's start-up. (In case you don't know: the letters LMS signify the name of the Railway Company: the 'London, Midlands and Scottish'.)

You've probably notice that the carters show little signs of giving way to the few motor vehicles impatiently follow behind. In fact, they show almost complete indifference, except for making what appear to be contemptuous glances over their shoulders now again - as if declaring prime right of road. I suppose they'd argue horses and carts were using roads long before motor vehicles were even thought of.

Although there's lots happening amongst this hurly-burly of traffic to hold our attention, we've much more to see; so let's turn away from this busy road and make our way down the slope of Buckley Street.

You'll find the traffic noises now giving way to the sound of people's voices and that of children playing. For instance, the group of children gathered on the cobbles at the entrance of the narrow street called Rhoda Street, immediately to our right, where the small and rather bashful looking girl stands at the centre of a circle formed by a mixture of girls and boys - all of them holding hands and facing the girl at the centre. They're circling around the girl, singing:

> *There stands a Lady on a mountain,*
> *Who she is, I do not know.*
> *All she wants is gold and silver...*

But now we've lost the next part of the verse in the sudden "wooooosh" from the train hurtling along the cutting behind the wall near the Stumps, to send a plume of smoke swirling high in the air. The children, completely undisturbed by the noise and smoke, continue singing; but in our urgency to move on, we've missed hearing if the song's expressed wants and needs will ever be met? However, what little we've heard declares the song arose from a realm where mundane matters have no dominion: a world where play continually mints afresh its own gold and silver - even in this crowded and smoke-filled world of streets we've come to visit.

Let's now take a few more steps down the cobbled slope, to see the full extent of the paved area we've now come to know as the Flags. It extends from the cobbles of Buckley Street to the base of the high, black-brick wall hiding the railway cutting. Also, at the far end of the Flags, built immediately in front of the railway wall, is an isolated house with a large yard to its side and rear. This house belongs to the family owning the coal-yard contained in the enclosure to the rear of the house. We'll call upon a similar yard during a later visit, to see what coal they stock and how it's sold.

On the subject of coal: there used to be a small coal-mine along Rochdale Road, not far from the top end of Buckley Street, before the street and its surrounds were built around the time of 1870. The mine existed in the period when Rochdale Road went by the name of Saint

George's Road. It belonged to a person with the title of Baronet Buckley: thus, no doubt, the name "Buckley Street".

Regarding names: the other streets we're about to visit seem to bear the ones of famous Victorians or city dignitaries. I tried to trace the source of the name "Heelis", but the only possible (tentative) connection I found concerned a family in the legal profession who may've been prominent in city affairs at the time the street was built. Also, Beatrix Potter's husband, William Heelis, may've been connected to that family; but in the absence of firm proof, the association of the family with the name of our particular street is speculative.

More to our present interest is the group of boys and girls of about seven or eight years of age playing on the Flags' expanse, between where we're standing and the house belonging to the family owning the coal-yard. Notice how they vigorously whip their mushroom shaped wooden tops - these tipped with a small metal button to make them spin more easily. This device and the efforts of their whipping make the tops bounce and spin rapidly along the paving.

Notice the whips they're using are made of a twelve-inch length of wooden dowel with a very thin leather strip of about the same length attached to its end. This strip curls around the top's stem as it's being whipped and then - by a quick and skilful sweep of the child's arm - the strip uncurls to drive the top spinning and bouncing in various directions. Each top is then chased by the possessor who whips it again and again with what seems like tireless energy. The children are too absorbed in their play to spare us even a glance. Their shouts and bursts of laughter as tops collide and spin off in unexpected directions tell how much they enjoy their activity.

See that top spinning nearest to us. It shows how the children have decorated the flat upper surface of each top with chalk and stuck-on bits of coloured paper obtained from sweet wrappings. This produces the bright, circular patterns on the upper surfaces as they spin.

Look! One of the girls whose top collided and has stopped spinning is about to start it up again. She's wound the leather strip around the stem of the top and is now placing its button-tipped end on the paving - holding the top in its vertical position with one finger placed on the head of the top. The quick sweep of her other hand holding the whip has caused the leather to unwind so that the top spins rapidly. She's laughing with delight as she whips it repeatedly to keep it bouncing and spinning along the paving. Her joyful skill could make us linger, but there's so much more to see.

For instance, that hubbub of sound coming from just over the other side of Buckley Street from where we're standing. The din is being made by that line of boisterous kids eagerly queuing outside the local cinema - whose sign above its entrance declares it's called 'The Rex'. They're waiting impatiently for its penny-matinee to start.

Also, notice the Walls Ice Cream tricycle standing by the curb a little way before the cinema steps and alongside the queue. The man in charge (the one wearing the white, peaked hat with the blue band and the white, blue trimmed coat) is attempting to entice any spare pennies from the boisterous line crowding along the pavement.

The sign on the large box positioned at the front of the tricycle - which contains the dry-ice to keep its contents frozen - displays the demand:

STOP ME AND BUY ONE.

Judging by the number of kids around the cart, it seems to be having its intended affect.

He's obviously parked in a strategic position on the corner; knowing the queue will progressively extend its length as groups of kids make their way up Buckley Street and from those adjoining. The queue forms a ragged line stretching from the wide stone steps fronting the cinema to then curl around its left-hand corner, where it's progressively filling the full length of the pavement in Bronze Street.

The manager, Mr Shaw (that's him - standing at the top of the steps and wearing the posh suit and a bow tie) has his own problems. He's trying to keep the line well behaved as it moves up the steps and into the cinema. He's warning the more boisterously impatient members of the line with possible exclusion unless they quieten down. And, like the Ice Cream Man's sign, this has its affect - but for a different reason and a different order of satisfaction.

Those coloured posters on the bare-brick wall at the rear of the open foyer indicates he's showing the next episode of "Flash Gordon and the Clay Men" along with a Laurel and Hardy film. No wonder the kids seem eager to get in!

However, we must leave this excited stream of life to walk a few more steps down the slope where we can glance to our left along the short length of Birtle Street. As you can see, all the houses in the rows on both its sides appear identical to those we've seen in Heelis Street. Also, you can now see how the other end of Birtle Street meets the top end of a street we briefly knew in a previous visit as Dalton Street.

The far side of the last-mentioned street contains the continuation of the railway wall we saw at the Flags. It's now much higher because it merges with the end of the viaduct we saw in our visit to Silver Street. All these structures maintain the level of the railway as it cuts obliquely across the district's slope to then enter the cutting beneath Rochdale Road. The far side of Dalton Street also contains a factory area - but we're unable to see this from where we're standing.

Perhaps you're beginning to wonder why I'm laboriously calling attention to all these features? However, if you bear with me for a while, their importance in shaping the neighbourly community we've entered will soon become obvious; so let's continue down Buckley Street to the next street on our left. This is called Worth Street and you'll notice it's built across the district's slope and therefore seems almost on level ground - like Heelis Street. You'll also notice it and the other streets we're about to see enjoy a reasonable quiet due to their distance from the railway and the noise of Rochdale Road.

The warmth of the afternoon sun has enticed a number of people out of their houses to stand in and around their open doorways to enjoy neighbourly chats. This can readily be done because the street - like the others in its district - isn't very wide and is therefore mostly free from vehicular traffic. The freedom from noise and vehicle intrusion permits conversations between next-door neighbours and even allows for quick exchanges between those across the street. But rather than risk creating our own intrusion by trying to catch the gist of these chats - even though they appear quite open and public - let's continue down the slope to the street we already know as Heelis Street.

Our walk will take us along its length. However, before doing this, you may like to examine more closely the gaslight immediately to our right. It's the one we saw standing just across the cobbles of Buckley Street when we glanced out of the front door of our house in a previous visit.

I suggest we take a good look at it now because it's the type of lighting found everywhere in our district and its similar areas in and around the city. Also, street lighting has a very important place in children's play, as we'll discover later. You can see it's identical to the one we saw at the other end of Heelis Street. It consists of the usual green painted iron post surmounted by a four-sided, glass housing tapering to its base and enclosing twin gas-mantles and their gas-tap positioned near the base. The housing has a pyramid shape cast-iron roof embellished with the small knob at its apex.

You've probably noticed that the crossbar just below the housing is brightly polished along its length - this because it's constantly use by the maintenance man to rest his ladder. If you stayed in the district, even for a short while, you'll see he calls regularly, as the well-cleaned glass panels testify. Gaslight isn't all that strong and grimy panels would reduce its effectiveness considerably.

One of the panels is hinged on its metal frame to allow replacing the mantles if needed. It also allows access for the Lamplighter to turn the tap on when lighting the gas each evening and then turning it off, next day, in the early morning. He uses a long pole with a hook at its end to open the hinged panel and then to manipulate the tap's lever. The end of the pole carries a small container to produce an acetylene flame for igniting the gas-mantles. They then cast a pale yellow glow over their part of the street.

Although lighting is done on every evening of every day, the kids of the district find it a continual fascination: so much so that there's always a group waiting to follow the Lamplighter when he arrives in the streets just before dusk. He looks like a warrior bearing a long, gleaming, flame-tipped lance on his shoulder as he strides down the street with the kids following behind and strutting along like his faithful retinue. They then gather around to watch as he lights the next streetlight. He doesn't seem to mind all this. In fact, he seems to find it amusing.

Anyway it's far too early for him to call, so let's move on. But before we do so, let's have a quick glance down the remaining length of Buckley Street to where its slope ends. The street you see running across its end is the one called Burton Street, which I mentioned previously. We'll see more of this in a short while; but before then, let's take our intended walk along Heelis Street. Here, again, we see various households taking advantage of the afternoon sun to chat with their neighbours. This time, we'll have to risk intrusion because of our need to walk the full length of the street's right-hand pavement.

You'll notice the people standing at their doorways will smile and nod a greeting as we pass by. Although their expressions will display an open friendliness, you'll also detect within it a hint of curiosity and wonder why. It's because in these small, compact and intimate streets, isolated from the main thoroughfares, strangers are not often seen.

These groupings of streets form the mentioned neighbourly enclaves within the city; each contained and defined by those features we've already noticed, such as railway lines; industrial buildings; busy main roads and the like. Similar features divide similar residential areas into intimate communities, wherein everyone knows everyone else; and the curiosity you detected arises from this condition.

You might feel a slight stir of embarrassment - as if you've strayed inadvertently into someone's home. However, as we progress along what they consider as exclusively their street, in their district, you'll find your mood responding to friendly glances as the people in and around the doorways lose their initial surprise at seeing strangers passing by. You might then feel an impulse to smile and return their quick nod of greeting.

Before walking the street's length, let's again remind ourselves of those defining boundaries previously mentioned, so that we'll be able to see how this sense of "village" containment we're beginning to notice is created.

As you've no doubt already gathered: the boundaries defining the community we're visiting are formed by Rochdale Road and the railway line sloping off at an angle from that road; then the Dalton Street factory area and then Buckley Street. The last mentioned street (occupying as it does the full extent of the slope we've just walked) forms its own boundary on the far side of the area from Dalton Street.

Finally, there's Burton Street which we saw cuts across the bottom of the Buckley Street slope to isolate the areas beyond that. All these features produce a natural demarcation between the group of streets of our visit and the localities beyond. If we visited other parts of the city, we'd find this geographical containment and the feeling it generates replicated in many areas - arising as it does from the numerous "accidental" boundaries of the kind we're seeing.

Adding to this sense of containment is the tendency for most people to seek employment in or around the place where they live. Moreover, when the people within these localities do their daily shopping, they'll meet mainly with neighbours. We'll see how and why this is so when we visit the shops they'll use.

Therefore, this natural enclave in which they spend most of their time causes its inhabitants to display that mild curiosity we noticed being directed towards us, in the same way people in a small village would react when seeing a passing stranger. Thus our feeling of being what their curiosity implies.

But we're nearing the end of the street and you're probably feeling reassured by the fact that - after the first enquiring glances - conversations continued with hardly a break and the kids playing skipping near the corner of the street we're approaching pay little heed to our presence.

You've no doubt gathered their ages suggest most of the older children form part of the queue we saw waiting for the Saturday matinee - leaving the younger ones full use of the street.

Let's approach their activity slowly and unobtrusively. This we'll do for two reasons. First, to avoid disturbing their game and, second, and more important to our interests, it'll allow a much closer and longer look at the way their game's being played.

The two girls of about eight or nine years of age, immediately ahead of us, are vigorously swinging a rope that they've stretched across the cobbles almost from curb to curb. They're chanting a rhyme as the waiting line of four or five girls and a mixture of a few boys of similar age take turns to dash into the rope's swing. On doing this, each performs a number of skips to the rhyme's beat.

The one skipping then dashes out of the rope's swing on the last word of the chant to then return to the end of the waiting line. The next in line immediately enters the skipping on the first word of the reiterated chant - and so on. All this must be done without impeding the rope's swing - which is kept in time to the words of the chant.

We can now clearly hear what they're chanting:

> *One, two, three, four, five,*
> *Catching fishes all alive.*
> *Five, six, seven, eight,*
> *Put the fishes on a plate...*

It seems that anyone getting themselves tangled in the swing of the rope by ill-timed skipping would represent a "fish" caught, who'd then have to retire from the skipping by (in the words explicit in the rhyme) being put "on a plate". You can see two boys and a girl excluded from the game by the assumed skipping errors sat on the far-side pavement, leaning against the wall and watching the line's progression. The last one remaining to skip would, it seems, be the winner - having escaped the "net" and therefore escaped the plate.

The game requires a great deal of agility and a good sense of timing, as you can readily see. Also, as in the case of the children in Rhoda Street and those on the Flags, the kids seem so absorbed in their play they appear completely oblivious to almost anything else. Their skill in judging the rope's swing and skipping to the beat of the chant seems quite astonishing. But we need to move on - and again risk intrusion because their play leaves limited room for us to pass by.

Our situation is made even more difficult because the game is being played with considerable energy and much dashing backwards and forwards. However, the children's brief glance in our direction as we attempt to pass barely disturbs their chant and the rope's swing. Moreover, the gap on the pavement left by the nearest girl swinging the rope allows enough space for us to reach the corner just beyond where she stands.

Having made it without the disturbance we feared, we now see the full length of Davy Street that runs at right angle to the end of the street we're leaving. You'll notice its short length follows its own section of the district's slope from Worth Street (a part of which you'll see to our left) to then end at the lower level of Burton Street that crosses the bottom of the incline.

The people living in the immediate area refer to Davy Street as "The Bruw". The only explanation I can offer for the word's usage is that it might have a connection with the old Anglo-Saxon word "Brue" - meaning a slope or incline? But this is speculation on my part. Yet, if true, it seems remarkable such an ancient word is found in the heart of a large industrial city - and be applied appropriately.

Another example of possible ancient origin is found in the term "midden-bin" (mentioned when we visited our house) used for what is usually called a "dustbin". Again, the word "midden" is Old English for a refuse heap, so it seems apt when applied to a receptacle for containing ashes and rubbish.

These comments are minor points of possible interest (if they are of interest, that is?). However, what you might find of greater interest is Agnes's Grocery Shop. That's the one just across the bruw and almost opposite, but slightly to the left of, the Heelis Street corner where we're now standing.

This shop may appear as an intrusion into the line of houses whose row it shares, but it really belongs in that row because it was, once, a house that became converted into a shop (a trend we'll see much more of in a later visit). Notice its front door is wide open - which, for most parts of the day during warm weather, it usually is. You'll notice that the two people on the customer side of the counter leave very little space for anyone else, since the shop's area is no bigger than the front room of our house.

The packages and jars you can see on the shelves fixed across the tiny downstairs window, to the right of the doorway, are really for decorative purposes. They're called "false packages", used for advertising. However and as previously mentioned, we'll hear more of this shop when we make another visit for another purpose. In addition, we'll see how and why shops of its kind came into existence. But, for now, let's turn right and make our way down the bruw's slope.

A few more steps beyond the rear-entry belonging to the row containing our house and the tall telegraph pole just past its opening takes us to Burton Street. The building on the corner we've now reached is the pub known as the Burton House. Notice the large, ornate windows of coloured glass on either side of its wooden door that opens directly onto the bruw. These bear the name of its rooms with a representation of a floral wreath enclosing each word. The Vault is on the left as you face the door and the Bar on the right.

If we went around the corner into Burton Street, we'd see a similar arrangement of door and windows. Also, we'd see the sign hanging above the door declaring the name of the pub.

Its Vault is used for men and women to have a companionable drink together whilst sat at its tables. The Bar is a smaller room where men (no women allowed) drink and play games of darts, cribbage or dominoes. It's also a place where those looking for work might get to know about possible vacancies. The proprietor's connection with the brewery allows access to such information, which he passes on to his "regulars". If they don't need the job, they'd probably know someone who does. The pub therefore acts as an informal employment information centre. This suits those who have an aversion to the rigid, governmental formalities and lack of choice that the Labour Exchange and the Unemployment Assistance Board offers.

Above the pub's doorways and just below the windows of the upper floor, you'll see the words BURTON HOUSE - ALES & STOUT set in light-brown tiles stretching the full length of pub in both streets. The proprietor seems to like this embellishment. You'll often see him up a ladder washing down its tiles.

Its doors are usually left partly open during hot weather. This applies to most of the houses - as we saw it does to Agnes's shop. In the case of the pub, it gives the kids an opportunity to have a bit of fun by peeping inside the bruw's doorway, then to dash away when spotted by the people inside.

One time, from the bruw's doorway, I saw my Gran'dad Jones having a drink at the Bar. When he turned round, I saw his moustache was covered with white froth and I called out:

"Gran'dad! Your moustache has gone snow-white!"

I didn't wait to hear what he said.

Anyway, it's closed at the moment so there'll be no kids hanging around to have a cheeky peep. So let's cross the cobbles of Burton Street to where a small passageway interrupts the line of terraced houses forming that side of the street. If you remember, it's the one my mother used when on her way to find work on that April morning in the early nineteen-twenties. The passageway's five or so well-worn stone steps takes us down to a short length of paved path starting just beyond the rear of the houses and at the base of the steps. This path follows the last part of the district's slope where it ends at Collyhurst Road.

Let's pause, for a while, at the top of this path, since it offers a good position to view our surrounds.

Across the cobbles of Collyhurst Road is the line of green painted iron railings bordering its far side pavement. These we saw on that Saturday morning's search for work. The most noticeable and dominating feature beyond these railings and therefore beyond the River Irk is the massive, four-storey block of tenements, standing in complete isolation in its own paved-over grounds. The building is locally known as "The Dwellings". This forms a neighbourly community in its own right.

The only access to the building is from Collyhurst Road by way of the narrow iron bridge you can see spanning the river, slightly to the left of the building. The veranda-like walkways along its extensive length allow access to the tenements on each of its upper three floors.

I believe the Dwellings were originally constructed to provided homes for the workers and their families employed on the local railway - a section of which you can see in the form of a high embankment a hundred yards or so beyond the building.

Its dark-brick, barrack-like structure with its forest of chimneys cluttering its long, flat roof might look somewhat forbidding. Also, the bright colours of the washing being aired here and there along the verandas and the white-lace curtains at some of the windows do little to relieve its somberness. Nevertheless, its occupants seem to like the neighbourliness the building offers.

The occupants leaning on the veranda rails and apparently gazing across the river in our direction are, in all probability, trying to catch any cool breeze the height of their verandas may chance to offer on this hot afternoon. Moreover, they'll use this out-door situation for having a chat with their neighbours - as we saw folks in the streets we've recently past were doing.

If you happened to be on a veranda with them, you'd notice the breeze carries a faint odour - like that of old linseed oil. You might detect this from where we're standing. It comes from the waters of the Irk and is caused by the waste dyes from the upstream mills entering the river. After a while, and like the people of the Dwellings, you'd hardly notice it - if notice it at all.

However, we'll see more of the Irk and the building later - there are a few interesting stories to tell about both.

What I've really brought you to see is the small piece of derelict land on the right-hand side of the path we've now reached; which - along with the path - follows the district's downward slope on its last thirty yards or so to Collyhurst Road.

This abandoned piece of land with its covering of sparse grass and outcrops of red clay is known, locally, as "The Fount".

At its lower far side corner, you'll notice a protrusion of large, stone blocks that may've been the foundations of an old building. Also - and on that same far side where it borders Delph Street - you'll see what appears to be the last remains of a massive stone wall. In addition, you'll notice the high and prominent wall made of blocks of sandstone at the top end of the land's incline. This was built at the same time as Burton Street to support the backyards belonging to the row of houses whose gap we came through. It also provides the support needed to level the street against the district's slope.

But returning to those buried foundations and the remains of the wall at the bottom of the Fount. Some say they're the last witness of what was once a large and spacious house, and the land that we now call the Fount used to be part of its gardens? If this is so, the origin of the name, "Fount" may be a diminutive of the word "foundations" - obviously suggested by the remains we're seeing?

Alternatively, there could've been a spring (a "fount") whose waters trickled down this slope into the River Irk, long before the surrounding industries and row upon row of houses dried up the land? But all this is, again, speculation - and a speculation you may think all the more inconsequential to even raise; because you're probably feeling that what I've brought you to see seems completely empty of any real interest or attraction?

Yet - if we let our eyes become those of a child - this unbecoming piece of land may take on another aspect. The dereliction we first perceived would quickly change into a bountiful place for play. And with our newly acquired eyes, we'd see stones and bricks to create our castles, and raw red clay to fashion the figures of our imagination - and bring them to life.

And this small and insignificant piece of land would undergo that remarkable transformation a child can always produce, no matter where that child may be. Where what little it may find can be turned into a vast and all-absorbing world of play.

At least, this is what the Fount was once to me - along with the streets and all the other unprepossessing yet wonderfully inexhaustible play-areas of that time.

Let's go back to that time, to find again its richness. To find again play's gold and silver that we saw being constantly minted amongst the children during our walk. Those riches children can always reveal in what seems but barren ground.

Let's go by way of the songs, rhymes and games imagined, learnt or invented by the children of that time.

But before we enter its setting, let's set the less-than-joyful economic scene of the Thirties. Then we'll explore the shops around the district - to know where they are and what it is they sell...

14
Earning A Crust

~~~~~~~~~~~~~~~~~~~~~~~~~~~~~~~~~~~~

The early part of the nineteen-thirties experienced large-scale unemployment. The figure for England and Wales reached something like twenty per cent of the total working population. However, as in the case of all statistics, such figures can be misleading if accepted without proper examination.

Certain areas remained comparatively prosperous whereas others (particularly those related to heavy industries such as coal, iron and cotton) were hard hit. The figures in these depressed areas therefore became substantially higher than the national average. For example: Jarrow had a rate of over 60 per cent.

The writer, J.B. Priestly, identified what he described as "The Four Englands".

First: the England of the Cathedral Towns and the Southern Counties, which Priestly represented as living in the genteel comfort of old Edwardian England.

Second: the bustling Home Counties around the hub of London; perceived by Priestly to be full of petrol service stations and factories, looking - as he said - like exhibition halls (i.e. the newly emerging car, light-engineering and domestic appliance industries).

Third: the declining areas of nineteenth-century industrialisation - identified by the Midland's silent blast furnaces and unsightly slag heaps.

And, finally, the most desperate of all the Englands. The Fourth England: the England of the Dole and the Means Test, typified by thousands upon thousands of "all alike" houses crowded around silent mineshafts and mills; the England of coal and cotton that once produced the wealth of all the Englands. This last England Priestly saw in the regions of Teeside and South Lancashire, where areas depending on coal and cotton seemed to be the worst hit.

Let's visit an area of this worst hit England, and - in its circumstances - see how folks strived to "earn a crust". But before doing this, let's set the scene wherein that crust will be earned.

At the time of Priestly's Englands, unemployment benefits were cut by ten percent. As a result, a married man, with, say, a wife and three dependant children, received twenty-nine shillings and three pence per week - this "benefit" being allowed during the first fifteen weeks of unemployment, after which the recipient became subjected to a Means Test. In this, the total and potential income of all members of the household (savings, possessions considered "unnecessary" or anything deemed possibly accruing income) was taken into account. This test of means determined whether the benefit should or should not continue. I'll use my mother's words to describe its workings.

"A visitor from what we called The Board of Guardians came to the house. They gave no notice of the day or time they'd come. The means-tester made a list of all he saw in the house that he thought could be sold and estimated how much they'd fetch, when sold.

"He also enquired about other members of the family who might be working or had any savings. He'd go all through the house, including the bedrooms, to list what he thought were unnecessary possessions. People dreaded the Means Test. They'd even suffered loss of Dole to avoid it."

She also told of some humorous incidents arising from neighbours subjected to its enquiries. For instance: one neighbour had an old and completely out of tune piano - virtually unplayable and kept more for appearance than for anything else. On the lady of the house being told the piano had to be sold, she exclaimed to the means test man:

"Oh, Mister! Not the piano! That's a family heirloom! It's our eldest lad's inheritance!"

Another household had a budgerigar they kept in a "stylish" cage. The bird possessed an erratic talking ability and - on it and its cage being put on the list of "saleables" - it happened to cry out:

"Wait a minute! Wait a minute!"

Whereupon the lady of the house said:

"There you are! It doesn't want to be sold! It's just said so!"

It seems humour was the final defence. If a person couldn't laugh, only crying was left. But to those forced to submit to its administrations, the means test wasn't really "funny"; and, as in all periods of adversity, the women of the family bore the brunt of most of its implications and consequences. Thus, many women in and around Heelis Street sought ways to augment the family income in case their "breadwinner" became unemployed. When and if this misfortune did occur, they'd strive to earn sufficient by their own effort to avoid applying for the Dole beyond its statutory fifteen weeks - the so-called "transitional benefit" determined by a means test.

On a previous visit, we saw and followed members of my family (my mother, her mother, and even my great-grandmother) in their efforts to support themselves and their families during difficult periods. As we saw in such instances: pride was a luxury enjoyed only by those able to afford its indulgence.

But we also saw one particular pride which only the most extreme circumstances could force them to abandon: this, the pride of self respect - which, to them, was as necessary for the sustenance of their spirit as food was for their body. To maintain this respect (one they'd describe as "standing on their own two feet") they'd suffer any task that others in their own particular versions of pride might see as being far beneath their dignity.

Now, let's witness these efforts. This time, amongst the women in Heelis Street.

An aspect of making ends meet emerged in the form of various households turning their homes into little transient shops (which we'll see happening during a later visit) for the sale of pies, soups, pickles, cakes, and the like. These they'd sell to anyone able to afford the offered goods. But for our immediate purpose, let's see how some sought the opportunities offered by trading and exchanging (commonly known as "Hawking").

One of the main sources supporting this activity existed at a warehouse known as Shufflebottom's, situated on Rochdale Road near Thompson Street and a little way past Gould Street gasworks. This stocked slightly flawed but otherwise good quality pottery (cups; saucers; dinner services; vases; ornaments and the like) which were offered at "bargain prices".

If a number of shillings could be raised for an initial stock, the items obtained could then be exchanged for other articles that would be well beyond the purchase-range of the households concerned - as we'll see later. Alternatively, the obtained articles could be sold elsewhere for more than initially paid. If all this buying, selling and exchanging resulted in a surplus of shillings above those dictated by household necessities, more stock could be obtained - thus allowing further trading.

Those in Heelis Street engaging in such transactions set off early in the morning with the pottery obtained on the previous day loaded in an old pram. Their most likely destinations would be the more prosperous areas along the upper end of Smedley Road and Smedley Lane. Also included were areas across Cheetham Hill Road from Smedley Lane and, sometimes, further afield to the upper reaches of Cheetham Hill Road and Heaton Park (a long push with a loaded pram - only done if the first and nearest areas proved fruitless).

The people in these districts were accustomed to this sort of activity and households would sometimes pay cash for attractive sets of pottery seemingly without blemish; or they'd exchange used but still wearable clothing for any items they fancied. The obtainer's family could keep the best of the exchanges for their own use and then sell any surpluses in and around Heelis Street to those needing such.

Some of the older girls of the involved families often became active in finding customers. Living as they did in a "closely-knit" community, they knew those in need of a particular article of clothing and what article would fit whom. Also, much of the clothing represented a substantial bargain, being of far better style and quality than could possibly be afforded by folks in and around Heelis Street.

But returning to those directly involved in this trading.

One such lady lived just a few doors up the street from our house, just past the gaslight mounted on the wall. She had no husband or children and trading happened to be her only or, at least, her main means of support. She used a market called the "Flat Iron" (I've no idea why it was called that) located not far from Strangeways Prison as her usual outlet for any second-hand clothes she obtained. This market offered facilities for auctioning such items, with a starting price of a penny or two for the less desirables and up to fourpence for the best - and, sometimes, even more for "specials".

Public transport represented a luxury not readily affordable, as we previously observed; and in any case, it'd be difficult to get a rickety old pram loaded with second-hand clothes on a tram - if, indeed, such was allowed. The lady of our concern - who'd left the advantage of youth far behind - was therefore faced with a long push of about three or four miles from Heelis Street to the Flat Iron. Since walking was the main and - for most purposes - the only means of transport, the long and arduous push over cobbled roads and up steep inclines would've been done as a matter of course and as an expected part of living.

The perennial problem of hard-earned and uncertain income, besides dictating the need for cheap apparel, also dictated a careful attitude towards all spending and, therefore, a need to know every source of cheap purchases - especially food.

In the context of the latter, my sister, Nellie, related her experiences at Smithfield Market; a place located on Shude Hill, near the city's centre and about a mile or so from Heelis Street - which, if you remember, we visited on a previous occasion. She told how, at closing time on a Saturday night, many of the stall-holders sold off perishable goods at a very cheap rate. A large rabbit could be obtained for threepence and sometimes even for less, depending on the "glut". Also, good quantities of fish could be got for a few pennies.

Additionally, fruit-stalls sold surplus stock whose ripeness appeared too near the limit for storing until Monday morning. Thus, a sizeable and still eatable quantity of bananas, oranges or apples could be obtained for a penny or two.

If you happen to recall a visit we made a couple of decades earlier than the time we're now considering, you'll recognise her experience at this particular market as being essentially the same as that of her (and therefore my) mother's experience when a child. So, it seems, only marginal economic changes had taken place between generations.

This need to forage for food is implied by figures produced at the start of the 1939-45 war, when the concern for "fitness" became uppermost - as we observed it did in the previous war. A survey directed towards assessing the Nation's health revealed the astonishing fact that out of every ten children, only three were adequately nourished, three were slightly undernourished and four were definitely undernourished. Therefore, this climate of constantly hovering deprivation made people on the margins of disadvantage mindful of the need for self-help, in order to avoid slipping into the worse category. This became an attitude of mind to the point of being almost habitual, as it must have been in all similar districts.

As a child, I once complained about a job I'd been given that I thought might interfere with my play. Our Dad said:

"Get on with it! There are no passengers aboard this ship. We're all crew."

That was the essence of it all - both in our house and in every house in and around the district. A "ship" constantly in difficulty couldn't afford passengers; it required "all hands to the pumps" - even if the hands called upon happened to be small. Everyone was and had to be crew, so even the young members of the family were expected to help keep the ship afloat in any aspect of its "floatability" - including finding cheap stock for the larder, as my sister did.

Also, earning your own pocket money to ease its demand on the household finances was another obligation, even though its demand in the usual scheme of things always happened to be one of extremely low priority.

One way the kids found of doing this "easing" consisted of selling firewood to the neighbours in our street and those adjacent. Therefore, any wooden boxes discarded by the local greengrocers along Rochdale Road or suitable wood found on the local municipal tip became highly prized. Chopped up into sticks of suitable size and bundled together into fire lighting quantities (about six sticks to a bunch) enabled selling at halfpenny a bunch - or a penny for three bunches (a business-like discount for quantity).

This service found a ready market around the streets, since - as we've seen - fire-lighting material always represented a household necessity. But wood supplies were never certain and, for most times, the needs of one's own family had first priority.

However, back to the activities of my resourceful sister: she and the other young girls around the district soon discovered Smithfield Market's habit of discarding wilting flowers could be a lucrative source of pocket money. Saturday evenings were the main flower clearing-out time. Blooms deemed droopy and therefore appearing incapable of lasting until the next selling sessions were thrown on a disposal heap.

The girls soon learned to recognise those that were less jaded than they appeared at first sight and might be revived by re-cutting their stems and standing them for a time in a bucket of cold water. They soon became experts at quickly selecting those likely to respond. These they hurriedly took home for an overnight bucket treatment. Those responding they tied into attractive sized posies the next morning.

The cemetery near Queen's Park offered a ready outlet for the resuscitated blooms (at a penny a bunch). The two miles or so walk was done using the usual pram-transportation to carry the stock; and arrival being arranged for just before the opening of the cemetery gates (usually 9 a.m.). Sunday visitors seemed glad of an extra - or their only affordable - bouquet to grace the graves of those they'd come to honour and mourn.

Although the activity of "unlicensed" selling in the streets went against the "letter of the law" (if the letter of the law felt it should be applied, that is) the local policemen knew most of the kids involved and turned the proverbial blind eye - as long as the practice wasn't too conspicuous or creating a nuisance. By this, both sides soon learnt the fine balance between law and leniency: the kids earning their pocket money - judiciously - and the police earning goodwill - sensibly.

Heelis Street and its district was, therefore - in practice and out of necessity - an enterprising culture: one embracing all ages and enough to gladden the heart of the most fanatical of Thatcherites (except the word then uppermost in people's minds was "surviving" and not "enterprising"). It was also, in many ways, a model of "recycling", enough to excite any present-day "friend of the earth".

In addition to these out-and-about ventures, other possibilities existed for work at home. Members of our family tried opportunities offered by a business we called Wolfe's (situated in the city centre, near Central Railway Station - as it was then). This work involved stitching together various size print-samples to make patchwork quilts for use as bedspreads. Some members of our family had an aptitude for this type of work and particularly my sister, Nellie, even when a young girl. Even my father acquired a good skill - after some practice.

The business provided paid-for materials only, and no equipment. However, our Dad obtained an old 'Jones' sewing machine he made serviceable with a bit of ingenuity - which he kept it in good working order with careful applications of oil and regular maintenance. This had a cast iron frame to serve as a support for the worktable holding the stitching unit. The sides of the frame contained cast representations of upwardly climbing stems of leafy vines.

In between and at the base of these embellishments pivoted the well-worn treadle, polished to a bare-metal shine by much pedalling. This operated the connecting rod attached to the machine's driving wheel; and although the mechanism operated as well as it could - after a good oiling - it still required fast legwork to produce good and close stitching.

Being six or so years of age at the time and therefore not much use in these activities (except for keeping out of the way) I found a tiny space in the corner of the front room, near the window. From there, I could watch the rapidly reciprocating rod driven by vigorous treadle-work; and listen to the chattering whirr of the machine as the multicoloured lines of stitched-together squares of material passed from under the needle and folded themselves into a basket on the floor. Such was the uncaring world of childhood in which everything seemed to exist just to satisfy curiosity.

But back to work. The materials obtained from Wolfe's Warehouse came in bundles of different size patches - varying from, perhaps, five up to eight or so inches square. And to make these into a finished quilt required lots of careful sorting into matching sizes and quantities (before stitching) in order to ensure producing the stipulated size of quilt with an even edge. This selection had to be carefully done, for if the finished article departed from the stated specifications, pay for that item would not be forthcoming.

Also, careful attention had to be paid to the quality of stitching. If on inspection at the warehouse missing or faulty stitches were found, the person offering the finished article had to "make good" any faults by close hand stitching, there and then, before being paid.

Because of these stringent demands, it could take something like a day's dedicated work to make a couple of quilts of the size and quality required - along with carefully checking all the stitching before delivery. This activity turned the house into almost a factory with the smell of powdery lime (which the prints had been, for some reason, pre-treated) permeating the house.

In addition, returning the completed work involved the further effort of transporting the finished articles to the Warehouse in a pram pushed by my mother and sister, with, of course, the same pushing of heavy bundles of prints on the return journey. The totality of this represented something like two or three miles of pushing.

All this effort and household disruption returned the astounding sum of five and one half-penny per quilt; and - at the rate of something like twelve quilts per week - this showed hardly enough margin on the money originally paid out to pay the rent.

Although working at home returned far less than its effort deserved, at least you were free to sing whilst working (if singing is what you felt like doing, that is). In the context of this expression of happiness, my sister told me of a place disinclined to permit its outflow - even in its most modest form.

Soon after leaving school in the mid nineteen-thirties, she took a job as a sewing machinist based on her quilt experience at home and the skills acquired; and being a new starter without knowledge of the "rules", she did what came naturally to her whilst working.

To use her own words: "I had a quiet sing to myself".

The Manager of the establishment happened to be passing during this expression of joy and told her she was there to work and not to sing; and if she persisted with the habit, she'd be dismissed.

It seems the conditions of work were in line with the Manager's disposition. For instance: you could go to the toilet if you asked permission. On this being given, you were "timed" whilst there. Also, you were permitted to have one week's holiday per year. But since you weren't doing any work, it had - obviously - to be without pay.

Other benefits such as Bank Holidays came as a matter of course. On these days, the business closed and you were, therefore, allowed the day off. However - in all "fairness" - since you weren't working on that day, you couldn't expect to be paid. But when you did work, you were, as a new starter, paid two-pence per hour. Obviously, no reason existed to jeopardise all these advantages by singing. (Forgive the cynicism.)

Not long after the incident forbidding my sister's impulse to add joy to her labours she found a job, which, if not completely "at ease" with the quality of her singing, did, at least, allow its expression.

But back to the quilts: after a couple of months of this work, my mother decided to abandon its not very rewarding efforts and return to the activity she'd done with, at least, some feeling of recognition and therefore satisfaction. She returned to the cleaning work that she used to do for the Jewish families living along Cheetham Hill Road, which offered more per hour than that earned from quilts - and for less effort and with no home "pollution".

So, our street, it seems, witnessed all sorts of activities to earn a crust. Also, hardly a household existed in it and all its adjacent streets without the woman of the house becoming the central figure - as she often does in all periods of difficulties.

But as far as we kids were concerned, all the activities the difficulties represented added interest to our lives; and if the activities were right before our eyes, the more interesting they became. Being free of concern for the future, we lived as all children do: forever in the present. Each day was "sufficient unto itself" and the extra money obtained from the efforts of our elders could mean, to us - on any particular day - an additional treat. We might have "Cake for Tea", to use a popular saying of that time, expressing a luxury. And because luxuries were a rarity hardly ever expected, they were all the better for their rarity - if and when they did come.

One thing I liked even better than cake for tea was tripe for tea. Not only because I liked the taste of tripe but mainly because we kids could go for the tripe ourselves.

It's nearly teatime, and we've been told by our Mam to get some tripe from the tripe-processing place: the one we call Paddy Jeff's. Besides tripe, Paddy'll sell us two pennyworths of pig's trotters, if that's what we fancied. (But we don't have to get any of those now.)

To reach Paddy Jeff's, we go down the bruw then turn left into Burton Street; then turn right at the end of that street. This'll take us into Dalton Street. Then, at the bottom of this street, opposite Saint Catherine's School, we turn left into where Dantzic Street meets the end of Collyhurst Road.

Paddy Jeff's is at the top end of Warford Street - that's on the left a little way along Dantzic Street and just before the gasometers on the opposite side of that street.

Paddy Jeff's is easy to find because it's the place with the big, wide-open, wooden doors. And when you go inside, it feels cool, even on a hot summer's day, because of the great big lumps of ice floating in the vats where the tripe's kept.

You'll see lumps of tripe floating amongst the ice. All we have to do is tell Paddy Jeff which piece we fancy. He'll fish it out, drain it off and wrap it up.

Our Mam said: if we hurry back, we could have it with a piece of black pudding, buttered bread and a nice hot cup of tea.

And, maybe, some cake afterwards...

TRIPE an' ONIONS

"Dash round quick to Paddy Jeff's...
See what tripe he might have left.
Tripe an' onions for our tea.
Y'dad's home soon –
and he'll be hungry.
Hurry up – and if you're good,
we'll also have some boiled black pud.
So dash round quick –
and come right back.
    Don't poke at the ice
    in the cold tripe vat."

15
Astonished Eyes and Ears

~~~~~~~~~~~~~~~~~~~~~~~~~~~~~~~~~

We've seen how the economic circumstances prevailing in the periods of our visits influenced life to make it, in many ways, immensely different from what we know now.

But before we continue along the path of time we've set ourselves to follow, let's reverse our direction for a while to go further back than we did in our last visit. By doing this, we can look at other aspect of life we now call technology and see how the many "wonders" that we now take for granted came on the scene. We can also experience how the people who first witnessed their arrival reacted.

A historian (whose name, unfortunately, I can't remember) once said: "If a citizen of Rome living at the start of the first millennium happened to be brought forward to the beginning of the eighteen-hundreds, that person would have little difficulty in adapting to its way of life and also understanding the things in everyday use."

For our purposes, let's say that citizen happened to arrive in France and then accompanied Alexis de Tocqueville on his visit to Manchester in 1835. In this case, he would, in all probability, feel the same trepidation his companion felt in the face of the never-before-seen great changes.

Yet, the melting and shaping of iron, the weaving of cloth and certain powerful machines were a familiarity going back to Roman times. Moreover, many of the people directly involved in the changes Tocqueville witnessed had, but a short time before, been forced by economic circumstances to leave an agricultural life essentially similar to that which our imagined citizen would've experienced in his own period. Therefore, the people who'd been forcefully pushed into the industrial milieu quickly made their own adaptations - as we assume Alexis de Tocqueville and his contemporaries did and the visitor from the previous time would.

But what if that same citizen happened to be brought forward to the time of now - some one hundred and seventy or so years later than the time of Tocqueville's visit? Making accommodations to the "strange forces" he'd encounter would be somewhat difficult, to say the least. It's easy to imagine he'd be startled almost to distraction; no doubt believing that demonic forces, witchcraft, trickery and supernatural manifestations had taken possession of the land.

Yet, although we cannot properly imagine the full impact such an experience would've had on the person suggested, we can get an inkling of the astonishment that person may've felt by calling upon my sister's memory. This because - as I've often remarked - she's fortunate enough to have recollections extending more usefully further back than mine, and was at the scene when many of the "wonders" which astonished those unaccustomed eyes and ears began to emerge.

My recollections are restricted to a time where the foundations of the age we know now were well established. The wireless (radio) had become a feature of everyday life - as you saw when visiting our house in Heelis Street - and had reached a reasonable level of technology. It had fast become an indispensable item in almost every household to the same degree a television set has in our present period.

In that particular visit, we also had a look at the technicalities of radio transmission and its development, and how the idea of "sounds coming out of the air and without wires" caused astonishment bordering on incredulity when it first occurred.

For a direct description of how it descended upon the scene in the nineteen-twenties, it is worth hearing my sister's amazement when first experiencing sounds coming from a Cat's Whisker wireless set.

(In her various tellings and in accordance with the colloquialisms of that time: "one an' six" means "one shilling and sixpence" and "twelve an' six" means "twelve shillings and sixpence". Also, the expression "t'pence" means "twopence"; and "thre'pence" means "threepence" and fo'pence means fourpence.)

Anyway, let her get on with the telling - just as she saw it:

"Our Dad made a Crystal Set. He managed to get all the parts needed, including the earphones, from going around various shops. He could afford to buy these because he'd got a job in the evenings, bagging up coal for a man named Mr Massey who owned a coal-yard in Cheetham Street.

"This job earned him a pound a week. He went to a shop on Shude Hill to get the cat's whisker - that's a very thin piece of special wire for making the connection from the crystal to the main parts, and that was the most important piece of the set. It cost t'pence.

"We were all amazed when he put all the parts together and we heard sounds and voices and then some music coming through the earphones. Nobody knew where the sounds came from. We thought it was our Dad playing tricks.

"I told all the kids in the street we'd a little box in our house with music and voices coming out of it, and I tried to explain it to them, but they didn't believe me. They said I must be barmy."

My sister also experienced the family's first acquisition of the original miracle's extension and its further developments. You saw a representation of this in the visit we made to our house in the nineteen-thirties. But, again, let her tell the story.

"Later on, proper wirelesses came into the shops. We managed to hire a three valve set from Walsh's, on Rochdale Road. We paid one an' six per week for its use. We found it very expensive to keep going - this apart from the weekly hiring payment. It needed a 120 volt Exide Battery or an accumulator to make it work, because we had no electricity in the house.

"We used an accumulator rather than a battery because this happened to be cheaper. But it had to be left at the shop to be recharged every week, and took two days before being ready. In the meantime, they'd loan you one for two or three pence, depending on its size - if you didn't want to be without one, that is.

"Sometimes, a valve burnt out. This meant taking all three to the shop for test to find the faulty one. The best valves lasted longest - such as Mullards - but each could cost as much as twelve an' six. Most times, we had to buy the cheaper valves because that's all we could afford. But they burnt out much sooner.

"When we couldn't afford a replacement valve, we had to do without the wireless until we'd saved enough money for what we needed. In the meantime, we'd make do with an old gramophone we still had - or fiddled around with the crystal set to see if we could get any sounds out of it.

"We were all glad when we got the wireless working again, because we began to miss it. All you had to do was turn a knob and you'd get entertainment. It seemed amazing."

So, by the time of my full awareness of the world, it seems the wireless was here, there, and virtually everywhere. Also, some of the miracles that became commonplace in the latter part of the twentieth century were emerging in sufficient form to be within the realms of credibility. Even "pictures through the air" (now captured by the TV screen) were - according to what we heard at school - becoming within the "it'll soon be here" expectation.

Moreover, even the more astonishing suggestion of space travel was presented on the cinema screens in the exploits involving Buck

Rogers and Flash Gordon. The silver screen was, it seems, preparing our minds for the many more wonders yet to come.

But as the birth of the wireless story indicates, my sister knew the time when miracles - now accepted as part of the everyday world and without the slightest feeling of astonishment - were conjured up before people's astonished eyes and ears. For instance: in the nineteen-twenties, the skies were virtually empty of what is now the commonplace passage of helicopter and aeroplane. To see a man-made artefact flying in the sky - even with the aid of gas buoyancy - was enough to bring people dashing out into the streets to stare in amazement.

My sister told me about seeing her first airship. However, her words rather than mine will give greater immediacy to the experience:

"One time, an Airship called the R100 flew over our street. The word quickly got around. Everyone became so excited they rushed out of their houses to have a look at it. Some were so excited they nearly fell down their front steps in a hurry to get out in the street, to see it, before it went by. We'd never seen anything like it.

"Afterwards - when aeroplanes began to appear now and again - all the kids came out of their houses and ran up and down the street, pointing to the sky, chanting 'Aera, Aera! Bon! Bon! Bon!' until it flew right out of sight."

On her telling me this, I asked if she knew the origin of the chant, but she didn't know where it came from or why it was used in that particular way and in that context. I asked the same of others who knew that period, but again they were unaware of its origin - although remembering the chant.

I then began to wonder if it might be a legacy of the - then - not long since First World War? Perhaps "Aera" is the diminutive of Aeroplane and, perhaps, "Bon" was originally "Bomb"? In those early days of flight, a plane's progress was slow enough to allow warnings to be shouted on its approach. A shout such as: "Aeroplane! Aeroplane! Bombs! Bombs! Bombs!" may've acted as an alert for the exposed to take cover in the trenches?

Perhaps the children of the immediate post-war generation had heard tales of such warnings from their elders; and - since all kids delight in rhythmic chants, whatever their origin and frightening intentions - they may've ascribed its transformed version to the sighting of any aeroplane?

It's interesting to note this chant happened to be in vogue when I became old enough to run up and down the street (nearly twenty years after the aforementioned war) to delight in a chance to chant the chant. But, by then, aeroplanes had reached a stage of technical development making them far more adventurously used - so flights across the sky caused much less excitement.

By the time of my birth, airway pioneers were in the process of exploring many new routes and possibilities. For instance, in May, 1930, the marvellously brave and adventurous Amy Johnson completed a solo flight (acting as her own mechanic) from Croydon to Australia, landing at Darwin in what was then the astonishingly short time of nineteen and a half days.

Before that, her longest flight was one between London and Hull, lasting for about two hours.

The two-year-old De Havilland Gypsy Moth biplane she used for the Australian flight had a maximum speed of 90 mph and a range of thirteen hours before refuelling. She navigated by checking the ground visible from the cockpit against a map she held on her lap.

Later, in 1932, she flew to Tokyo by way of Siberia in ten days.

These events caused a sensation; so much so that it impelled a popular song called "Amy! Wonderful Amy!" performed by Jack Hylton and his Band on the wireless after the first flight - this to be eagerly imitated by many popular bands and singers thereafter.

In addition to this artistic and sophisticated musical accolade, it seems our district also contributed to the enthusiasm - although at a different level of expertise. My sister told me of a song made up and sung by the kids soon after the Australian event. It went like this:

Amy Johnson flew in an aeroplane,
She flew to Sydney
And all the way back again.
She flew in an old Tin Lizzie,
Enough to make her dizzy.
But she looked sweet,
Sat in the seat,
Of an aeroplane made for two.

This being sung to the old music-hall tune of "A Bicycle Made For Two" - as most made up songs seemed to be in those days.

Again, this song still enjoyed popularity in my time and that of my playmates when we all delighted in such ditties - I suppose it was too good a ditty for the kids to let go. (By the way and in case you don't know: "Tin Lizzie" means a rickety old contraption.)

The somewhat silhouetted photo offered on the previous page - taken immediately upon her landing in Darwin - appeared in the May 26th 1930 edition of The Daily Telegraph.

However, various developments were taking aeroplane technology far beyond the Tin Lizzie stage. By the mid-thirties, they'd become versatile enough to be used in what was, for that time, highly sophisticated advertising. Biplanes frequently traverse the clear sky drawing a long, canvas trailer behind them to carry a slogan promoting a product such as:

CARTER'S LITTLE LIVER PILLS.

These new additions created a resurgence of excitement sufficient for we kids to follow a plane's progress across the sky and to render that old and previously mentioned chant with the same joy and enthusiasm as before. This time, the word "Bon" being delightedly used in the same spirit as the French word signifying "good".

In addition to all this came the more exciting aerobatics of skywriting done by the same type of biplanes; scripted in the upper atmosphere with a smoke-trail when the air happened to be calm enough to hold the results for a reasonable time. This again being done to emblazon the virtues of some desirable product across the high heavens.

We'd gather in the street, open-mouthed, to watch the message unfold as the plane twisted and turned to shape each letter.

So, in my sister's experience, "machines that flew" had emerged from the miraculous to the commonplace and - in addition - she had the privilege of being astonished by pictures that not only moved but even talked; and then to see this amazement become commonplace.

Again, let's hear her tell about the first event:

"When I was about seven or eight, Granny Corrigan used to take me to the local cinema which we called the Cinny - a short name for cinema. It was the one at the top of Buckley Street. She did this once a week. They showed black and white silent films. I'd read the words for Gran because her eyesight wasn't too good.

"The showing took place from quarter to six in the evening until about eight o'clock. After the showing, Gran went to bed almost straight away - she had to be up at half-past-four in the morning, for work.

"After a year or two of my reading out the words, the Cinny decided to change over to talking pictures. But we weren't quite sure what that meant. The place closed down for about three months and during that time they did it up a bit and gave it a posh name, 'The Rex', but we still called it the Cinny.

"Gran missed going to the pictures during this closure because of it being her main entertainment. But when the Cinny opened again, everyone sat in amazement. Talking pictures! We didn't believe it! Someone said they'd got some people to stand behind the screen - singing and speaking the words.

"Anyway, they didn't need the piano player any more, and I missed her, because - if a film wasn't all that interesting - I could at least watch her playing the piano and listen to the music.

"We were glad the prices stayed the same - still t'pence for the front seats. These were long, hard wooden benches with a hard wooden back-rest. They'd pack as many as they could on each, and if you sat on the end, you had to hold tight to the edge of the seat on either side of your legs when you felt the row of sitters being moved along. If you didn't hold on, you could get pushed off the end.

"The rear rows - where I sat with Gran - were still thre'pence. These were single seats fixed together in rows and provided with padding on each seat and its backrest to make them more comfortable. The Cinny also had a small balcony, but Gran couldn't afford this. It cost fo'pence.

"The outside of the building hadn't changed. They kept it as it was before the closure - more or less a long, high shed with a brick front and rear and with sides clad in corrugated iron sheets. Kids in the district used to drag a stick along the corrugations - thinking it great fun - and this made a terrible rattle inside.

"This hardly mattered when pictures were silent because of reading words; but when the talking pictures came, you couldn't hear a thing. Eventually, the manager had to go outside to watch out for mischief. Anyone caught had their name taken and weren't allowed to attend the cinema for weeks. This stopped the nuisance - or, at least, it didn't happen so often."

So this is the way the "talkies" came on the scene at the Cinny. In the context of this, it's interesting to note how technical changes can impose new ways of evaluating behaviour - as in the case of the stick-rattling changing from a minor to a major mischief. Also, it's interesting to note the age wasn't free from sudden redundancies due to technological changes (the dismissal of the no longer required piano player, for instance).

But by the time I became old enough to attend the cinema, to sit up and take notice, talkies had, like the aeroplane, become commonplace and many films such as the Mickey Mouse escapades were being produced in full and glorious Technicolor. So again I missed out on seeing it all burst forth in its fresh and original excitements.

Yet it always seems the case and is - apparently - the driving force of "progress": one set of novelties tends to generate the next. In the pressure to keep the pennies flowing in the box offices in a steady and expanding stream, advances came in various combinations of the spectacular. These again were displayed mainly in Technicolor and culminated in what was probably the most spectacularly colourful film of the nineteen-thirties: the 1939 'Gone With the Wind'.

Before this abundance of colour started to flood each screen and the eager and excited eyes of each cinema-goer, I remember being taken to the Cinny (its posh name, the Rex, still hadn't caught on) to see the first great and really spectacular presentation of the early nineteen-thirties: 'King Kong'.

I happened to be of an age young enough to cower against my mother when the giant Kong appeared on the screen in all its terrifying black-and-whiteness - giving the film a frightening starkness which, I believe, colour would've much diminished.

This raises another "note" of interest. Advances are, it seems, not always total gains and can sometimes bring losses: as, for instance, my sister's previously mentioned loss of her favourite piano player and also the possible "distraction" colour can have on the impact of various images.

It's interesting to note this became recognised in the film 'Schindler's List' which employed black and white right up to the final scenes, because of its stark affect.

However, advances - or whatever we wish to call them - will come, whether we like it or not. Because - again, whether we like it or not - and in the closing words of a Newsreel popular in the nineteen-thirties:

"TIME MARCHES ON..."

16
As a Matter of Interest:
The Airship R100

~~~~~~~~~~~~~~~~~~~~~~~~~~~~~~~~

In our last visit, we witnessed how newly arrived wonders, such as the wireless, talking-pictures and air-flight, astonished the eyes and ears of the people who lived at that time. In addition, I told you about the incident when my sister saw the Airship R100 as it sailed directly above Heelis Street.

Its dramatic appearance not only astonished the eyes of our little street but also the whole of Manchester's.

For an on-the-spot description of this happening, I can do no better than quote Thursday's edition of The Manchester Evening News, whose headline on the 22nd of May 1930, stated:

R100's SURPRISE VISIT TO MANCHESTER.
MIDDAY THRILL FOR CITY CROWDS.

The report went on to say - and I quote from the newspaper directly because it seems well worth a hearing:

Britain's giant airship R100 passed over Manchester in brilliant sunshine soon after 11:30 to day.

During the night, the airship had been cruising over the East Coast and this morning headed inland from Hull.

When the airship appeared over the city, Manchester was taken by surprise. She was flying so low that the noise of her engines drew thousands of people to mill and office roofs and windows. The airship's number could be plainly seen. In the suburbs, housewives ran to their doors.

Travelling from the north, the dirigible came over Corporation Street and Cross Street and, watched by thousands of eyes, circled round the Town Hall with a wide, graceful sweep. It was a beautiful sight, the sun glinting brilliantly on the airship's hull. Then she turned her nose north, dipped a little, and sailed away over Salford.

Long after she had passed, the roar of the engines could be heard gradually diminishing until it became a faint buzz and was lost in the sound of street noises. But thought the airship had gone, crowds of people in Market Street, Cross Street and Deansgate stood peering into the sky in the hope that she might pass over again on her way to Cardington.

A report in The Manchester Evening News some months previously - Monday December 16th 1929 - told how the ship carried a black cat as a mascot on its first flight. It's highly likely this symbol of luck had its presence in the ship during its reported flight over Manchester and, if so, it certainly carried luck to the city regarding the weather and the sighting it made possible.

So, it seems: "they came out in their thousands" - just as my sister said. But what sort of object was it that made them "fall over themselves" to pour out into the streets and then peer upwards into the brilliant blue sky - in open-mouth astonishment?

Imagine an object with a length equal to that of two football pitches, shaped like a massively long, fat cigar-shaped dart, cruising at what would seem almost rooftop height, with its silvery outer-skin gleaming in the May mid-day sun and moving so slowly that it seemed to hover. Well! I put it to you: such a sight would stop traffic even now; and to an age hardly used to air-flight, it must've appeared awesome.

A book I came across in my local library ('Airship Saga' - from which I extracted various details included in the following information) gives an idea of its technicalities and again of its size.

The ship R100 (shown on the left in a somewhat faded photo) was essentially composed of a lightweight metal frame covered by a weatherproof canvas. From tip to tail it measured 709 feet (216 metres) and at its mid-section measured 130 feet (39 metres) in diameter. The interior contained 15 gasbags of a total capacity of 5,156,000 cubic feet of hydrogen. Below and towards the front of the frame a Car or Gondola carried the crew - usually comprising five personnel with room for up to forty-five passengers.

The propulsion units (six Rolls-Royce Condor engines, capable of generating 4,200 horsepower) were slung below and central to its mainframe - propelling the ship at speeds up to 83 miles per hour.

An aviation consortium called 'The Airship Guarantee Company' (of which Vickers held the major share) built the ship at Howden, near Kingston-upon-Hull, under the supervision and design skills of Barnes Wallis (the person famed for his Dam Busting Bomb in the Second World War).

Another (later famous) person involved with the R100 and working as an assistant to Barnes Wallis happened to be a person named Nevil Shute Norway - who later became a distinguished novelist using the less exotic name of Nevil Shute. He made his contribution to the airship's construction by doing most of the complicated mathematical calculations for the engineering design team.

One of the ship's test voyages involved sailing into a thunderstorm, in which a great gust carried the vessel 1,800 feet upward in less then a minute. Nevil Shute Norway - using the dramatic skill that later served him well as a novelist - described an incident during this alarming turbulence, thus:

The ship was so far nose down that it was necessary to hold on, apparently plunging straight into the ground in thick cloud and rain, with the altimeter going madly the wrong way, completely out of control. At that moment, in the faint orange light, a torrent of sticky red fluid resembling blood poured down into the control car. Grand Guignol could not have done better.

As a matter of interest: Grand Guignol happened to be a theatre in Paris that specialised in dramatically gruesome presentations.

The mentioned red fluid came from a tin of red dope used for repairing the canvas outer skin. This spilled over in the workshop above the control car and then seeped through the deck to provide the theatrical and somewhat horrific effect described.

Additionally, the mentioned book revealed that the R100 had a sister-ship designated as the R101 - shown on the left at its mooring tower. It happened to be built more or less at the same time as the R100 but at the Royal Airship Works situated near Cardington, Bedfordshire.

The R101 caused Manchester a great disappointment some months before the mentioned R100 flight, when, on its second trial flight, it headed north and could have - but did not - sail over the city.

However, the disappointment would've been even greater if it had sailed Manchester's way, because it poured down during the crucial period - as the Monday, December 16th 1929, edition of the Manchester Evening News interestingly and somewhat amusingly reported:

As soon as the news that the R101 was probably flying to Manchester became know to the city, there was a general tendency for everyone to gaze skyward. The Manchester Corporation Gas Committee was sitting in the Town Hall, and so eager were the members to see the airship that, at noon, when someone inform them it was close at hand, they adjourned their meeting and went out in body into Albert Square - giving Manchester citizens the unusual spectacle of a mass of city fathers craning their necks towards the heavens.

Clerks in the Town Hall who could snatch a moment to spare followed the Gas Committee's example. However, nothing appeared in the sky except clouds, and a heavy shower sent the watchers scurrying for shelter.

So, it seems, the "city fathers" responsible for the city's gas didn't see the gas-filled object they thought might sail above their heads. However, and as we've seen, they had a chance to redress their disappointment some five months later when the R100 appeared out of the blue on that glorious spring-time day (that's if they, the city fathers, concerned about gas, were around to see it - as thousands of awe-struck people were).

I do not know if the R101 likewise had a black cat for a mascot, but it certainly needed luck from any source in the terrible circumstances of its end - as reported in the Daily Mirror of October 5th 1930:

Disaster struck the world's biggest airship last night when the R101 exploded in a fireball as she hit a French hillside not long after setting off on her first journey to India. A total of 44 people, including Air Secretary Lord Thomson, are known to have died in the crash near Beauvais, with just eight surviving. The King has expressed his horror at the tragedy, and although a full investigation into what caused the crash has yet to begin, it seems likely the disaster will set the cause of airships back years.

Indications are that heavy rain may have been to blame, forcing the 777-foot-long airship to lose height. Engineer H.J. Leech said: The rain suddenly came down, and so wetted the ship that she answered badly to the helm. Twice she dipped dangerously and then on the third occasion she ran nose first into the hill and burst into flames with a tremendous explosion. The officer in command became aware that the £600,000 airship was dangerously near the ground and he sent an urgent message 'Slow down' to the engine car but it was too late. The five and a half million cubic feet of hydrogen on board exploded. Within seconds she was reduced to nothing but a skeleton of twisted steel.

Eyewitnesses, woken from their beds by the roar of the crash, told of a great yellow glare shot with tongues of flames. Another engineer, A.V. Bell, explained how a water-tank burst above his head on impact and its water came drenching down to save his life.

So that was the end of the ill-fated R101. And although the R100 of our sighting fared much better (completing a flight to Canada and back in the July and August of 1930) the terrible disaster encountered by her sister-ship cast a great gloom over the British Airship industry, to make the R100's Canadian flight its last. In the November of 1931, the great ship that awed Manchester was taken into a shed at Cardington and dismantled, then to emerge as £450 worth of scrap. Thus ended the British Airship adventure.

What was thought to be the air-travel of the future received its final blow by a disaster even more startlingly dreadful than that of the R101. This happened when the German ship, Hindenburg, exploded as it began to dock at its mooring mast on arriving at Lakehurst, New Jersey on the morning of May 6th 1937. The headlines of the May 7th edition of The Daily Telegraph stated:

DISASTER TO GIANT AIRSHIP: 50 DEAD.
HINDENBURG DESTROYED BY EXPLOSION.
HELD UP IN STORM: CRASHED IN FLAMES.

It went on to report:
For an hour the giant Zeppelin had cruised around with a thunderstorm making it impossible for her to land. When the weather improved, she approached the mooring mast. It was then the explosion took place. The flames spread with great rapidity. The airship collapsed to the earth and was soon a mass of twisted wreckage. There were 100 occupants aboard, of whom about half of them perished.

The actual numbers of fatalities were 35 passengers and crew out of a total of 97 people aboard. It seems remarkable that so many survived when disaster struck so suddenly.

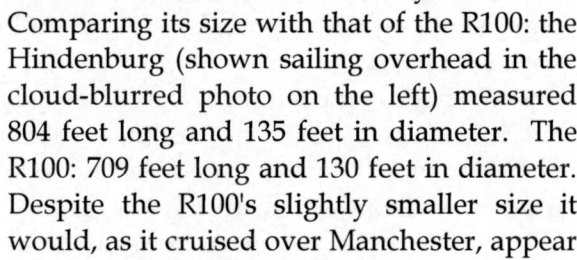

Comparing its size with that of the R100: the Hindenburg (shown sailing overhead in the cloud-blurred photo on the left) measured 804 feet long and 135 feet in diameter. The R100: 709 feet long and 130 feet in diameter. Despite the R100's slightly smaller size it would, as it cruised over Manchester, appear very much like the Hindenburg portrayed in the photo.

The fate of these floating giants ended the Age of the Airship. Their story became a reflection of the 1930s: an age of rising hope ending with a disaster, which drastically changed the ways of thinking.

But we needn't think of that now. Instead - and in our next visit - we'll take a walk around the shops over which the R100 must have sailed...

17
A Walk around the Shops

~~~~~~~~~~~~~~~~~~~~~~~~~~~~~~~~~~~~

Our next viewing involves the district's shops. We'll see how they form an important aspect of the neighbourly community previously mentioned. Before returning to when they existed, it might be useful if we review the type of coinage we'd find in everyday use.

Prior to the changeover to a decimal system - effected on the 15th February 1971 - the coinage had a history going back to the Middle Ages and even before that time. It had its beginning when a pound weight of silver was divided into 240 pennies. (The word "penny" being derived from the Old English "penig" - first associated as a unit of coinage with King Penda - c 577-654 - the overlord of an area in Anglo-Saxon England called Mercia).

By the time of the Middle Ages, the currency became based on the Pound Sterling. The term "Pound" originated from the mentioned pound-weight of silver and the word "sterling" from the Old English "steorling", meaning a "small star". It became customary to stamp this star-symbol on the early silver penny to guarantee the purity of its metal. The symbol '£' signified the pound (comprising 240 pennies), the symbol 's' signified the Shilling (comprising 12 pennies) and the penny, itself, had the symbol 'd'. Therefore, to indicate an amount comprising, say, two pounds, eleven shillings and six pence we'd write: £2. 11s. 6d.

So the basic composition of the currency before the big "change" (no pun intended) effected by decimalisation was represented by the symbols £, s, d - pronounced "el, es, dee". This is the system of currency we'll find in use during our visit.

The symbol £, s, d, derive from the Latin words Librae, solidi and denarri - respectively. This came about because Latin happened to be a universal language in the Middle Ages and the Lombard Bankers - invited to London during that period to help organise financial matters - consolidated the use of the Latin terms. As you can see, the currency symbols and the actual currency we'll be observing during our visit had a "rich" and extensive history (one that was "criminally killed off" by decimalisation - some might say).

However, to move away from moral and academic issues and get down to matters of "hard cash". We'll find sub-divisions of the £, s, d in the form of a half-a-crown coin (two shillings and sixpence, or colloquially: "two an' six"). This represented half the value of a coin once known as the Crown - distinguished by a heavily embossed crown on one of its sides; but that particular unit of currency became defunct prior to our intended visits due to its cumbersome size.

There's also a shilling coin (colloquially know as a "bob"); a two-shilling coin (known as a Florin but colloquially as "two-bob"); a sixpenny coin (known simply as a sixpence or, colloquially, as a "tanner"); a three-penny coin (known colloquially as a "thre'p'ny bit"). There's also the penny and halfpenny along with the farthing (one quarter of a penny). In addition to the pound note, we'd find in common use a ten shilling note (known colloquially as a "ten-bob note"). We might also see the infrequently used large, white, five-pound note - which could represent a week's salary for, say, a head-teacher. So we'd more than likely see this being exchanged in the districts where such "highly paid" people live, and not in the district we'll be visiting.

Also in use - but again not often seen in the district of our visit - is the "gold guinea", minted in gold and representing one pound and one shilling. This coin had its origin in 1817 but became superseded by the "gold sovereign" of the same value. However, the term "guinea" persisted until 1971; being used to price expensive items, especially in the arts world, and for billing professional fees.

You'll also need to know colloquialisms for two-pence ("t'pence"); three-pence ("thre'pence"); four-pence (fo'pence); a halfpenny ("ha'p'ny"); a halfpenny-worth ("ha'p'nyworth" or "ha'p'orth") and a penny-worth ("penn'orth"). The same colloquialisms would describe one shilling and three pennies as "one an' three". This style of abbreviation applies throughout the shilling and pence combinations; as, for instance, the "two an' six" (two shillings and sixpence) mentioned previously. Therefore, throughout this narratives and those to follow, the colloquial pronunciation for the coinage and its various sub-divisions will be used - this to enter the period of our visit with the "correct currency", so to speak.

As all these complexities indicate: an enormous changed took place in the currency used during my mother's lifetime. The connecting thread of currency that I knew as a child, and my mother knew as a child, and her mother knew as a child, and so on and so on, became broken in 1971 - again indicating an aspect of the "great change" theme weaving its way through all these narratives.

Along with the change of currency (although not directly related to it) the mode and style of shopping represents another of the most remarkable contrasts between the first and second half of the century we're considering. The first half is characterised by the small corner shop and the second by increasingly vast and constantly expanding "Emporiums".

A remarkable aspect of this enormous change lies in the fact that anyone from, say, the mid-Victorian period would have little difficulty in understanding and using the shops we'll see in our visit. Also and as previously indicated, they'd find little difficulty with the coinage in use. However, that same person would be completely baffled and possibly somewhat alarmed by what the second half increasingly presented (especially the astounding practice of using a small piece of strange, flexible material as a substitute for "hard cash").

Our proposed visit to the nineteen-thirties will be one where we can experience the conditions our imagined Victorian would find comfortably familiar. However, again we need to see things mainly through the eyes of a child and by way of its perceptions and interpretations - which, as previously suggested, can provide certain advantages.

One of the main advantages in this case arises from the fact that the shops projected an intensely personal appeal to the children of that time. Each shop possessed its own particular character; whereas it would be difficult to imagine the now ubiquitous and impersonally large emporiums holding the same qualities for children - or, indeed, for anyone else - except, perhaps, for the vast quantities of "goodies" inviting an over-indulgence?

Anyway, let's make a start. Our intended excursion will take us along Rochdale Road, which is the main shopping area of the district. On our way to the first of its shops, we can have a glance at any entertaining places we may've missed during our previous visits.

So, assuming the eyes of a child, we'll leave Heelis Street and turn right into Buckley Street - staying on its right-hand pavement.

A few steps up the slope and over the other side of the street you'll see a house belonging to a man named Mr Curry. You might've noticed his downstairs window on our previous walk, because it contains a shelf full of stuffed birds and small animals - which he seems to like because he's got lots more inside. You'd hardly be able to move around his front room without one staring you in the face. When he leaves his front door open in the warmer weather, the word quickly gets around. The kids gather to have a good gawp inside his front room. He doesn't seem to mind this as long as they're not making a nuisance and don't stay gawping too long. Anyway, his door's closed at the moment so let's move on.

Next door to his house is a little pub called The Friendship. You'll notice it's not much bigger than the houses whose terrace row it shares. In fact, it went through much the same process as that of Agnes's shop: once having been a house but, in this case, becoming a pub. Again, like Agnes's, you can tell the original purpose by its windows. They're the same size and shape as those belonging to the houses on either side - especially its upstairs window that looks no different from all the others in the row. The main change to its exterior produced by the conversion is the ornamental glass pane fitted to the downstairs window - containing the Brewery's name 'Groves and Whitnall', framed by the usual etched wreath of flowers.

The Pub has two well worn stone steps leading up to its small front door; well worn because people in our district pop in and out as soon as its open at eleven in the morning. Most of its customers take a jug to be filled with t'pence-worth of frothy beer, which they take home to drink with their mid-day meals. Many people in our street like to do this - especially on a Saturday.

The shop we've now reached (the one over the other side of the street and at the top end of the pub's row) is called Globe's. We call it Globe's because Mrs Globe owns it. Its door is on the corner of, and set at an angle to, Buckley Street and Almond Street. It has two large windows on either side of the doorway and therefore one in each street. Here you could buy a ha'p'orth of crystals - lemon flavoured. You put these in a jug and then fill it with hot water. After filling the jug, let it stand on your scullery windowsill for a while. The drink tastes better if the crystals are allowed time to dissolve and the water gets really cool.

Another thing you might like to know about Globe's is that it sells a Woodbine cigarette along with a match for a ha'p'ny, but only to those she thinks old enough to smoke - otherwise, if you ask her for what you're not supposed to have, she'll tell your Dad. But this doesn't affect us, so let's move on - there's lots more to see.

We'll stay on the right-hand pavement and take a few more steps to the corner of Worth Street where we'll see the full extent of the building belonging to Miller's Raincoats. It's just across Buckley Street's cobbles from where we've now reached.

Perhaps you've noticed a long length of blank brick wall in Almond Street, nearly opposite the window of Globe's shop. It belongs to Miller's. Lots of kids use this wall for playing bounce-ball - that's throwing the ball against the wall and catching it on rebound. But if you happen to bounce it too hard and miss the catch - so that the ball bounces near Globe's window - you'll get told off.

She once had a window broken by kids who'd chalked a wicket on the blank wall and then played cricket using a hard ball. The Dads of the three kids involved had to pay for the damage and they weren't too pleased. Ever since, all the kids have been very careful. They'll use a tennis ball - if they've got one - but this doesn't stop Mrs Globe getting worried if a ball bounces too hard and goes near her window. So let's move away or she'll think we're hanging around to play cricket or bounce-ball - and start getting anxious.

The next street on our right up Buckley Street's slope is Birtle Street. It has a very important shop on its corner opposite to the one we've reached. It's known as Cogh's and is owned by Mr Coghlan. It sells all sorts of things, but its main business is selling food. You may've heard a rhyme the kids in the district often chant, which goes like this:

> *In the morning,*
> *When you waken,*
> *Go to Cogh's*
> *For your eggs and bacon.*

We reckon Mr Coghlan made this up, himself, and hopes to spread it around to make his shop more popular. He's written it on the wall inside his shop. Sometimes, he'll chant it to you as you leave his shop. We shout it loudly when we pass his door, just for a bit of fun. He seems to like us doing this - although he never gives us anything for the free advert we give him: not even a broken biscuit! Also, you may've heard the girls using the same rhyme in their skipping games, but with a few more lines added to make their skipping a bit more lively. It goes:

> *In the morning,*
> *When you waken,*
> *Go to Cogh's*
> *For your eggs and bacon.*
> *When our Mam goes*
> *Up to Cogh's,*
> *She always wears her*
> *Shawl and clogs.*

Some of the kids made up another version. We use this when we feel a bit cheeky. It goes:

> *Coghlan's bread*
> *Is as hard as lead.*
> *Take one bite*
> *And you'll drop down dead.*

Mr Coghlan doesn't like this, at all - and gets very annoyed - so we don't do it all that often.

Anyway, let's not worry about the quality of Cogh's bread. Instead, let's look at the adverts on the wall outside his shop. You'll see they're mostly simple images with short statements enamelled on a metal sheet - mostly in blacks or blues on a white background. They seem mainly for decorative purposes rather than advertising.

The four you see there now are "Typhoo Tea, for Indigestion"; "Tizer the Appetiser"; "Colman's Mustard" and "Nestle's Milk".

Other times, you might see: "Hudson's Soap"; "Bile Beans"; "Home and Colonial Tea"; "Lipton's Tea"; "Robin Starch. Does not stick to the iron". Also: "Fairy Soap"; "Monkey Brand Household Soap"; "James Dome Blacklead - as used in the Royal Household"; "Zebra Blacklead"; "Reckitt's Blue Bags for Whiter Whites"; "Carter's Little Liver Pills - for general well-being".

Of course, you'll never see all these all at once (there's only room for a few). In any case, I'm not sure Cogh's sells all the things I've mentioned; but you might see most of them, from time to time because Mr Coghlan would sell almost anything if he thought it worthwhile. He'll then change his panels to suit. However, whilst we're looking at those now on display, let's have a few thoughts about adverts in general.

You'll probably feel the ones we're now seeing seem completely naïve, compared with the highly sophisticated, lavishly presented and heavily financed "persuasions" used in the time from whence we came? It may be that such lavishness only arises when society reaches the (fortunate?) financial position allowing people to afford things they don't really need - and therefore have to be tempted to buy what they wouldn't otherwise buy.

As you know from our previous visits, such adverts would be a waste of time in the district we're exploring. You can hardly entice people with very little cash to spare into making purchases above those they'd consider essential. What money they may have they'd use for necessities - and people hardly need persuasion to buy necessities.

If you were to tell folks in the district we're now visiting that a future time would see spending made by people like themselves move from the essential to the indulgent, they'd raise their eyebrows in surprise. If you were to add that a cause for concern would be the poor becoming too fat and the rich too thin, they'd laugh uproariously and think you're attempting to become a comedian. So, in this case, it's best we say nothing about what they'd consider to be a preposterous reversal of normality, for fear of ridicule.

However, look at that small dispensing machine - the one painted green - on the outside wall of Cogh's shop. From this you can get three Woodbine Cigarette for a penny. You may think this contradicts what's just been assumed about spending, because it could be argued it's a purchase people with hardly anything they'd call spare cash really need to make. This indicates "need" can be an arguable concept that can provoke discussions going on for ages - so we'll avoid starting one. But if you stood around in the evening (not for ages, but - perhaps - for ten minutes or so) you'd see the machine very much in use. This especially by the "just-started-work" young lads wishing to acquire what they think is the grown up habit of smoking - and thereby demonstrate they *are* grown up.

You might've noticed the shop is very much like Globe's: a doorway set at an angle to both streets and a large window in each of the streets. This gives it a favourable corner position inviting custom from each direction. The invitation the door and windows make (and also the enticement of his rhyme - as Mr Coghlan would have us believe) seems to succeed, because its single stone step appears as well-worn as those belonging to the Pub in Buckley Street. But it isn't folks coming for a jug of ale to have with their meal who cause the wear, it's people going there for eggs and bacon (when and even after they've wakened) along with other things they might need. Anyway, its door's wide open, so let's take a peep inside.

If you see Mr Coghlan stare at us whilst he's serving the woman from Worth Street - as if he wants us to move on - just chant his rhyme (the proper one) in a low voice and he'll smile. The woman might also be amused. He'll then let us stay long enough to have a good peep.

Whilst peeping, the first things you'll notice is that the wooden surface of his counter is bleached white from constant scrubbing and - on the end nearest the window - there's a large set of brass scales and a bacon-slicer. Also, the wall behind the counter has wooden shelves stacked with all sorts of goods in jars and packages; and the wooden floor is covered with a generous sprinkling of sawdust - which he sweeps out just after he closes the shop in the evening.

He puts new sawdust down every morning, before opening. He mixes the old sweepings with coal-dust to burn on his living-room fire.

The plywood chest on the floor on the customer side of the counter contains tea. Also, you'll see a sack of flour and a sack of sugar to the right of the doorway. All the contents of these he serves using a metal scoop left in the sacks or chest for that purpose. The amount the customer requires is scooped out and weighed on the scales. Then Mr Coghlan displays his skill of quickly forming a bag from a sheet of thick brown paper. He does this by rolling the sheet into a conical shape - like a dunce's hat. He then closes the pointed end by twisting it tightly. It's a cheap and handy way of holding quantities of sugar or tea - usually bought in amounts of a penn'orth or two.

One time - when I went to his shop for two penn'orth of tea our Mam sent me to get - he asked if I knew where tea came from. I said it was a place called Indiana; and, instead of putting the tea in the conical bag he'd just made, he stuck the bag on my head - saying it represented a dunce's cap - then gave me a biscuit. He said he hoped it would nourish my thoughts to give better results. I didn't mind this because I thought I'd got the right answer - and I'd also got a biscuit.

When I asked our Dad if the answer was right he said it wasn't, because the answer was India; but I should've got another biscuit for knowing there's a place called Indiana.

Talking about biscuits: of greater interest to the kids than where tea comes from are the broken biscuits he keeps in a large bin behind the counter. He gets the biscuits as rejects from the CWS Factory in Hazelbottom Road - near Crumpsall Hospital - and must think this good business, because lots of hungry mouths in and around our street can't afford proper biscuits. He sells what he gets as quickly as he can get it. You can buy a penn'orth of these at a time, which he serves in his quickly-made paper bag. If you're lucky, you might find some bits of chocolate biscuits in the portion he serves you.

Anyway, let's not bother about broken biscuits at the moment. Instead, let's go up the slope a little way for another look at that very important place we saw on our previous walk: the Rex Cinema - which, as you know, the local folks call the Cinny. Its stands across the cobbles just beyond Birtle Street where we've now reached. Its building covers the complete block contained by Bronze Street and the next street up the slope of Buckley Street, called Rhoda Street (that's the street where we saw the kids playing the game called 'There stands a Maiden on a Mountain'). Brass Street, at the rear of the Cinny, completes the block.

In our previous visit, you probably noticed that the Cinny has five stone steps built into the slope of Buckley Street's pavement, so that the length of the bottom three steps are progressively shorter than those above. These steps lead up to its open foyer, which is nearly as wide as the building, where it displays the usual paper posters on its bare-brick rear wall. The well-worn steps and long queue you saw during that visit no doubt made you realise it's the district's main place for entertainment. Even so, it still has to be careful about what it offers. Folks are reluctant to waste their pennies looking at films they don't want to see. They'd stay at home and play snakes and ladders, or sit by the fire and listen to the wireless, or read something interesting. Because of this, the Cinny goes to great efforts to put on what it thinks might appeal.

Sometimes, it makes more efforts than seems necessary. For instance: the manager, Mr Shaw, put on a display to attract people to see Johnny Weissmuller in Tarzan the Ape Man. He had a person standing at the top of the steps dressed in a leopard skin (supposedly like Tarzan) making Tarzan calls as people walked by.

The man stained his body with brown lotion to look as if sun-bronized, but the kids soon noticed it was streaked and made remarks about it. The man got cross. But despite the streaky make-up (and also the man getting cross) the effort seemed worthwhile because the Cinny had a full house. However, I found the man pretending to be Tarzan more entertaining. Especially his Tarzan calls - even though they were a bit croaky.

One attempt we didn't like was when Mr Shaw arranged a singsong during a Saturday afternoon's matinee - to fill in time before showing the main film. He hired an accordionist to stand on the cinema stage and play popular tunes for the kids to join in. But this wasn't at all successful because the kids created a protest - which made him withdraw the well-meaning entertainer and put on a Three Stooges (Curly, Larry and Moe) film, instead. We'd seen the film before, but thought it better than listening to the accordion.

We don't mind a singsong now and again; especially the ones where words are projected on the screen - line by line - and a bright white ball bounces from word to word in time to the tune. We then feel we aren't being cheated because, after all, it's films we'd come to see and this type of singsong is like a film - because it's on the screen.

We can see an accordionist for nothing when Dominic Rae, the Italian, comes into our street to play his accordion for any pennies he might attract - which we kids don't have to give: because we haven't got any. However, Dominic Rae is someone we might see on another visit. For now, let's take a closer look at the posters.

There's a Buck Jones cowboy film starting next Saturday, along with a Flash Gordon serial and a Loony Tunes cartoon. Save your pennies: it'll be worth seeing - especially the Flash Gordon serial.

Anyway, now we've seen all the excitements to come, let's take the last few steps to the top of Buckley Street to the corner where we started our first walk around the district. From there, we'll walk along Rochdale Road in a direction away from of the city centre, to see some of the shops and places of interest along that part of the road. It's where people in our district do shopping for things they mightn't be able to get from the more local shops.

Before we do this, I'd like to tell you a bit more about the place we've just passed. It's the place we know as the Flags. It probably got that name because it resembles the Flags near Charter Street - which we came to know during one of our visit. Many people now living in our district came from the Charter Street area and probably gave the name to a feature similar to one they knew in their old location. Also - like the Charter Street Flags - it's used as a place for children to play, as we saw on our walk around the district.

But that's just a bit of information in passing; so we can now take the last few steps to the top right-hand corner formed by Buckley Street and Rochdale Road. It's where we can see the first shop I want to tell you about. It's just across the road and in the middle of the row to the left of the wall that forms a parapet to the railway cutting beneath the road. This shop is known as Slater's and always has baskets of fruit and vegetables outside on the pavement - as you can see.

This shop sells large bags of mixed vegetables (potatoes, carrots, swedes and onions) for thre'pence. We often go there because our Mam makes a good stew from these vegetables, along with three-penn'orth of scrag-ends or cow's cheek. You only need to go a short distance along the road, to the next row, to get the scrag-ends or cow's cheek from Hall's butcher shop. But we needn't do that now - because no-one's asked us to - so let's stay on the side of the road we're on and cross the cobbles of Buckley Street, to reach its opposite corner and its large, three-storey, assembly hall with an ornate parapet and windows. There's a tale you might like to hear about this building.

One night, the word rapidly spread that a strange looking bird had perched on a ledge at the top of the building. When I got there, a big crowd from all the streets around stood looking up to where it sat.

We'd never seen a bird like it; and a man in the crowd said it was an owl, strayed from the countryside a long way away. We stood staring up at the ledge until way past bedtime. But it just stayed there doing nothing - except twisting its head now and again from side to side as if it didn't know where it was or what to do. And when we went back the next night, the bird had gone. We never saw it again.

However, you might find where folks do their Rochdale Road shopping more interesting than the stray owl. So let's walk a little way along the road to the opening of a passageway called Inland Place. It's now on our left and has Yaffee's second-hand shop opposite the first corner we've reached. You'll see the shop has a doorway set at an angle to that corner and also has a large window on either side of its doorway - like Cogh's. In this case, one window is positioned in Inland Place and the other in Rochdale Road. You can see both are filled with all sorts of useful bits and pieces.

I'm mentioning this shop because my aunt Sara Jones lived there for a while as a domestic-help-cum-shop-assistant. Because of this, she was able to get the second-hand pram that allowed me see the wider world whilst being wheeled around the district. However, an even more import benefit than getting my pram was the living-in arrangement the shop offered. This eased the accommodation problem in her own home. She had four sisters and two brothers at the time and - as you know - the houses in our district aren't very roomy.

A brief comment: I suppose this opportunity had its parallel in the "living-in-servant" arrangements available in the South of England, where it became almost an industry - employing more young girls than all the Mills of the North. One report concerning the nineteen-twenties indicated well over 340,000 young and not so young females were employed in domestic service in the South. No doubt such occupations demanded long days of hard work. Nevertheless, the normality for most people belonging to their background was exactly that: long days of hard work. At least the living-in arrangement had the compensation of allowing the person to share some of the comforts and "elevated" way of life enjoyed by the families they served.

However, let's get back to Yaffee's. It provides many useful and cheap household items, such as second-hand pots and pans, second-hand furniture and the like. These in addition to the pram I mentioned, whose stout wheels and axles eventually became part of a "guider" when the rest of the pram became worn out by long use.

You'll see lots of guiders in and around our district. The kids use them for play and for many other purposes that we'll see later. But in case you don't know what a guider is, here's a quick description.

It's a type of cart made up of a wooden plank about four or five feet long, about fourteen inches wide and at least one inch thick - which, for descriptive purposes, we'll call the "main board". This board has a hole drilled near one of its ends and in the middle of its width. A wooden crosspiece about two feet long, three inches wide and one inch thick is made to pivot on a bolt passed through this drilled hole and one drilled in the centre of the crosspiece. The bolt is secured by a locked nut - which is left loose enough to allow the crosspiece to pivot freely.

A pair of pram wheels, fitted to their axle, is secured across the underside of the pivoting crosspiece - using nails or screws. This arrangement becomes the steering end of the guider. The other axle obtained from the pram - also with its two wheels fitted - is then fixed firmly across the rear of the main board.

The front pivoting piece has a length of rope tied to each end - just inboard of the wheels - to act as the steering control: somewhat like a horse's rein. The rider can then sit on the main board with feet resting on the protruding part of the pivoting crosspiece. Thus seated and holding the steering rope, the driver can control the guider with rope and feet to ride down the many bruws (slopes) in our district. Or - if on a level stretch - can be pushed along by someone at the rear.

Also, if the guider has a strong main board and stout wheels, it can be used for transporting coal from the coal-yard, thus avoiding the need for returning the cart lent by that yard (an activity we'll see later).

Some "posh" guiders have a seat cushion fitted - usually obtained from an old chair. Also, the chair's backrest can be fitted if usable.

The owner of a guider is much envied by the rest of the kids who haven't got one - especially if it's a posh type (the guider, I mean - not the kid). They're home-made and you'll need to get your Dad to make it for you; or someone else in your family who's just as able? But you might be able to make it yourself - now that you know how.

However, back to the shops: along the same side of Rochdale Road and just past Yaffee's is another shop you'd find useful - at least it is to the kids. We call it Irving's because Alma Irving owns it; and its large window to the left of its doorway is full of toffee apples displayed in neat rows on metal trays, with their sticks uppermost.

When Irving's makes the toffee apples, they push the stick into the core of the apple and then dip the apple into a melted dark-red, sweet, sticky, treacly toffee - all this done in the back room of the shop. It's a pity we haven't the money to buy one now. If we could, we'd ask for the large one with the thick coating. That's the one at the front of the left-hand tray and the one they probably dipped first.

You can now see why it's best to be at the shop when they put new trays in the window: you can have first pick.

Anyway, if you can't afford a toffee apple, you can always stand outside the shop to savour the sweet smell of melted toffee pouring out of the shop's doorway. This, along with the display on the trays, causes wide-eyed, mouths watering, lingering at the window on the part of the kids in the district. But this makes them want the toffee apple they're drooling over, but can't afford, all the more.

On Saturday afternoons, those with a penny above the one needed for the Cinny's matinee usually buy a toffee apple for eating whilst waiting in the queue. It's better value than the penny 'Snofrute' got from the Walls Ice-cream man - because it lasts much longer. But as you saw during one of our last visits: the queue's usually packed with boisterous and excitable kids engaged in animated discussions about what might happen in the next Flash Gordon serial - or whatever.

If you happened to be positioned near a kid excitedly flourishing their toffee apple - and you're not sufficiently alert - you'd find it accidentally dabbed in your hair or smeared against some part of your clothing. Nevertheless, this slight contamination of the toffee apple seems to go completely unnoticed by the possessor; and the adherence of hair or fluff on the treacle coating doesn't deter the continuation of its consumption. However, ignoring the particular discomfort of being accidentally made sticky, or eating a hairy toffee apple, let's consider another - alleged - discomfort.

You might hear the Cinny being described as the "Flea Pit". But this isn't a true description of the place. You'll usually hear it from those who've failed to save the penny for the Saturday matinee and are thereby feeling disgruntled. Nevertheless, you'd soon cotton-on to the reason for their disparaging remarks and therefore ignore the attempts to deter you from what you'd saved up for, all week, to enjoy. So let's not concern ourselves too much about such people's peculiar dispositions. Let's continue our look at Irving's shop.

If you can't afford a toffee apple, it's useful to know that the shop sell bags of "waste" for a ha'p'ny. That's a bag of the bits and pieces of treacly toffee left on the display trays, or the old toffee gone into a solid lump in the dipping pan and then broken up into small pieces to clear it out. A bag of waste - if there's any available - is the next best thing to a toffee apple and it's much easier to eat in the Cinny queue.

A warning: don't leave it in the paper bag too long, otherwise it forms a solid lump and sticks to the paper. Also, eating the waste can cause your fingers to become very sticky so that they nearly glue together. You'll need to lick them a lot to clean them up. But you'd soon discover this for yourself.

Another useful thing you might like to know is that Irving's shop has a toffee apple stall at Hall's Crescent market. That's the market located opposite Eggington Street, about a quarter mile or so along Rochdale Road from their main shop - whose widow we're now looking at. We briefly saw this market during an earlier period when we followed my mother's search for work. You'll find it's well worth a visit, because, amongst the many stalls, there's one selling second-hand comics such as the 'Dandy' the 'Beano' and the 'Boy's Own' - the last mentioned being full of all sorts of perilous adventure involving daring lads.

Also, you can get second-hand copies of the 'Adventure'; the 'Wizard'; the 'Rover'; the 'Hotspur' and the 'Skipper'. All of these contain gripping stories with exciting characters such as "Lionheart Logan the Canadian Mounted Policeman" and "Wilson the Wonder Athlete". Also, there's an exciting story called "The Wolf of Kabul".

Wilson is an orphan who lives like a hermit on the Yorkshire moors. He brews special herbs that he discovered growing on the moor, and only he knows about. They keep him very fit and strong. He needs only two hours sleep each night. He does amazing athletic feats and goes around the world to challenge all the great exploits of the past. He does all this entirely in secret. One time, he went to the ancient Olympic Games arena and exceeded all the recorded achievements. He did this in the early hours of the morning when no-one was there to see him. He's not interested in fame - only in beating records.

The Wolf of Kabul is an intrepid Englishman who disguises himself as an Afghan. His mission is to discover what the tribes are planning, and especially if they're gathering to invade India. He has a Gurhka servant who carries a club made of an old cricket bat that's bound with copper wire. He's frighteningly fierce if attacked and has to use it. Lionheart Logan goes to all sorts of perilous places and always "gets his man". You wouldn't put any of these stories down until you'd reached the last exciting word.

All the stories are really serials; but each story is more or less complete in itself, so it doesn't matter if you buy an out-of-date copy. People say that university lecturers and ex-army officers earn extra money by writing the stories, under assumed names. I don't know if this is true or not; but all of them are so well and excitedly written, it could easily be true.

It's always a good idea to have a large stock available for rainy days, when you can't go out to play in the street and there's hardly anything else to do but read. When you've finished the stock you have, you can do a swap with other kids and get some you haven't read. Or, if the ones you have are in good condition, you can exchange these at the market. But they only give two for each three you bring - and only if they're in really good condition - so it's much better swapping with other kids: one for one.

Anyway - now that you know how to prepare for a rainy day - let's change the subject to re-ironing our clogs. We can see where we get this done by going along the road a few shops beyond Irving's.

This particular shop is very important because, when the irons on your clogs wear out, you'll be walking on the soles that are made of wood - which wears the clogs out in no time. Therefore, it's always best to get the clogs re-ironed for thre'pence rather than have the expense of a new pair of clogs, costing as much as three an' six for a really hard-wearing pair.

The cobbler - Mr Seddon - has a box of irons of all sizes, so he'll soon find a set to fit your clogs. They're shaped like horseshoes - especially the ones for the heels - and he'll let you sit on the bench in the shop to watch him nailing on your new ones.

When passing the shop, you can look through the window and see him working - as he's doing now. He'll give you a nod and a wink if he recognises you - that's if he's not too busy to look up. However, he's busy now so I'll tell you about what you can do with newly ironed clogs. Kicking the pavement with a sharp, glancing kick makes sparks shoot out from beneath the clog. Although it's much fun to do this, it isn't if you get caught. Our Dads get very annoyed if they hear we're wearing out new irons only just been done for a cost of thre'pence; so we go behind the Cinny, in Brass Street, where we're less liable to be seen; and have a competition to see who can make the most sparks.

But let's move on to where we might find a bit of excitement we're allowed to have. This time it's at a butcher shop called Wolstencroft's. It's a little way along the road from Seddon's. It's especially worth visiting before New Year's Day, because the butcher puts a pig's head on a tray in the window. He puts an orange in its mouth and parsley around its neck and the kids crowd around the window to stare at it. Also, if you happen to be a customer when the shop first opens at the start of the New Year, and say to Mr Wolstencroft "Happy New Year", he'll give you an orange. But you'll need to get there early, because he's only a few to give away to first callers.

Anyway, let's quickly walk past the next two streets on our left - Copper Street then Zinc Street - to see a shop just beyond the last named street, called Donelan's. This accepts Board of Guardians Mean Test Vouchers - the ones given to the unemployed allowing them an allocation of groceries. The vouchers contain a written warning stating that it cannot be exchanged for non-essentials - such as cigarettes, or any luxuries, such as butter. They'll let you have margarine, instead. But we needn't concern ourselves about the Means Tests and its misfortunes at the moment. Let's go to a shop that helps to keep us cheerful. It's just a short distance away along the same side of the road we're on and just beyond the next two streets: Gorton Street then Norman Street.

You can now see its window's crammed full of valves, speakers and bits and pieces of wirelesses. It once sold gramophone but now deals with wirelesses because most people want one - as the shop soon found out. It's where we bring our accumulator to get it re-charged. You can smell the acid-fumes from the ones on charge in the back room. At times, the fumes seem to pour out of the front doorway like an invisible fog. It's always busy because most people rent an accumulator even if they're able to afford to buy one, outright. They do this because the shop lets you have a fully charged replacement immediately you take the old one back. But if it happens to be one you own, you'll have to wait the couple of days until it's recharged.

Of course, the rented one must be in proper condition when you bring it back, otherwise you pay for any damages; and you're not allow a replacement until you do. Because of this, you need to be careful when bringing the old one back and taking the new one home.

As I mentioned when we visited our house: the accumulator contains acid and its glass casing is very easily broken if jolted or dropped. We use our guider - the one I told you about - for taking our accumulator to and from the shop. We put the accumulator on a thick pile of newspaper, making sure it's well tied down with string. We then pull the guider along by its steering rope - careful to avoid jolting when crossing the cobbles and negotiating the curbs.

So, now you know what to do and where to go if your accumulator needs re-charging. Also, we've come as far as we need on this side of the road, so let's cross over and take a look at some shops on the opposite side as we make our way back to Buckley Street. Be careful when crossing the road; and watch out for that tram; and that horse and cart; and that car; and that man coming towards us pushing his old handcart piled high with bundles of rags - it looks a bit wobbly.

Anyway, we've made it, and we're now on the side of the road opposite Kinsey's shop and near the corner of Whitley Street.

Just past this corner you'll see Walsh's cycle shop where you can get second-hand bikes. However, more important than Walsh's is the shop on the next corner formed by the road and Franklin Street. People in our district call this shop "Dirty Lizzie's". I'm sure the name has nothing to do with the lady's personal habits but probably due to the shop being so untidy that there's hardly any room to get in. And when you do get in, you'll find its wooden floor is very much worn and there's a strong smell of oil and wax.

She sells lots of things quite cheap, such as plates, dishes, cups and saucers and many other things you might need for your house; and although the inside of the shop appears chaotic, she seems to know exactly where everything is.

No doubt her given name is because she always has grubby hands, a dirty apron and a smeared face - probably due to handling the dusty, waxy things piled high inside her shop. However, the reason I've brought you here is because Dirty Lizzie's is a sort of reference point in our district. When giving directions, people might say: "You know where Dirty Lizzie's is? Well, it's near there"; or, "It's only a few shops beyond Dirty Lizzie's"; or, "It's just across the road from Dirty Lizzie's" - and suchlike. She has a good laugh about this, and about the nickname.

Another reason for showing you this shop is because of the important items Dirty Lizzie sells. The one you'll need the most is a gasmantle. It's that delicate, lace-like, dome-shaped, thing you fit over the gas-jet, to glow incandescently immediately the gaslight is lit.

When three or so years of age, I lay ill in a cot in the downstairs front room - near the fire for its warmth. I remember staring up at the gaslight, whose soft, mellow glow had a soothing quality. Also, by listening carefully, you can hear the soft hiss of its gas. I believe its soothing light and soft sibilance somehow helped ease the illness. At least I remember feeling its restfulness - and this must've helped with my getting well?

However - and back to the shop. Whilst outside the less than soothing, window-crammed, and not so brightly lit shop we now know as Dirty Lizzie's, you'll notice adverts on the wall to the right of its window similar to the ones we saw at Cogh's. In this case, there's only two. One tells about "Royal Daylight Lamp-Oil" and the other refers to the item I've just mentioned: "Ironclad Gas-Mantles". But anything less "ironclad" than a gas-mantle is hard to imagine. You've got to be very careful when fitting one to the gaslight or you could easily damage its delicate fabric. The mantle is so delicate we were warned by our Dad not to jump out of bed in the mornings (our bed is immediately above the gaslight in the downstairs front room) because the jolting might damage the gas-mantle.

One time, I forgot about this in my eagerness to get downstairs for tea and toast and became responsible for a damaged mantle, just fitted the day before. I had to use the penny I'd saved for the Cinny matinee to help pay for a new one. I missed the next episode of Flash Gordon and the Claymen.

But let's push this sad event immediately from our mind and consider something you may find amusing. Just along the road from Dirty Lizzie's is a very narrow passageway between two shops. People call this "Squash Belly Entry". It leads to the streets at the back of Rochdale Road; and for some extremely portly people it can be a bit of a squeeze to negotiate the tight passageway.

A story has it that a very large person got himself stuck in an attempt to get along its length. They said it caused him to become very upset. He had to shout to people passing by to help get him loose. I don't know if this is true or not; but if you know any large people, warn them about this particular passageway. Tell them how it got its name.

On second thoughts, we shouldn't see such things as amusing (the gentleman concerned wouldn't have thought it funny). Instead, let's return to Dirty Lizzie and see what other things she sells.

She has plenty of useful things such as oil-lamps, wicks for oil-lamps, candles and candleholders. The candles are especially needed in our district because most houses have only one gaslight therefore the other rooms need an oil-lamp or a candle for lighting - as is the case in our house. So when we go to bed, we use a candle in a candleholder - both got from Dirty Lizzie's.

She also sells "Pan-mends" - six on a card for t'pence. I'll explain what these are just in case you don't know. But before explaining, one thing you already know is how people in our district keep things in use for as long as possible - due to shortage of cash. Because of this, many items (some bought second-hand and others passed on from family to family) become very much used, or even over-used.

As you saw in the visit to our house: pans are often placed on the open coal-fire and the sulphur in the coal has a corrosive effect that causes the metal to deteriorate. Also, the gas-stove - having coal gas for its fuel - produces the same affect. So, due to a pan being used both on the fire and stove, it could eventually develop a leak where its metal becomes corroded. In this case, it would hardly be sensible to throw away a pan just because of a little leak. And in any case, it's more than likely the owner of the pan can't afford a replacement.

In that situation, the answer is a pan-mend. This comprises two metal washer plus a hard rubber washer and a small nut and screw. One metal washer is placed on the outside of the pan - at the leak - then the rubber washer is placed on the inside of the pan, to match, and over that is placed the other metal washer. The screw is then passed through the small holes in the washers and thereby through the wall of the pan where the leak is. Then, using the small nut (best positioned on the inside of the pan) the assembly is tightened to make the pan leak-proof. And once again the pan becomes fit for use - until, of course, it requires another pan-mend.

As a matter of interest: my sister, Nellie, said she saw a pan still being used with seven pan-mends, but the most I ever saw was one we owned that had four fitted.

So now you know what to do if your pan develops a leak: trot along to Dirty Lizzie's for some pan-mends. Six on a card will keep your pan going for some time.

But let's move on to another street that you might find interesting. It's known as Osborne Street. It's a little way along the road from Dirty Lizzie's and directly opposite Copper Street - a street we needed to pass soon after leaving the shop that re-irons our clogs.

On the corner of Osborne Street (the one nearest Buckley Street) is the three-storey, stone-clad Pub called the Osborne House. It always has a sharp, spicy smell of hops pouring from its cellars. You might be able to detect this as we approach. You'll notice the pub has an entrance in both Rochdale Road and Osborne Street. Also, its ground floor has high, arched windows with stained glass panes similar to those we saw in The Friendship Pub in Buckley Street - but with more elaborate glass and, of course, very much larger panes. The pub's very popular because of having various entertainments in its large, ground floor room.

However, what you might consider much more interesting than the pub's entertainment and smell of hops are the Baths and Washhouses in Osborne Street. Here you'll get a tangy smell of fresh soap and hot water. You can see its large building a little way up the street - just beyond the tobacconist next door to the pub. Lots of kids regularly go to the Baths. It's where I learnt to swim. It cost a penny to get in and you can soon earn a penny by fetching coal or running errands. It has hot showers and lots of red, carbolic soap smelling clean and tangy.

You have to go through the showers before they'll let you in the pool. But I like having another shower after the cold pool because it warms you up. You're allowed to do this as long as you don't stay under the shower too long; otherwise the Attendant gets annoyed - especially if you hold up those coming in for the first time.

The pool has changing cubicles on three of its sides - all having swing-doors. You can see over the top of these and watch the swimmers already in the pool, whilst getting undressed - that's if you stand on the wooden seat fixed to the wall at the back of the cubicle. I do this especially when I'm getting dressed. The tiled floor is always wet so standing on the seat allows you to dry your feet properly, before putting on your socks. Of course, grown-ups can easily see over the top, even when they're standing on the floor.

You can leave your clothes hung up in the cubicle whilst having your swim. There's no lock on the doors but the clothes are safe. And you needn't bring a towel because the Baths provide one. They're a bit rough but not too bad if you don't rub too hard.

The other part of the Baths (the Washhouse) is in the same block as the swimming baths, but its entrance is in the next street along Rochdale Road - the one called Victor Street. Our Mam said she'll be taking some blankets and a large pile of washing to the Washhouse, next Monday morning. She'll hire a cubicle called a "scrub". This'll cost fo'pence for a couple of hours of use. As mentioned before, it's far better and far easier than doing a big wash at home, especially during the winter - if you're able to afford the cost, that is.

Each cubicle has a large sink with a ribbed board fixed at one side that you can use for scrubbing. On the other side is a rectangular boiler - heated by gas - for boiling clothes. Also, there's a pummeller for agitating the washing whilst it's being boiled. This is a pole with what looks like a three-legged stool fixed to its end. It's similar to the one you saw in our house, but the washhouse one is much bigger; and there's a cross-handle fixed to its other end so that you can twist the pummeller to agitate the boiling clothes. This makes it easier when doing a heavy wash.

There's also a pair of wooden tongs for lifting the scalding hot clothes out of the tub and into the sink and a scrubbing brush and some bars of hard Sunlight Soap for doing items that need a good scrub before being boiled. All this activity makes the place full of steam, so that the washroom seems filled with a wet, warm fog all day.

After boiling, the articles are rinsed under the tap then allowed to drain in the sink. Then the wet clothes can be put in a bowl and taken to the spin-drier, called "the big whizzer". This is worked by an electric motor. The washing is not completely dry after the spin; but, for a few extra pennies, you can put the clothes on the racks in the drying room. This gets really hot because of the large steam-pipes around its walls. However, the washing has to be put in the big whizzer before you're allowed to do this.

If there's not many people waiting, you can leave all the articles in the room until they're really bone-dry; then you needn't hang them on the ceiling-rack, near the fire, when you get home - where it can be a bit of a nuisance as you saw when visiting our house.

Anyway, we've seen all we need to see for now, so let's return to Buckley Street. And mind how you cross the road...

18
And Even More Shops

~~~~~~~~~~~~~~~~~~~~~~~~~~~~~~~~~~

We've now returned to the Rochdale Road end of Buckley Street and if you care to join me on the next walk (using the same eyes as before) we'll take a look at more shops. You'll find these are of a very different kind from those we've already seen. Also, you might find them startlingly different from the ones we know in our present time.

The shops we'll see are the ones previously mentioned: those arising from time to time out of the economic circumstances the period we're visiting imposed upon the district. Whilst seeing these, we'll no doubt come across further aspects of our neighbourly community that we can (for want of a better word) call "street-life".

All the shops, events and incidents we'll witness in our exploration must be put in the context of a time when a schoolteacher, with years of experience, received a salary of about £300 per annum - an amount that would provide a reasonable standard of living. Commensurably, to have a "penny in your pocket" meant having the ability to make a satisfying purchase - especially if that pocket belonged to a child. However, much of a person's interests and entertainment would be found in situations and interactions occurring "naturally" in the community in which they live, and therefore provided adventitiously and without cost.

With this in mind, we can start our walk.

A good place to start is at the corner formed by Buckley Street and Birtle Street. If we walk a little way down the last-named street, on the opposite side from Coghlan's shop, we'll see a tiny shop known, locally, as Evans's. Again, it's really a house of the same type as all the others in the district, and not originally intended as a shop. In fact, it's not even fitted up as a shop. Mrs Evans uses her front room - just as it's furnished for living in - for selling her commodities. In the winter - when it gets really cold - she'll let you come inside and stand by the fire whilst she serves you with your ha'p'orth of toffee or lemon drops - or whatever you fancy - from the varieties she keeps in the large glass jars on her scullery shelves.

This type of house-cum-shop is not at all unusual in our district - as you'll soon see; and you might be wondering why so many come into existence as they do? This especially in an area where the quantity of money most people have available shouldn't allow even a suggestion of exuberant spending. However, the many varieties of shops in and around the streets are not there to mop up surplus cash. They're there for two reasons. First: not many people have the facilities for preserving food in the "raw", so they need to do regular day-to-day shopping. The second reason is exactly the opposite of the indulgent spending the many services suggest. The transient and semi-shops arise because money isn't plentiful; and the ever-present pressure to acquire the crucial extra few shillings directs people into all sort of activities to make ends meet. Thus, houses offering services similar to that of Evans's come into existence almost overnight, as and when domestic circumstances allow or dictate.

In Heelis Street, for instance, the lady at number three obviously saw she could usefully employed her talent as a cook to supplement the family income. She started selling cakes, pies, soups and pickles - all produced on the premises. One morning, when we got up, there they were in the window: all the "goodies" arranged on a table and positioned so that passers by could readily see the tasty display, along with the listed prices.

Perhaps you're beginning to wonder what official rules and regulations governed such activities? Well, if there were any, nobody seemed to bother. And none of the established shop seemed to bother, either; no doubt because these small and transient activities had little affect on their main business - one supported by the established shop's capacity to maintain reliable stocks of constantly needed commodities.

So now that you know what is and what isn't a shop is determined mainly by circumstance and convenience, let's return to Buckley Street and walk a little way further down its slope to Worth Street. Near its corner, we'll see another variation on the same theme. This time, it's one instigated by Mrs McBride. Although it's been in business long enough to be considered a permanent shop, the fact that Mrs McBride's husband needs to work on the Railways to supplement whatever returns the shop provides indicates its less than financially supporting ability. However, it attracts many kids in the district with a penny or two to spare.

Amongst its saleable items are peashooters used as a blowpipe for blowing hard peas. This device is made of a tin tube with a mouthpiece at one end - something like a smaller version of one you'll see on a trumpet. They cost a penny each - and you get a little bag of dried-peas with it. The purchase makes it possible to indulge in a pea-shooting activity much liked by the kids; because they know if someone shoots a pea at you it doesn't hurt - much. It just gives a bit of a sting (most times).

Instead of peas, you can use brown Indian corn obtained in a bag from the Crescent Market - mainly bought by those in our district who keep racing pigeons (our Dad kept some, once, in a small roosting shed he built in our backyard). The corn is cheaper than peas and conveniently happens to be about the same size. However, you'll find it's got a very hard skin that makes it sting a little bit more than a pea.

The pigeons that wander around the streets (because nobody owns them) like Indian corn being used. They ignore the peas but eat any corn left lying around after a peashooter battle. They'll gather around on the rooftops waiting for one to begin. So, it seems, from every situation someone derives benefit - even if it's only a pigeon. However, pigeon-treats don't happen as often as these hungry birds would no doubt like. If people find themselves harder up than usual, they sometimes use Indian corn to make a soup. At such times, the pigeons have to look elsewhere. Anyway, pigeons are capable of looking after themselves, so we needn't worry about their situation; so let's get back to McBride's.

Her shop also sells kazoos. These costs a penny-ha'p'ny (that's one and a half pennies). Here's a brief description of a kazoo, in case you might be wondering what is. It's a device for making tunes by blowing down the mouthpiece and raising and lowering the notes by the same method you'd use when whistling. It doesn't make a whistling sound but a buzzing sound - like one you'd get from blowing through a comb whose other side is loosely covered by a strip of thin brown paper. But a kazoo makes a much louder and sharper sound than that. It consists of a tin tube blocked at one end but having an opening at the top of the tube at the blocked end. This contains a reed. The reed vibrates to make the buzzing sound when you blow through the mouthpiece.

All the kids like to buy a kazoo if they can. We form a band and play tunes such as "Rule Britannia"; "Hay, Hay, Farmer Gray"; "Yaaka Hula Hickey Dula"; "Tiptoe through the Tulips" and whatever we think makes a good kazoo tune. We sit on the corner of our street near the lamppost to do our concerts. Nobody in the nearby houses ever complain, even when we get a bit out of tune - as we might do, sometimes.

The shop also sells ha'p'ny clay pipes we use for blowing soap bubbles. Also, you can get caps for your cap pistol. These are sold in a long, red strip with spots of gunpowder along its length, contained in a small round, red, cardboard box costing a ha'p'ny. And when you load your cap pistol the striker hits each spot, in turn, on each pull of the trigger. You can fire continually until the strip runs out. It's just the thing for playing Cowboys and Indians - especially after seeing a Tom Mix or Buck Jones film at the Cinny matinee.

She also sells tiny celluloid dolls about two inches in length. These cost a penny. But there's a sad story to tell about one my sister, Nellie, bought after earning some pennies for running errands for various neighbours.

Shortly after buying the beloved and much treasured doll, it suffered damage because someone accidentally sat on it when it was left lying on a chair - squashing it nearly flat. (It wasn't me. Honestly!). But they're easily squashed due to the celluloid being so thin. In this particular case, the squashing happened to be very severe because a damaged doll can usually be brought back to its original shape - near enough - by placing it in a bowl of hot water. The heat expands the air contained in the doll and pushes out the dent (that's if the doll has no holes or splits).

Unfortunately, the damage to this particular doll didn't allow the "cure" and, in the absence of money to acquire a replacement, imagination had to devise a substitution. Her still unsatisfied maternal longings were partly relieved by drawing a tiny face, using a pencil, on her left-hand thumbnail. She then wrapped that particular arm from wrist to elbow in a towel and - with fist clenched and thumb uppermost - cradled this arm in the bend of her right arm, nursing it like a sleeping baby. This indicates an important rule: when the pressure of necessity is so strongly felt, it can, sometimes, be the real "mother" of invention.

But not all of what McBride's sells is so easily damaged. For instance, a very popular toy is one we kids call "Boxers", which cost t'pence. These are made from the type of wooden clothes-pegs called "dolly-pegs" - that's the peg shaped from one piece of wood and formed to have a cleft at one end and a knob-shape at the other. The prongs formed by the cleft are sawn off and then nailed to the body of the peg - this to make a pair of legs pivoting on their respective nails at the "hip" part of the peg.

The knob has a representation of eyes, nose and mouth, painted in black, and is topped with the same paint to represent hair. To finish it off, the hip part of the peg and the top part of the pivoting legs are painted in a suitable colour to represent boxer shorts. Two "boxers", wearing different coloured shorts, are then joined together to face each other by means of two slender strips of wood, representing extended arms - these nailed to the body of the peg to allow pivoting at the "shoulders". Then - finally - a small hole is drilled through the centre of the wooden strips.

Now! Here's the clever bit! To use the boxers, you thread a length of string through the holes made in the arms. One end of the string you tie to a suitable anchorage - a chair leg, for instance; or if you happen to be playing in the street, the base of a lamppost or the bottom part of a gutter-drainpipe. You then hold the free end of the string taut enough to support the figures in a standing position but also to allow a continuous jerking of the string's held end. This agitates the figures into a leg swinging, shoulder lurching, dancing and cavorting tussle; just like boxers engaged in a vigorous bout - which provides the lucky possessor and those watching with a great deal of amusement.

I'm not sure whether or not the McBrides, themselves, made the toy, but some ingenious person in our district certainly did.

However, let's pause for a while in our walk around the shops, in order to offer a comment on the reason why this toy became so popular in our district.

It no doubt arose from the fact that boxing exists, unavoidably and constantly, in the minds of the Collyhurst community. The famous (or infamous?) Collyhurst "Blood Tub" (a Boxing Gymnasium located at the Rochdale Road end of Collyhurst Road) is not far from Heelis Street. You'll also see similar establishments in Churnet Street and Osborne Street - both a little way across Rochdale Road from Buckley Street.

The Collyhurst district produced numerous prominent boxers, amongst which were some of the most dynamic fighters this country has ever seen. Jackie Brown and Johnny King, for instance, became national and even international names - both of whom were born and lived a good part of their lives in the Collyhurst area. Jackie Brown lived for a while in Dalton Street, and Johnny King lived not far away on the other side of Rochdale Road - near Saint Patrick's Church.

On a lesser, but by no means diminished scale (at least, to the people in Heelis Street) we had Walter Ross living at number eleven. He became well known for his successes in the boxing booths held on Albert Croft - an area just off Queen's Road and not far from the top end of Collyhurst Road.

He also engaged in bouts at places that had large attendance, such as Blackpool and Fleetwood. He became listed on the books of Mr Harry "Kid" Furness - otherwise known as "The Manchester Matchmaker". To reach this high prominence indicated a great deal of talent. Many experts in the business considered he possessed the potential for being a very promising middleweight. However, he turned away from this possibility when his fighting impulse diminished in the face of a committed, romantic, interest.

Be that as it may or as it may not be. Although much of the local boxing seemed - to us - heroic, a reminder of its less glamorous aspects became embodied in a young man, known as Arthur, who delivered newspapers around our district. The job was given to him by a local businessman after his employment as a sparring partner at the Blood Tub caused him to be what was then called "punch-drunk" (a condition recognised in a later age as "brain-damaged") leaving him partly paralysed down his left side.

All these incidents (tragic and heroic) were common knowledge in our neighbourhood. But whatever misgivings and reservations people may've felt, boxing appeared to offer opportunities for fame and fortune for those able to face its demands. Otherwise, they'd probably find themselves in some menial, low paid occupation. Or even - and not at all unlikely - with no regular job at all.

Thus, boxing offered the possibility to escape from poor economic circumstances - as present-time parallels illustrate. And those who "made it" spurred on the efforts of others wishing to do the same; since the successful ones enjoyed a life-style unobtainable by any other legitimate means offered by the scope of their background.

The successful ones remained very much appreciative of the community from whence they came - one they felt had given them support in their "fight" for a better life. This they showed in their desire to return, from time to time, to the district of their origin, to display the success they'd achieved. Far from causing envy, these visits were immensely enjoyed by the folks in the neighbourhood.

I've a recollection of Jackie Brown as a particular example, when, at the peak of his World Flyweight Championship, he visited our street. I must've been about four or nearly five years of age at the time, but even at that tender age - when the affairs of the adult world commanded no particular interest sufficient to interrupt my busy-at-playing world - he made an impression powerful enough to make me pause and take notice.

I later discovered that he may've called to see a friend - perhaps Walter Ross because of his contact with boxing. I remember he wore a beige fur coat (known as a "teddy-bear" coat) and a trilby hat (an unusual dress-style amongst the "cloth-capped" Collyhurst working class - let alone the teddy-bear coat) which made him all the more commanding and remarkably different from anyone I'd ever seen in our street.

My sister told me he possessed at that time a very large, red sports car. This I didn't see; probably because Heelis Street and those around were not wide enough and a bit too crowded for such a vehicle to safely negotiate. She also told me of another visit he made a year or so previously which - even if witnessing - I regretfully can't remember.

In this, Stanley Trulio's brightly painted horse-drawn ice-cream cart happened to be in the street and Jackie Brown went to all the houses and called the kids out to form a queue at the cart. He then bought the whole lot of them (and there were a good many) an ice-cream followed by second helpings. This emptied Stanley Trulio's tub - to the delight of Stanley Trulio. The kids weren't too upset by this depletion because, by then, they were all well satisfied.

He also handed out half-crowns to any old lady he saw in the street, saying: "Here, Ma! Buy yourself a treat!" As we've seen: half-a-crown (two an' six) represented no mean sum - especially to the old folk.

But we've strayed away from our main purpose: this because the wealth and variety of happenings in those more than full and much lived-in streets makes wandering along the multitude of active paths each event opens up very difficult to avoid. So let's get back to the particular path we're supposed to be following.

We'll let Mrs McBride carry on with her selling whilst we walk a little bit further along Worth Street - where, half way down the street and on its left-hand side, we'll see another curious little "house-cum-shop", known as Goodwin's. Here, Mrs Goodwin sells paraffin lamp-oil at a penny a half-pint. This she serves from a large tank (painted red) kept in the scullery at the back of the house (bring your own bottle).

The tank is fitted with a tap for running the strong smelling liquid into the receptacle you've brought with you. She uses a funnel that causes a misty spray as the lamp-oil froths around its sides then pours into the bottle. If you stand too close - to watch the bubbles swirl and dance in and around the bottle - the mist makes your eyes water. Also, it leaves its smell in your hair and clothes.

She keeps a large jar of pear-drops and will give you one - after she's served the lamp-oil. The pear-drop usually tastes of lamp-oil; but if you suck it for a while (the pear-drop, not the lamp-oil) the oily taste soon disappears. However, we don't need any lamp-oil at the moment, so let's cross the street and walk the short distance to where the top end of Davy Street (that's the bruw, which is now on our right) meets Worth Street.

Just beyond the bruw we'll see the top end of a street known as Coulman Street. Here, Emily Archer's Fish and Chip Shop is situated end-on to the Coulman Street row nearest the bruw, so that its front door and large window (to the right of that door when looking from the street) faces into Worth Street.

It's also situated almost exactly opposite to a coal-yard, called Hollingworth's. You can't fail to notice this because of its large green painted wooden door opening directly on to the street and its wide upstairs window immediately above that door. I'm mentioning this because religious meetings are often held in its upstairs room. You can hear hymn singing on some evenings whilst waiting for your fish and chips. It sounds quite nice - sometimes.

The "scent" in the air tells that Emily Archer is now doing fry-ups in readiness for her opening time, so let's savour this appetising smell of fish and chips drifting through her half-open doorway - it's much better than Goodwin's lamp-oil. And with this aroma following us, let's walk the short distance beyond the top end of Coulman Street to where Worth Street meets the upper part of Dalton Street.

You can now readily see how Dalton Street slopes away at a slight angle to our right, to end at the lower level of Collyhurst Road. But more to our interest is the large expanse of black-brick wall over the other side of the street and directly opposite to where we're now standing. We saw this from the far end of Birtle Street on our previous walk.

It's the last part of the - now much reduced in height - Manchester to Leeds railway viaduct that ends at the cutting made through the top of the slope formed by the Irk Valley. This cutting is the one Rochdale Road spans near the area we know as the Flags.

The part of the wall almost directly opposite to the end of Worth Street contains the entrance to an underpass. This you've probably already notice. It allows access to the other side of the railway lines.

Let's cross the cobbles for a closer look, because there's a few tales concerning various places on the other side of the underpass.

You'll notice that both of its tunnel-like sides are covered with reddish-brown tiles up to where the arch of the roof starts, which is then clad with white tiles. These help to reflect the light from the two gaslights fitted one at each end of the roof's extent. Also, you can see the start of a dozen or so stone steps at the far end of the passageway.

If we climbed these steps, there'd be - to our right - the beginning of a pathway running between the railway wall and the backyards of a long row of houses. This pathway is officially known as "Railway Path" but to the people in the district it's known as "The Long Entry". Following its length for a short distance would take us to the end of Limer Street - where we saw the unhappy event of Elizabeth and her newborn baby.

Not far beyond this sad reminder, we'd see the Long Entry running on a gradual downward slope to hug the base of the viaduct's increasing height for two or three hundred yards or so. It continues to do this until ending at the lower reaches of Gould Street Gasworks - a feature we saw during the visit we made to Silver Street.

If we had time, you might be interested enough to walk its length; this because the viaduct creates a series of high archways used as workshops for blacksmiths; clog-makers; cobblers; cartwheel repairers; carpenters; barrel-makers and all sorts of trades. We kids often go there to stand at the entrances of any workshop we might find interesting. The workmen don't seem to mind this as long as we keep well out of the way whilst they're busy.

The blacksmith's forge is the one I like best. On a warm day, its large wooden doors are left wide open. You can see the fire burning fiercely in its brick-built fireplace located in the corner of the workshop. Its blaze casts a red glow on the smoke-blackened arch of the brick roof; and you can smell and taste the acrid coke-fumes in the air. Now and again, you'll see the blacksmith's mate using leather bellows to force the fire's blaze. This makes it glow so bright you can hardly look at it.

You might be lucky enough to be there when the blacksmith is making a horseshoe or a metal part to repair a machine. This he grips with iron tongs to thrusts it into the fire's centre, which becomes a yellow glare as air is forced through the glowing coke. Then the blacksmith quickly withdraws the white-hot metal to place it on the anvil. Sparks fly with each clang-clang-clang of his hammer as he beats the white-hot piece into shape. Sweat rolls down his soot-stained face and soaks his shirt.

Sometimes, he'll throw a quick glance to us watching kids and grins as the bright sparks fly from his hammer. He then plunges the red-hot metal into the barrel of water. It hisses like a fierce snake whose steamy breath rises from the liquid to twist and turn in the air.

If you're even luckier, you might be at the door when he's shoeing one of the giant carthorses from the LMS Yard, just beyond Charter

Street. He grips the horse's fetlock to his thighs whilst his work-mate quickly heats the shoe so that it burns into the horse's hoof, to make it a firm fit. The horse stand impassively as if unaware of the hot metal burning its shape into its hoof and the stream of smoke smelling like charred leather pouring into the air.

The blacksmith rapidly nails the shoe to the hoof whilst the metal is still hot. He takes each nail from the cluster he holds between his lips as he wields the hammer with his other hand. The horse gives a snort and a toss of its head from time to time - but again seems not to worry about what's being done.

One time, we kids marvelled at this and said to the Blacksmith: "Hey, Mister? Why doesn't the horse make a fuss when you're nailing its shoe?"

He replied: "They're big, strong horses; who aren't cry-babies - so they don't make a fuss." He then laughed and said:

"I bet you kids make a fuss when you get soap in your eyes - when your Mam washes your hair!"

We said we didn't.

But let's forget about hair-washing - with or without fuss - and let's get back to the archway. It's a popular place to play on a rainy day and therefore to keep out of the wet. Also, if you run along its length and shout, it makes a loud echo. So now that you've heard about the Long Entry, the blacksmith's shop and the echo in the archway, we can go look at the two shops occupying each of the corners formed by Worth Street and Dalton Street. They're just across the cobbles from the archway and both have the same door and window arrangement as Coghlan's.

The one on the corner to our right - looking back along Worth Street - is known as Ford's. It's here you could buy a ha'p'orth of fresh milk (bring your own jug). Alternatively, you might want to buy a can of that thick substance that looks like white treacle and is known as condensed milk. The variety they sell is called "Cow Brand". It has a picture of a happy-looking cow on the label. It's mainly used for milking tea and lasts a long time without going off. The people in our district use it a lot because we've no such thing as refrigerators.

To keep fresh milk fresh, we need to put the jug or bottle in a bowl of water and place it in the coolest position we can find in the house. Also, it helps if we put some muslin cloth over the top of the jug and let its edges dangle in the water. Even then, the milk soon goes sour. That's why condense milk is so popular.

The other shop on the opposite corner is Anderson's. There, you can buy a packet of tea for a penny and - amongst many other things - a "Dosser's Wedge" for the same amount.

In case you mightn't know what a Dosser's Wedge is, I'll explain.

It's basically a triangular sandwich about an inch thick, consisting of a sticky mixture of dates, raisins and currents contained between two layers of soft, treacly, pastry. It's large enough to make a meal - almost. Its shape looks like a wedge, which explains the second part of its name. The first part probably came about because the dosser's wedge is much favoured by those inhabiting "Doss Houses".

Just in case you don't know what a Doss House is, here's a quick description. It's a cheap, dormitory type, lodging houses, costing about two or three pence per night - just for a bed with no meals - and usually inhabited by men travelling around looking for work.

Those making use of such places are therefore called "Dossers" (Doss meaning, "To bed down"). The itinerants haven't much cash to spare, so they probably find a Dosser's Wedge makes a cheap "filler" for a stomach having to be content with less than adequate provisions.

Anyway, you could try one for yourself if you've a penny to spare - if you like that sort of thing, that is. They're quite tasty and well worth the money.

However, let's direct our thoughts towards doing what we're supposed to be doing. Let's return to the street that we previously saw (the one called Coulman Street) then walk down its short cobbled slope to where it ends at Burton Street.

At the bottom of Coulman Street and on the right hand corner we've now reached is the house where Donkey Dan lives. He obtained his name because of driving a cart pulled by a donkey, which he employs in his rag-and-bone trade. This gave rise to a rhyme and - like the one about Cogh's - is one used for skipping. It goes:

> *Dan, Dan, the Donkey Man,*
> *Washed his face in a frying pan,*
> *Brushed his hair with the donkey's tail,*
> *Scratched his belly with his big toe nail.*

He doesn't seem to mind this rhyme. He just laughs when he hears the kids say it. And when he's at home, he'll sell you a penn'orth of winkles or a penn'orth of goos'gobs (gooseberries). He'll sell you these even if he knows you're one of the kids who might chant the rhyme. Anyway, it looks as if he's out with his donkey and cart at the moment, so let's continue just a short way along the right-hand side of Burton Street to the Burton House pub at the bottom of the bruw.

We saw this pub on a previous visit, but I've brought you back because I want to tell you a bit more about its activities.

During the summer months, it arranges day's outings to places such as Blackpool, for those who can afford it. When this happens, the kids in the streets gather around because the group going on the outing have a booze-up in the pub before the chara (short for Char-a-banc) arrives.

As soon as it comes, they pile into its seats in a very happy state of mind; and, as it pulls away, the affect of the ale and the prospect of their day out make them feel generous. This they express by throwing ha'p'nies - or even pennies - out of the windows for the kids to grab. This results in a mad scramble as the coins bounce off the cobbles. At one of these outings, I managed to grab thre'pence. But you need to be quick: some kids catch the coins before they hit the ground.

However, let's finish our exploration by walking Burton Street's remaining length to where it meets the bottom end of Buckley Street - which we saw on a previous visit. I didn't make comment at that time about a sad event concerning the fish-and-chip shop you can see facing up the slope of Buckley Street from the opposite side of Burton Street. But since we're near the shop, it seems appropriate to tell about an incident that happened one winter.

On an icy day, a horse that couldn't hold its cart on the slope of Buckley Street's cobbles broke through the shop window.

However, on second thoughts, I think I'll stop telling you about this because it doesn't seems right to mention an injured horse after talking about the happy business of Donkey Dan (I'll tell you about the incident another time). So back to the shop itself. A lady called Annie Hallows owns it - and therefore it's known as Hallows's.

My Uncle Edward Corrigan had a part-time job in this shop - peeling and chipping potatoes - whilst waiting for a full-time occupation as a tram-driver. But that's by the bye. What I really want to tell you about is that the owner of the shop is known in our district as "Madame Vaseline", due to the habit she has of using this preparation to keep her hair in place whilst serving fish and chips.

This name isn't given out of any unkindness because in our district - where everybody knows everyone else - those with an unusual habit, occupation or appearance invariably get a nickname - as in the case of Donkey Dan and Dirty Lizzie; and in the case of another character called Charlie Chuck.

Now that I've mentioned Charlie Chuck, I'll tell you about him. He lives in Almond Street and keeps hens in his backyard. This gave rise to another rhyme - again used for skipping or just for the heck of chanting a tongue twister if it's said very quickly. It goes:

> Charlie, Charlie, chuck-chuck-chuck,
> Had ten chicks and one white duck.
> The duck died,
> The ten chicks cried,
> Charlie, Charlie, chuck-chuck-chuck.

Anyway, we needn't feel too upset by the thought of Charlie Chuck's duck - what it says in the rhyme probably never happened. Also, I don't think he even had a duck? So let's now walk up Buckley Street, keeping to its right-hand side, to reach the first corner of Heelis Street.

Just before reaching that corner, you'll notice another house-cum-shop, called Kemmer's. It's situated end on to the Burton Street row and has its door opening into Buckley Street and its window on the right of that doorway, when looking from the street.

Again, you'll see it's just like all the other houses except for the display of jars and packages in the downstairs window. Here you could buy a penn'orth of pickles or a penn'orth of pickled cabbage, or a penn'orth of jam - most of these having been made on the premises. (Don't forget to bring a cup or an empty jam-jar, or Mrs Kemmer won't serve you.)

But let's continue our walk to the corner of Heelis Street where you'll see a shop called Wood's. This again is similar to Cogh's; having two large windows - one in each street and a doorway set at an angle to its corner. There's a tale to tell about this particular shop that you might find interesting.

Those who knew the district years ago say the shop began as a Pub called the 'Live and Let Live' (it still has a cellar where they kept the beer). It must've been a very small pub because it seems none too large as a shop. However, the one we saw in Buckley Street - The Friendship - is a lot smaller and is still in business; so what happens to be a pub becomes similar to what happens to be a shop: just a matter of convenience and circumstance.

As you can see in this case: circumstances have turned it in to a shop. The only thing it sells remotely resembling what it once sold is ginger beer. This it sells in what people call a "stone jug", which is sealed with a screw stopper. In actuality, the jug is made of a sort of thick pottery, not stone. Some people use it as a hot water bottle when they've emptied it of its original tastiness. If you do this, be careful you don't accidentally kick it out of bed: it easily breaks. Also, don't fill it up with very hot water: this causes it to develop a crack and it then makes your bed wet.

The shop also sells lots of other things aimed at tempting pennies out of the most guarded of pockets - such as treats which last a long time and therefore seem good value. For instance: you can get a bundle of liquorice roots for a ha'p'ny - containing four thick sticks. These can be sucked and chewed for ages and the juice produced in chewing and sucking makes a taste very much enjoyed by the kids.

A comment: I discovered some years later that liquorice roots have valuable medicinal properties, especially for the digestive system. It seems our pennies were more wisely spent than we knew. But back to the shop: there's lots of trays in the window, containing slabs of toffee of many flavours: banana; liquorice; treacle; caramel and lots of other temptations. There's also an advert on the inside wall of the shop about the content of one of these trays, which declares:

Sharp's Super Kreem Toffee Speaks for Itself.

When I became able to read, this declaration puzzled me because of its incorrect spelling of "Cream".

I started school at Saint Catherine's - know as Saint Cath's - at the age of three (that's the school you saw near the Dwellings on Collyhurst Road and by the River Irk). Early schooling happened to be a general educational policy and the first years consisted of various simple lessons - such as how to tie shoelaces, learning to add up simple numbers, learning the names and then the sounds of each letter of the alphabet. Then, having learnt the alphabet, you progressed to reading words by putting together the sounds of the individual letters.

A comment: this mode of learning - abandoned in the early 1960s - was simply known in the time we're visiting as "learning to read". There's now an attempt, in the period from whence we came, to reintroduce its method under the fancy title of "synthetic phonics". Sometimes, progress requires retracing steps - it seems.

But back to Saint Cath's. In the early afternoon, after a play-session, we had stories followed by a mug of hot milk and an hour's sleep. We had our sleep on folding camp beds and rough, but not all that rough, grey army blankets were used to cover us up.

Our school-teacher-cum-carer was a lady named Miss Worthington. She had a crippled foot that must've been painfully awkward; but when she softly sang us to sleep, she did so with the sweetest and most tender voice imaginable. The sweetness of her voice must've arisen from the sweetness of her nature. I'll never forget Miss Worthington.

Because of this early schooling, I quickly learnt to read and - like all children when they first learn - became very pedantic about "correctness". No doubt the intention of the advert's idiosyncratic spelling was to catch attention. But in the money-careful days we're now visiting, if the commodity didn't "speak for itself" any attention-catching gimmicks would prove a complete waste of time. Nevertheless, the Super "Kreem" toffee quickly became one of my favourites on its own merit, and - like the proverbial pudding - the proof was in the eating (in this case, the sucking and chewing).

To make the toffee easy to serve, the shop breaks the slabs into manageable bits with the aid of a little brass hammer with the word "Toffee" cast along it handle. Then the amount you want is weighed on a small set of brass scales - using little half-ounce and one-ounce brass weights. If you glance through the window, you'll see the scales on the counter at the back of the shop. You'll also notice the layout is very much like Cough's - except there's no sawdust on the bare but frequently scrubbed wooden floor and no tubs, bags or chests.

When we're in the shop buying our toffee, we watch the weighing, intently, with our noses level with the scales. Mrs Wood smiles to herself as she, very slowly and carefully, piles the selected pieces, one at a time, in the weighing tray. We hardly dare breath in case this influences the weighing to our disadvantage. We "will" the scales not to tip until a goodly pile of pieces accumulates. Then - grudgingly satisfied - we hand over our tightly clasped penny to the smiling Mrs Wood and dash out into the street to enjoy the newly acquired treat.

Another favourite is a bag of sherbet, costing a penny - which has the word "Kali" (pronounced "Kaylie") printed on the bag. It's supplied with a black straw made of liquorice to allow you to suck the sweet-tasting powder straight from the bag. This warrants a further comment: again some years later, I made another discovery about the word "Kali" being associated with the saltwort plant whose extracts are supposed to be beneficial to the digestive system, in a similar way to that of liquorice roots. So, again, our spending had a medicinal return and we were - unwittingly - wiser kids than we thought.

But back to the shop: you can also get large, round, brown coloured things we called "Gobbers". You'll see them on the counter in a large glass jar. They cost a ha'p'ny each; but we think they're well worth the money because they last such a long time. A single one is big enough to fill your mouth. The Mams and Dads of the district favour these because they tend to keep the kids quiet for a while.

We congregate at our favourite place on the corner of Heelis Street - that's on the opposite side of the street from our house and at the bruw end, near the lamppost, where there's a length of blank wall. We sit on the pavement and lean against the wall, sucking our purchase in a state of silent bliss; unable to speak or engaged in any other activities - thereby providing the adults of the street with a respite from our usual boisterous play.

You may think it strange we sit so readily on a bare pavement, without any concern? We do this because - as mentioned in one of our previous visit - the pavements in our street and all those around are considered an extension to each house. The people of each street therefore feel obliged to keep their area of pavement almost as clean as they would the interior of their own home. Having a dirty pavement immediately outside the house reflects badly on the house itself; and as we previously saw: on every washday the doorsteps and the pavement in front of each house are washed with soapy water left over from the laundering. Also, the steps are "donkey-stoned" soon after this washing down.

In case you don't know what a donkey-stone is, here's a quick description. It's a soft, pumice-like, brown or cream coloured stone that is wetted and then applied to the ends of each step. This creates a bright and easily seen edging. It's also used on the stone windowsills to provide a nice decorative effect to brighten up each street. The stones can be got from Dirty Lizzie's (a penny for a large stone) or from Donkey Dan when he comes round with his donkey and cart: one stone for a few rags, a couple of jars or some scrap metal.

The stone gets its name because a popular brand has an image of a very strong-looking donkey moulded on its top surface. I suppose this is intended to indicate it can stand hard work.

Many of the young girls in the district eagerly seek the work of stoning steps and sills - thereby earning a penny or two for buying whatever treats they fancy. My sister, Nellie, was much in demand by the people of our street as a quick step-stoner; so much so that the constant kneeling on the bare flagstones made her develop a mild case of "housemaid's knee". So - at the early age of twelve - she had to retire from employment, for a while, because of housemaid's knees.

However, back to sitting on the pavement. You might also notice there's no litter lying around in the streets. This is because almost everything is either used for some purpose or returned to a place where it could be re-used - a practice now much encouraged in the time from whence we came and has the fancy title of "recycling". In the time we're visiting, this process is considered a natural and sensible part of life - so it doesn't have a name.

For instance: if burnable, it's fuel for the fire; and if durable - such as jam-jars - valuable ha'p'nies could be earned by taking these items back to the shop. Large mineral-water bottles are - again as we've seen - useful for holding lamp oil. Medicine bottles - green or brown - can be taken to Stoba's, the Herbalist, on Rochdale Road (that's a shop almost opposite Dirty Lizzie's) where you'd get a penny for each bottle if they're clean and not cracked or chipped. Also, and as you've already seen: a stone ginger-beer container (not returned to the shop to claim its refundable penny) can be used as a hot water bottle.

So, in the district we're visiting and those of its kind there's no such thing as rubbish. Almost every item has its value or use. If someone happens to be daft enough to discard a bottle; or a jam-jar; or a jug; or burnable material of any sort; or old rags (useful to exchange for donkey-stones) someone would soon make use of its "gift".

Those virtually indestructible plastic bags, bottles or containers - so widely discarded in the time from whence we came - have not yet intruded into the general scheme of things. There are no empty drink-cans to throw away and no large purchases with all their elaborate wrappings and hard-to-get-rid-of containers. There are no supermarket trolleys to abandon and no pizza boxes to carelessly drop. So, and as you see: in this there's-nothing-to-throw-away or should-ever-be-thrown-away environment, no-one would have the means or the cheek to litter anyone's pavement with their "unwanteds" (even if they had anything they considered unwanted) no more than they would toss rubbish through the open doorway of anyone's house.

Thus, the streets are clean; and we kids sit on the pavement, the doorsteps, the pavement's kerb, or anywhere in the street we think convenient to sit, almost as naturally as using the furniture in our own houses - in a street we all see as an extension of our own home.

Whilst we're sitting comfortably on the pavement, resting our back against the wall, and sucking our gobbers, let's consider the shop just across the bruw. The one I showed you on a previous visit. The one called Agnes's. As you noticed during that visit, it's just like all the houses in its row and had its beginning as one of those "overnight" shops we've seen coming and going around our district.

Due to its convenient position, it enjoys continual use and therefore a reasonable prosperity - and therefore permanence.

This brings to mind the wedding held from Agnes's not so long ago. Then we saw cars in our street - an amazing sight for kids whose street mostly sees nothing grander than Donkey Dan's rag-bone cart or Stanley Trulio's horse drawn ice-cream cart; or the less grand horse draw Corporation dust-cart that comes to empty our midden-bins each week.

Let's drift back to the time of the wedding to see what happened on that day. After that, we can take a peep at Donkey Dan and then Charlie Chuck's backyard...

AGNES'S:

(the busy shop –
the one that's at the top end
of the bruw)
would offer tick to those she knew;
and those who'd pay back
pretty quick.

And in her shop,
there's jars of treacle sweets;
and all those other tasty treats.

And on her daughter's
wedding day,
two cars came
and then they drove away.

The kids gaped
at all the fine array.

And cars weren't often seen
down cobbled streets –
which gave the kids
a further treat.

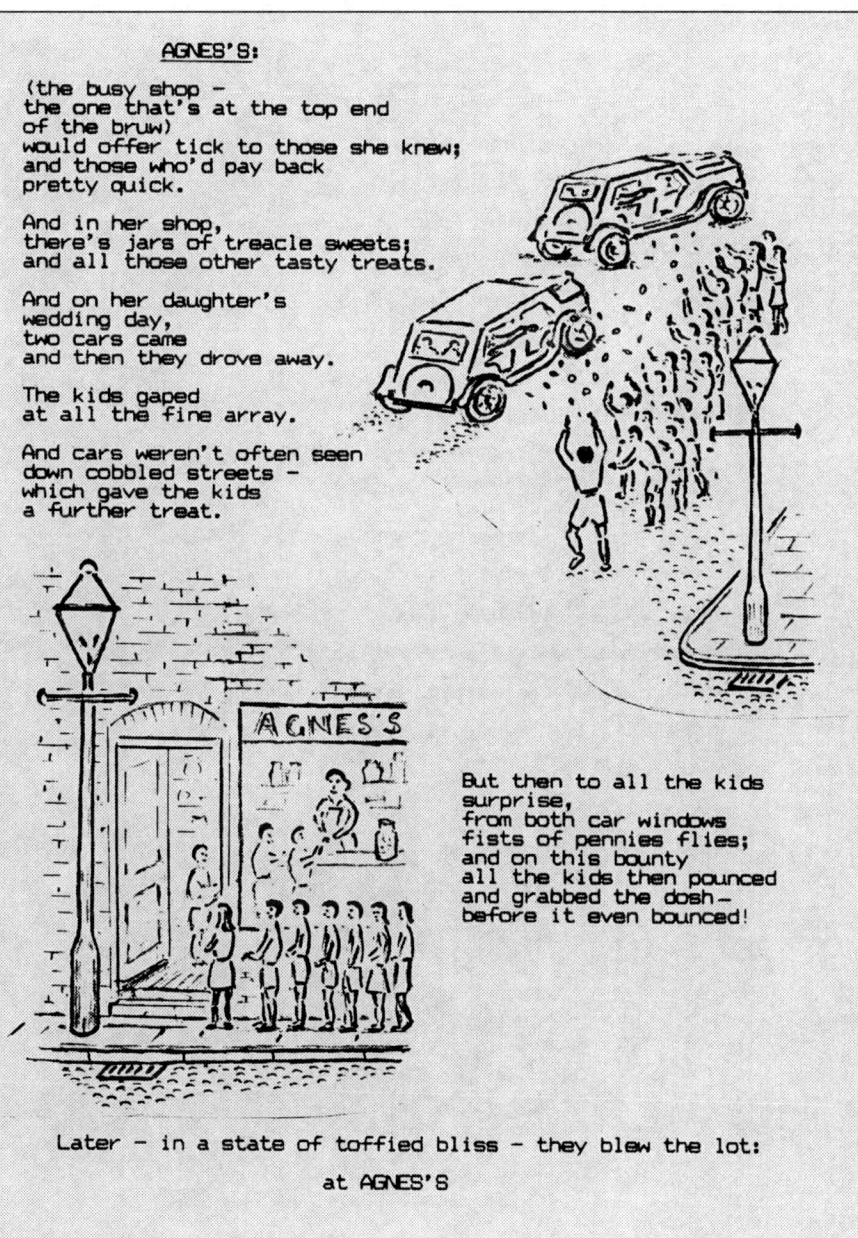

But then to all the kids
surprise,
from both car windows
fists of pennies flies;
and on this bounty
all the kids then pounced
and grabbed the dosh –
before it even bounced!

Later – in a state of toffied bliss – they blew the lot:

at AGNES'S

Balloons & Fishes – Rags & Bones

       Donkey Dan,
       the Rag-bone Man;
       catch him, catch him,
       while you can.
       For the rags and bones
       you kept,
       he'll give you stones
       to clean your steps.
       And if you've got an old
       iron bed,
       he'll give balloons
       or a fish instead...
Dan, Dan, the Donkey Man,
washed his face in a frying pan;
combed his hair with a donkey's tail;
scratched his tummy with his big toe nail.

CHARLIE CHUCK

Charlie, Charlie,
Chuck, Chuck, Chuck,
kept ten chicks
and one white duck.
The duck died;
the ten chicks cried.
Charlie, Charlie,
Chuck, Chuck, Chuck.

* * *

The hens were kept in Charlie's yard –
behind wire netting, and a guard.
And fed on oats, and Indian corn;
and scraps of meat to give them brawn.
His cockerel was an 'Island Red'.
It crowed all day, from on the shed.

Charlie's chucks went: "cluck-cluck-cluck".
We never saw the big white duck.

19
A Matter of Life and Death

~~~~~~~~~~~~~~~~~~~~~~~~~~~~~~~~~~~~

Let's digress, for a while, from the active business of living to examine another marked contrast between the first and second half of the century we're considering. This concerns medical advances and the associated facilities each period could provide.

We can also look at the health aspects of our present time that the period we've just visited would see as being almost beyond belief. For instance: the medical advances would, in themselves, elicit amazement; but the now accepted right of access - regardless of cost or the financial means of the person benefiting - would evoke complete astonishment.

To gain an insight into why such reactions would arise, let's return to the circumstances of that earlier period.

In the communities of our visits, most people would treat at home, as best they could, whatever ailments came along - unless it seemed impossible for them to do so. A call on the doctor could cost as much as two-an'-six; and as we've seen, to many people in that time this represented a sizeable sum.

Two-an' six could, for instance, buy a goodly amount of essential coal, and if a household kept the fire reasonably low, and "recycled" the cinders by augmenting these with a mixture of coal-dust and burnable rubbish, this could keep the fire going for the best part of a week - which, in winter, was the best way to ward off ills and chills.

Since most households in the districts of our interest had virtually all their weekly income allocated to prime necessities - such as rent, food and keeping the fire going - making provisions for unpredictable illnesses could hardly assume a prior place in a limited household budget. Therefore, if ailments made an unwelcome visitation, all but the most serious had to be treated from the household medicine chest. This usually contained a wide variety of cheap "do-it-yourself" cures supplemented by treatments from the local herbalists (or pharmacist, as they would now be called).

Some of these I well remember in actual practice and especially the "chesty" ones because - as we'll see later - dampness and air pollution seemed to be the "normality" during winter periods. Therefore, a chesty complaint could easily develop amongst those susceptible.

However, let's hear my sister's words about the dark months of the year and the ailments that could arise during its chill:

"Winter was a dread; especially if your house happened to be damp and draughty, as lots of houses could be in those days. Most people couldn't afford a visit to the doctor, and - least of all - for a doctor to visit them for any length of time; even though some doctors in less well off areas allowed you to pay back the cost at sixpence per week. Therefore, people had to do their own doctoring and treat themselves in the best way they could. Or - better still - do things to protect themselves against getting ill.

"Most elderly folk tried to avoid chills in the cold weather by covering their back and chest with Thermogene: this being a pad of compressed cotton-wool impregnated with something that made the protected parts feel very warm. You could buy this from the Herbalist along Rochdale Road. The pad had an orange colour and looked as warm as it felt.

"People only removed the pad when they washed, then put it back on again immediately afterwards. They had to make it last as long as possible and only make a change when the pad started to break up. No-one could afford replacements too often.

"Also, they'd buy pills called Fenning's Little Lung Healers to ease chesty complaints - that's if they could afford them.

"During the winter, parents of young children with a tendency to catch chills put pads of thick red flannel on their back and chest next to the skin - these to be worn all day. Also, most homes had a stock of Wintergreen Ointment to rub on the chest before putting on the pads.

"The older folk used Sevens Rubbing Oils or Sloan's Liniment to rub into aching joints caused by cold and dampness. Winter was always a worry - especially for the elderly."

These, then, were the ways of warding off winter's chills and their associated aches and pains. Another great concern lay in the lingering Victorian obsession with the business of "inner cleansing".

Again, I'll use my sister's words:

"If people had bowel trouble, they'd take a cup to the Herbalist to obtain some Black Draught or Cascara (I don't know where the Black Draught came from, but I believe the Cascara came from the bark of a tropical tree).

"The Herbalist - Stoba's - that's the one along Rochdale Road at the top end of Copper Street - kept these liquids in large, brown-glass bottles on the shelves behind the counter. He'd sell amounts to put in a cup you brought, in accordance with what you could afford. He also sold Senna Pods - which were dried leaves brewed like tea - and Brimstone and Treacle laxative, mixed to suit your taste. The Herbalist soon got to know everyone's taste.

"All sorts of shops in the district sold Bile Beans; Beecham's Pills; Carter's Little Liver Pills; Back and Kidney Pills and suchlike - these were to keep your innards toned up and make you feel well."

My sister has now told us what remedies we need to ward off - or at least, to ease - any chesty complaints we might get during our visits. Also what we might need in order to keep our "innards" properly cleaned. However, if financial circumstances can't stretch to the ready made and bought from the herbalist concoctions, we'd find many well tried and tested "make-it-up-yourself" treatments available. Most of these no doubt had their origin in Victorian times and some from times long before that.

None of these "folksy" treatments seemed to have any side affects - except, perhaps, to make the treated people smell of applications such as tallow wax, mustard, or camphor oil. But friends and neighbours would no doubt be ready to forgive these strong "fragrances" in the interest of the person getting well - especially since they, themselves, would, more than likely, carry the same aromas from time to time.

Let's now look at these remedies and, perhaps, mentally compare them with the highly scientific and sophisticated drugs offered in our present period. Drugs that cost a fortune to produce and are inclined towards producing all sorts off "wobblies" as side-affects and - at times - generate much questioning about their long-term consequences.

By contrast, and as previously inferred, the worse side-affects of all the treatments we're considering lay in their possible interference with personal relationships that their "pong" might cause.

As, for instance, in the treatment for:

Chesty Complaints: Cure 1. Make a mixture of mustard and camphor oil and rub it all over your chest before going to bed. This is especially good for chesty colds. Cover the area with red flannel to hold in the heat and stop the bed-sheets from getting "mustardy".

Cure 2. Take a sheet of brown paper and rub tallow wax all over one of its sides. Put the paper into a warm oven to melt the wax until it's absorbed into the paper. Wear the treated paper on your chest next to the skin. This keeps out chills.

(Note: if you haven't any tallow wax, soak the paper in lamp-oil and let the oil become dry enough to wear next to your skin. It's not as good as the wax treatment, but will suffice if it's all you have available. At least, it's better than having nothing - perhaps?)

Cure 3. Wear red flannel on your back and chest, next to the skin, after rubbing these areas with Wintergreen Ointment. This eases chesty conditions and helps keep the lungs warm.

Cure 4. Mix a teaspoonful of mustard into a cup of very hot milk and quickly drink it down. This relieves lung congestion.

Cure 5. Slice up a raw onion in a bowl. Sprinkle this with a good amount of brown sugar. Pour boiling water into the bowl - enough to just cover the contents - then breath the fumes deeply. This eases chest congestion. And whilst the water is still hot but cool enough to drink, use a large spoon to sip some of the onion and sugar mixture. This is also considered helpful in easing a sore throat.

Whooping Cough or Chestiness (especially in infants): Take the child to where there's roadwork in progress and the workmen are spreading hot, melted tar. Hold the child over the tar in a position to ensure breathing the fumes. The workmen always stop work whilst you do this - or spread more tar, if needed. The infant might cry and protest, but this must be endured because the fumes will be inhaled more deeply and thereby enhance the "cure".

A quick comment: I've certain doubts about this one. I've a vague recollection of it being done to me. All I can recall is an image of bubbling hot tar, a cloud of smoke and being scared stiff. However, at that time it was - it seems - "the thing to do". It must've shown some benefit - even if limited - otherwise this treatment would hardly maintain its credence for so long, to the extent that some doctors advised its application.

It seems the trust in its efficacy lay in the claim that workmen constantly exposed to the hot tar-fumes rarely got chest complaints - or so it was believed.

A comment: Whooping Cough (caused by the bacterium Bordetella Pertussis) prevailed as a major complaint amongst infants even up to the 1950s, when the early years of that decade had something like 160,000 notifications. Children under the age of two were particularly at risk to the point where they could die if the condition was neglected. Fortunately, the advent of a vaccine in the latter part of the 1950s dramatically reduced incidents. The characteristic and distressing "whooping cough" made when the child choked and gasped for breath - which everyone distressfully knew before the vaccine arrived - became blessedly rare.

However, let's consider complaints far less serious yet distressing enough for those afflicted.

Stomach Upset or Colic: Fill a cup with warm water then take a red-hot cinder from the fire. Drop the cinder into the water. Drink it down as hot as possible (not the cinder, of course). This eases stomach pains.

Sore Throat: Roll up a sheet of paper to make a tube. Put about a third of a teaspoon of powdered sulphur (obtained from the Herbalist previously mentioned) into the end of the tube. Open your mouth very wide and get somebody (preferably a person you really like) to blow the sulphur to the back of your throat. Leave the sulphur in the throat for as long as possible. (Mind you don't choke.)

You can also try the sugar and onion treatment mentioned previously.

Sore or Stiff Joints: Make a thick mixture of mustard and margarine (or, better still - if you can afford it - camphor oil). Apply the mixture to the affected joints then rub well in, leaving it as long as possible to "soak" deep into the skin. (You'll have to remove any surplus treatment because it'll make a mess of whatever you intend to wear - as you've no doubt guessed.)

Chills: Fill a bowl with hot water - as hot as the hand can bear. Put two large spoonfuls of mustard into the water and mix until dissolved. Place your bare feet in the bowl and soak until the water starts to cool. Wipe your feet and put on thick socks then go to bed immediately Note: put plenty of blankets on the bed - enough to cause a good sweat.

A Warning: you might have to change the bed-sheets next day if you happen to be particular about sweaty, mustardy sheets.

A Tonic: Buy a bottle of thick black Stout - if you can afford it. Pour this into a glass then plunge a red-hot poker into the liquid. Drink it down straight away before it cools. (A lot of people like this: so much so that some might claim the need of a tonic when it's not - perhaps? - really warranted.)

Loss of Appetite in Illness: Eat "pobs" to keep up your strength. (Pobs are made by breaking bread into small pieces in a bowl, then pouring very hot milk over the pieces until they're well soaked, and the milk covers the bread.) Eat the pobs slowly, but before the milk cools.

Depression: Sing a cheerful song. This, perhaps, may not effect a complete cure but it has been known to relieve the symptoms. (A possible side affect is the causing of depression amongst those who happen to be listening - depending on the quality of your singing, of course.)

A note in passing. During the last years of conversations with my mother, she told me (maybe as a leg-pull; but knowing her disposition, perhaps with a serious element of truth) that the way she tackled depression caused by being "hard up for cash" (if, again, to use her words, she ever found time to be depressed) was to walk to the city centre and look in the various shop windows. She'd then see so many items she didn't really need - and therefore seemed such a waste of money - she'd feel glad about not having the cash to allow temptation to buy any of them. She'd then go home feeling more cheerful.

I suspect this do-it-yourself treatment echoes a folksy mode of "counselling", appropriate to that stiff-upper-lip time, which would suggest:

"Get yourself out of yourself and do something to make you forget about yourself".

This rather direct and uncompromising recommendation might be unacceptable to the present period's more sympathetic and non-judgemental mood. Nevertheless, holding its advice and the other suggested remedy in mind, we must also recognise that, despite all our efforts, even the most diligently applied treatments can sadly prove not enough. To paraphrase the Book of Common Prayer: "In the midst of life, there's always the fact of death"; and, in that first half of the century we're considering, death - as a fact of life - existed far more extensively in people's awareness.

Illnesses and their possible fatalities were always highly visible since most occurred and were dealt with in the home. Even during what should be the joyous event of birth (which, again in the communities of our visit, mostly occurred at home) fatalities could sometimes result - as the unhappy event of my grandmother's sister, Elizabeth, showed.

But even in the decades somewhat later than that sadness and in the time of my childhood, infantile mortality continued to be extremely high; so much so that statistics for the industrial areas of Britain indicated little change to the situation prevailing at the turn of the century. For instance: whooping cough was - as noted - almost an expectation; and sudden afflictions such as diphtheria and meningitis (words spoken in anxious whispers in every home with young children) could, in cases occurring soon after a previous debilitation, bring about fatalities within hours.

In the type of districts of our visits, the biblical three score years and ten seemed no more than a promise and, in many cases, not even an expectation - or even a near expectation. So, in these circumstances, funerals and the events leading up to that finality came within everybody's experience from a very early age.

One particular incident stays etched in my mind, although being no more than five or six years of age when it happened.

A family in our street had the distressing experience of nursing, at home and for many weeks, a severely ill member of that family. This involved a young woman who eventually died. I particularly remember the event due to overhearing a conversation held in Agnes's shop whilst waiting to make a purchase.

Being a little chap, I barely reached the height of the counter and, it seems, my arrival wasn't even noticed during the intense conversation taking place between two woman customers from our street and the owner of the shop. Despite my impatience to be served, the compelling curiosity which all children possess made me listen carefully to what I sensed was an important and emotional adult matter.

However, before telling you about the conversation, I need to explain a feature common to the houses around our district (if you're not already aware of it, that is) so that certain aspects of the conversation will be more readily understood.

Most houses in our district had lace curtains but no "pull-together" drapes, because of the expense. The more usual provision for night-time privacy was a pull-down roller blinds made of thick, durable, beige-coloured paper. With this in mind, let's return to the conversation. The part I heard went something like this:

"She was only a young woman. I knew she'd gone when I saw their gaslight still lit in the early hours of the morning. I could see the shadows on the blind as they washed the body..."

The last sentence held my attention because the fleeting shadows cast upon the blinds made by the people in the house as they moved between the window and the source of light (the gaslight or the fire in the front room) was, to me, a source of fascination.

The conversation quickly evoked a vivid picture of the softly lit blind with its wavering shadows in the darkness of the street - a darkness only relieved by the glow of the gaslight on the street corner nearest the house. I must have been staring up, intently, at those conversing, for their talk suddenly ceased when they noticed my presence. However, by then, I'd understood the essence of what they'd said.

Again, the last few words of the conversation may need explaining. They concerned the expectations a family suffering bereavement had to meet, amongst which was the washing of the body immediately or as soon as possible after death. Again, let's hear my sister's voice, since her greater span of experience allows a more detailed telling:

"If someone in a family died, the body had to be laid out in the coffin in the front room for a number of days. This allowed people time to pay their last respects. The window had to be covered on the inside with a sheet of white linen to make a subdued light in the room. This covering also indicated to anyone passing by the house that it had suffered bereavement. Mirrors in the house also had to be covered with the same cloth.

"Before being laid out, the body had to be washed by a female member of the family or a close female relative and then dressed in clean, white linen. Sometimes, a neighbour would do this if no suitable family member or relative happened to be available.

"At least one member of the family - or someone close to the family - had to sit in the front room all night until the day of the funeral. They called this a 'Wake'. No fire could be lit in the house whilst the body was laid out. The family had to rely on neighbours or relations living nearby for hot water and cooked food.

"Neighbours and relations called at any time to pay respect, and extra chairs and cups and saucers (which the family mightn't normally possess) would be needed for this. If the family or neighbours were unable to supply these, the Undertaker arranged a loan of whatever happened to be required.

"The Undertaker also supplied a tea-urn required during the all night sitting and also for any callers' refreshment. He could also supply white linen to wrap the body and to drape the windows and mirrors - if the household hadn't any available, that is.

"People seeing the covered windows showed their respect by walking as quietly as they could as they passed by. Men removed their hats. Children weren't allowed to play near the house during the time involved."

These are the details my sister recalled. People with experiences confined to the age in which we now live will inevitably see such "rituals" very differently from the way they were then perceived. However, in the time we're considering, they were part of normal custom and expectation. I cannot say if such expectations prevailed in other areas, but they certainly did in the districts I knew. So, as you readily see, bereavement in our district and those of a similar nature could never be a closed and private affair. It involved the whole neighbourhood.

This "openness" may've produced many beneficial effects. The public - and therefore obvious - rituals surrounding the bereavement made everyone in the affected neighbourhood feel they could share or at least be openly sympathetic to the grief. Thus, any comforts the neighbours could offer to those bereaved came readily and without traces of embarrassment.

In addition, since all the rules and expectations concerning these events were well understood and impossible to hide, this and their visibility evoked the appropriate behaviour from all members of the community - including the children.

For instance: shortly after the overheard conversation, I strayed in my play too near the doorstep of the house suffering the particular loss. Although probably well aware it wasn't the right thing to do, I suspect my straying may've been partly driven by that deep curiosity overhearing the conversation first evoked. However, I was soon "told off" - quietly and gently - for my infringement.

So, the facts of death and the proper behaviour expected in the face of its visitation were soon learnt early in life, along with all the expectations concerning the funeral itself. As we previously saw: the still lingering Victorian dread of a Pauper's Grave with all its stigma shaped such expectations and also raised the anxiety to meet any demands. It was therefore considered a matter of honour for a family to provide a "proper" funeral for any of its members. As indicated in a previous narrative: making provisions for such could mean a considerable expense, far beyond the capacity of the family's immediate resources.

One way of guarding against this was the Burial Club - a form of protection offered by various Trade Unions or other fellowships. Also, some Insurance Companies provided coverage for something like two or three pence per week for a family - depending, I suppose, on assessed risk and the number of family members.

The "Burial Man" (the name ascribed, locally, to the Insurance Representative who called to collect the pennies) became a regular visitor to most homes. Our family had a man named Mr Ingram calling regularly each week. This he did over a number of years and because of his long association became almost a friend of the family. He'd stay for half-hour or so on completion of his collecting, to sit by the fire, have a cup of tea, smoke his pipe and have a chat.

My memory of him is particularly vivid - this because he smoked a rather elaborate looking pipe with a curved stem, something like the one I'd seen depicted in a picture of Sherlock Holmes. Our Dad said it must've been expensive because its carved bowl was of a special pottery made at Meissen, in Germany. He added (jokingly and not in the hearing of our visitor, of course) that the curved stem was to keep the pipe from setting fire to his moustache.

The style he cultivated was the more luxurious variety of what we'd now call Edwardian. Being of an unsophisticated age, I took the possibility of an incendiary event literally; and during the winter evenings - before my bedtime - I would, if I could, find an unobtrusive position in our small front room and watch him smoke his pipe in the expectation of a possible conflagration.

Another aspect of this process that commanded my attention was the thick cloud of smoke he puffed from the bowl then being drawn by the fire's draught and sucked up the chimney in a long stream.

That's by the bye and not immediately related to our main subject concerning health matters. Although, perhaps, it would be in our present period in which Mr Ingram's habit would hardly receive the open welcome (and the interest) it then did.

However, and returning to the main theme. The area he covered was such that he knew most of the neighbours in and around our street and all its adjacent areas along with most of their troubles; and, at times, became almost an unofficial and unpaid counsellor for those needing the advice his experience could give. He always avoided naming individuals but offered the experiences of people he knew as a "general principle" - mentioning possible solutions that he knew had been used for particular difficulties. This made him more trustworthy and also effectual as a confidant and a source of advice.

But returning to funerals: the one I particularly remember was that of my Granddad Jones, in 1936. I recall staring in awe at the lacquer-black coach with shining windows and silver lanterns polished to gleam sharply in the afternoon sun; and the pair of towering, coal-black horses with tossing, jet-black plumes upon their heads; and the coachmen all in black wearing shiny top-hats. Then the clatter of hooves and rattle of wheels on the cobbles as the coaches drove away; passing a line of neighbours - all with heads bowed.

Such was my absorption at seeing this arresting display that any thought of what the funeral represented was pushed way down in my mind. The curiosity that takes hold of the child to the exclusion of all else held me; so much so that a vivid memory can easily be recalled after all these years.

Sometimes, the circumstances of death does have its impact even on a child; sufficient to penetrate that barrier of protective curiosity and raise in the child's mind those powerful feelings of impotence and confusion - those we later learn to deal with by adult resignation.

In that long-ago-time I had a school-friend, named Gerry Myers, whose death raised such feelings.

Let's go back to the schoolroom, as a child - to feel again that incomprehension...

"Please, Miss;
Where is Gerry Myers?
He's our chum;
why hasn't he come?
Is it 'cos his coat got tore?"

"They say he... died...
Just after four...
Please...please...
I can't say more."

"But, Miss?
Why?
Why did he die?
When he fell, in the playground,
he'd never cry."

"Please, children...
Please...
I cannot say...
Please...it's nearly time for play..."

20
Kettle, Coal and Soft Gaslight

In our last visit, we saw how a warm house was an essential for maintaining good health during the winter months - this requiring a fire constantly stoked up to the top bar of its grate.

In previous visits, we saw how the fire provided the main means of heating water and cooking food; and, because of this, how the fire and its oven were in constant use in our house and the majority of houses in and around the district. Also, we saw how - as in most houses - a large iron kettle always stood in the recess on the oven's top; simmering gently and waiting to be moved closer to the fire to boil, for making tea.

Because of its important position in the house, the fire's grate and the oven's door, with its decorative cluster of embossed flowers, took on a dark, pewtery shine in the fire's light - having been treated with Zebra Grate Polish over the many years the house had been occupied.

And so the fire burned constantly in our small front room, from early morning until late at night, and only on the hottest of summer days would it remain unlit.

My earliest recollections are of sounds associated with the fire. Even now I can recall the feelings of lying in a warm bed on a winter's morning, then hearing the quite sounds of my mother rising to go downstairs whilst the day was still dark.

I'd lie in bed, watching the flicker of candle-light making dancing shadows as she passed the small front bedroom where I lay, and then hear the sound of the fire being gently coaxed into life. Eventually, when called to get ready for school, a bright blaze roared softly in the fireplace and the iron kettle whistled its cheerful song. The smell of hot toast and freshly brewed tea filled the room to tempt an eager appetite - one reawakened from having drifted back into a quietly interrupted sleep.

On a quiet winter's evening and at the closing of the day, when the gaslight was turned low and the fire's blaze made flickering shadows on the walls, our small front room became like a warm cocoon, as if holding and protecting those within its confines from the darkness of the outside world. We'd sit before the fire's glow, seeking images amongst the blazing coals; gazing almost hypnotically at the flickering-flames and the shifting, incandescence shapes the coal contained. Remarks would arise such as:

"Look! See, there - amongst those bright cinders. There's a shape that looks like a face."

Or:

"That flame - that bright, shimmering flame in front of the large lump of coal. It looks like a dancing figure."

The fire's entertainment seemed almost endless; conjuring up within the minds of those who sat around its hearth images as vivid and as varied as the dancing patterns within the flames.

However, the fire had its demands. In return for the constant visualisations it evoked and the comfort it gave, it had to be fed. Coal had to be got; and as our visits constantly showed: the days of the Thirties weren't noted for surplus cash. Most families lived, and had to live, on a single weekly income that hardly lasted until the next; and because the fire was an essential almost equal to that of food, its demands could cause constant anxiety. Coal was affordable only in small quantities; and this never allowed a "comfortable" reserve to be maintained. Whatever limited supply the household held needed careful management.

Ashes from the previous day's fire were assiduously raked and put through a riddle to sieve out any reusable cinders. Material such as wood or paper were never thrown away but used to supplement the fire's fuel. For instance: the wax-proofed wrapping paper from a sliced loaf - after exhausting its extended purpose of wrapping sandwiches for the working members of the family - would be employed in lighting the morning fire.

People lacking experience of those times may find it difficult to appreciate the anxiety a low supply of coal could create. Or - conversely - when a good supply was obtained, to know the delight of a fire stoked up to the capacity of its grate and filling the room with the continual roar and warmth of its blaze. Moreover, how having a new stock of coal could be an "event" relished to its full.

This almost perpetual anxiety about necessities, even to the extent of maintaining a fire's blaze, causes social commentators to describe the districts of our visits and those of similar circumstance as areas of deprivation - and, within the expectations of our later period, they probably were. Also, the previously mentioned Rowntree Report and Priestley's comments on the 'Fourth England' seems to suggest that they were - in reality - exactly what the commentators thought they were.

Yet, as a child, along with all the other child-companions I then knew, the concept of deprivation as it is now perceived hardly entered our awareness. As kids, we fully realised that being "hard up" represented an ever-present condition under which we lived. We realised this because of constantly having to learn the discipline "hard-upness" demanded: which - in simple terms - meant learning to be satisfied with what you've got and doing without that which you couldn't have.

Awareness of deprivation can only arise when people believe there's something they could have but have not got - which usually comes from making comparisons with the more plentifully endowed. But in our closely contained and busy-being-children world, we had no such comparisons to make: we were washed, we were fed, we were clothed, and we went out to play. And all of us: we were all the same.

During the conversations with my mother, I progressively began to realise the sometimes-chronic difficulties and anxieties those times must have created for people with children. I asked how she really did cope with what must've seemed a series of day-to-day worries. After a few moments reflection, she smiled then said:

"Well! We just had to feel grateful for what we had and what we managed to get - and be happy with that; and do the best we could under those circumstance."

Her answer seemed to sum up the very essence of that time. As I remarked in one of our previous visits: she could make a glorious meal out of half a cabbage and a few penn'orths of ribs. Even the water in which the cabbage and ribs were boiled became part of the meal. We kids drank it.

Perhaps it might've been more difficult for those of her kind to maintain such equanimity if they'd known a previous period of better circumstances - these to impose upon them the sort of comparisons I mentioned earlier. However, since no-one in the district seemed to have experienced such conditions (or, at least, I never heard tell of this) grounds in which seeds of discontent could establish themselves and grow didn't exist. For most people in our street, the life they then knew would seem an improvement over the circumstances of their own childhood and most certainly over those known by their parents.

Thus, the people I knew all around me appeared, in the main, "cheerfully appreciative" of what, to them, seemed a reasonable way of life. In this setting, how other people beyond the boundaries of my world lived was, to me, hardly a speculation. My own world seemed as full as it could be and therefore provided no room for thoughts about other possibilities.

I did eventually become aware of large and spacious houses substantially different from those in the tightly packed and seemingly endless row upon row of two up, two down dwellings of my own world. These existed some miles away from where I lived; and, in the latter years of my childhood in Heelis Street, my mother took me to one such place.

It happened to be a house for which she'd obtained the job of doing a day's cleaning in preparation for a family party or function. I retain an impression that the house may've been somewhere near Heaton Park - an area beginning, at that time, to form a prosperous outer suburb on the northern extremities of Manchester.

I particularly remember this event because it involved the treat of travelling to the place by tram. But I never saw the occupants of the house - or, at least, cannot remember seeing them. Moreover, the day gave little opportunity to think about the type of people who lived there; or to explore that very remarkable thing the house possessed (the garden). Nor was there time to wonder about the spacious district in which it stood; or whether it was - as a place - usual or unusual in the greater scheme of things. My being there was to assist my mother in whatever way I could helpfully do and to avoid doing anything to disturb the place and to be as quiet as I, as a child, could possibly be.

However, these demands were not in any way felt as restrictions but part of the normal discipline expected of children at that time: a discipline sustained in this case by the awe I felt from being in what was, to me, a strange and remarkable place. Adding to this appreciation was the feeling that its circumstance offered my mother an opportunity to earn the very valuable extra few shillings to provide for the next bag of coal, or for an added luxury to enhance the next meal - or even to pay the rent.

This feeling particularly arose from my mother's general air of cheerfulness as she went about her work; and I remember becoming as cheerful as she seemed to be, since children readily pick up the moods of their parents - and, in this respect, I was no exception.

In this way I obtained the first experience of a place existing as it did in its own "unusualness"; outside of the vast expanse of rows upon seemingly endless rows of terraced houses and paved backyards and occupying a vastly different world from that of my own.

I later discovered the area of my revelation was part of the Jewish community in which my mother had worked for some months. From this she'd bring home such things as pickled herrings, pickled gherkins, and those hard, dry, 'Passover' biscuit the Jewish people eat during their religious observance, and - one time - much to my amazement and delight - a large jar of boiled sweets. My childhood palate couldn't accept what was, to me, the harsh taste of pickled herrings and gherkins. However, I liked the Passover biscuits - and, of course, the sweets.

Yet, in spite of the obvious advantages these places enjoyed, they never seemed to cause envy or discontent - at least, I never heard my mother make comments suggesting such. They were, to her, places offering a welcome opportunity to earn the much-needed extra few shillings.

Later, and towards the end of my brief in years but seemingly eternal childhood in Heelis Street, I again wandered occasionally into areas similar to the one of my earlier but suspended curiosity - this time with other child-companions. But even then, my own world of intensely neighbourly streets still seemed to contain the real "reality"; and I suspect this was so for most people in our area.

Those without experience of the massive conurbation comprising the inner cities of the nineteen-thirties may feel surprised, and, perhaps, even amazed, at the insularity these comments imply. But the ease of mobility now existing was not then available. For the people I knew, a visit to places beyond walking distance required transport and consequentially represented a journey making demands on limited finances - and therefore done only out of necessity. Even the thirty or so miles to Blackpool seemed a formidable distance whose expense restricted its travelling to rare "treats" confined to a single day; and London's distance seemed so great as to make it unreachable.

I remember my mother once saying she'd love to see London but supposed she never would. However, she did, subsequently, in 1956; but in the nineteen-thirties, such possibilities seemed just a dream; and the dreams of those days - although, perhaps, wistfully enjoyed - were rarely given credence.

The affluence to support the cheap, readily affordable and now commonplace "Package Tours", offering an easily opened door to the outside world, had yet to appear. The widespread perception of the world being a place of enormous and restrictive distances must therefore be seen in that context. Many areas of the globe - that the wide-open window of television now constantly overlooks, allowing those who sit before its screen to view with complete familiarity - were areas of mystery and obscurity. Also, no orbiting satellites existed to photograph every inch of the world's surface in minute detail, to thereby diminish its once perceived vastness.

In the early Thirties, it was astonishingly discovered that something like a million people lived in the central highlands of New Guinea whose existence was never suspected by Europeans. Conversely, the inhabitants of that area had never seen a white person and never suspected or had any indications that white people existed.

It is said that when the inhabitants first saw Europeans in all their "paleness", they believed they were seeing spirits of the dead and ran away in panic. (But who can blame them! Some people are very frightening - even when their identity is known!)

However, to be serious: the Amazon, into whose dark and tangled grotto the explorer, Lieutenant-Colonel Fawcett, disappeared in 1925, was still a blank area on the map. Likewise were parts of Africa portrayed in Joseph Conrad's Heart of Darkness, written in 1902 - impelling the description "Darkest Africa" to attach itself to such obscure areas even up to the nineteen-thirties. Also, the excitements of Henry Rider Haggard's novel, King Solomon's Mines, written in 1885, still retained its half-believed mysterious possibilities well into the Thirties.

Airflights, now exposing every corner of the globe to safe and easy access, then represented perilous adventures. Attempts to fly over the "dark areas" could result in aircraft "disappearing off the map". Large tracts of the Polar Regions, Tibet and China were likewise uncertain. For instance: the early nineteen-thirties film of James Hilton's Tibetan fantasy, Lost Horizon, seemed credible because the remoteness of its area allowed such figments to be - if not completely believed - at least considered as "maybes". So, to the minds of most people in the Thirties, the world was a place of many vast and mysterious zones.

But most influential of all - and returning to the theme of being content with one's "position" in life - no TV existed to thrust itself into our self-contained lives that other aspect of its potency: its capacity to impose multitudinous images of many places where everyone seemed to be going and where the viewer ought, likewise, to be going. Or additionally to generate desires for the new, shiny, thingamabobs which everybody else seemed to be getting and which the viewer ought to be getting - if wishing to be envied and admired.

In the no-TV-world of the nineteen-thirties, the nearest we ever got to seeing other ways of life came through the flickering, tinselled glamour Hollywood presented in our weekly visit to the cinema. But we knew its images were only entertainment that had no relevance to the world as really lived, by real people.

Even the newsreels of that time had a sense of unreality, in that they existed side by side with Hollywood's main phantasmagoria. The images of places all this revealed seemed too brief and too unusual to have any real relevance or even substance as far as our lives were concerned.

But we've now strayed too far out into the wider world and away from our main business: that of getting coal. So let's return to that task to see where and how coal can be got.

We previously took a quick glance at some coal-yards in and around our district and found they'd sell small quantities of coal in amounts of a quarter; half; three-quarter; or a full hundredweight at a time - to suit the customer's means. A half-hundredweight represented the most popular purchasing quantity. If you've gone metric, a half-hundredweight - 56 pounds - represents 25.40 kilograms. Also, a half-hundredweight would cost two and a half pennies of today's currency - sixpence in the old coinage.

Typical coal-yards in the district were Burke's (the one we saw situated on the far side of the Flags where the children played whip-and-top) and the one in Worth Street owned by Mrs Hollingsworth and her son. The last named we saw at the Dalton Street end of Worth Street and opposite Emily Archer's fish and chip shop. But this time, we'll go to a yard you've not yet seen.

However, before we do this, let's return to Emily Archer's fish and chip shop whilst I tell you something you might find interesting.

It's always a favourite place for the kids in the district, even in which to queue and wait patiently whilst doing so. You may wonder why this is - especially since patience, especially in queues, is not an attribute readily displayed by many kids. Well, in the case of Emily Archer, she may - if you happen to be what she'd call a "well-behaved queuer" - give you some tasty scrapings (the little bits of fried batter and bits of chips accumulating in the trays above the fryers). Of course, its treat came as a matter of chance - but one occurring with sufficient regularity to make it a good possibility, and thereby calling forth the appropriate behaviour to receive its benefit.

Moreover, the shop contains another attraction besides the possible treat and the delicious fragrance of frying fish and chips. High on its walls are a number of large stuffed carps in a glass-fronted case. The unblinking and remote stare they maintain whilst suspended amongst the imitation fronds of a still and timeless sea demands an awe-stricken attention. So any quiet queuing I happened to exhibit wasn't entirely due to a possible reward, but also due to the hypnotic fascination the motionless but seemingly live creatures created.

Again we're straying too far from the main theme, so let's get back to the business of getting coal. Saturday morning (the morning immediately after pay-day) is the main and therefore the busiest time for this activity, allowing the many eager kids of the district to earn a penny or two for the afternoon's matinee at the Cinny. This possibility was one extended by families without children "hiring" the services of those belonging to other families who were willing to do the job.

In order to assist this kid-centred activity, each yard possesses a number of small, wooden carts able to hold a hundredweight of coal at a time. Each one of these is fitted with a single axle set mid-way to the cart, and their cast-iron wheels are kept well greased to make for easier pulling. In addition, they have a 'T' shaped metal handle set centrally to the front of the cart, thus allowing two children at a time to pull the conveyance along. Purchasers of coal are given a free loan of a cart to deliver the coal to the household concerned. At times, it may happen that all the available carts are in use - resulting in a possible long wait for one to return. To avoid this, it's a good idea to be at the yard just after eight o' clock when its doors swing wide open for business.

Another imperative for arriving early is the not too uncommon situation of a household being almost "on its last cob" but desperately needing a good fire to cook the Saturday dinner for the returning, hungry, Saturday morning workers (a morning most workers had to do). Under these circumstances, a long wait for a cart could mean, if not a disaster, at least a great inconvenience.

My sister, Nellie, when age about twelve, found herself subjected to this urgency - one made more acute because the reward for fetching the desperately needed coal was conditional on a quick return with the requirements. A cart wasn't available so she decided to carry the half-hundredweight of coal (weighing 56 pounds) on her back with the help of some friends.

She recently told me (jokingly?) that she could still feel the large, sharp, cobs digging into her tender parts - even after all these years.

Nevertheless - and irrespective of how your tender parts may be affected - even after many years - coal getting represented the main means of earning the funds for the mentioned Saturday matinee. Therefore, mere physical discomfort could hardly deter the gaining of the necessary pennies permitting the witnessing of its excitements.

Being deprived of the main highlight of the week - the continuation of the Flash Gordon or Buck Jones serials - would represent a suffering far more acute than any imposed by a half-hundredweight of sharp cobs carried on one's back. So, to gain the necessary finance and thereby avoid such awful deprivation, a convoy of wagons rattled and rumbled to and from the coal-yards every Saturday morning.

Even without its monetary gain, the task - in itself - presented immense enjoyment: one usually shared with other kids and therefore invariably turning into play. The many slopes of the district demand the strength of at least two children for controlling the weight of a fully loaded cart down the inclines. In this, you could both imagine you're part of a wagon train transporting valuable supplies to some besieged fort - and facing the dangers of ambush around every corner. Or you were strong horses pulling a great cart over rough terrain and possessing the strength to hold its weight - even on the most steep and perilous inclines.

In addition, the yards, themselves, are a fascinating place to the kids. Each yard has a large set of scales composed of a strong cast-iron beam pivoting between a pair of iron post, set vertically in a solid iron platform. This assembly runs on four cast-iron wheels, allowing the scales to be moved around to the various heaps of coal stored within the yard's shed - these varying from tiny pieces of "nutty-slack" to great, big, shiny black lumps called "best cobs". (They're the ones that dig into your back if you try to carry a sack-full.)

A large steel scoop - whose metal is polished bright from the many shovelling in and tipping out of coal - is suspended from one end of the beam. On the other end - and supported by four chains fixed to an eye-bolt set in the underside of the beam - hangs an iron tray for placing the weights needed to balance the coal the scoop might hold. These weights are solid cast-iron blocks of various sizes with a recessed handgrip set in their top. A number cast on the side of each block indicates their weight, in pounds.

Let's go to the yard I previously mentioned - the one you've yet to see and the one I particularly like - which our Dad reckons gives the best coal. Mr and Mrs Markey own it and it's on the corner formed by Brass Street and Bronze Street, just by the cinema. You'll soon notice the yard because its large, green painted wooden doors are left wide open all day; revealing the coal-shed occupying the bottom part of its two-storey building whose upper floor the Markeys dwell in.

Whilst waiting to be served, we try lifting the heavy weights kept just inside the yard, by the door, to Mr Markey's invariable comment:

"Thar'll ne'er lift that, lad! Not 'til tha as big as tha Dad."

Then, when it's our turn to be served, he places the weights needed to balance our order on the tray with a clang; then shovels the amount we've ordered into the scoop. He'll increase or decrease the amount of coal until the balance is just right: not a cob more; not a cob less.

Mrs Markey - dressed in her long-skirted, Victorian style, black dress - over which she wears an apron made from a coal-sack - and with her hair done in a tight bun - holds open the mouth of the strong canvas bag placed in the cart she's selected for us to use; then braces herself whilst Mr Markey locks the beam and tilts the scoop to discharge its contents into the waiting canvas. Whereupon a thin cloud of tiny coal particles spirals upwards, glinting and dancing in the shaft of sunlight slanting through the open doorway.

Mr Markey - straightening up with what seems a dignified slowness (but what may be a careful movement demanded by an aching back) and with teeth gleaming in a coal-blackened, moustached, face - then makes his other invariable comment:

"That'll do thi', lad. An' if tha's going down Buckley Street, watch 'ow tha go. An' don't forget t' bring 'cart back! Now! Where's y'u' brass!"

His cautioning about Buckley Street was apt. As I mentioned on a previous visit: during an icy winter, a horse with its cart lost control on the cobbled incline and finished up through the window of the fish and chip shop - that's the one we saw in Burton Street and at the bottom of Buckley Street's slope. The word quickly spread; and I remember running from our street to see the terrible scene.

Being a small lad, I managed to push my way to the front of the gathering crowd to view with the compelling curiosity of a child the jagged glass and the blood stained horse lying on the cobbles in pain. However, my quick removal from the scene by an adult denied further witnessing.

Despite this awful incident, any cautioning, although respectfully heard, could be lost in a task eagerly converted into play - especially those requiring a modicum of "recklessness". We'd set off down the street with the iron wheels rumbling on the cobbles; then much pushing, shoving and manoeuvring from pavements to cobbles and cobbles to pavements until the household needing the coal is reached.

The impatiently waiting householder lifts the bag from the cart we'd manoeuvred down the narrow back-entry and tips its contents in the backyard storage space. Then the quick return of the bag and cart to the yard (a great crime not to do this - you'd never get another loan) and if we'd earned more pennies than admission to the Saturday matinee requires, a dash to the local shop for whatever extra treats our fancies dictate.

Let's imagine it's a winter's evening and we're sat in our small front room. We've a good supply of coal and our Dad's returning to the front room with a bucket-full of cobs he got from the scullery's storage. He's now taking two large shiny cobs out of the bucket and placing them on the glowing blaze.

Flames lick eagerly around the fresh coal. The little spurts of smoke issuing from their heated surface catch alight with a soft roar.

We feel its warmth.

The gaslight is turned low and shadows are dancing on the wall.

Let's sit, for a while, by the fire...

KETTLE, COAL, AND SOFT GAS-LIGHT

Gas-light sighs would pacify
the darkened hours of winter's day;
the long, contented, sibilant sigh -
like surf surging far away.

Kettle resting on the hob
would sing so softly from its spout,
as the coal's heat-fissured cob
breathed small plumes of white smoke out.

Then these plumes would catch alight,
from the fire's glow, spreading more,
making dancing flames - blue bright -
start a soft and soothing roar.

Thus, when all was quiet within
the warm snug room on winter's night,
homely sounds would then begin -
from kettle, coal, and soft gas-light.

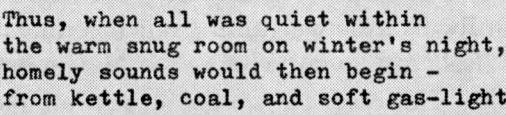

21
Gasworks and Games

~~~~~~~~~~~~~~~~~~~~~~~~~~~~~~~~~~~~~~

In the days when most people saw central-heating as an expensive peculiarity, used by Americans, and the terms "double-glazing", "draught-proofing", and "cavity wall insulation" were not yet invented, the household fire was - as we've seen - virtually a life-saver.

Nevertheless, coal had its "darker" aspects - these bringing about conditions that the time to which we now belong would deem horrific.

Before this reaction arose, the less than pleasant conditions were accepted with the passivity only a visit to that earlier time could effectively convey. The outpourings of innumerable domestic fires merging with the voluminous discharges from vast numbers of factories, causing the characteristic smoke-haze covering most major towns and cities, was seen as something that cities were supposed to have. It was, therefore, hardly an issue warranting much comment.

Concern only pushed itself into awareness as the November chill produced its usual results. The cold air of the upper atmosphere sometimes trapped and held down the outpourings of factories and domestic fires to produce "pea-soupers" (a name given to the fogs of that time due to their density and sulphuric tinge). These could blanket the city for days. Nevertheless, although comments often arose about the discomfort and disruption it caused, hardly any were offered about its possible elimination, since the whole of industry and the comfort of the home depended on coal. To get rid of its adverse affects would mean forbidding an ingredient upon which every aspect of society depended - this causing just as much social and economic disruption as would the banning of oil in our present time.

With the wisdom of hindsight coupled with the power of technology, later periods became aware that such fogs (or "smogs" as they came to be known - from the combination of the words "smoke" and "fog") were avoidable. In this process, the changeover from coal to oil and natural gas substantially helped to "clear the air".

The need to banish what was once resignedly accepted became an imperative after the London experience of December 1952. Smog producing circumstances created by the mentioned atmospheric conditions became more severe than usual and persisted for nearly a week. Even at mid-day, visibility was no more than ten yards or so; and - as you can imagine - this brought traffic to a virtual standstill.

Over 4,000 deaths were indirectly attributed to the pollutants that the fog represented; and although the unfortunate victims were mostly elderly (already suffering from respiratory diseases such as bronchitis and pneumonia) nevertheless, this calamity rightly horrified the nation - so much so that rectifying measures were demanded.

A nation in the mood to insist upon a far better world than that existing before the 1939-45 war expected "something to be done" by the political order elected to "do something". The response emerged in the form of various Clean Air Acts primarily directed towards eliminating the use of coal in its "raw" form. Smokeless fuels, such as coke and anthracite, were made readily available along with enclosed fireplaces designed to produce more efficient combustion - this because the new fuels burned less easily in an open fireplace than the cheaper coal.

Also, the Clean Air Acts accelerated the progress of central heating as a domestic feature - using oil, gas and the previously mentioned smokeless solid fuels, made to burn in unobtrusive heating units. Consequentially, fireplaces were "designed" out of most newly built houses.

But as noted before: in gaining something we lose something. The open fireplace once found in every home - that held attractions in the form of warmth and comfort sufficient to gather the family around its setting in the evenings, to chat and exchange their experiences - virtually disappeared. The TV set - whose nature demanded from its viewers the minimum of chat - supplanted the fireplace as the domestic focal point.

Family meals moved from a shared table of conversation to a tray balanced on the laps of mostly silent individuals; each TV isolated member waiting for a commercial break to compress within its interruption any brief verbal exchanges thought necessary.

This decline of leisurely and informative family conversations became even more so with the increasing range of choices offered by the new lure. Members of the family who wished to exercise their own particular preferences escaped to their own particular rooms with their own particular TV sets and entered their own particular and isolated ambience. In many cases, the families portrayed in those episodes given the name of "Soaps" became more familiar and therefore even more "real" than the family to which the viewer belonged. In this respect, the social nature of domesticity underwent a subtle but drastic change compared with what it used to be - and once needed to be.

Additionally, the growth of "take-aways" - ideally suited to the new mode of mealtimes - displaced the "housewife" as the skilled provider of appetising and much appreciated nourishment. She thereby lost her central and crucial role when the proficiencies she once possessed became less needed and therefore much less valued.

As the home became less demanding in care, culinary and cleaning skills, there seemed very little left for her to do inside the home; so paid outside work seemed the only way to justify her existence. This became an increasing necessity in order to raise the finances for all the had-to-be-got appliances to keep the household chores to a minimum; also to purchase the latest and more exotic TV sets; digital video recorders and the take-aways required to fill the gap caused by the decline of cooking. Funds were also needed to obtain all the gizmos and goodies TV displayed as "must-be-got-desirables". Thus faded - or even ended - that Victorian vision of the frugal family and the "mother in the home", as expressed by that archetypical Victorian poet, Tennyson, who declared in his poem 'The Princess':

Man for the field and woman for the hearth.

A statement whose implications and intent would've been received with a satisfied nodding of heads up to the time of 1939, but with a increasingly emphatic shaking of many heads thereafter.

The present period's perspective might exclaim: "The views just expressed are as stuffy and gloomy as a gas-lit Victorian parlour. They ignore all the social benefits - such as the person once restrictively called a "housewife" being freed from Tennyson's old, obdurate, prescription. She can now choose activities other than a constant attendance at the kitchen sink and be as economically independent as she wishes. Moreover, we needn't all huddle around a fire in draughty houses. And there's no fogs!"

Well, this challenge must be put in the context of the suggested "gaining and losing". Great concern exists in the present period about the loss of family cohesion and the problems this creates. And regarding visible pollutants: technological changes have, in their turn, produced invisible pollutants not unduly worried about until fairly recently, but much worried about now. Before these worries, they were tolerated as a consequence of desired economic circumstances in the same way as atmospheric conditions resulting from industrial processes and domestic necessities were perceived before 1952.

Although the pre-1952 conditions sometimes causing disquiet, the consequential fogs were seen as just another aspect of the season's weather that had to be accepted along with other "natural" manifestations - such as rain, high-winds, hail and snow.

One of the most visible and persisting consequence of industrial fogs (the smoke-blackened exteriors of the city's stone buildings) was likewise seen as "natural", to the extent that no-one seemed to make comment about this defacement. In fact, as a child, I thought black must be the natural colour of the stone from which the buildings were made. Therefore, we inner-city dwellers never seemed to see even the most severe manifestations of industrialisation as something that should cause undue worry or complaint. Its "discoloration of the atmosphere" had been a feature of the manufacturing cities from the beginnings of the Industrial Age; and when a condition persists for a considerable time, it seems pointless to make comments or undue complaints about it.

Just as rivers were seen as the obvious and natural means of carrying away industrial wastes of the liquid variety, so air was considered the obvious media for carrying away waste of the gaseous kind. Where else could that natural consequence of burning coal go, other than into the air? And if it so happened that atmospheric conditions stopped the smoke from clearing away at the rate it usually did, then this was a normal result of the weather. You just had to wait until a change of wind or weather cleared the atmosphere - as it would do, eventually.

As previously suggested: this "relaxed" attitude allowed pollution to be put up with to an extent we'd now deem irresponsible. Moreover, the fog-exacerbated ailments were endured with a fatalistic resignation that our later time would, within its own circumstances, find incredible - as we saw in a previous visit.

But it's all a question of awareness. The deleterious effects of cigarette smoking, for instance, were ignored until comparatively recently. Tobacco intake was considered to have beneficial affects recommended by many "smoking" doctors, especially as a "tranquilliser" - as the troops in the First and Second World Wars emphatically and gratefully accepted. This and the health-quality of air we breathe became more the concern of our later time, as determined by its own considerations.

It may be that such concerns for health, over and above what they were in previous times, arise more intensely when the belief in a compensating and eternal life in a realm beyond declines. The life many began to believe would be the only one they would ever know became the important one to be preserved and extended so that it could be enjoyed as long as possible - with all the worries this entails.

Along with the shifting beliefs about the "value" of life, advancing medical and scientific knowledge began to indicate that pollution could threaten everyone and reduce the life of anyone. This applied even to people living in green and pleasant places, where those with the power to effect changes usually live, and not just those living in the industrialised inner cities.

You may think this a cynical observation, but a similar shift from puzzled indifference to urgent concern came about in the 1860s when Prince Albert died of typhoid. This resulted in a massive programme to clean up all water supplies, under the powerful realisation that typhoid could be borne by the water everybody (the rich, the poor, the politically impotent and the politically powerful) had to drink.

So, it seems, the advance of social awareness, knowledge and the political will to react to these realisations are the essential ingredients required to bring about changes, along with giving due considerations to any adverse economic affects such changes may produce.

However, such deep social, medical, ethical, economic and political matters were too profound to impinge upon us kids living in the industrial nineteen-thirties. Nor did we ever consider whether or not humankind is motivated essentially by self-interest or altruism. We accepted the circumstances just as they were. Sufficient onto us was the fact that certain "worse" aspects of the inner city produced conditions we saw as positive enhancements to our lives.

Let's go back to that time - using once again the accepting eyes of a child - and experience how these eyes could transform what would appear to the present time as the worse aspects of inner-city life.

Imagine we're now in the nineteen-thirties. We've decided to go along Rochdale Road where we can stand at the main gate of Gould Street gasworks, just opposite the railway-yard situated on the other side of that road and where a line crosses the road from yard to gasworks. If we're lucky enough to be there just at the right time, we'd see the bustling stream of traffic brought to a halt; causing the gigantic cart-horses amongst the trams and lorries to snort and toss their heads restlessly whilst held in check by their carters. Then the shuddering creak of the large wooden gates belonging to the railway-yard swinging open; immediately followed by the squealing of the gasworks' enormous iron gates pivoting on their hinges.

And then: excitement! A towering locomotive, belching steam, smoke and sparks, emerges from the railway-yard; pulling its iron wagons filled with coal to feed the gasworks' hunger. Then the clanking, fire-driven giant crossing the road amidst outpourings of steam and smoke - with fireman's face painted a lurid-red from the fire's glow as he stoops and plunges like some demented devil to frantically stoke his charge. And then to watch it clanking its awesome, squealing way into the canyons between the towering blackened buildings of the gasworks. Clanking and screeching into the smoke filled labyrinth of ovens and gasometers - as if even this mightiness of iron and steam squeals out in terror at the prospect of being enveloped by the smoke and confusion within.

Then the gates of the gasworks clanging shut and the nervous traffic moving forward again, to leave us peering through the rails in wide-eyed wonder; trying to catch a glimpse of the engine and wagons we still hear squealing within the massive, smoke-shrouded labyrinth behind the iron gates.

And yet another time, we might see the scorched, gigantic doors of the coking-ovens just beyond the gates open, to feel the heat from the disgorging of angry red coke sweep towards us. And then a confusion of noise and darting figures amid steaming cloud of sulphurous smoke: like the inside of the Hell we'd heard about at Sunday School - a concept which frightened but at the same time held us in awe.

Thus, we experience the intoxicating mixture of fear and excitement: the stimulant the child seeks as eagerly as an alcoholic seeks theirs. However, in our inner-city life, the intoxication is all around us in endless cocktails - waiting for us to drink it all in. And the noise, smoke, turmoil and activities fermenting it all is the awe-inspiring normality of city life, whose world we accept as all children do: just as it is and with all the fears and excitements it can offer.

And so it is with the fog and its capacity to excite and scare. Sometimes, I'd lie in bed waiting for the distant muffled bang of the railway's fog-signal (the small explosive charges placed on the railway lines, detonated by the train's wheels to warn workmen and those operating the signalling of a train's approach).

This sound - coming from Rochdale Road's part of the railway - seemed to emphasise the silence of the impenetrable world swirling and pressing itself against the small, dark, window of my bedroom; making me pull the bed-sheets even tighter over my head; to hide myself from the ghostly images the fog might contain. This I would do until drifting into the deep sleep of childhood - a sleep as deep and enveloping as the fog itself.

Moreover, in our waking and constantly active hours, we could use the fog's presence to mix another intoxicating cocktail. Before offering this for you to experience some comments might be helpful, to set the scene.

A view from the present would deem it incredible for anyone to permit young children to play in the streets, as we kids did, without it causing anxiety - and especially in fog. But as you've already seen, very little traffic intruded into the residential areas away from the main roads to create concern. Also and as stated previously: the harmful affects of the less extreme fogs upon the healthy were not fully realised. But most of all - and again as you've already seen - in those close-knit neighbourly communities many friendly adult eyes seeing to their daily activities would always be around during the hours kids played.

Adding to this feeling of safety, as far as children were concerned, was the absence of that all too familiar fear arising more intensely in our later period: the possibility of child abduction. This never seemed to enter anyone's awareness. The widespread possession of cars into which strangers could entice children, to take them quickly away from the area where they belonged, wasn't a feature of that time. And again - and as you've already seen - if a car did appear in our street or any of its adjacent streets, it caused immediate curiosity.

But an aspect most relevant to the feeling of safety in these communities was the fact that they were too "public" to hide misconduct. As you saw during our visits: everybody knew everyone else, so the persisting presence of a stranger would soon be noticed. More especially, there's always the long serving bobby-on-the-beat who knows the area and everyone in it and is therefore part of the neighbourhood - and usually lives in or comes from that locality.

It's commonplace to see the local policeman stopping for a conversations with those in our street and its adjacent streets; knowing many of the people by name, along with those of their family, friends and relations.

One of the most comforting feelings I ever experienced was the warm grasp of the local policeman's gloved hand when, as a small child, I'd adventurously strayed a little too far from my own street and was led back home to where he knew I belonged. It always seemed we lived in a safe community - as safe outdoors as it was indoors.

In this setting, we played a game called "Rally-O" (a name probably derived from the hunting cry: "Tally-ho!"). We'd play this in the dim light of the early evening, just after the gaslights were lit and with the fog swirling around the small area of visibility the streetlight offered.

We'd divide ourselves into two groups: one group to be the hunters, and the other: the hunted.

The lamppost is the rallying point and the area beyond: a fog enshrouded hunting ground of fog-blurred shapes and shadows.

Let's drift back into that early evening's fog.

Let's play Rally-O....

RALLY-O!

On dark nights when fog descended
(a fog so thick
that figures blended
into its dark and yellow smoke –
outpourings from the coal and coke)
the kids would play at
Rally-O:

One gang would wait while others'd go
into the fog,
where they would hide.
The first gang – by gas-light –
would bide
their time until
they'd counted ten;
and on that count, but not 'til then
(they'd promised by a 'cross-my-heart')
the hunt would start.

Around the street, each hide-away,
each known retreat where kids might stray,
they'd hunt for fog-hid fugitives;
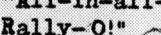
then take them where gas-light would give
a fitful but sufficient glow
to tell who's friend and who was foe.
When all were captured
calls would go:
"All-in-all-in.
Rally-O!"

And those still searching
would return
to where the yellow
gas-lights burn.

For hours,
this game,
the kids
would play.

(The thick-fog-smoke did not dismay)

22
As a Matter of Interest:
Coal, Gas and Steam

~~~~~~~~~~~~~~~~~~~~~~~~~~~~~~~~~~~~~~

The coal, gas and steam of the Victorian age still held their dominant position right into the nineteen-thirties, as our visits showed. Oil, natural gas and electricity were only just beginning to spread their influences, to finally bring in the age of energy and power that we now know.

Some of our visits revealed how the not-yet-displaced coal, gas and steam could hold great fascination, despite their less than pleasant aspects. They also indicated how this fascination could especially apply to the kids of that time - being, as they were, less mindful of the noise, smoke and smell.

In our environmentally conscious age, with its concern for clean and renewable energy, the idea that the previous period's conditions could hold any attraction whatsoever might appear to many people as ludicrous. Yet such is the enduring appeal of coal and steam - irrespective of its noise, smoke and smell - numerous dedicated Railway Preservation Societies keep it very much alive.

The gasworks and the arrival of its coal-supplying train we saw in our visits represented a typical arrangement for virtually every industrial, and even not so industrial, town and city of that time. The increasing need for gas went alongside the growth of the Victorian conurbations and their rapidly expanding populations. For instance: from 1801 to 1851, the demand for workers resulted in a three-fold increase in Manchester's inhabitants. During the same period, England and Wales doubled its numbers from nine to eighteen million.

So, this pouring of people into the constantly growing towns and cities impelled the construction of numerous gasworks with their massive gasometers (such as the Manchester example shown on the left) in all industrial and not so industrial centres. These structures were primarily placed where outputs in the form of gas and coke had direct and immediate consumption. And, as the photo indicates, their presence could substantially dominate the area in which they were constructed.

In our present concern about environmental matters, the placing of such enormously polluting and unsightly complexes right in the centre of any habitation would now meet serious challenge. So, since those gigantic and dominating gasworks are no longer a usual feature of our townscape, and even landscape, it could be interesting to go back to the time when the one in the Gould Street of our visits had its beginning. By this, we might gain insight into how and why it was thought right and proper to build it there in the first place.

As a point of reference, we can return to the period when the French gentleman we previously met - Alexis de Tocqueville - arrived in Manchester in 1835. On his arrival, the road we knew in our visits as Rochdale Road went by the name of Saint George's Road. Gould Street (already existing and possessing that name) had a position related to this thoroughfare as it does with Rochdale Road in the present time.

The other nearby feature (Saint Michael's Church - constructed in 1789 along with its burial ground) was more than likely seen by the French visitor as he surveyed what was, to him, the alarming, predatory nature of industry. Although built just a short period before his visit - as the "life" of a church goes - it had declined into a fast fading remnant of its former glory. The increasing industrialisation of its once pleasant area impelled the well-to-do "gentlefolk" - who inhabited the Georgian houses in Angel Meadow and used the church for their religious expressions - to move elsewhere.

As a matter of interest: Saint Michael's stood intact until the year 1935 when its demolition began as the district entered its last stages of decline. It became finally reduced to rubble by 1936 and the site left derelict until comparatively recently. This area has now become attractively landscaped - thus fulfilling the hesitant and restricted attempts made to the church grounds some hundred or so years earlier.

In terms of original buildings: only the Charter Street Mission still endures as a last witness to the substantial edifices that once gave "grace" to the area.

However, the church's humiliation began when the once genteel neighbourhood first experienced the many foundries and workshops, crowding increasingly around the church and pushing outwards from existing places such as Hargreaves Street and Rogers Street. This unremitting pressure soon destroyed any semblance of an area that could claim the high-esteem it once had. It had rapidly become part of the scene that the French visitor saw with a certain amount of alarm - as his "gloomy" description of Manchester, offered at the beginning of these narratives, indicated.

Just a few years before he penned his sombre view, the increasing demand made by all the expanding areas of industry to be supplied with gas and coke became a possibility. The pressure of demand caused the existing "City Fathers" to realise "something must be done" in that direction. This more so because - in addition to the fast growing need for furnace-coke to feed the expanding factories and foundries - an increasing pressure arose to supply gas as a means of lighting the fitfully illuminated buildings and dark streets at that time. Doing this would, it was believed, reduce criminal opportunities. It soon became obvious that only a large and substantial gasworks could supply the enormously expanding requirements.

Well before the problem of gas-supply was thrust upon the "City Fathers", a Scottish engineer by the name of William Murdoch used coal-gas to light his house as early as 1792. By the period of our main consideration, the possibility of applying its techniques to lighting the main streets of towns and cities seemed more than a possibility. This casting of light where once night-time darkness prevailed began to appeal to many streets and buildings. For instance, Manchester's Theatre Royal and nearby Fountain Street became gas-lit in 1819.

However, it soon became apparent that the existing small and scattered sources of supply, arising haphazardly and restricted to each individual demand, were becoming increasingly "not up to the job". The conveniently piped and more illuminating alternative than the expensive candles or smelly oil-lamps, previously used in the domestic settings, had won the day (and night) so to speak. Thus, the wide demand for gas was one that the City Fathers had to meet.

At this stage, it seems appropriate to mention certain devices allowing the widespread success of interior and exterior gas lighting. The most important innovation that finally transformed the not very bright naked gas-flame into a satisfying level of illumination is one we've already see. It came in the form of the delicate, fabric-like hood mentioned many times in our various visits, which eventually became known as the "gas-mantle".

Before this ingenious and comparatively simple invention arrived on the scene - to brighten up peoples' lives - numerous attempts were made to increase the gas-flame's illumination. The first viable effort came in the form of a device known as the Argand Burner. This had already been extensively employed in oil-lamps and therefore its tried and tested principle became, in 1809, transferred to gas-light. It worked on the basis of a cup-shaped flame, achieved in the case of the oil-lamp by a circular shaped wick.

Its application to gaslight took the form of a circular arrangement of the gas-jet, allowing the maximum amount of air around the flame and thereby providing for more efficient burning - and, of course, greater illumination. The glass "chimney", found as a necessary part of the Argand Burner principle, when used for oil-lamps, also added its induced airflow to improved gas combustion. This arrangement of cup-shaped flame and glass chimney became the standard method of gas lighting up to the latter part of the Victorian period. However, its level of light still failed to satisfy, and numerous devices to produce something like the gas-mantle were tried with varying success.

It seems the first effort approaching a satisfying practicality appeared in 1878, when the American inventor, Thomas Edison, coated a woven platinum wire-mantle with oxides of zirconium - this to place over the flame to then glow brightly in its heat. The final and more affordable effort came with an invention produced in 1885 by a person named Carl Auer Von Welsbach. This took the form of a woven fabric (cotton or rayon) impregnated with a solution of thorium and cerium nitrates. Its advantage - besides being cheap - also lay in the fact that its flimsy construction immediately gained strength by the chemical reaction created by the burning process. This innovation continued to reliably produce what was then considered to be a highly satisfying level of light for most homes and streets, until the arrival of brighter and cleaner electricity ensured its final "turning off".

But back to the production of gas: under the pressure to satisfy demand, those responsible for the city's gas supplies obtained - in 1824 - a vacant and convenient nine-acre site in Gould Street, no more than a mile or so away from the city centre. The plan then drawn up consisted of a processing complex capable of serving as a major gas producer for that area - with the possibility of eventually supplying areas beyond.

This new site received the name of St. George's Station, employing eighteen men. By the time Alexis de Tocqueville arrived to contemplate the scene, and write his gloomy view, it had reached a production of 50,000 cubic feet of gas per day. Such was the arduous and dangerous nature of this crucial task that each employee received a quart of ale every day and was offered a free coffin - if needed.

The latter "benefit" arose from the undoubtedly perilous process involved in heating coal to extremes of temperature - this being done in airtight ovens, known as retorts. These allowed the coal to release its gas without igniting. The main constituents of the released gas consisted of the highly flammable and poisonous methane, hydrogen and carbon monoxide combinations.

At Gould Street, the resulting gas had its storage in a cluster of three massive gasometer - the final one being erected by the time of 1850. These had a design-capability allowing the storage and then the controlled discharging of their contents into the ever-expanding network of gas-mains and branching pipes, built according to demand. In such complexities, explosions could easily occur from escaping gas. The early stages of the gaswork's construction and its subsequent development resulted in many accidents. In one instance, a man suffered a fatality and thirteen received severe burns.

These dangerous possibilities inevitably became part of the undertaking and resided in its nature. The gasification process ended with each retort being emptied of the carbonised lumps that we know as coke, necessitating the handling of material giving off sulphurous gases at extremely high temperatures. Therefore, it wasn't surprising that a coffin "if needed" was offered as part of the job; and the men involved probably thought the offer very generous and not in any way unusual.

In addition to the inherent dangers, it seems these industrial units became targets for sabotage during periods of "unrest". For instance: in the Chartists disruptions of 1824, the Gould Street works - then in the early stage of construction - came under attack, resulting in its newly built sections being damaged. Further attempts at sabotage occurred in 1876, on the part of the Fenian Movement (an Irish-American Republican secret society, first emerging in 1858 as the forerunner to the IRA). After this incident, many of the Gould Street workers were granted the power of special constables "to act in any way necessary and according to the situation". No doubt the offer of a coffin also gave "consolation" in these circumstances?

In the early stages, another condition exacerbating the arduous situation was the absence of trains - such as the one that we saw crossing Rochdale Road in one of our visits. This had to await the extensive railway complexes built some decades after the gasworks' construction. Therefore, in the early stages, the coal required to feed the constantly increasing demand for gas had to be laboriously transported by horse and cart, which became a limitation on output.

With the arrival of railway transportation, production leaped from the original 50,000 cubic feet of gas per day to the staggering figure of 7,000,000 per day. By 1860, this needed a constant 400 tons (about fifty wagonloads) of coal each day to generate the necessary volume of gas and coke - requiring the employment of 700 men to maintain its output. This level of output became possible because of the enormous amounts a train could immediately deliver straight from the mines. Thus came into being the everyday crossing of Rochdale Road with the train entering the gaswork's fiery, smoke filled labyrinth.

But let's prepare for our next visit. This time to see the River Irk when it bore its own unmistakable signs of industrialisation...

23
The River Irk

~~~~~~~~~~~~~~~~~~~~~~~~~~~~~~~~~~~~~

During our previous visits, we saw how air and water were looked upon as the obvious media for carrying away what was then seen as the "natural waste" of industrial processes - or "industrial pollutants", as they would now be called.

The River Irk seemed to be mainly used for this purpose - chiefly to carry away the liquid effluence many mills and factories along its banks wished to discharge. In our district, the upstream dye-works sometimes caused the river to flow a bright green and, at other times, a dark blue or yellow; but, for most times, a sombre reddish-brown.

In later years, I learnt if numerous colours are mixed it always results in a tone towards brown; and the red, being the most powerful tint, can bias that tone towards its own coloration. This probably explains the predominance of the reddish-brown we often saw, which gave the river a more forbidding look than it might otherwise have possessed if its tone had been more "cheerful".

However, moving away from the river for a while, to comment about what will be the main theme of this narrative.

It's main concern is how children adapt to and make use of any situation they find around them and how they use whatever they do find to develop their imagination. Also, even the most casual observation suggests children have an in-built imperative to quickly become a product of their time. Their intense and innate curiosity facilitates this process as they rapidly absorb all that they experience. This they do without inhibitions about whether or not things should or could be otherwise.

Although they absorb all aspects of their "born-into-period" - and thereby become a child of their time - they also become immensely inventive in utilising whatever features their surrounds happen to provide that might further their play-purposes.

In the context of this, one of the most conspicuous differences between the first period of the nineteen-hundreds and the period thereafter is in the mode of children's activities and the explorative freedom each period provided and allowed. Children of earlier times had far fewer ready-made devices and distractions, whereas the later period provides all sorts of commercialised pre-programmed packages - many of these directed towards indoor and solitary play.

In the tightly packed streets with its continuous outdoor activities we witnessed in our visits, children's play had to be - by the nature of its setting and the provisions it offered - constantly companionable. These associations of highly active children generated many ritualistic rules, mostly invented by the children themselves. Such inventions added excitement to their play and, by this, tightened the companionable bonds. An active example of it all we'll see in a later visit, at a place called the "Dark Arch", where the suggested bonding between companions involves the completion of a mandatory task.

This rule-bound and ritualistic play seemed to be a universal feature of that time and wasn't restricted to the industrial settings of the kind we visited. The 'William' series written by Richmal Crompton in the 1920/30 period indicates a realistically portrayed rural example.

Although related to a drastically different context from the one that we're about to enter, nevertheless, the "William" activities illustrated the almost uninterrupted society that period allowed amongst children and the emergence of the bonding rituals appropriate to such conditions. Just as William and his gang had their unstained ponds and streams to provide excitement and curiosity, we had our much less "pure" but nevertheless rich-with-the-same-powers, River Irk.

In addition to what seemed to us its unpredictable potency to change its hue, it held other fascinations arising from the fact that we were warned from a very early age about the river's dangers. However, in the world of childhood, that which is deemed dangerous invariably excites intense curiosity.

I suspect this disposition stems from another deep-seated feature of human nature. Anything threatening or appearing to threaten seems to impel a need to see and understand all its aspects and sources. Witness, for instance, the crowds invariably gathering at road accidents or where other misfortune may've happened; and how this curiosity associated with a particular happening can persist long after its occurrence.

However, back to the river: between some of its deep stone and brick built banks its waters flowed with a fast and turbulent speed, especially after periods of heavy rain. Despite this and all the other highly visible confirmations of the river's dangers, the dominant feeling held by the companions whose play I shared was mainly that of a compelling curiosity. This became tinged with apprehension arising from the cautions constantly stressed by the adults around us. The resulting confusion of feelings induced amongst us numerous weird and sometimes frightening scare-stories, elaborating upon all the visible and verbal warnings. Nevertheless, these served only to excite our curiosity. Under its compulsion, we'd stand at the railings along Collyhurst Road, staring at the swirling currents some four or five feet below pavement level, as if, by this, we could defy any dangers the river represented.

Nevertheless, this cloak of defiance couldn't prevent the more acute warnings from penetrating our awareness. We knew the river could suddenly conjure up a fearsome challenge of its own. This we witnessed after some days of heavy rain when its waters rose alarmingly to flood our area of Collyhurst Road to a depth of two or three feet. Its murky overflow reached halfway up the railings bordering its banks and spread across the road to swirl against the Fount's lower slopes. Then, to our awe stricken dismay and then amazement - rising to a growing delight - we saw the flood had made attendance at Saint Catherine's School impossible.

The only access to the school - the narrow iron bridge spanning the river - had become partly submerged along with the adjacent bridge giving access to that block of tenements known as the Dwellings, which you saw during one of our previous visits. However, our main attention centred on the school's bridge and the release from school its condition implied. In our growing sense of freedom from any responsibilities or adverse consequences related to the river's capriciousness, we could rejoice in the flood's results.

Others had a different "view"; especially those occupying the row of terraced houses on the opposite side of Collyhurst Road from the school. Being built partly into the bottom of the district's slope, the row required a raised foundation at its front to level its flooring. This resulted in the front doorways of the houses being seven or so feet above the pavement's level.

To provide access to the doors thus raised, a walkway - not unlike a long veranda - ran along the row's length. When viewed from the front of the building, and with the input of a modicum of imagination, this resembled a theatre stage with the coming and going of the inhabitants appearing as if they were actors. The previously mentioned impulse to ascribe descriptive names to unusual features impelled the inevitable giving of this row the name of "The Stage".

The raised foundations also provided for a number of basements beneath the veranda; these built partly above and partly below the level of the road and having access from the front of the row by way of a flight of stone steps leading down from the pavement. A small window at the side of each access door allowed daylight to penetrate what would otherwise be gloomy interiors. Thus made less gloomy by natural light, the basements became converted into small workshops for occupations such as cobbling and carpentry.

Their below-pavement situation caused them severe flooding. This affected the father of a play-friend who used one of the units for his shoe mending occupation. His Dad's anxiety about the materials and equipment stored in the basement conveyed itself to us by way of our play-friend, and was the nearest the river's action came to mitigating the flood's excitements.

A few days later, when the murky waters began to recede, we watched the firemen pumping the sludge out of the basements and back into the River Irk, to reveal much of their contents ruined. Before this, we'd "enjoyed" the safety of the Fount's upper level from where we observed the swollen river as it flowed with a frightening rapidity along the inundated length of Collyhurst Road.

We watched with a mixture of awe and anxiety as the firemen - with the turbulent waters swirling around and dragging at their wader-clad legs - attempted to cross the narrow bridge that gave access to the Dwellings. The watching crowd that had gathered on the Fount offered reassuring waves to the inhabitants lining the verandas who were anxiously observing the firemen battling to reach their flood-isolated building.

Some days later, when the water finally receded to its usual confines, we congregated at Collyhurst Road's railings to watch the debris flowing by - tossing and twisting in a current almost as fierce as when in full flood. If we'd possessed adult sensitivities, perhaps we might've seen some of the debris as quite gruesome. The body of a pig, for instance, carried into the city from that other, to us, curious outside world beyond ours, floated by: twisting and turning in the fast flow.

As town dwelling children of not many years of age, it was the first time we'd seen a pig "in the flesh", so to speak. And being free from the inhibitions adult sensitivities impart, we were able to give complete rein to the wide-eyed "take-it-all-in" curiosity of childhood. We watched, fixated, as the creature's body twisted and turned in the racing current; then raised excited shouts as it got caught in a tangle of debris jammed on the far side of the river. And, as the numerous stories about the river came to mind, we felt that growing disquiet on seeing the awesomeness its waters could capriciously inflict.

Although this disquiet was, for most times, held deep down in our awareness, it could nevertheless rise rapidly to the fore. This it did a year or so previously when the police dragged a section of the river with grappling irons to recover the body of a young lad whose home was in a nearby street. They eventually found his body a mile or so downstream where the Irk's waters plunge over a steep fall to then flow beneath the vastness of Victoria Station at the city's centre - this by way of the frightening "Dark Arch" we'll visit later.

It seems the unfortunate lad climbed over the railings at the end of Warford Street to gain access to the river. He may've done this in an attempt to retrieve something washed up on the mud banks formed along that stretch. In those throw-nothing-away times, local lads earned the occasional few pennies by making bundles of firewood needed by householders to light their morning fire. Anything useable for this purpose (for instance, a wooden crate washed up on the mud-bank) tempted the less than cautious. Nevertheless, whatever the reason for the lad's tragic action, its dreadful result again brought to our minds the awful "reality" of the river.

Yet, when the anxieties associated with this unfortunate event subsided, the river's fascination seemed to increase; but this never completely stilled the anxieties always ready to surface. In order to dissipate the tensions the incipient disquite generated, and thereby allow us to continue giving way to the curiosity the river impelled, we used a prescription which, I suspect, has been used by children in its various forms ever since time began. We conjured up "phantom shadows" of the fears in our minds. Then, when these reached a disturbing intensity, we ran away from the source of the fears until reaching a distance where we felt we'd escaped their clutches - thus reassuring ourselves these fears had no real power to catch us.

On our way home from school, we'd sometimes stand peering through the railings at the dye-stained waters swirling some four or five feet below the pavement level, until our lurking disquiet rose to such a degree it began to wash away the curiosity affixing us to the spot. At this "critical" moment, someone amongst us would give voice to the cry:

> *Jinny, Jinny, Greenteeth*
> *Has a sharp knife.*
> *If you see her coming:*
> *RUN FOR YOUR LIFE!*

The loudly shouted last line released us from our fixation, to permit dashing away from where we stood. We did this with that half-laugh, half-excited yell of a child who feels a real terror yet at the same time knows the terror has no real substance. We'd run until we felt "safe" and then - washing away our fear with laughter - turn to some other activity quickly catching our attention. Thus - armed with this instinctive and called-upon-when-needed therapy - we were able to face our fear whenever we felt inclined to do so; and once again experience the excitement of a fear taking hold of us and then for it to be banish with the same incantation.

In later years, I often wondered about our ritualistic rhyme and why it seemed particularly related to the river? Then - purely by chance - I came across a book of folklore in a jumble sale. On browsing through its pages, I found to my astonishment that Jenny Greenteeth (not Jinny, as we pronounced the name) was an ancient Lancashire scare associated with lakes and rivers, which the book claimed went as far back as Celtic times.

This malevolent spirit seized unwary children in her long, green fangs to drag them down into the depth of her dark and watery realm. However, this baleful spirit was, according to the book, pacified by the sacrificial throwing of valuable possessions into the waters - an instinct that seems to have "trickled down" in the action many people impulsively display when they throw coins into pools and fountains?

It could be that the ancient lore came to be believed by those long-ago people and possibly emphasised to make children wary of dangerous waters? But whatever its origin and purpose, it seems astonishing this folklore, originating aeons before industrial cities ever began, could have persisted and penetrated into the industrial heartland - and be so aptly applied. This without knowing its why and wherefore; and applied with our own particular invented rhyme - even to the point of including a "sacrificial knife"?

Also, the similar play-society experienced by preceding generations may've used the same image in the same manner; and the continuity of companionship - then an essential aspect of children's play - allowed it to be passed down to those who came afterwards? But whatever the case: in addition to constructing this type of imagery, there appears to be a powerful impulse for children to give their fears "real flesh", so to speak. This, it seems, makes them eager to project associated images onto any person who happens to offer a "ready embodiment".

The Dwellings, situated as it was by the River Irk and thereby associated in our minds with the dangers it represented, and possessing many winding stone stairways, long verandas and corridors, became a mysterious place, and therefore one tempting exploration. A lady we knew as Mrs Wilky (who seemed to our young eyes as extremely ancient) took on the role of deterring any non-residential kids from boisterously using the building in a way that could disturb the peace. By the fact of her living close to the river and being a person who "disciplined" she became our eagerly sought-after embodiment.

Although, to us, she presented a formidable appearance, she was, in reality, a very kindly soul - as my mother and those who knew her affirmed. But the power of our imagination was such that all her kindly attributes became submerged in the images we projected upon her. And with the "power" our imagination bestowed, she maintained a very effective peace around the Dwellings. A few words of chastisement from her made all potential offenders scurry away. She exercised this power with - again to us - an awesome potency although possibly unaware of its origin.

An aspect adding to its effectiveness resided in the fact that each upper floor of the Dwellings had a number of chutes used to deposit household waste into bins located in bays at ground level. This feature of high-level living was an arrangement whose purpose we kids, not belonging to the Dwellings, didn't really understand.

We came to believe that those apprehended in misbehaviour would be "put down the chute" and thereby finish up in the River Irk: an awful prospect filling us with great dread. This we elaborated into all sorts of terrifying images. Therefore and thereafter, if we ever needed to approach the Dwellings, we did so with great trepidation.

Let's go back in time to an incident as it actually took place; one carrying with it all the affects that this fear produced. Again we must - in order to experience its "reality" to the full - take on the eyes, ears, imagination and feelings of a child.

It's an early evening just after school. John - a playmate of ours - has been charged by his mother to deliver some second-hand clothes to Mrs Wilky's dwelling. We sense his great anxiety and his need for a companion to give support in the fearsome task he's forced to face.

We succumb to the temptation he offers: if we join him, he'll reward us with a portion of Sharp's Super Kreem Toffee when he receives the spending-money promised by his mother on completion of the errand. Although the fear of Mrs Wilky is formidable, the pledged reward holds great temptation. With this uppermost in mind, we set off to begin our frightful mission.

The darkening clouds gathering overhead seem to deepen our feeling of foreboding as we make our way down the bruw and then the steps leading to the Fount. In a silence generated by a rising apprehension, we warily cross the cobbles of Collyhurst Road. We hesitate, fearfully, at the railings along its far side, where we see the Irk flowing swiftly between its banks of green-slimed stone. Its dark-red waters appear more threatening than ever; and just upstream, the reddish-brown froth created by the small weir brings chilling thoughts of blood.

We shudder as the images take hold. The resolution that the promise of Sharp's Super Kreem Toffee had kept steadfast begins to waver. We tremble as we glance across the Irk to the line of railings along the edge of its opposite bank; then beyond these to the massive, forbidding bulk of the Dwellings - where Mrs Wilky could be waiting.

Warily, we glance to the upper floor where she dwells; and then along the line of verandas to see if she's watching; then quickly shift our gaze to the narrow bridge crossing the river - the only way to and from where she lives.

As we approach its span, a dreadful chill creeps over us: in crossing the bridge, we could be confronted by the lady of our fear. Or even worse: what if we cross the bridge and - on our way back - she confronts us, and we cannot escape?

We become even more fearful as we see John clutch the bundle of clothing tightly to his chest as if for protection. And again that almost overwhelming impulse to desert the task takes hold. But, John - with a face gone pale - begins to move forward.

Instinctively, we know he's weighing the fear of his mother's admonition on failing to complete his errand against the chances of seeing Mrs Wilky; and we know that we - ourselves - must likewise move forward; clinging to the thought of Sharp's Kreem Toffee as tightly as John clings to the bundle of clothing.

We cross the bridge as if in a dream, fast becoming a nightmare. We glance fearfully along the dark line of verandas. Then that dreadful climb up the dimly lit flight of steps at the far end of building with its dark corners - around which, at any moment, we could be confronted by the one we most fear.

Apprehensively, we follow John who still clings desperately to his bundle; then - after a nightmare of hesitant steps - we reach the veranda with the chute and its ghastly possibilities.

John makes a backward glance as if pleading for our support, but no words leave his lips. We make a feeble gesture - urging him forward. He moves as if struggling against some great paralysis; then his tremulous, choking shout as he knocks on Mrs Wilky's door:

"Mrs Wilky! Mrs Wilky! Here's the clothes! The money'll do tomorrow!"

He drops the bundle and we run as fast as our legs would allow. Fear floods into laughing relief as we reach the safety of distance.

But now that we're safe, let's see the image that caused us so much dread...

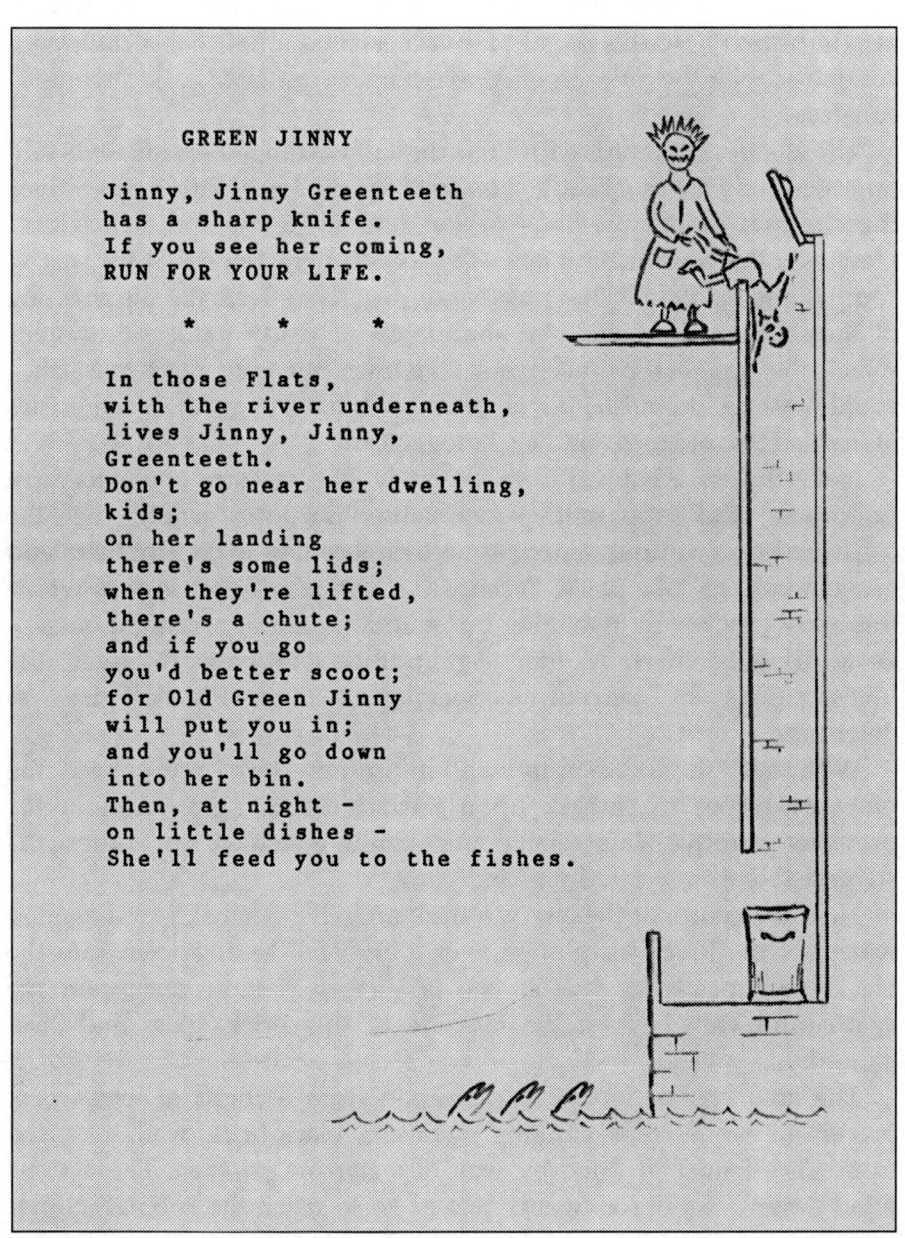

GREEN JINNY

Jinny, Jinny Greenteeth
has a sharp knife.
If you see her coming,
RUN FOR YOUR LIFE.

    *   *   *

In those Flats,
with the river underneath,
lives Jinny, Jinny,
Greenteeth.
Don't go near her dwelling,
kids;
on her landing
there's some lids;
when they're lifted,
there's a chute;
and if you go
you'd better scoot;
for Old Green Jinny
will put you in;
and you'll go down
into her bin.
Then, at night –
on little dishes –
She'll feed you to the fishes.

24
The Dark Arch

~~~~~~~~~~~~~~~~~~~~~~~~~~~~~~~~~~~~~

Our last visit showed how fears and excitements could be "played out" in the child-centred activities that the nineteen-thirties allowed. It also indicated how this social play represented a noticeable difference compared with the more isolated experiences our later period seems to construct.

The electronic games, with their digitally arranged excitements and fantasies, may act as a ready substitute for the imaginative projections the children of the previous period had to devise for themselves? However, this substitution lacks the social interactions that we saw in companionable play. What positive or negative affects the diminishing of these interactions and the abundance of ready made situations - which the imagination need not construct but only react towards - could have on individual development will have to await the enquiries of learned Sociologists and Psychologists.

Nevertheless, whatever form play may take, perhaps one of its most important and apparently instinctive purposes could be the construction of various settings in which learning to control fears and excitements can take place. Perhaps the lack of play settings in which this early practice in managing our emotions can occur might emerge as a disability in later life? Again, this will have to await the investigations of perceptive Sociologists and Psychologists to determine.

With all these assumptions in mind, let's return to the nineteen-thirties to embark upon the adventure I proposed in the previous narrative. This offers an incident in which we can witness the suggested learning actually taking place.

Near the centre of the city is a dark arch. It's where the red-stained waters of the River Irk plunge over a high fall to disappear into the blackness beneath the vast spread of Victoria Station; not to emerge again until way beyond the far side of this brick, glass and steel enormity.

The arch can be looked down upon from a flight of well-worn, precarious stone steps clinging against a black-brick wall, accessed from Cheetham Hill Road by way of a narrow passage. These steps wind down steeply for twenty feet or so to reach the cobbled corner formed by Verdon Street and a row along the river's bank with the simple name of Scotland.

From the top of these steps - with but a flimsy iron rail between you and the hard cobbles below - you can look into the awful blackness of the tunnel where the Irk's waters plunge and foam over the fall.

Below the fall and against the far side of the tunnel's opening is a bank of black mud formed by the swirling waters plunging into the tunnel's maw; where - it is said - rats living along the water's edge scavenge for washed up waste.

The blackness that lurks just inside the tunnel seems to swallow any light straying into its depth, and the dark-green slime seeping from its walls appears to consume what little light tries to escape.

To add to this awfulness, the previously mentioned boy who suffered the terrible misfortune of drowning in the River Irk was found just below that fall. This, and all the frightening thoughts the place could conjure up, made the Dark Arch and its flight of steps the most terrifying place we kids knew.

Let's turn away for these steps and the awful arch, for a while, to explore an aspect of childhood explaining the ordeal we're about to face. This, I believe, instinctively appears in various forms in all times and places where children play together. It is also an aspect of play that the time we're about to visit appears to have given greater scope.

This play-aspect consists of a powerful impulse for constant companions to form amalgamations we generally call "gangs" - as we saw portrayed in the fictional 'William' of the Richmal Crompton stories and in the factual examples we witnessed in our previous visit. This impulse may echo a long-ago tribal instinct, wherein one of the essentials determining the extent of a particular grouping is a constant association amongst its members - this association arising from living in and identifying with a specific, communal, location.

In our district, the boundaries we saw during a previous visit defined our area to make it distinct from those around, thereby offering the conditions in which companionable association could readily be formed. Gangs thus formed devise their own tests for initiation and therefore continuation of membership. These tests - if failed - could lead to exclusion from the gang, with all the felt shame and isolation this could bring about.

One of the most terrifying of tests to prove "worthiness" to become a fully-fledged member of the clique centred on the Dark Arch. Those facing its rigours were compelled to demonstrate their courage by leading the way down the long flight of frightening steps where - on each step - the fearsome blackness into which the waters plunged could be seen.

Now it's our turn to perform this test. And, becoming the child allowing us to do so, let's weave the same cloak of defiance that we did when facing Jinny Greenteeth. Wrapping its protection around us, we'll challenge the Irk's fearfulness once more: this time at the terrifying Dark Arch.

It's a late Sunday afternoon with a sky whose clouds seem to absorb the sun's light in the way that the Dark Arch swallows the light straying into its depth. From the top of the high steps whose flight we must now descend, we glance fearfully through the flimsy iron rails to the rain-swollen waters plunging over the steep fall. The worn steps feel slippery beneath our feet and the muffled roar issuing from the tunnel's mouth sounds as if some gigantic throat is ingurgitating the swirling waters.

We feel the thump-thump-thump of our heart as those behind urge a move forward. We have an almost overwhelming impulse to turn and push our way back to the top of the steps; but the shame this could impose compels a moving downwards with a nervous placing of each foot on each step. We cling for support to the flimsy iron rails edging the steps whilst at the same time trying desperately to avoid looking at the awful sight below. Our feet move from step to step in what seems a never-ending descent into a fearful, waking nightmare. And all around: the roar of water.

Suddenly we find ourselves at the bottom of the steps, not knowing how we got there. The relief bursts from a stifled breath in a tremulous shout. We glance quickly at the surrounding faces - hoping nobody realised just how terrified we were.

Impulsively we turn and run the length of Verdon Street and away from the Dark Arch - all of us laughing at an ordeal ended...

This event lived powerfully in my memory, so much so that during the course of this writing I drew the sketch that you'll find on the next page - this to give "life" to the incident. The added verse arose from the same impulse, with the voice and simplicity of the child whose experience the event was; and, because of this, the result came in the form of an emotional expression rather than an exact portrayal.

Nevertheless, I believe the sketch captures the "feelings" of the event in a way that a less spontaneous representation might be unable to depict.

Shortly after completing the sketch, I needed to make a quick visit to Manchester. Having a few hours to spare and being near where the ordeal took place, I decided to see again the setting that lingered so powerfully in my mind for all these years.

I wanted to see if the place validated the sketch and also the feelings I tried to resurrect.

This suited my purpose: I felt I could "absorb" the scene and return, in my mind, to that long-ago experience without the distractions of people passing by.

I found the steps in the midst of an extensive neglect. All the industry of that long time ago had gone, and the subdued light caused by the thin, high clouds of a late autumn afternoon seemed to accentuate the area's dereliction. The only sound leaving any echo of the past was that of water plunging over the fall.

Nevertheless, I felt if I stood there, alone, at the top of the steps, the intense feelings about the place I experienced all those years ago would soon return.

Yet, although the main features of the scene were essentially the same as those existing at the time of my childhood experience, none of the expected feelings arose. Uppermost in my mind was the unsightliness; and although a special journey had been made to see this place, I felt reluctant even to walk down the steps so central to my recollection - appearing as they did a nuisance to descend and then to inconveniently re-climb.

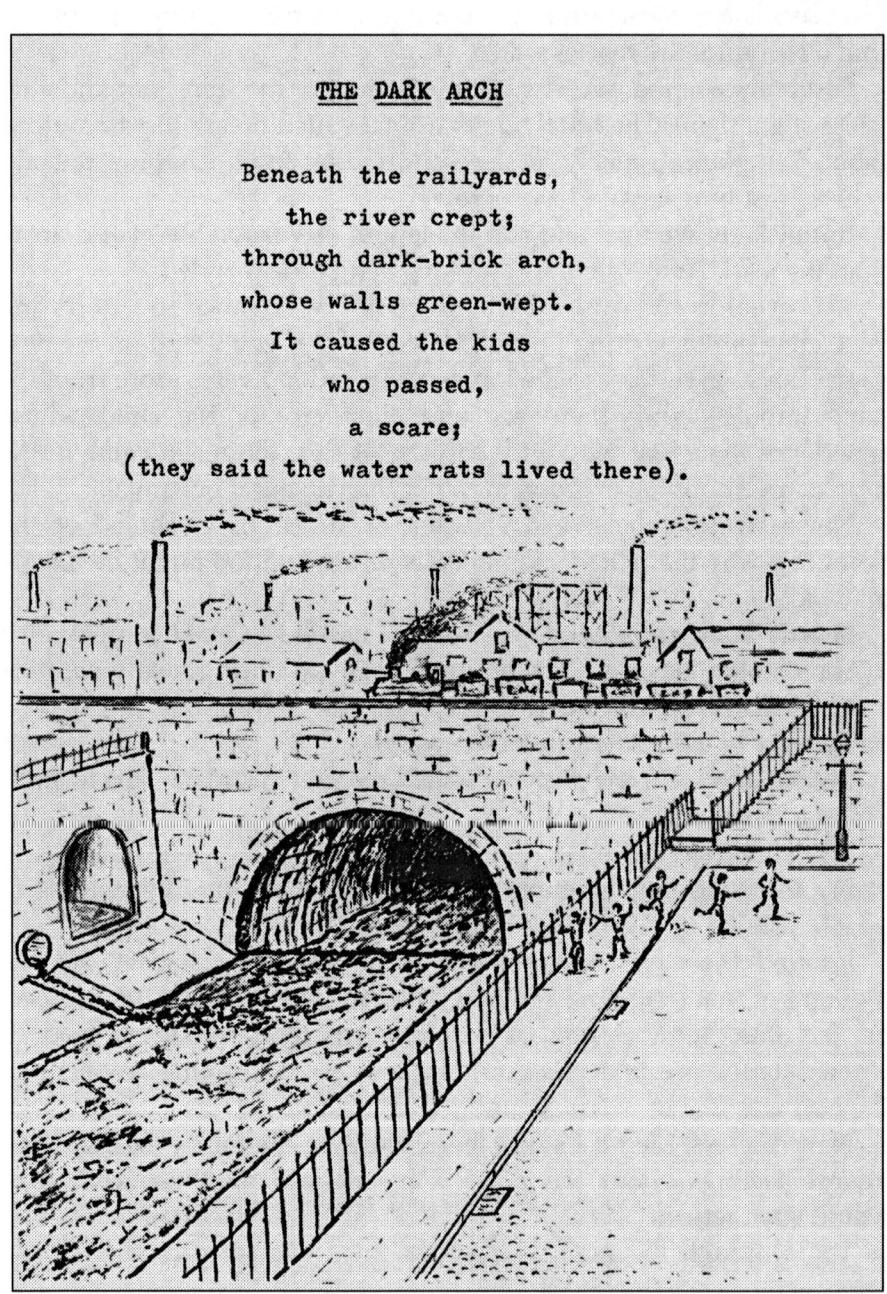

The visit happened to be on the same day of the week as that of the ordeal, and probably because it was a Sunday no-one seemed to be around.

I began to wonder how it was that this setting, existing so powerfully in my memory for so long, had no affect upon me now - so much so that it appeared to declare my memory and its associated feelings had no validity?

But then I realised I was obviously seeing the place through a different set of eyes and a contrary set of feelings to those I had as a child. And it may well be that what was "played-out" during that time had achieved its purpose of eventually destroying the fears and fantasies which arise so readily in childhood. Out of this emotional transmutation comes the "realistic perspective" which, as adults, we pride ourselves on possessing.

From the perspective that growing out of childhood confers, I knew this drab flight of stone steps represented an obstacle whose descending I would do only out of necessity - and not for some "childish" reason. And the tunnel - far from being a terrifying incomprehension - represented an unsightly means of directing the river under the road and the buildings beyond.

It seems our adult mind not only habitually projects this "realism" onto all the things we see (and therefore excludes those childhood fears and excitements along with their emotions) but also expects the world to appear "orderly and understandable" - or, at least, contain that possibility. Only when the world fits in with this way of seeing does it "comfortably make sense" and can be easily accepted.

However, I also knew that the child who'd experienced this place all those years ago didn't see the world in quite that way. The incomprehensible aspects of the world, which "sophisticated" intellectuality wasn't there to "explain", were left for the child's imagination to grasp; and because of this, nearly everything had its potential to awe and excite.

It seems, as we grow out of the capacity to see the world in this special way, it loses much of its wonder. Instead of awe and excitement being all around us - even in the simplest of things and the most improbable of places - we have to search far and wide to find it - and may never find it at all?

The imagination we once had, with its freedom to wander wherever it may, becomes something we must learn to control and direct along "sensible" paths. We must not become too imaginative and allow the latitude imagination might possess to raise fears or fantasies with no real substance.

But as previously suggested, it may well be our childhood-play is to teach the emotional restraints we, as adults, must have. And within these restraints, we no longer want - nor would it be "proper" for us - to splash in puddles; or run excitedly over a vacant piece of land; or even allow ourselves to conjure up fears whose excitements can chase us along the street.

Yet, it seems that part of us wanting to do these things never really dies. Perhaps in this lies the strong attraction of places like the seaside where we can uninhibitedly run and splash. Also fairgrounds and theme-parks that permit us to feel once more the intoxicating mixture of fear and excitement we so readily knew as children: those feelings and emotions we possessed in that exciting, extra-ordinary world in which we once lived, and now and again try to recapture.

In this place, where I could stand and allow all these thoughts to come, I then knew that my memory was "real" and belonged - in truth - to that time; and that all my other memories shared the same "reality". And the simple sketch with its unsophisticated verse echoed the feelings as they once were, in all their "childish" veracity.

In the midst of these thoughts came faint stirrings of that long ago event and of a childhood now lost.

The dereliction that first offended faded from my awareness; and - instead - I felt affection for the drab stone steps with the rickety iron rails; and even for the dirty old Irk whose continuous flow seemed to defy the passage of time...

25
Child's Play Isn't...

~~~~~~~~~~~~~~~~~~~~~~~~~~~~~~~~~~~~

The childhood realm of the nineteen-thirties we've so far observed revealed a world of imaginative invention; where the children of that time used whatever they found around them to create their own amusements.

We saw how various tasks, such as embarking on a shopping errand or fetching coal, were readily turned into adventures; and how the numerous lampposts in the district became the focal points for activities such as the game of Rally-O.

Rope discarded from orange-boxes and obtained from the local greengrocers or throwaway lengths from the nearby Mills or railway yards became skipping ropes or lamppost swings. In the case of the latter, an agile kid tied the rope to the crossbar - normally used to support the maintenance man's ladder - then fashioned the free end of the rope into a loop to suit the swinger's sitting position.

The happy creator of this device propelled themselves around the post until brought to a halt by the resulting winding of the rope; then to reverse this process until being brought to a halt again - each time bantered by the next in line awaiting their turn. This went on and on and on until the rope wore out or the participating kids became exhausted from their efforts. Usually, the rope wore out first. The posts were strong, solid, cast iron constructions well able to withstand the load; and no doubt this is why the adults of the streets seemed not to object.

As these and others activities we've so far seen show: the way children played in the past is vastly different to the way that children play now. In the hope of gaining a deeper insight into the whys and wherefores of this, it might prove worthwhile to probe these questions:

Do the attitudes and beliefs of the period in which play takes place influences the nature of play? What impels its activities? Is it a childish diversion of insufficient importance to warrant attention, or is it a crucial part of a person's development - that needs to be "played out" in whatever way and whatever the period?

Even attempting an answer to these questions implies a formidable task; since play and how it relates to the period of its enactment perplexes whole cadres of psychologists. For instance, an eminent member of that profession, Jean Piaget, once said:

To understand the intricacies of nuclear physics is child's play, compared with understanding child's play.

Nevertheless and despite this caveat, we can, perhaps, claim some entitlement to raise the suggested questions, since most of us began life absorbed in play.

Perhaps a start could be made by considering a statement offered by another eminent person: the poet Wordsworth; and the person who penned that oft-quoted phrase: "The child is father of the man". Or, to avoid the gender bias demanded by our present period: adults are the products of the children they once were.

His statement shouldn't cause too much surprise, because it well accords with much of the thinking emerging in the child development and educational theories arising with great emphasis after 1945 and continuing well into our own time - as we'll see later. And as the learned Psychologist implies: even the most casual glance indicates that play has a purpose all of its own and is far from being the random activity that a first glance may suggest.

This is particularly indicated when a well-intentioned adult tries to coax a child into accepting what they assume the child would like; to then find the carefully selected and probably expensive plaything firmly rejected.

Even more frustrating is when the child discards the expensive offering to then play happily with the "throw-away" carton.

In one of my frustrations, I became tempted to write to a particular manufacturer to suggest that the toy and carton should be sold separately, so that the buyer could discover which mostly appealed to the child - with the option of trying the carton first, of course.

But returning to the serious and practical: this seems to raise a variation on the old adage about leading a horse to water. You can give a child a plaything but no amount of persuasion can make that child accept that item if it seems unsuited to its "need". What this need is, the child - and only the child - can possibly know.

It therefore follows that the purpose of play can only be fulfilled when the child is allowed a large degree of freedom to choose how and with what it plays. If an adult tries to push play in a direction not in accordance with the child's wishes, this, more than likely, will inhibit the playing - and, possibly, making the child sulky and resentful?

I believe the play-world in the period of our visits was largely free from adult impositions and therefore its actions and choices had a great deal of latitude. Most adults of the pre-1939 world (largely unaware of the mentioned eminent psychologist's view about the complexity of play) viewed its activities through an extremely relaxed and even dismissive perspective. They generally saw play as a purposeless whiling away of time that all children do before becoming mature enough to engage in more constructive activities.

Providing their play seemed harmless, it was generally felt that children should be left to select or find their own playthings and utilise these as and when they wished. The concept of "educational" play emerging in the latter half of the twentieth century had not yet arrived on the play-scene and - in the absence of the anxieties this brought about - the unconcerned attitude then existing seemed to allow a spontaneous process to unfold.

Assisting this process was scarcity of money to buy ready-made items. Most children in the neighbourly communities of the type we visited were face with the necessity of inventing and fashioning what they felt they needed - this from whatever materials they could obtain without cost. But even in circumstances where financial restriction didn't apply, no particular views prevailed about correct playthings. As implied: children were generally left to chose or indicate the item or items which most appealed out of the traditional proved-to-be-suitable range.

All the concerns arising in the second half of the century about what came to be known as "gender roles"; "stereotyping"; "societal indoctrination"; "attitude formation"; "self-image construction"; "identity creation" etc., etc., etc., and the part play plays in all of this had not yet emerged. Thus, no special academic, commercial or political interests ready to promote such concepts existed. And if they did exist, they weren't noticed.

Additionally (and mainly arising from the same perspective as the one related to play) an essentially free attitude prevailed in the realm of stories. Debates about what was "right for the child" hardly arose; since the stories available followed the traditional theme children had read or had read to them over many generations. Parents therefore probably reasoned (if reasoning in this respect ever seemed necessary) that since innumerable eagerly attentive children throughout the ages had found these stories satisfying, they must be suitable on that basis alone.

These traditional stories mainly centred on conflict between the good and the bad - which seemed to most people the right and proper theme. This theme largely accorded with long established Judeo-Christian attitudes and moral concepts (or the interpretations thereof) which long held sway. Therefore, their suitability had this additional and authoritative support.

Thus, the traditional stories prevailed: stories in which the good must always triumph over the bad; and - within this - those who did wicked deeds must meet with unfailing "comeuppances". Also, those who did good deeds must always - and unfailingly - be rewarded.

In this setting, the later period's tendency to question, probe and rewrite the long accepted stories - to make them more "acceptable" - never seemed to occur to anyone.

The impulse to rewrite came to my awareness when browsing through various books in order to purchase one for a grandson; and having an attitude firmly entrenched within an age where the traditional stories' inviolate correctness remained unchallenged, it came as a surprise.

In one version, the old theme of 'The House that Jack Built' had departed from the original nonsensical and bouncy play on Jack's whimsical nature. Instead, it commenced with an enthusiastic declaration on the wonders of the countryside; then to conclude with an environmental caution about the violation factories create by being built in its green and pleasant setting.

Having been born in an area surrounded by industry such as we saw in our visits - and whose employment provisions were very much welcomed in an age of unemployment - I wondered if it seemed fitting to suggest to a child that the "problem" resides in factories, per se. It appears to me that the real problem is not "factories" but our apparently insatiable desire for what they produce.

To me, the story seemed to represent a displacement of the essential cause: like blaming food and the providers of food if we find ourselves putting on weight, instead of attending to our own appetites.

Also (because environmental issues have, as implied, a conflict between what we should collectively deny ourselves for the long term good and what we, as individuals, desire for our own immediate satisfaction) the story could raise many "ifs", "buts" and "maybes".

These environmental uncertainties have such complexity that most adults find them difficult to unravel. This more so when they become subjected to rival and changing scientific suppositions, more liable to confuse than enlighten; raising issues that are hardly understood by adults, let alone a child. And as suggested: this is particularly compounded by the fact that factories offer a life-style we'd loathe to be without - as any child would soon realise. Furthermore, when unemployment threatens, we demand as many as possible should be built (anywhere?).

In the wider context of life-style, there's also the fact that the travelling we all love to enjoy is done at enormous and invisible cost to the pure environment we insist must be maintained. For instance: one jet-flight from, say, Manchester Airport to Florida's Disney attractions creates as much pollutants, per passenger, as would each person driving their car for a full year's average mileage - in the biggest of cars. If a suggestion should arise that this and similar flights should be restricted, it seems to me that many people would suffer a certain degree of "restlessness".

Additionally, a certain unhappiness would ensue if it happened to be proposed that a far greater contribution to the reduction of environmental pollution would be made by abandoning the "casual" (or even the total) use of the car. Moreover, if the suggestion also arose that we should all go to our beds when it starts to get dark and get up when sufficient daylight allowed (thereby saving enormous amounts of electricity with its corresponding reduction in pollution) adverse reactions would surely result. Not only would the affected people be "disturbed" by this idea (as sensible as it may seem) but many industries would be more than disturb.

However, back to the story's revision. It obviously intended to raise in the child's mind what many would think was a proper concern about the affects of industry being built in areas we consider unspoilt countryside - which seems a proper concern to create. Nevertheless and as we've seen: it's an issue containing many moral and economic complexities; and these complexities impel responses that some may find less then acceptable.

As an example: one of the present time's response to its concerns about energy use is to construct wind-farms in - by necessity - the most open countryside and on the most prominent and unobstructed places. By this "necessity", we create noise pollution along with scenic pollution in what were once green, pleasant and tranquil areas - and, in certain conditions, disrupt wildlife.

This illustrates the rule of gaining and losing, losing and gaining. It's always a case of assessing, on society's proverbial swings and roundabouts, the fine balance between what we want and the cost of what we want.

However, problems and confusions arise in any period; and at the core of most human problems there usually lurks a moral conflict. In most cases, this involves a reluctance to accept that "painful" aspect of morality called self-restraint. This appears to be especially indicated in the case of the suggested strong individual desire for the goodies factories produce versus collective concern about the damage such desires may generate.

This - in what may seem a roundabout way - brings us back to the implications of child's-play. Perhaps a more lasting method of creating a positive and responsible attitude to the environment or anything else - in any period - may be by way of fostering the child's developing social and moral sense and its capacity for self-control.

Wordsworth's observation about the child being the father of the man - and, by implication, the sense of morality and social concern the man eventually develops - puts childhood experiences at the centre of this issue. His observation, however, appears to suggest that the hoped-for positive development is not easily formulated but must emerge as a spontaneous process, arising from the child's innate and unrestricted impulses.

This again introduces the previously mentioned Jean Piaget's observation about the complexities inherent in child's-play. Nevertheless, and more fitting to the questions first raised, his investigations concerning children's moral development might provide some tentative answers.

Particularly applicable to the play that we previously witnessed - and will again be witnessing - is his term "The Morality of Co-operation". This, in the context of our concern, simply means that the child reaches, or should reach, a stage where he or she sees the rules concerned with acceptable behaviour as an essential means of regulating their social relationships.

As our visits showed: the first "society" in which a child encounters this type of regulating morality, in any meaningful sense, is when it enters a companionable play-world in which adults with the power to impose rules are absent. In this setting, whatever conformities play demands becomes accepted on the basis of a willing consent amongst equals. This acceptance starts with the common-sense realisation that disregarding any rules necessary to the play that a child wishes to enter threatens the continuation of that activity - and, as a consequence, the goodwill of playmates.

The insistences associated with this acceptance arise naturally in companionable play. They usually take the form of: "you mustn't cheat"; "you mustn't be a spoilsport"; "you mustn't be unfair"; "you must stick to the obligations of the game"; "you mustn't try to gain unfair advantages"; "you mustn't complain if the rules go against you"

- and so on. These are the "moralities" without which play couldn't progress in any social sense.

Also, these moralities must have their equivalents in the wider society for that society to be viable; and the more consistently and unambiguously such rules are generally expressed in the child's wider community, the more readily they can be applied by the child in its own activities.

In their efforts towards trying to understand what should be done and what should not be done, the children, in whatever period, have an enormous task bordering on the miraculous, considering the way they mostly succeed.

In a few short years - with no prior knowledge or previous experience - they need to absorb and make sense of a whole culture with its language, customs, institution, values, forms of behaviour, distortions and contradictions. They've no time to be deceived about its real nature, whatever that may be; for this - whatever it may be - they must absorb and become.

As far as the period of our visit is concerned, harmony of rules largely prevailed - with, I believe, play being consequently more relaxed. This harmony had additional support from the felt approval given to the children's self-created play by the adults around them.

Their approval no doubt arose because the rules of play generally centred on behaviour prescribed within the framework of the - then - still very much entrenched Victorian ethos. A forceful aspect of this stressed obligation determined by the needs of society rather than those of the individual. Its values, therefore, supported the attitudes necessary for companionable play to take place. The concept of "Individual Rights" in their own "right", so to speak - without any direct association with individual responsibilities - is a concept that emerged with any degree of recognition soon after the 1939-45 war, when it then began to expand into a "universal principle".

Before that time, the idea of unconditional rights would've been almost incomprehensible. Therefore, the primacy of obligation over and above individual inclinations allowed the children of that time to expect that any playmate should strictly conform to the rules of their games. They thereby tended to display immediate intolerance towards anyone deviating from these rules and - if necessary - were supported by adults in this attitude. Participation in a game therefore became dependent on the player recognising their obligations to maintain and uphold the rules, and thereby the orderliness of the game. The "right" to participate was conditional on the acceptance of these obligations and the responsibilities they demanded.

As previously suggested, our later period developed a substantial shift of perspective: seeing self-expression as the desirable, if not the chief, regulator of behaviour. But since in self-expression what is suitable behaviour is - by definition - that which the self desires, and is therefore for the self to judge, children of our later age absorbed the logical consequences of this. They become subjected to one of its main anxieties: that of avoiding being "judged" as "judgmental".

Arising from this came a desire to perceive deviations from rules as requiring a non-judgemental acceptance rather than rejection and condemnation. This, reflected in play, may make that activity become less rule-centred and more casual than it was in the past. And - perhaps - this may explain why the later period's play appears to lack the impulse to generate highly structured rules and rhymes of the type we've seen and will see again in our visits.

However, returning to the question of being non-judgmental: I found its implications emerging in another revised tale - again found during my search. This time, concerning Grimm's 'Hansel and Gretel'.

The new version no longer had the "Wicked Witch" banished in no uncertain terms for the evil she intended towards the children. Instead, the Witch, after exhibiting her frightening intentions, then "promised to be good". Thereafter, the children, to quote from the story:

...loved living with her in her delicious house... where she'd never try to eat them again.

From that previously mentioned perspective formed within an age believing the old stories required no corrections, I found myself out of tune with this version - as in the case of the other revision. This - rightly or wrongly - wasn't because of any fundamental disagreement with the environmental message implied by Jack's behaviour, or the kindly forgiving contained in the new Hansel and Gretel. It was because both departed from what the period forming my attitudes led me to believe should be the implicit intention of most children's stories. Which is: to present a world containing simple certainties with clearly presented and readily understood portrayals of the "harmful" and "fearful" - whose embodiment will be, in the course of the story, unfailingly and unambiguously banished.

By this, the child - in what must, at times, seem a frighteningly confusing world - can feel the reassurance that, when evil is cast out, "all will be well in the end" and people can live "happily ever after".

In departing from this principle, the revised Hansel and Gretel seemed to slide into all sorts of confusions. This no doubt arising from our later period's attempt to find behavioural frameworks that weren't considered necessary in previous times.

For example: the Witch had enticed the children to enter her house by trickery. Also, Gretel, by trickery, imprisoned the Witch to thereby extract the "promise to be good". If, as the story implied, trickery is a "legitimate strategy" - verified by the fact that the heroine also used deception - how would the child know that the Witch was not practising another deception in making her promise, and thereby waiting to do evil all over again?

The adult - with an adult's capacity to readily separate fact from fantasy - can, perhaps, laugh heartily and then dismiss this proposition. However, in the child's mind, stories take on a "reality". They are - for the time of the story - not fantasy but fact.

In the context of this, it seemed to me the old version free from the frightening uncertainty of a reformed Witch far better served the child's need. This need requiring the embodiment of evil to be well and truly eliminated in a way that the child can readily understand as final. This reassuringly affirmed by the triumphant cry: "The Witch is dead", as proclaimed in the old version - which, as a child, I liked, and which, I believe, a child's emerging moral sense demands.

There's nothing strange in this desire for a satisfying ending. If we - for instance - as adults - read a reconstructed version of Dracula in which the final dispatching with the stake was withheld on Dracula's promise "to be good", we would, to say the least, be bemused - or even slightly disturbed.

Furthermore, the revised Hansel and Gretel denies the child the implicit moral message of the old version, which is: only by being wary of evil and eradicating it wherever possible will good triumph. Instead, the child is presented with the subtleties of "reformation" and having faith in this guaranteeing no "recidivism": issues which baffle the minds and even, at times, frightens the whole of our political, moral and legal system, let alone the mind of a child.

I therefore believe what the child asks is reassurance, even if this only applies in the make-believe world that the child likes to believe is - for the time it needs to make-believe - the real world.

At this stage, you may ask where our enquiry is going? The answer is where it must be going in order to ascribe any purpose other than just aimless entertainment to the play we'll soon be witnessing.

In its activities, we'll see that the rules arising in the various games demand that the infantile impulses every child possesses, in the beginning, must give way to socially harmonious and constructive impulses. If the conflict between the self-centred and the self-ceding is not allowed to play itself out in the child's first society of play, an aspect of its failure may be seen in that frightening, infantile, manifestation we now call "Road Rage" and in other types of behaviour indicating the self's loss of control.

As previously implied: it seems an obvious assumption that this conflict between the self-centred and the self-ceding will be more readily resolved if the essential rules of behaviour, in the individual's immediate and supportive community, are consistent and thereby easy to understand. This we'll find to be the case in the community of our proposed visit.

By contrast, our later period offers a multi-channelled, multi-sourced complexity whose "messages" are so numerous as to be almost impossible for them to remain consistent. Out of all this, the still being formed young try (as they must always try) to determine what rules of behaviour are acceptable and elicit most approval. Sometimes they find that even the idea of rules appear to have little significance.

Part of the answer to our original question is, perhaps, implied in the following rule. The real "good" each period should ensure is the enhancement of the individual's capacity to live in society and, by this, sustain the individual's protecting entity: society itself. The real "bad" is that which does the opposite.

Each period is face with the enormous problem of ensuring its neonates learn to be successful members of its collectivity. Or, to use the eminent psychologist's concept: they must learn "the morality of co-operation".

Most societies perceive this as achieved when each of its individuals becomes less self-centred and more community conscious. Therefore, the conditions any period constructs for that crucial process we call "child's play" to play itself out must be judged on that basis.

So the conclusion's crux is: child's-play isn't... It represents a complex process that must be permitted to unfold in its own time and in its own way, in conditions that allows (to paraphrase the previously introduced phrase) "the child to become the effective parent of a socially desirable man or woman".

In the play we'll soon be witnessing, we should be able to detect this processes unfolding spontaneously in its various activities - these unregulated by anything other than the rules generated by the activities themselves and what those engaged in the activities will willingly accept.

The only adult demand we'll notice is one insisting that all activities must be orderly.

With all this in mind, we can start our visit to the play-world of the nineteen-thirties...

26
Swings, Steps, Slides and Skipping Ropes

~~~~~~~~~~~~~~~~~~~~~~~~~~~~~~~~~~~~~~

In our next visit, we'll see activities taking place in the way that the previous narrative suggested. Many of these will arise from a variety of possibilities, some discovered or invented by the children themselves, and where the games we see being played are those that the participants feel most inclined to play - in whatever way it seems, to them, appropriate. Also, we'll see how and why these activities are a product of their time.

In all the activities, boys and girls play together or go their own way, as and when they feel inclined to do so. Swinging games - such as the one around the lamppost - are shared by both sexes. Games, such as "rag-ball", which we'll witness later, are mainly played by boys.

Skipping activities are mostly - but not exclusively - the province of the girls. This activity we'll see performed in the same way our previous visit showed: in groups, using a length of rope sufficient to reach across the street from pavement to pavement, with enough slack to allow two players to swing the rope.

So let's return to the nineteen-thirties, to see it all in action.

That skipping game, for instance, now being played near the bruw, in the same place we saw a similar activity during our previous walk. Again, it's the type much favoured by the younger kids because of its simplicity and the vigorous beat of its rhyme. This version attracts younger sentiments because of the "elevated" message implicit in its chant?

Listen to the words:

> *ONE-two-three-four-five-six-seven*
> *All good children go to Heaven.*
> *Five-six-seven-eight*
> *See them skipping through the gate.*
> *Eight-nine-ten-eleven*
> *Who is next to go to HEAVEN!*

You'll soon notice it's played under the same rules as the game we witnessed in our previous visit. Those waiting their turn to skip form a queue whilst those swinging the rope chant the rhyme and swing the rope to the rhyme's beat. The first in line waits until the rope allows a dash into its arc, on the word "ONE", then to dash out on the word "HEAVEN" - both these words chanted with emphasis to act as a prompt for entering and leaving.

Again, as in that previous game, the dashing in and out of the rope must be done without interrupting its swing. Then the next in line must enter the rope's arc with the minimum of hesitation whilst the one just completing the skip joins the end of the queue - and so on and so on and so on - until the kids get tired of playing the game. But as you can readily see: they don't tire easily.

In all such skipping games, the main skill is judging when to dash into the swing of the rope, complete the skip and then dash out of its swing to the other side. To disturb the swing in either instances or during skipping means taking a turn on the rope or dropping out of the game. The version we're seeing incurs similar penalty - in this case, for an unsuccessful attempt to get through "heaven's gate". Even a brief glance shows that the game demands a great deal of co-operation between all involved; this along with strict obedience to its rules and a proper acceptance of "turns".

A more elaborate variation is played under essentially the same rules as the one we're seeing but invariably attracts more boys - this no doubt due to its dramatic rhyme; which goes:

> *PADDY on the railway*
> *Picking up stones.*
> *Along came an Engine*
> *And broke Paddy's bones.*
> *Oh said Paddy,*
> *That's not fair!*
> *Oh said the Engine,*
> *I don't CARE!*

Its rhyme may've originated from the time when large gangs of Irish navvies built Britain's railways - thus the choice of the name "Paddy"? It may also be a social comment on the fact that compensation was rarely, if ever, forthcoming for the many injuries that occurred in such highly dangerous conditions - as implied by the words "I don't care". However, this is speculation on my part.

Yet even in the time we're now visiting, the same circumstances applied. This came to my awareness at an early age, when my Uncle Joe (my mother's brother) suffered a fatal accident whilst working on a building site. Also, when a close friend of his from just across the street - named Charlie - died not long afterwards, after falling into a vat of near-boiling quenching oil at a local steelworks.

No compensation was, it seems, forthcoming in either case although the "fault" appeared to lie with inadequate safety measures. A great deal of cash and access to a lawyer or solicitor would've been required to pursue such claims. Most people in their situation had neither.

Although I felt the loss of a favourite uncle (who made me many a toy and let me listen to his gramophone) I particularly remember the event of my uncle's friend. He'd been brought home soon after the accident, where he survived for many days despite his horrific burns. The nature of the injuries and his prolonged suffering caused great distress to family and neighbourhood.

As previously inferred: treatment in hospital depended on the ability to meet the cost. Since the finance wasn't available he had to be treated at home by a local doctor - which also had its cost but one far less than the hospital treatment that he should've had if circumstances had allowed.

A further comment: life has many twists and turns. My Uncle Joe worked at the Ford Motor Company - then located in Manchester, at Trafford Park. The company decided to transfer its activity to Dagenham, in the South, probably because the area of the proposed relocation happened to be where the newer industries were developing - whereas, in the North, industry seemed to be in decline.

My uncle rejected the Company's relocation offer; this because of his reluctance to leave his friends and especially the girl he happened to be "courting" (to use a term which our later period may find archaic, and therefore meaningless). What would've happened if he'd made the move and thereby avoided the circumstances bringing about his end? How many years above those short twenty-five would he have had?

But let's return to happier considerations.

As you've no doubt noticed: all the games are extremely active, played out of doors and mainly arising from a "no money to spend so amuse yourself" situation. None of the indoor and isolating entertainment the children of later times find readily available have yet intruded to change this mode. So, for nearly all of the summer and a good part of the winter, it's "out playing".

Another thing you may've notice is the lament, "I'm bored", never seems to enters the kid's vocabulary. Such is the range of ongoing activities open to any willing participant that it leaves no scope for even a brief spell of idleness. Even a short interruption caused by a shower elicits a restless impatience. But even in this, the kids turn impatience into play. If irresponsible and intrusive weather curtails enjoyment, the younger children retreat to the shelter offered by the threshold of their open doorway, to chant:

Rain, rain, go away! Come back another day!

This phrase - derived from an old nursery rhyme and embodied in a popular song of the time - being repeated over and over again until the shower ceases. On one such day, the whole length of the street on both sides echoed with this incantation; even more so because the many rhyme-using games the children habitually play creates a strong sense of unison - giving their chants a "penetrating" effect.

The adults of the street displayed an amazing tolerance for this behaviour, since none complained. Maybe they hoped the "primitive magic" would soon work, allowing those making the chant to leave the shelter of the doorway and return to their rightful occupation of playing in the street. To those households whose threshold happened to be used for shelter, this would be a far better outcome than the constant chant from their immediate doorway.

In this particular instance - and much to the relief of the households involved - the "magic" worked and the sun shone strong and bright again. This proof of the chant's potency encouraged the use of its incantation whenever it seemed necessary.

Anyway, all is sunshine at the moment, so let's continue our walk. Again you'll notice the most conspicuous feature in all these activities is the utilisation of materials readily available - at no cost. You'll see discarded pieces of rope; lengths of wood; bundles of rags; slates; tiles; empty boot-polish tins; an old brick or two; stubs of chalk, or whatever the kids find applicable to their play. Each item selected, fashioned and used according to the game's requirements.

Also, because the street "belongs" to all the kids, and a wide range of talent is required to invent games and to fashion the materials employed, virtually all the activities develop as a group involvement. Nevertheless, when, for whatever reason, a large group is unavailable, games to suit a few players can be called upon. These activities are simple in their rules and material requirements; and, because of this, can quickly terminated if more kids appear on the scene. If they do, activities involving all those arriving will soon occur.

These transient games can be just as absorbing as the more extensive activities, and - like them - needs the inevitable setting of the street. Two such games (one called "Ciggies" and the other "Merricks") we might see in action during our walk. But in case we don't, here's how they're played.

The game, Ciggies, makes use of cigarette cards - as the name suggests. Every packet of fags contain a thin card the same size as the packet; and since smoking amongst male adults is a usual habit, cards are always forthcoming from family members or from visiting friends.

Most cards have an interesting topic or event presented as a picture on one side and some interesting information about the topic on its reverse. They usually take the form of a series for collecting, based on categories such as 'Ships of the British Navy'; 'Uniforms of the British Regiments'; 'Flags and Symbols of the World'; 'Railway Locomotives'; 'Great Explorers'; 'Animals'; 'Aircraft'; 'Great Inventors' - and so on.

The more expensive cigarettes offer very elaborate cards made of stiff cloth containing a picture woven in silk - unsuitable for the game mentioned but highly attractive for collecting.

I managed to obtain a set of the colourful "Flags and Symbols of the World", but lost interest in the collection when I succumbed to other attractions. Yet I wish I had that set now - they'd be worth a bob (a shilling) or two - as a saying of the time we're visiting would have it.

But away with such useless regret! Let's continue the game of Ciggies. This requires at least two boys, both with an ample supply of the plain type of cards. (The girls seem not to bother with this game or even the cards involved - probably because smoking happened to be mostly a male habit and the cards therefore reflected male interests.)

The game requires a length of wall to restrict the cards to a manageable space and a section of pavement. Each player stands a determined distance away from the wall - usually at the pavement's curb. They then, in turn, place a card on their open hand and flick it towards the base of the wall with the middle-finger of the other hand. The moment a card flicked by a player happens to cover one lying on the pavement by at least two thirds of its surface, that player can then claim all the others previously thrown. This clears the pitch and the throw starts all over again - if both players still hold cards, that is.

It's a popular game because it allows increases in a player's stock and enables swaps of any duplication with other card-holders, thereby offering the opportunity to acquire a full set of a particular series.

The other game - Merricks - is one probably known to most people as "Marbles". I've no idea why we called marbles merricks? Merrick may've been the name of the manufacturer? However, the rules of this game are as simple as Ciggies. To start the game, you draw a circle on a part of the pavement that you know will be free from interruption.

One of the players places a merrick on a marked spot at the centre of the circle and the other tries to knock it out of the circle with their merrick.

They have to do this by resting the merrick in the crook of their forefinger, with their supporting thumb behind it. They then rest the knuckle of the forefinger on the ground at the edge of the circle and flick the thumb so that the merrick shoots at the one in the centre.

If you knock it out of the circle, you win it. If you fail with three goes, the other player has a go at one of your merricks. The game continues until both players are fed up or until one of the players becomes more than fed up - having lost all his merricks (marbles?).

There are many transient games of this sort involving variations too numerous to relate; so let's take a look at other activities not related to losing your marbles - but, perhaps, causing the greater discomfort of losing a reputation for possessing a "daring spirit".

Some of these make use of the numerous flights of steps in and around the district: one being a steep climb known as Barney's Steps, which you'll find located on the Collyhurst Road side of the high bridge spanning the Manchester, Whitefield and Radcliffe railway lines. These steps lead up to the top of this bridge and provide access to a large and derelict area found on its far side - an area known to our locality by the same word given to the steps: i.e. Barney's.

But before we go to see if the steps are now being used for any of the suggested daring activities, here's a bit of relevant history.

I came across a map (the one dated 1922 and offered in a previous narrative) showing three extensive brickworks covering the derelict area we know as Barney's. The largest of these had the name of Baronhill Brickworks; and, possibly, the name Barney's may've been a corruption of Baronhill? However, this is speculation on my part.

All three sites must've been active in the year of the map's production; but by the time of my first awareness of the area, the clay had become exhausted to leave the brickworks and their surrounds completely abandoned - and, to the kids, all the more exciting.

Anyway, back to the main point - with a bit more local history thrown in.

Barney's is reached from Heelis Street by way of the Fount's path then by turning right to follow Collyhurst Road to where you'll find the Municipal dry refuse tip a few hundred yards or so on your right. This feature, known locally as "The Tip", is a massive depositing of waste and rubbish (what our present period calls a "land-fill"). It extends from Sand Street, which you'd find on the far side of the tip from Collyhurst Road, at a level considerably higher than that road. From there, the tip reaches a front approaching within a hundred yards or so from the road's pavement.

The continual advance of the tip's face forms a steep slope of loose earth, bricks and various intermingling of rubbish rising to thirty feet or so above the level of the road. Its top, level with Sand Street, is compacted by the trucks and horse-drawn carts arriving from time to time to reach the tip's face to then dump their various loads. The continual compacting caused by these vehicles resulted in the formation of an extensive plateau offering scope for a "daring activity" - to be mentioned later.

On the right-hand side of this tip - as seen when facing its front from Collyhurst Road - is Vauxhall Street. This runs at a right angle to the road and limits the tip's advance along that side.

The land the tip progressively covers was once the site of an extensive and spectacular pleasure garden - known as Vauxhall Gardens. Its area centred on a natural, picturesque dell sloping down to the bank of the then pure (or, perhaps, reasonably pure?) River Irk. This place of pleasant leisure existed in all its glory up to the time of the eighteen-seventies - three or four decades before the final humiliation the tip imposed.

No doubt the advance of factories, mills and dye-works along the banks of the river reduced the dell's attractiveness as a place of verdant enjoyment. It then became a sand quarry to supply the iron foundries moving into its area. When exhausting its use in this respect, it became a convenient place for dumping some of the town's unwanted rubbish. Convenient for the Municipal Administrators, that is, but not for those living nearby.

The original garden obviously gave its name to Vauxhall Street - a street finally consisting of the tip's high mound on one side and the long, dark-brick front of a dye works on the other. The name Vauxhall therefore became the last echo of a once-upon-a-time area of lush lawns, tree-lined paths, fountains and flowerbeds.

Sand Street - a later construction at the top end of the fast disappearing dell - no doubt derived its name from the final digging out of the metal-moulding sand from the heart of the dying gardens. In all probability, its four adjacent streets - Zinc, Copper, Brass and Bronze - derived their name from the same association.

But in the spirit of the nothing-must-be-wasted attitude existing in the time of our visit, the tip became a source of supplementary - or the only - income for the area's unemployed; subjecting each dumped load to an avid combing for scraps of metal or any other reclaimables. It became commonplace to see a gathering of men and boys waiting at the top of the tip for the next dumping; then their scrambling to rake through the pile; even before the rubbish tumbling down the steep slope in a cloud of dust had hardly come to rest.

In the hygiene conscious age from whence we came, many would view the tip's environment and its activities with horror. But even in our enlightened times, it's now recognised that excess hygiene could carry a "cost" and those subjected to its extremes may be unable to develop early resistance against allergies and infections. So, it may've been advantageous for comparatively healthy folk to be exposed to a "bit of dirt" now and again, so to speak. Therefore, the age we're visiting, with its apparent lack of thought, may've done certain things unwittingly right. However, there's a limit to everything and the balance between any extremes (in this case: excess of hygiene and excess of its opposite) is always a problem in whatever period.

Returning to the previously mentioned daring activities: with the remorseless advance of the tip, some of the long buried waste combusts now and again in places deep below the surface of its plateau. Walking across these "smoking hot spots" offers one of the dares. Because it proves too discomforting at times, it represents an activity we kids don't seek very often - unless challenged. So let's go where we intended to go in the first place: the mentioned steps leading to the top of the bridge giving access to Barney's. And then we can have a look at the wide-open space beyond.

These steps are little way past the tip and on the opposite side of Collyhurst Road, and are accessed by a narrow iron-bridge spanning the River Irk. On the other side of this bridge you'll see a short length of cinder path rising on a steep slope to the foot of the steps. Bordering the left-hand side of this path is a fence made of heavy wooden railway-sleepers. The path's other side has a narrow rectangular strip of vacant land lying between it and a Paper Mill that extends from the bank of the Irk to the base of the railway embankment. The bridge - comprising four smoke blackened brick archways - surmounts the embankment's high mound.

The steps worn by innumerable feet and leading to the top of this bridge rise steeply from the cinder path to a short level stretch interposed halfway up its climb. This gives some respite when negotiating the steps' steepness. The climb then continues until reaching the pathway forming the top of the bridge. My sister, Nellie, counted the steps whilst on her way to work and made a total of seventy-seven. Thereafter, she always referred to them as "the seventy-seven step".

The pathway she walked on completing this dedicated counting is entirely pedestrian - probably constructed to allow the many workers access to the brickworks that once gave them employment. No doubt these workers produced the millions upon millions of bricks needed to build the many thousands upon thousands of houses forming the vast labyrinth of streets in the area we're visiting.

Another feature of the bridge you might find interesting - in the context of daring play - is its massive buttress sloping down from just below the right-hand parapet as you reached the top of the steps. This provides a dare as compulsive to enact as similar challenges would be for all kids in their own particular time and place. It involves a climb over the wall then a scramble down the steep, stone-clad slope the buttress forms and then to climb back again to its top, and finally over the wall onto the pathway. Completion of this act affirms, to the watching kids and to those participating in the same dare, the fearless and adventurous nature possessed by the climber. The agility of those involved is sufficient to ensure no harm results - except, perhaps, for the occasional bruised knee or torn trousers.

Let's now cross the bridge to see Barney's open spaces. Here you'll find a paradise of almost unlimited possibilities for play. A place of steep slope formed by abandoned clay diggings; tumbled down brick buildings; long, arched tunnels of old kilns; discarded iron wagons once used to transport clay from diggings to brickwork; wagon lines supported by timber trestles running down long inclines. And here and there, amongst the many excavations, you'll find ponds filling their hollows. Some of these - over the years and by means, mysterious - became populated by frogs and stickleback fish.

To kids brought up in an enclave of brick, slate and cobblestone - where the only other life is the ubiquitous pigeon, sparrow, cat and dog and the less interesting human adult - to be able to explore this rare, other world of life, existing accidentally but in its own right, offered a constant source of wonderment.

And always, we have the sailing of boats: boats home-made or fashioned there and then from whatever material lay at hand. Boats produced by a wide variety of skills ranging from those possessed by the kids themselves or by the adults of the family - usually the dads or elder brothers. Boats ranging from simple constructions made from bottle-corks joined together with matchsticks - to form a raft fitted with a makeshift sail of cardboard - up to skilful attempts at carved wooden hulls with lengths of dowel-rod for masts. The more elaborate constructions come bedecked with cross-riggings and cloth sails; and great excitements lay in seeing if each home-made attempt floated successfully on its first launch.

If, for a little while, all the excitements offered by Barney's lose their attraction, there's always the other great climb of steps at the top end of Vauxhall Street. These are known as the "Fifty-three Steps" (someone else assiduously counted these - not my sister) or called the "Umpteen Steps" by those unaware the count had been made - or didn't care and preferred the pre-count name. These steps possess a long and continuous tubular iron rail supported by iron posts set down their middle, with the climb eased in places by a wider step where the rail becomes level for a short distance. The rail and the easing of the slope offer - as in the case of Barney's steps - a respite for those having to make the long, steep climb up to Sands Street.

If you happened to be there when the steps are being used for play-purpose you'll see the kids of the district - with the seemingly boundless and inexhaustible energy childhood bestows - need no such rest or assistance. They dash up the steps time and time again, to slide down the series of rails whose metal gleams bright from polishing by the trousers and skirts of multitudes of kids whom, over the years, had taken the long, exhilarating series of slides to the bottom of the steps.

But if climbing these steps also loses its interest, for a while, we can return to Heelis Street where the games available are so numerous we can always select one to suit our mood. We can play the game of "Rag-ball"; where the ball is made from a bundle of rags tied together with string, and used either as a football or a throw-ball - which, besides overcoming the lack of cash for the proper item, also has the advantage of being permitted for playing in the street. Its lack of bounce makes it less liable to get out of control and damage windows.

Yet even in this setting of tightly packed houses you'll notice the kids are generally left to be as boisterous as their games demand. However, they can be severely checked by the adults of the street if any play becomes unruly. This "rule" is well understood and its transgression avoided, so its sanction is rarely applied.

One game I should mention which the kids are very much inclined to play - but dared not play in the streets without bringing upon their heads the sanctions mentioned - is one called "Peggy" (some call it "Piggy"). This, we reserve for the wide-open spaces such as Barney's.

The game makes use of two pieces of wood, usually obtained from a discarded broom handle rescued from its more likely role as fuel for the domestic fire. From this we cut a length of about five or six inches, which we then sharpen to a point at one end. The remaining, much longer, length is employed as a bat - held and used like a baseball bat. The short peg is placed on a hard surface - a brick or suitably raised base - and its pointed end struck sharply with the end of the bat in order for it to fly up in the air, so that it can be immediately hit again with the bat.

The main skill of the game is in being able to strike the resting peg with one blow to raise it sufficiently for the second hit. This can be difficult, but three tries are allowed. The peg is then propelled with the successful hit to or beyond a set distance indicated by a marker - usually a brick standing on its end or a stick stuck in the ground. If the batter succeeds in their effort, they're allowed to continue batting; but if the peg fails to reach the marker, the other players chase for its retrieval. The retriever takes over the batting - all players "straining at the leash" just before each hit for the opportunity to do just that.

Since batting is the most exciting part of the game, much competition ensues. The batter therefore tries to maintain this role by hitting the peg for as many hits as possible; propelling the peg to or beyond the marker whose position is set by the practicality of reaching it's distance. During the game, this distance can be extended if it proves too easy for one of the players.

This readjustment may cause many disputes because of it making the playing more difficult for the less skilled; but in the interest of getting on with the game, disputes are quickly resolved - sometimes by a system of agreed handicaps suited to the various abilities. The winner then becomes the one who scores the highest number of hits beyond the marker. The game ends by common consent - usually when someone is the indisputable winner.

However, let's now drift back to the street to see what games are taking place. There's one called "Ticky-hit" being played halfway along its cobbles where an area has recently been marked out for its playing. Those two lines drawn across the cobbles and about twelve feet apart is the space containing its activity.

One player has been nominated "Ticky" whose role is to chase and touch any one of the participating kids - as he's attempting to do now.

But we've missed the nomination process that took place at the beginning of the game. It's usually done by a mode of selecting you probably know. However, the one used in our district goes like this:

Eenie, Meenie, Minie, Moe.

Put the baby on the poe.
When it skrikes, let it go.
Eenie, Meenie, Minie, Moe.

An explanation: no doubt you know the word "poe" is slang for chamber-pot, so that part of the rhyme always causes the kids a giggle. However, the word particularly relevant to all the games is "skrike". In our district, this means "crying in a complaining manner". It's a word carrying a powerful stigma. Nobody likes being called a "Skriker" and this inhibits the behaviour implied by that word - thus assisting the harmonious playing of our games.

Getting back to the business of selecting: this requires the person chanting the rhyme to touch each members of the group, including themselves, consecutively upon each word. The one touched on the last word is the one nominated (in this case as Ticky) who then has to chase all the other players. Those chased have to stay within the chalked area and avoid being touched - i.e. ticked. The one caught by being ticked, or who inadvertently leaves the marked area in trying to avoid being ticked, then becomes Ticky.

Although simple in its rules, this game nevertheless provides much fun. All children find great excitement in being chased and the weaving and dodging to avoid being ticked produces constant fits of laughter - as you can readily see.

Another favourite game similar to Ticky is called "Statues". This again requires a nominee, in this case to be "Puller". The game commences with the remaining players - all extending an arm - forming a line against one chalked along the cobbles. The nominated Puller then vigorously and unexpectedly jerks a player out of line by their extended arm. The Puller then shouts: "Statue"; upon which the one pulled has to freeze in whatever position they happened to be at the time of the shout. They may be hopping on one leg or bent over in some uncomfortable contortion, but they must hold that position - without even a wobble.

The Puller continues jolting his victims out of the line until one of the "statues" fails to make the pose or wobbles whilst maintaining a pose - as one eventually will - upon which the failed poser or wobbler then becomes the Puller and the line reforms. The Puller's skill is in making unexpected pulls with enough vigour to create the maximum imbalance for the one so pulled and in shouting "statue" at the most inopportune moment for the "victim". This game demands a great deal of individual control in holding a balance for what could be many minutes, however awkward the pose, and the agility possessed by most children results in some bizarre and comic postures.

To watch eight or so kids playing the game can be quite amusing - so much so that adults in the street sometimes come to their doorways for the entertainment of watching the antics taking place. In fact, a player will wobble just because of the giggling brought about by seeing the contortions of others in the game.

Whatever the cause of the wobble, it's a wobble; and as we've seen: all rules of whatever games are strictly imposed and carry the mandatory penalty of being excluded from play if not obeyed. But even worse: also having the shame of being thought a spoilsport; or worse than that: being called a skriker; or even worse than that: being called a cheat. Therefore, each player is mindful of the game's rules and especially of that final rule, which demands being mindful of every rule. Thus, within this mindfulness, most games appear orderly - even allowing for disputes bound to occur amongst vigorous kids.

Now that we've seen how Statues is played, let's look at another game in action. There's a group living in Buckley Street now enacting one we've not yet seen. They're gathered opposite the entrance to Heelis Street and near the lamppost on the far side of the cobbles. Three of the lads are standing before the group of five sat on the pavement's kerb, just to the left of the lamppost. The three standing are performing all sorts of movements and stances.

You'll probably find it difficult to tell what these actions are supposed to signify from our position halfway along Heelis Street. Rather than moving closer to the game, and thereby appearing intrusive, I'll offer my interpretation.

The game they're playing is called "Three Labourers". One of the lads has taken on the role of Gaffer - having been selected for that role by the method previously described. He's the one standing to the right of lamppost and near those sitting on the kerb watching the action. Those performing what looks like weird contortions in front of the watchers are the three Labourers. On selection, the three remove themselves a little way from the others to decide what "work" they'll perform. Having decided, they appoint one of the three to act as a representative who approaches the Gaffer, saying:

> "We are three Labourers out of work.
> Please can you oblige us."
> The Gaffer asks: "What doing?"
> The spokesman replies: "Anything!"

The Gaffer says: "Show your skills!"

Immediately, the three Labourers mime their task.

At this moment, they're performing actions as if they're building a brick wall - or so it seems from where we're standing. One of the Labourers appears as if he's laying bricks, another mixing mortar, and the last going backwards and forwards from the invisible wall to an invisible pile of bricks - pushing, filling and unloading an invisible barrow he's pretending to use.

The purpose of the game is for any one of the observers to guess what the three Labourers are doing - individually and co-operatively. The successful guesser can then take on the role of Gaffer and nominate three others to act as Labourers - or, alternatively, select two others to act out a task along with himself and leave the existing Gaffer in that role; or even nominate another Gaffer. Correct guessing allows lots of options; and if the successful one selects the role of Gaffer, this confers the final word in any dispute.

A comment: you may've guessed the game arises from the prevailing social circumstances. Job seeking and demonstrating ability for whatever happens to be offered is something the kids would know from talk they'd often hear amongst the adults around them. The game is based on one generally known as 'Charade' - as you've probably guessed.

Anyway, in addition to the "fun"; the "acting-out"; the "daring"; and all the other games we've seen, there's lots of ball-games based on snappy rhymes - demanding much skill of hand and eye. A favourite amongst the older girls is one using a nursery rhyme, called "Cobbler", but modified to give a sharper beat:

> *Cobbler, Cobbler, mend my shoe,*
> *Have it done by half-past-two.*
> *If you stitch the loose sole down,*
> *Then I'll give you half-a-crown.*

This game requires a blank wall and two tennis balls.

As it happens, it's now being played at the bruw end of Heelis Street, near the lamppost, where there's the useful length of blank wall. All three girls gathered there are involved. There's two watching and one active. The active girl is holding two tennis balls, one in each hand, and throwing these continually and consecutively at the wall - catching each one on its rebound and throwing it immediately back at the wall. The thrower is singing the rhyme whilst throwing the balls. If she drops any of the balls or her throw isn't kept synchronised with the rhyme, then a waiting player, in their turn, takes over. The aim is to do as many uninterrupted repetitions of the rhyme as possible.

Some players keep the two balls bouncing rapidly and consecutively off the wall for an amazing length of time, to a point where those waiting for a mistake to happen become impatient. Because of this, the more highly skilled girls who happen to be lucky enough to own the necessary tennis balls tend to play the game by themselves; sometimes with an admiring group carefully watching - wishing to observe and possibly emulate the player's skill.

However, a much more demanding variation of this game, played by the really skilled, is one employing the rhyme:

> *Nebuchanezzer, King of the Jews,*
> *Bought his wife a pair of shoes,*
> *When the shoes began to wear,*
> *Nebuchanezzer began to SWEAR!*

A comment: perhaps this rhyme would cause difficulties in the more "sensitive" period from whence we came; but to the kids we're observing, the meaning of the words are incidental. What matters most is the wonderful rhythm created by the words and especially that marvellously tumbling off the lips and tongue word: Ne-bu-chan-ez-zer. This game is played exactly as the Cobbler game, but with the added challenge of the player quickly twisting around on the emphasised word, SWEAR and then having to catch the last ball thrown; then to repeat the process without pause or hesitation.

Some of the girls develop an ability to do this to the point of astonishment - resulting in competitions to see how many SWEARS can be done before a player finally drops a ball. This becomes a new "record" to be challenged by those with sufficient confidence.

You may've notice the rhymes these ball-games employ are eminently suitable for skipping and are often used for that purpose.

Yet another bounce-ball game requiring a high degree of skill is one called "Alera" - again being played exclusively by the girls. In this, they use only one tennis ball. This is bounced continually on the pavement using the flat of the hand as a bat. The rhyme used during bouncing is:

> *One, two, three, ALERA!*
> *I saw Sister, Clara,*

> *Walking with my auntie, Sarah*
> *One, two, three, ALERA!*
> *I saw Sister, Clara…*

And so on and so on, for as many continuous repetitions of the rhyme that can be completed without error.

I've no idea of the origin or meaning of this rhyme. Speculation suggests the term "Sister Clara" could refer to a Nun. The part of the city we're visiting possesses a number of Catholic schools along with their churches. These hold annual walks of impressive pageantry wherein Nuns and lay-people join together in procession along Rochdale Road - usually on Whit-Sunday. The word "Alera" - whatever it's meant to mean - has an Irish "ring", perhaps giving credence to the suggested origin? (By the way: other denominations also hold walks just as spectacular but on different days.)

But let's get back to the way the game is played. As mentioned, the ball has to be bounced on the beat of each word; then, on the emphasised word "Alera", the player has to cock one leg over the ball on its rebound without interrupting that particular bounce and its subsequent "re-batting". The object of the game is to maintain the bouncing in time to the rhyme without any pause, and to do as many Aleras as possible. If the player hesitates in the rhyme or a bounce fails, another player takes over.

A comment: when this game is being played, you'll see some of the girls unabashedly tuck the hem of their dress into the leg of their knickers, in order to avoid the dangling dress getting in the way of the action necessary to the game. This act of "convenience" produces much amusement on the part of the lads, along with teasing - to the irritation of the girls. But it's a brave lad who takes the teasing beyond what the girls will allow. So, any lads: Beware!

In addition to the various ball and skipping games, the girls play many versions of "Hop-flag" and "Kick-stone". These require chalking a pattern of connecting squares on the pavement - each one being consecutively number, usually up to ten, with a square marked "Start" immediately before square one.

In the Hop-flag version, the player selected to start the game throws a piece of slate or tile or an empty shoe-polish tin from the start-square to land on the number one square. They then hop to that square to pick up the thrown item. The player then hops back to the start-square to repeat this action for the next higher number and then back again to the start - each act continuing until a disqualification occurs.

Disqualification involves actions such as missing the intended square; throwing the tile, slate or tin onto a line; hopping on a line; losing balance; dropping the throw-piece in the process of carrying it back to the start position - or any other action agreed to be faulty. In such cases, the other player takes over. If that player then suffers a disqualification, the first player again takes up the game - starting at the number they'd previously and successfully reached.

The winner is the first player to complete the process to the highest number and reverse the actions back to number one. If it happens there's a group watching the game, another person could challenge the winner or selections made by the "Eenie, Meenie, Minie, Moe" method.

Kick-stone is similar in its rules and way of playing. This again requiring a flat object - usually a flat stone or something easy to slide, such as the much-favoured empty shoe-polish tin. However, this game is more exacting in its demands and requires greater skill than the version just described. Again hopping on one leg, the player has to slide the tin or stone from square to square with one kick of the supporting leg. This is done until reaching the highest number and back again without disqualification - all the actions being under the same rules and carrying the same penalty as Hop-flag. In this game, however, the piece must not be picked up and must be moved to its appropriate place by kicks only.

Another comment: at a certain stage, the lads begin to find most of the girls' games tedious. Perhaps this is because they find it difficult to achieve the high degree of expertise the girls managed to display? Nevertheless, and despite this, I surreptitiously paid much attention to what we lads called "girls games" because of the rich variety of rhymes employed.

Research indicates that girls acquire a more sophisticated use of language earlier than boys - which, perhaps, explains the greater utilisation of rhyme in their play. However, you may've notice that the lads - impelled by their own development and following their own inclinations - appear not to mind this instinctive segregation. In fact, they seem more than happy to go their own way to play what the girls call "silly games" - these involving a great deal of rough and tumble and vigorous physical competition.

However, despite the disdain the girls develop for these "less refined" activities, certain games - although considered exclusively the girls' province - must have the participation of at least one young lad. When this situation arises, the girls always manage to overcome their growing reluctance to associate with the "less refined group".

One such game - which all the masculinity of my young years dreaded - was the one we briefly glimpsed in our first walk down Buckley Street: the one using the rhyme "The Maiden on the Mountain" and called by that name. Participation is particularly feared because of it being played by girls who seemed to have reached what might be called a romantic stage. Whether or not this stage was and is fostered by nature or nurture would be, I suppose, open to many debates in the "gender equality and inclusive" age from whence we came. However, in the time we're visiting, such debates hardly ever occur; since if a particular manifestation seems to arise with each generation it's assumed to be "natural" and therefore indisputable. This also applies to the previously mentioned inclination towards selective companionship each gender appears to display at certain stages.

Nevertheless, whatever the case or cause, the lads became nervously alert to the suggested romanticism, which they warily detect as it emerges. This wariness occurring even more so because the lads seem - whether by nature or nurture - to lack its sensitivities.

However, back to the dreaded game. It's played in the way you saw in a previous visit: requiring a girl to stand at the centre of a ring composed mostly of girls but having to contain at least one boy - but preferably more than one boy. All those in the ring hold hands as they face towards the centre then circle the standing figure, singing:

> *There stands a Maiden,*
> *On a mountain,*
> *Who she is I do not know.*
> *All she wants is gold and silver,*
> *All she wants is a nice young man.*
> *Choose your lover,*
> *Choose your lover,*
> *Choose your lover, Fair Maid!*

On the word, "Maid", the singing and circling stop. The girl at the centre then chooses one of the boys - or the only boy - in the ring to join her at the centre. Those forming the circle are required to express surprise and admiration at the choice - the emotional depth of this depending on the participating girls' favourable or unfavourable view of the unfortunate lad chosen. Then - and as I experienced as a "trapped" victim at the centre of what was, to me, an unnerving circle - the singing and circling starts again, with the verse modified to:

> *There stands a Maiden,*
> *On a mountain,*
> *Who she is I do not know.*
> *Now she has her gold and silver,*
> *Now she has her nice young man.*
> *He's your lover,*
> *He's your lover,*
> *He's your lover, Fair Maid!*

The game then starts all over again from the very beginning with another girl at the centre and another lad, if one is available, chosen. Or the only lad in the game is again commandeered for the enactment.

Oh, the embarrassment of it all! If the word gets around that the game is to be played, the lads - who by then deemed such games "sissy" - vacate the street as quick as their legs can carry them. Within seconds, the street clears of possible candidates. Lingering could result in being bullied, or - if that strategy fails - being finally bribed with a toffee or similar temptations the girls thought might entice participation.

In my "fall", I yielded when my addiction to the offered Sharp's Super Kreem Toffee overcame my fear of humiliation. However, I felt acute embarrassment when I saw the lads of our gang - who'd managed to escape - or those whose strength of character had saved them from succumbing to any bribes - peering around the far corner of the street during the play, with delighted, sadistic, grins on their faces. I never did really understand the object of the game - or possibly did not want to - unless it was to cause discomfort to us captured lads.

It may be the game had a sublime and romantic intent that my lack of sensitivity never allowed me to see. I only knew it took some time to live down my part in its enactment, which resulted in chants of "there stands a maiden on a mountain" whenever the other lads happened to catch sight of me. Any unfortunate victims caught in the act of participating in the game suffered the same, unnerving, torment.

Because attitudes and perceptions are somewhat different in our later period, certain aspects of the game and the rhyme employed needs explanation. For instance: in contrast to our present aversion towards accentuating differences, young lads of the time we're visiting highly value a perceived "macho image" - to use the current term. If this image suffered "damage", the mental discomfort felt from teasing by the other lads for being involved in "girls games" would be acutely felt. This, no doubt, because lads seem to acquire strong gender identifications at a certain stage, which they'd assert with great intensity. As implied, this identification process seemed to pertain to both sexes.

In the time we're visiting, it usually develops as an aversion to each other's activities. Its more direct and vocal expressions you might hear emerging in our visit take this form: girls see boys as "rough and gormless"; boys see girls as "soft and sissy". Thus, this shapes choice of play - and, of course, identities - and thereby determines with whom one plays.

Yet again the question of nature or nurture rears its formidable and contentious head. However, I'm relating how things are in our visit and not affirming it could, should, should not, or might be otherwise.

My belief - for what it's worth - is that this stage has its beginning during nascent puberty, when the formation of firm gender identification seems to become - by nature - an imperative. Humankind is composed of two halves: male and female. When these two halves mature and "come-together", it completes the species. It may be that the period of instinctive separation permits the appropriate identifications to emerge and became firmly established, without distraction? Many so-called primitive tribes seem to be aware of this and insist on a ritualistic separation at the time of puberty.

In all associations, the species is then perpetuated - or so it was in our long evolutionary history - through the firm establishment of "opposite" identifications and the subsequent mutual attraction of these opposites. This was, of course, before our later period's science introduced a possible, impersonal, by-pass process.

However, and despite science's intervention, I believe children are impelled to follow the imperatives that brought them into existence - or so it seems to be the case for most of them. Fortunately, for our ease of mind and the enjoyment of our games, and the formation of our relationships, nobody told us kids - who happily played in the time we're visiting - it should be otherwise.

But returning to that "dreaded experience": one just had to hope someone else would suffer a similar entrapment, thereby diverting attention from your own "disgrace".

I'm glad to say that my disgrace had what could be described as a positive(?) outcome. From its suffering I learnt a valuable lesson which provided for my subsequent "salvation". If weakness of character allows succumbing to temptation and thereby the taking of a bribe, make sure the value of that bribe more than compensates for what you may have to endure as a consequence of its taking. Abiding by this principle, I began to demand an exorbitant price for participating - such as a full bag of Sharp's Super Kreem Toffee, or a penny for the Saturday matinee.

It seems my price became too high for whatever value I contributed to the game. Much to my relief, the girls labelled me as "not worth the bother" and thereby released me from temptation; thus enabling me to join those leering around the corner at our "weaker brethren".

Before moving away from this sad tale of weakness and corruption, you may find a comment relating to a word pertaining to the boy's role could further our understanding of attitudes, sentiments and beliefs prevailing in the time of our visit. Concerning the game in question, the word "lover" is romantically and innocently meant: simply meaning "one who loves". Therefore, the word suggests more of an emotional state rather than a physical expression.

In our later period, its meaning seems to have suffered a substantial shift towards a more overt sexual implication and would probably be less freely used in children's play, if used at all. Its usage must be put in the context of an age wherein an over-lingering kiss shown in a film and lasting more than thirty seconds is considered to be bordering on "explicit sex". By contrast, our later period developed a more "advanced" perspective. Even the film's first kiss can lead, immediately, to the frantic divesting of apparel with hardly any time for a formal introduction; and what happens after that leaves little scope for imagination to exercise its capabilities.

Again, by contrast: in the age we're visiting, it's also considered "not proper" to show a male and female sharing the same bed. Even those portrayed as right and properly married (as it would be thought proper for them to be) have - where a bed scene cannot be avoided by the film's plot - to be shown in single beds. Each person being "decently" covered in buttoned-up-to-the-neck pyjamas for the male and a properly concealing night-dress for his lady wife.

The portrayal of sex in the time we're visiting is always "properly covered up" and questions about what "lay or took place beneath the covers" are virtually left unanswered. Therefore, in the context of our visit, the word, "lover", has its meaning directed by this innocence (or, some might say, naïveté). Whether or not this attitude contributed to or distracted from individual happiness and the proper workings of the society in which it prevailed (compared with our later period's believed liberating effect of a leave-nothing-to-the-imagination treatment of sexuality) I really do not know? This question needs, I believe, extensive analysis by those qualified to decide whether it's even capable of an answer.

Nevertheless, many learned people in our present time opine that a definitive answer is available. It resides in the belief that gaining greater knowledge and a deeper insight into our own nature allows the awareness deemed essential for the development of fulfilled individuals. This belief carries the implication that such individuals will inevitably construct a more satisfying society. The conviction is now implicitly embedded in our education system - particularly concerning those matters that the period of our visit wished to keep "restricted and unmentioned".

Yet as we saw in the visit to the "Dark Arch": what is not known makes demands on the imagination. The imagination may mislead or misdirect; but if its role is constantly being diminished by "extensive revelations" this may stultify its capabilities. If this happens, the viewer needs more and more of the picture in more and more detail.

At the extreme of this process, nothing but the actuality in all its particulars can fully satisfy - if it ever does, in actuality, fully satisfy? This may lead to demands for further embellishments of the actuality in order to diminish the boredom of the "already known".

By contrast, a fully exercised and developed imagination allows a person to "control the picture" that they - themselves - can create, modify or adjust to their own "satisfaction".

When television first came on the scene, it came to those who'd long since relied upon imagination to "fill in the picture" required for many aspects of reading and listening to plays on the wireless. People whose imaginations had thereby been constantly exercised by the demands of a pre-television age often remarked that they preferred radio to television because "the pictures were so much better".

This use of imagination also applied to viewing films that the cinema censors had "adjusted" to suit "proper taste". For instance: in the time we're visiting, the present period's detailed displays of "action" following the previously mentioned first kiss receives a screen fade-out dramatisation - thus leaving unlimited scope for individual imagination to go where it will.

However, our nature appears to have an impulse to follow what seems the easiest and less demanding way. Ready made images require far less effort than imaginative constructions we have to create for ourselves. It's long been recognised that there's a universal law directed towards the conservation of physical energy. It may be the case, therefore, that there's a corresponding individual inclination which demands the conservation of mental energy; this conservation continuing until it begins to result in the dystrophy that the conservation of physical energy eventually produces?

But these are abstract and philosophical issues. More direct and applicable to our present interest is the part imagination plays in the process of play. We saw its essential role in the imaginary worlds many of the games we witnessed demanded. We also saw its constant application in formulating rules that ensured "the morality of co-operation" mentioned in the previous narrative.

In addition, we saw imaginative inventiveness being constantly employed in utilising the bits-and-pieces used in games involving swings, steps, slides and skipping ropes - and all the other excitements.

However, what should be especially noted is that some of the games we saw were played within an innocence that time ordained. This allowed their playing to possess a romantic and imaginative sentimentalism, completely undisturbed by realism's anxieties; thereby allowing such play to be as free and as natural as it could and should possibly be - or so it seems to me.

Let's exercise our imagination. Let's again immerse ourselves in the marvellous experiences offered by the steps; of Barney's; of the lampposts; of the infinite varieties of games we can play in the street or wherever we may find an opportunity to play.

We can play games inspired by what we've seen in the cinema: those endless and always fascinating struggles between "goodies" and "baddies"; in which the goodies always win and everyone fights fair - even the baddies. We can play games arising from times long ago or invent new ones of our own.

Listen! Can you hear the children's voices calling us to play?

They're calling us to build a boat, to sail on Barney's ponds; and, on our way back, to have a slide down Barney's steps.

And afterwards, we'll return to our street where we'll have a swing around the lamppost.

Come on! They're waiting for us....

Let's go to the Burton House Pub,
To find some corks in their yard's entry.
If they're clearing out their yard,
We might find plenty.
We'll join the corks with some matchsticks
And Barney's pond, our ship, we'll sail on.
We'll use some cardboard for a sail -
Just like a galleon.
We'll sail our ship to treasure Isles,
Across a wide and perilous sea.
But we'll not sail away, too far:
We must be back in time for tea...

On Barney's many granite steps -
Divided by the stout iron rail -
Leading to the high-arch bridge
Made so it would long prevail
Against the surge of smoke and steam,
The wear of feet, the rain's hard teem.
The kids from all around the town
Will play the game of up and down.
Up and down -
They laugh and shout -
It never seemed to wear them out.

Swinging round the lamppost,
Faster - for a dare.
Making shadows on the wall,
Big enough to scare.
If there's someone passing,
Don't get in the way.
If you do, they'll tell your dad -
And he'll not let you play.

27
As a Matter of Interest:
Ring and Pretend Games

~~~~~~~~~~~~~~~~~~~~~~~~~~~~~~~

Our last visit allowed us to witness a large variety of games. One of these resembled the type of game generally known as charade and another involved the formation of a ring and the singing of a rhyme.

I often wondered about possible origins of these activities and only when I found a little book, at an antique fair, did I gained any real insight. This compilation - written in 1916 and edited by Frank Kidson - had the title '100 Singing Games, Old, New and Adapted'.

It contained an almost identical portrayal of the "Three Labourers" we witnessed being played at the top end of Heelis Street and also two versions bearing a strong resemblance to the ring-game using the song "The Maiden on a Mountain" that we first saw in Rhoda Street. The book's preamble states:

The antiquarian interest in ring games is very great. In many cases they represent bygone customs and ceremonies from a very remote period...

This implied antiquity of many children's games is supported by the well-known "Ring o' Roses", whose theme suggests a connection with the Great Plague known as the Black Death. People believed that the scent of a floral posy provided some protection from contagion. Also, its symptoms happened to be severe sneezing with the resulting "falling down" - as the end-line of the verse declares.

Again, the assumed antiquity is supported in the case of the "Three Labourers" that we saw being played in Buckley Street. The book presents a variation of its enactment under the title "The Labourers out of Work". Its portrayal has a rural setting and therefore suggests an origin predating our industrial version - probably arising from the times of the Agricultural Enclosures and its resulting dispossessed farm-workers?

Its enactment takes the following form (and I paraphrase the book):

One player represents the Farmer whilst the others impersonate displaced farm labourers. Advancing to the Farmer, they all sing:

> *Pray, Master, can you find for us,*
> *Some little job of work?*
> *We'll hold the plough, we'll thresh the corn,*
> *And nothing will we shirk.*

> *We've wandered here, we've wandered there,*
> *At last we've come to you;*
> *We are poor starving labourers,*
> *For we have no work to do.*

The leader of the labourers asks: "Can you give us a job, Master?"
The Farmer says: "Well, what can you do?"
"Anything, Sir," the leader replies.
The Farmer then demands: "Well, let's see how you set about it."

The leading labourer then mimes a particular kind of work connected with farming. This could be milking, guiding a plough, driving a horse, sowing seeds, reaping, mowing, etc. The person representing the farmer makes a guess at what the mime indicates.

If that guess fails, a forfeit has to be paid. The rest of the labourers, in their turn, then perform mimes of their own devising - which also require a guess and a possible forfeit.

In order to compare the variation we witnessed in Buckley Street with the one the book presents, here's a summary of the enactment we saw:

The chosen three labourers removed themselves a little way from the Gaffer and the group observing the game. They then decided what work they'd perform. Upon deciding, they appointed one of their number as a spokesman to approach the Gaffer, saying:

> *"We are three labourers out of work, please can you oblige us."*
> *The Gaffer asks: "What doing?"*
> *The spokesman replies: "Anything!"*
> *The Gaffer says: "Show your skills!"*

The three labourers then mimed their task.

There's no doubt that the game we witnessed is derived from the original rural version. The major change in our industrial variation is in the first introduction. This presents a direct: "We are three labourers out of work, please can you oblige us." In addition, our variation involves a more complex and co-ordinated miming process involving three players, rather than those performed on an individual basis.

In the context of origins: the method of selecting the various roles in the games that we witnessed has an astounding antiquity. It seems the words "eenie, meenie, minie, moe" represent an ancient counting system pre-dating Roman times, and possibly going as far back as the building of Stonehenge.

One wonders if the children of that time played a game similar to the 'Three Labourers' and if one of the mimes concerned the building of the great ring of stones? However, that's one of my nice-to-imagine fantasies. Let's now consider the ring-games, whose intriguing complexity is interestingly suggested in the book's comments:

The ring game is one of the most common types of the marriage games, and with more or less variation it is well known in all parts of Europe. This kind of game is a great favourite with little girls, amongst whom ring games are the most popular. Antiquaries date many of these, with the traditional actions that survive them, from a very remote age.

The book presents two examples very similar in content and action to our "Maiden on a Mountain". One goes by the name of "Poor Widow of Babylon" and the other "The Lone Widow." The latter displays the greatest similarity to the version we saw in our visit to Heelis Street. The book's portrayal is described as follows - and I quote directly from the book:

"A ring is formed. One little girl, representing the Widow, being in the centre. Going around her, all sing in chorus:

> *Here's a poor Widow she's left alone,*
> *She has no one to marry upon,*
> *Come choose the east, come choose the west,*
> *Come choose the one that you love best.*

"The girl in the middle now chooses one from the ring and they both stand at the centre of the circle of players. Again the ring goes round with the children singing:

> *Now they're married we wish them joy,*
> *Every year a girl or boy,*
> *Loving each other like sister and brother,*
> *We pray the young couple to kiss one another.*

"The action is suited to the words and the game is continued with another child as Widow."

Again to remind and compare the action and song the book portrays with the one of our visit - which took the following form:

A girl stands at the centre of a ring composed mostly of girls, but having to contain at least one, but preferably more than one, boy. All those in the ring face inwards and - holding hands - they then circle the girl, singing:

> *There stands a Maiden,*
> *On a mountain,*
> *Who she is I do not know.*
> *All she wants is gold and silver,*
> *All she wants is a nice young man.*
> *Choose your lover,*
> *Choose your lover,*
> *Choose your lover, Fair Maid!*

On the word, "Maid", the singing and circling immediately stops. The girl at the centre then chooses one of the boys - or the only boy - in the ring to join her at the centre. This requires the others to express surprise and admiration at the choice. Then the singing and circling starts again, with the verse modified to:

> *There stands a Maiden,*
> *On a mountain,*
> *Who she is I do not know.*
> *Now she has her gold and silver,*
> *Now she has her nice young man.*
> *He's your lover,*
> *He's your lover,*
> *He's your lover, Fair Maid!*

Our game appears to contain a greater complexity than the book version and, perhaps, suggests connection with an even earlier setting - possibly medieval? It also presents the loneliness and the abandoned nature of the girl more dramatically than does the variation described in the book - this by the words: "There stands a Maiden on a mountain, who she is I do not know". In addition, it states the practicality of ensuring financial provisions for the forsaken maiden - this contained in the song's request for "gold and silver".

Before leaving these ring-games, there's one we didn't see during our visit - this because it needed a minimum of twelve or so children for its effective playing. It has the title "The Farmer Wants a Wife" and requires the mentioned number of boys and girls to willingly get together to enact the game.

This situation didn't occur in our visit; however, its enactment is worth describing in full because it also suggests an ancient origin and a rural connection.

Although a ring-game - which the book suggests mainly appeals to girls - the farmer-game could, nevertheless, attracted the willing participation of many boys. I suspect this is because the boys believed they could dominate the game, due to it containing far more boisterousness than romance.

It also had the dominating role of "farmer", which the game implied had to be a boy. Nevertheless, the romance implicit in the title appealed to the girls who would, for the sake of the game, put up with the boys' attempted domination and the usual rough and silly behaviour that the girls believed was an incurable affliction boys have. (The writer being excluded from this assumed disability, of course.)

The game starts with the usual ring containing a boy at its centre. The circling then commences with those in the ring singing:

> *The farmer wants a wife. The farmer wants a wife.*
> *Ee aye. Ee aye, the farmer wants a wife.*

The circling then stops and the "farmer" chooses one of the girls in the ring to be "wife" - to stand with him at the centre.

Again the circling starts with the singing of:

> *The farmer has a wife. The farmer has a wife.*
> *Ee aye. Ee aye, the farmer has a wife.*
> *The farmer wants a dog. The farmer wants a dog.*
> *Ee aye. Ee aye, the farmer wants a dog.*

The circling stops and the farmer chooses a "dog" from those in the ring. The circling then continues with the same pattern and theme to select a "horse", a "cow" then a "pig".

When the pig is chosen, the singing declares:

> *The farmer has a pig. The farmer has a pig.*
> *Ee aye. Ee aye, the farmer has a pig.*
> *The farmer wants a cat. The farmer wants a cat.*
> *Ee aye. Ee aye, the farmer wants a cat.*

The cat is then chosen and those circling sing the last verse:

> *The farmer has a cat. The farmer has a cat.*
> *Ee aye. Ee aye, the farmer has a cat.*
> *The cat will chase a mouse. The cat will chase a mouse.*
> *Ee aye. Ee aye, the cat will chase a mouse.*

On the last word, "mouse", the ring breaks up and the "cat" darts from the centre to chase anyone amongst the excited and evading children showing a possibility of being caught. The caught "mouse" then has the penalty of getting down on hands and knees to do a mouse imitation - involving sniffs and squeaks. This evokes much laughter and lots of fun. The "pantomime" is terminated when someone in the group shouts, "The farmer wants a wife".

Although it's entertaining to watch the mouse's antics, the shout arises when someone wishes to claim the role of farmer and thereby command the making of selections. The game then recommences with the self-selected farmer revealing who will be the wife, the various creatures and, finally, the "mouse".

In all of these games, revisions, complexities and adaptations no doubt developed with the passage of time; but for games to persist and be accommodated to new settings, they must contain enduring appeal.

The ones we saw in our visits and those the book described seemed to have all the ingredients children find appealing: rules, rhymes, songs, physically activity, companionship and the playing out of human and social situations. And, finally, they must contain the appeal above all appeals: they must be entertaining.

In our next visit, we'll see entertainment in its wider setting - arising spontaneously from day-to-day activities occurring in our street...

28
All the Street's a Stage:
With Nancy Dickybird, Dominic Rae and the Hurdy-gurdy Man.

~~~~~~~~~~~~~~~~~~~~~~~~~~~~~~~~~~~

The Jubilee Party (which we've yet to witness) is a good example of how the streets in and around the district could be used as a ready setting for entertainment. Apart from this nationally orchestrated event, our street had its day-to-day role as a constant "stage" for an endless round of spontaneous games, diversions and amusements.

Many of the most enjoyable "offerings" came in the shape of entertainers wandering into the street for possible pennies appreciative residents might be able to spare. Others would arrive in the form of visiting tradesmen with the explicit purpose of selling baked potatoes, muffins or roasted chestnuts; or swapping commodities such as a donkey-stones or balloons for bundles of rags or pieces of scrap metal.

These street-visitors invariably arrived with a snappy quip or rhyme to announce their trade and were welcomed as part of the street's recreation.

The street, therefore, always seemed to be a melodious kaleidoscope of sound: the calls of tradesmen; the sound of children chanting rhymes; the singing or playing of instruments by visiting entertainers; the clatter of metal buckets as people washed their steps or windows; the sound of neighbours gossiping or having a laugh about something - all this mingling with the music from gramophone or wireless issuing from open doors. Doors wide open in what, to me, seemed the endless summer days of the financially poor yet community rich period of the nineteen-thirties.

In the crowded, terrace streets of our district, privacy represented a condition the inhabitants seemed not to expect. Therefore, the buzz of noise created by the constant comings and goings in and around the street never seemed to cause objection or complaint - mainly, I suppose, because folks accepted this as a natural consequence of living.

Whether or not this lack of privacy, when compared with the virtual anonymity members of present-day society enjoys, was a good or a bad thing is a debatable matter. But from the earliest days of childhood, the inhabitants of our street and its many similar locations were born into a notion that play and entertainment - and, indeed, most of life - was mainly a public affair. And by the nature of things, the street to which they belonged became its natural settings.

In this constant hubbub of street-noise, no particular sound tended to dominate (with the exception, perhaps, of the one made by the hurdy-gurdy man - an experience we'll "enjoy" later). Therefore, life in the street produced a harmonious merging of sounds quite pleasant to most ears.

The nearest present-day experience is, perhaps, the buzz of sound in the vehicle-excluded environments of the open-air shopping precincts; where sounds never seems to be intrusive but become background noises one can attend to or not. In this setting, a person soon learns to select and then direct their attention to any particular source - a piece of music; the call of a familiar voice; a conversation, or whatever - and isolate that sound from all the rest.

And so it was in our street. However, ours was the age of gentle sounds: of voices; of wireless; of gramophone; where each sound seemed to harmoniously complement all the other sounds. No roof-shaking, twin speaker, sixty-watt ghetto blasters and similarly intrusive inventions to rise above the comfort of the human ear yet existed.

The wireless we saw in the visit that we made to our house had a speaker-power that just about filled our small front room. The gramophones mainly available at that time played their melodies not by way of electronic amplifications but through the acoustics of its "horn", decoratively fashioned to look like a large flower. If, for some reason, you wished to quieten it still further, you just "put a sock in it".

Another method of adjusting its sound-level was by using a different grade metal needle. For instance: a "soft" needle (fitted to what a later age would call the "pick-up" but was then called the "soundbox") produced a result gentle enough for an ear to be placed at the mouth of the horn. This you'll see portrayed by the quaint advert of a well-known Company showing a dog named Nipper attentively listening to the sound issuing forth.

To me, the cosy, softly echoing, muffled pleasantry of the gramophone had the acoustic equivalent of soothing gaslight; and in my mind, the two go together. I remember my uncles Joe and Edward (both living next-door-but-one to our house) playing records in the evening after their day's work. Sounds of 'Good-night Vienna', played by Jack Payne and his band and sung with the melodious voice of his resident singer; or 'Sweet and Lovely', presented by the rich tones of Russ Columbo; or 'Serenade in the Night', rendered by Tino Rossi; or

'Ramona', sung by Layton and Johnstone, drifted from their front room as the evening gaslights were lit.

These are my particular recollections; but as stated previously, my sister, Nellie, had the advantage of a memory able to delve further back in time than mine and can therefore recall far more details. I can, for instance, clearly remember the music along with most of the lyrics, but had to rely on my sister to provide some of the names of the bands and singers involved.

She also told me of her excursions to the Woolworths - situated along Rochdale Road - to buy records and packets of gramophone needles for the mentioned uncles. 'Mimosa' and 'Victory' records containing tunes such as 'In a Monastery Garden'; 'Lady of Spain'; 'In a Persian Market'; 'Happy Feet'; 'Tiptoes through the Tulips'; 'The Laughing Policeman'; and a great favourite of mine at the time, 'Teddy Bears' Picnic', were all sixpence each. Needles to play them cost t'pence a packet, containing a quantity of fifty. These were made of soft steel and the instructions on the packet advised using one needle only for each side of a record - this to avoid a worn needle damaging the record's grooves.

Although the gramophone and wireless had their undoubted fascinations, the greater fascinations were, to me, those previously mentioned "turns" of ordinary, everyday life provided by visitors to our street. However, even more enjoyable were the spontaneous entertainment provided, incidentally and sometimes unintentionally, by the inhabitants of the street, themselves.

In this setting, a sound never failing to compel my attention drifted now and again from number nine, just across the road from our house and next door to my Granny Jones - who lived at number seven.

The "man of the house" would - after his day's work and whilst waiting for his evening meal - sit on a wooden stool just inside his open front doorway where a cool breeze might chance (as previously mentioned, the mid-thirties had long, hot, summer days). From there, he'd entertain himself on his concertina - producing melodies such as: "To be a Farmer's Boy" or "Hay, Hay, Farmer Grey", which drifted across the street to be enjoyed - or not - by those attentive enough to listen.

The multitudinous sounds of the street continued whilst those well used to his performance went about whatever concerns or enjoyments each had at that time. The children - whose chants and rhymes, shouts and laughter, made them oblivious to any sound other than those important to their play - continued their activities. But the melody would be there for those who cared to hear. And as it began to float from the open doorway, I'd quietly move away from whatever game I happened to be playing to take up a position across the street and near our front door, where I could watch with wonder the squeezing and rolling of the concertina and the strong, stubby fingers on the keys as the tune drifted across the cobbles to where I attentively sat.

But compelling though his magic was, it sometimes became overshadowed by the flamboyant, accordion playing visit of a man named Dominic Rae - whose appearance, in itself, was enough to command attention. His usual attire consisted of an Italian-style, dark coloured pin-stripe suit and matching trilby hat with a "flashy" white band. And, of course, he sported the - then seemingly obligatory - thin black moustache that folks imagined Italians should sport.

From a commanding position in the centre of the street, his dazzling performance of "Oh, oh Antonio, he's gone away!" and "Serenade in the night, 'neath a fair lady's window..." cascaded along the full length of the row to entice any pennies his appreciative listeners might be inclined to give.

Yet the sounds from number nine remained my favourite because it belonged to our street; even if, for most times, there came only the one tune, with its key theme yearning for a rural life:

"To be a farmer's boy, yoy-yoy-yoy-yoy, to be a farmer's boy..."

But we all have our preferences. My sister's favourite visitor to the street was Nancy Dickybird, who eventually became a member of the Salvation Army - thereby extending her voice to reach a much wider audience. My sister didn't know if "Dickybird" was the lady's real surname. However, in a district prone to rectifying such uncertainties by ascribing a nickname, it was - in all probability - a nickname. The lady possessed a very high, sweet voice and no doubt the reason for the conferred title?

It seems she visited the street before I'd reached the age to take notice. However, any sensitivity I possessed in my early years was insufficient to fully appreciate a sweet voice, from whoever and wherever it came. To me, the workings of instruments such as gramophones, accordions, ukuleles and banjos seemed far more compelling. But more especially compelling was the barrel organ - which the kids called a "hurdy-gurdy" - as played by the previously mentioned miracle tune-maker: The Hurdy-gurdy Man.

His visits commenced with the pushing of his highly decorated two wheel contraption to a position half way along the street, to the same commanding spot favoured by Dominic Rae. Then, resting the cart on its struts, his energetic turning of the brass, tune-producing, handle reeled off voluminous rolling sounds of: "When it's spring-time in the Rockies" and "Oh I wonder, yes, I wonder, when it's time to go up yonder, will the angels play their harps for me..."

These and the other melodious sounds issued forth whilst we kids gathered around - spellbound; and only the receiving of a coin would momentarily slow the turning of the highly polished handle. Then, upon sufficient coinage being received (or no more judged to be forthcoming) his handle-winding would cease and a wheel-rattling progress made along the cobbles to the next street, to seek further gratuities.

Years later, as the passage of time took away my childhood "innocence" - to replace it with adult cynicism? - I wondered if the pennies were readily given not so much out of musical appreciation but more as a bribe for him to go elsewhere: his hurdy-gurdying happened to be the loudest of all sounds. Nevertheless, his ready production of tunes in all their marvellous loudness attracted the kids, and we'd follow this awe inspiring maker of music to the next street for another rendering. The Hurdy-gurdy Man couldn't have had a more tireless and appreciative audience - even if cashless.

Another visitor I greatly enjoyed was one we kids called "The Banjo Man" - also known in the street as "Mr Plink-Plonk". (Again, this must have been a nickname!) He specialised in George Formby renderings and one I particularly liked began with the words: "I'm leaning on the lamppost at the corner of the street in case a certain little lady passes by". This seemed particularly apt to our street - which, as you know, has a lamppost at its corner.

Although the concept of "courting" implied by the song wasn't readily understood by me at that time, I'd noticed the lamppost was - in actuality - leaned on, at various times and for some purpose, by those I'd call "big lads"; and this had something to do with the eventual arrival of a grown up girl. But the main reason for particularly noticing this occurrence was because it sometimes interfered with certain games we might be playing around the lamppost; and we kids saw the lamppost as specifically our property.

However, and returning to the main subject: I never saw the Banjo Man receive any pennies and, as far as I remember, he received mostly "butties" (buttered bread) and cups of tea for his efforts. He'd sit on the donor's front doorstep to enjoy his "reward", which he appeared to very much appreciate. Perhaps that's why he came to our street?

Perhaps he knew our street provided particularly tasty butties and a good brew of tea?

Another frequent visitor with entertainment intentions was one we kids called "The Chicken Man". It seemed he'd received an injury or had been crippled in some way (because of the war?) which resulted in a withered right arm and a twisted right leg. Also, his voice had a peculiarly high pitch sound - probably due to a throat affliction (a gas attack in the war?) which made his singing appear to us like the squawk of a chicken. This along with a hand withered to resemble a claw - like that of the chickens' displayed in the butcher's shop - no doubt gave cause for the ascribed name.

This naming arose not out of any unkindness (there wasn't any shown nor would we dare show it) but solely from the impulse children seem to posses that impels them to liken or describe an unaccustomed concept within the terms of something already known.

The words of what he sang and what tune it represented couldn't be made out, and this added to the curiosity motivating us to follow his progress along the street - again not out of intentional unkindness but because of the deep curiosity deformity seems to produce in children. I think this is because any departure from the "norm" generates perplexities compelling a desire to understand.

I'd dash home to try to obtain a penny or ha'p'ny to give before he reached the end of our street: this again not out of any sentimentality or feelings of charity, but - possibly - because that mentioned perplexity seemed to impel some response.

It seems to me that a child's mind is disposed to make almost anything (revulsion, embarrassment, sympathy or any refined social emotions we learn later in life) subordinate to curiosity. Children do acquire the "finer" emotions quite early in their development - or, at least, have the potential for such - but in the beginning, it's curiosity that reigns supreme; and so it was in the case of the Chicken Man.

Returning to the previously mentioned entertainment occurring unintentionally. (My use of the word "entertainment" arises from a child's point of view; the adults of the street may've offered a different definition.) Virtually everything attracts a child's attention; this because it's governed by a curiosity that will focus on the smallest of detail, which an adult's "sophisticated judgement" would find trivial - and therefore fail to see its fascination.

For instance, another visitors to the street happened to be a person we called "The Sharpening Man". He came with a one-wheeled contraption, like a wheelbarrow, surmounted by a structure containing a large grindstone connected to a foot treadle. The lower part of the stone ran in a shallow tray of water for wetting its edge when operated by the treadle. In the manner of all our visiting entertainers and purveyors of trade, he'd take up a commanding position in the centre of the street to rest his contraption on its struts. The kids immediately stopped their play to wait for him to rise to his full height, draw a deep breath and then sonorously call out: "Kniiiifes... Scissoooors... Any kniiiifes... Any scissooors... To shaaaarpen...!"

His drawn-out cries - as he pivoted to project each cry along both halves of the street - immediately gathered the kids around him; eagerly hoping someone required his services. And when hopes were fulfilled, an open mouth staring at the stone gathering speed as he treadled faster and faster, making the tray of water fill with miniature tidal waves. Then the intermittent streams of tiny shooting stars when metal met patches of not quite wet stone - these to silently explode and miraculously vanish.

Unfortunately - and in spite of running into the house to persuade our Mams to offer something for sharpening - this event occurred far less often than we hoped. Nevertheless, this highlighted the treat when it did happen.

It cost t'pence for a carving knife and thre'pence for a pair of scissors - which most people in our street thought a bit too much to afford. Therefore, most people saved their pennies by sharpening the more frequently used knives themselves - usually on the stone front doorstep. However, he had the monopoly on scissors: these didn't fare too well if subjected to front doorstep treatment.

My sister - always an astute observer of any scene - told me the action of sharpening a carving knife on the said step, on a Sunday morning, was a way of telling who in the street happened to be temporarily "well off". Just before the mid-day meal, the man of the fortunate household might, and usually would, sharpen the carving knife in the manner mentioned - and therefore in full view of anyone in the street who cared to observe.

This action "signified" a household preparing to enjoy a joint of meat on that particular day, instead of the usual scrag-end stew most households in the street might have to face - which probably would've been the fare of the observed household if it hadn't been blessed with the assumed joint of meat.

My sister maintained this sharpening proved a reliable indicator because, in addition to the doorstep action, the aroma of roast-beef wafted from the opened doorway.

Of course, the sharpening action - by itself - could represent mere show on the part of those implying a status not really deserved. But if supported by the aroma of roast-beef? Well, the visitation of good fortune couldn't be denied!

However, who could blame those in a time and community - wherein the wheel of monetary fortune didn't frequently turn to a more favourable position - for engaging in a modicum of conspicuous display? At least, those in the immediate vicinity shared some of this fortuitous turn of the wheel by being "treated" to the delicious aroma of roast beef!

Nevertheless, if good fortune happened to be a rare event, the chance of having "the glitter of gold" displayed on your front door could occur for a very small price. From time to time, a man came around the streets, offering to refurbish - there and then - the house-numbers (these being drab, cast iron letters nailed to the front door) in gold paint for the sum of a ha'p'ny each house. Again, in the absence of knowing the person's real name, we kids gave him the name of "Mr Glitter".

We never failed to appreciate his capacity for making miraculous transformations, even after constant repetitions. We'd follow him from house to house to see his glitter being applied; then to gaze in wonder as the drab metal unfailingly changed into gleaming gold. Even if all that glitters is not gold, nevertheless, the magic he performed in transmuting dull, base metal into a lustrous marvel certainly impressed the wide-eyed kids.

But let's avoid being too restrictive in our descriptions of good fortune. Although the previously mentioned roast beef would, at that time, be highly rated on any scale of reckoning, we kids had other measures; and these extended into realms not fully appreciated by adults. Because of this, good fortune made - for us - frequent visitations.

In the age before the casual flick of a switch could flash images of the world into each closed and private living room, the street represented our wide-open window on the world and all that mattered. Also, it was a window all the more fascinating because of its immediacy.

To my reckoning, one of the most supremely immediate of all the performers in our street was a lad just a few years older than I happened to be.

Let's see if he's putting on his own speciality. His house is at the end of the street, near the bruw and by the lamppost on its corner. He's got a passion for doing song and dance routines seen on the local cinema. The pavement by the lamppost is his stage and its adjacent cobbled area is where he attracts his audience.

Look! He's out there now! Let's see what song he's about to do!

And after we've seen his show, the Hurdy-gurdy man might come...

DANCING TOMMY

In that end house just near the brow,
lived that rum lad:
Tom Donoghue.
And if you asked him as a dare,
he'd do a dance like Fred Astair.

But then his mother would lean out -
and from their window call and shout:

    "Tommy! Tommy!
    Stop your row.
    Y'dad's home soon...
    I'll tell him how
    y'think we're here
    for doing nowt
    but getting shoes
    that you'll kick out.
    Y'know he says
    he'll not have debt.
    If you keep on,
    then clogs you'll get."

Tom would stop;
then with his grin would dance
again (when she'd gone in).
And then he sings,
with gleeful beat:

"A - jig - in - clogs -
 would - be - a - treat."

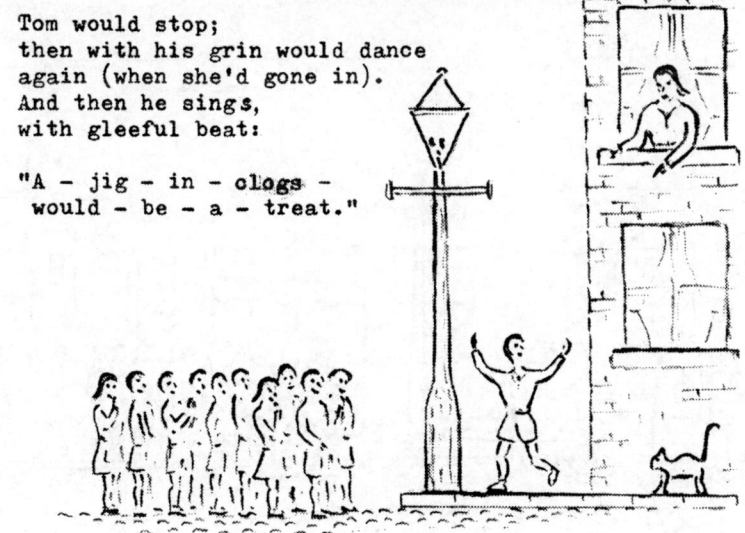

HURDY-GURDY MAN

Amongst the hurly-burly of street trade,
the hurdy-gurdy man's tunes bravely played:
'Oh! oh! Anton-i-o,
he's gone away;
left me all alone-i-o; all on my own-i-o...'
'Follow, follow, follow,
the merry-merry pipes of Pan...'

But every time these cheerful sounds began,
into the street would come the ice-cream man;
and Hurdy's handle whirled round even faster,
to hold his crowd – and stave off his disaster.
For music – that sweet food of love – now vied
with other fares – which ice-cream man implied.
Though Hurdy turned
and turned
(not to give in)
it always happened:
love of food would win.

29
The Jubilee and Cake for Tea.

~~~~~~~~~~~~~~~~~~~~~~~~~~~~~~~~~~

We can now join the event that, to me, as a child, was the highlight of the mid-thirties: the Silver Jubilee Celebration of King George V in the May of 1935. The photograph on the right shows the king as he was some months before that event.

His national role happened to be "brought home" to the people of the country on Saint George's Day, April 23rd 1924, when he made a speech at the opening of the British Empire Exhibition at Wembley Stadium - newly built for that purpose at a cost of £750,000.

The recently constituted BBC relayed the speech to the estimated six million homes that possessed a suitable receiving device. His voice was also heard by many thousands without the necessary device - this due to the opening ceremony being relayed by way of numerous loudspeakers positioned in public places throughout Britain.

The 'Daily Mirror' reported how these many thousands of listeners all over the country stood in bareheaded silence (it was customary at that time to wear a hat when outdoors, and remove it for situations requiring "respect") whilst the bands played the National Anthem during the relayed opening, then to be followed by the King's speech. This broadcast happened to be the first time that people in general had heard his voice and thereby "felt" his presence.

But very much felt in the country's psyche was the dominance of the Empire. For instance, the first day of the Exhibition attracted over a hundred thousand visitors who wanted to be there when the King spoke and also to "see" the Empire in what was then the biggest display Britain had ever staged. The total cost of it all represented a sum exceeding £10,000,000 - an enormous amount for that time.

The composer, Sir Edward Elgar, added to the "pomp and circumstances" of the occasion by conducting massed choirs rendering his specially arranged 'Land of Hope and Glory'. Such was the popularity of the Exhibition that the organisers decided to open it again in the summer of the following year. The two years combined saw an attendance of over twenty-seven million visitors.

So the people, it seems, were "Empire minded" and the institution no doubt appeared to them as enduring as the Rock of Gibraltar. Even Winston Churchill must have had this concept in mind when - during the first years of the war to come - he could suggest the possibility of "the British Empire lasting for a thousand years".

However, we now know something he did not know at the time of his apparent optimism: what had taken hundreds of years to construct would start to fall apart in no more than three decades.

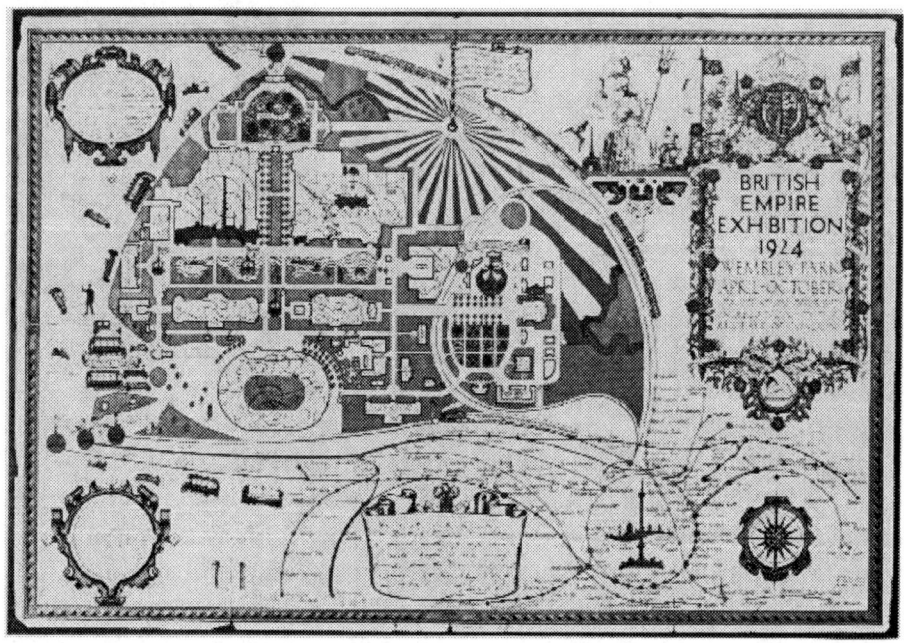

The expected enthusiasm for the exhibition is implied in the elaborate poster published to announce its coming. This represented a stylised map of the area's intentions and layout, which - when presented in its full-size and colour - must have looked somewhat compelling. The oval shape near the lower left-hand side of the poster shows the stadium's position relative to the other avenues and buildings, specially constructed along with the transport network.

But let's return to the Jubilee celebration mentioned at the beginning of this narrative. In its preparations and subsequent street-parties, we'll notice many of the values and beliefs cherished in the period in which it took place contrast dramatically with those our later time developed. So let's focus on the Jubilee Party, to examine some of its sentiments along with their implications.

At that time, and during the Empire Exhibition a decade earlier, various "dissenters" - somewhat disturbed by what they considered the immorality of colonisation - expressed their dissatisfactions. These emerge with far bolder emphasis as the idea of "King, Country and Empire" began to tarnish during the increasingly adverse economic circumstances of the early Thirties. For instance, an article in the 'Daily Worker' complained bitterly about spending large amounts of money on "celebrations" whilst millions were on the dole. They deemed this "irresponsible wastefulness" as "Royal Squandermania".

Other critics inferred that the Jubilee concept and its publicity represented nothing more than a pre-election gimmick on the part of a then unpopular Government. (Who but the cynical could suspect politicians of such a devious trick - I ask you?) But whatever the truth of the situation - honourable or otherwise - virtually the entire Nation seemed to embrace, with great enthusiasm, the prospect of celebrating the Jubilee - except, of course, for the, then, vastly outnumbered dissenters.

However, we kids, being free from the distortions politics can inflict upon perceptions, were hardly touched by any machinations of the adult world - even assuming the possibility of being able to understand their confused intentions. All we knew and all we wanted to know was that wondrous preparations were taking place - everywhere and all around us. We wandered through the streets with eyes astonished, to see erstwhile blank-brick walls being painted in patriotic reds, whites and blues; and to be further astonished by portrayals of the Union Flag, various coats of arms; and - in one street - an awesome wall-painting of Saint George battling with a fearsome dragon.

We were told at school about the national implications concerning all these widespread and energetic activities; but, for us, this hardly registered. All we absorbed was the magical word "Jubilee"; and that this word meant parties in the streets and we'd all get a free Jubilee Mug with a picture of the King and Queen on it! Therefore, with the practicality all children possess, we absorbed the essential "essentials". With all the knowledge of the Jubilee we required, we went around the streets enjoying the exciting preparations carried out with impressive eagerness by the inhabitants of the streets themselves - which seemed, to us, mainly for our benefit.

No doubt the declaration that a prize would be awarded, district by district, for the most innovative street-decorations enhanced the enthusiasm. So, as the day of celebration drew near, all the eager and enthusiastic folk obtained additional materials and longer ladders to bedeck each street higher and higher and wider and wider with more and more national flags, balloons, buntings and bright wall paintings.

We kids knew not from whence the money came to produce, in that financially restricted time, all the displays along with the forthcoming party. Nor did we really care. To us, and no doubt to all the children in all the other streets, the necessities seem to come from heaven; and we were not inclined to concern ourselves, overmuch, about the why and wherefore of heaven's blessings. Sufficient unto us was that they had come and we'd be suitable and appreciative beneficiaries.

Later - with the passing of years bringing about their inevitable concerns about cash - I marvelled on realising that most of the money raised to produce such widespread and miraculous transformations came from the "not very deep" pockets of people in each street. Yet much can be done with very little. For instance: buntings were easily produced from scraps of coloured cloth cut to triangular shapes and tied to lengths of string - these joined together to span the street from each opposite upstairs window.

Also, lime-wash (the principle and ubiquitous means of backyard whitewashing) came cheap and only required the addition of other hues such as dolly-blue (normally used in the washing of linens) to produce bright blues and henna powder to produce deep reds. And there you had it: reds, whites and blues to gloriously transform every erstwhile drab wall - with hardly a brick left untreated.

The food for the party came by way of the home-baked efforts of the streets themselves; and local shops - mindful of their "patriotic image" and therefore customer goodwill - made contributions, adding to the ever-increasing supply.

Again, in retrospection, it seems incredible that the people who'd borne the brunt of deprivation (brought about by economic depression and the corresponding failure of their nation to provide, for many of them, even the rudiments of prosperity) could respond to this event with such patriotic fervour? However, our parents were part of that historic long line which saw Britain as a world power second to none - a perception not yet shaken by the economic trauma of a war to come.

Just as a person's past shapes the awareness of their present-self, in terms of confidence and worth, so does a country's history shape a nation's perception of what it is, what it means and what the people composing the nation think of its worthiness (and therefore of their own worthiness). In the case of our parents, their perception of the nation was firmly fashioned by nigh on five hundred years of history, wherein the might of its naval power was - in thought and many times in deed - eventually equal to that of all the other powers combined.

This perception emerged in numerous popular songs, such as: "We've got a Navy, a fighting Navy, that made Great Britain great..." and, last but not, least "Rule, Britannia, Britannia rules the waves".

Those in our street and the streets around who eagerly sang such songs would know of nothing to contradict the sentiments these tunes expressed. This would particularly apply to the last mentioned "glorification", which held its popularity ever since Thomas Arne wrote its verses for his opera 'Alfred', in 1740. Therefore, this and all the other songs were sung with an unshakeable conviction supported by a long series of affirmative years.

Such vainglorious vocalising may sound jingoistic and even embarrassing to our later age, nervous of anything hinting of "Nationalism"; but to our parents, and therefore to us, these represented songs everyone felt perfectly entitled to sing, without embarrassment or fear of contradiction.

As previously implied: the unease that grew to great proportions in our later period about the possession of Empire was virtually absent in the minds of most people of that time. The attitude towards its possession appeared to focus on its "civilising and peace keeping mission" succinctly expressed by a teacher at our school.

In the extensive lessons he presented about the Nation's history, he likened the British Empire to that built by Rome. Supported by a map of the world prominently fixed to the wall of the classroom - depicting large areas coloured pink to indicate British "possessions" - he "explained" the map's rationale in near enough these words:

"Just as the Roman Empire brought civilisation in the form of literacy, law, learning and numeracy along with science, trade, communications and road building to large areas of backward Europe, so did the British Empire confer similar benefits to many parts of the wider world. Also, its Pax Britannica maintained law and order in areas previously knowing only tribal warfare and much barbarity."

This explanation may not "fit" perceptions formed in our later period and some would reject it emphatically: asserting that many related actions were not always civilised. However, the "civilising mission" was the way our teacher and many others of his time saw the British Empire and its role in the world. He'd probably reply to the mentioned criticisms by saying that many mistakes were no doubt made, but attempts were also made to rectify such whatever they happened to be and wherever they happened to appear.

So, although perceptions about colonisation were to shift dramatically within a comparatively short time, the period wherein our teacher presented his view was part of a virtually unbroken and assertive line of history - as the Empire Exhibition appears to indicate.

In addition, the perception our teacher seemed quite happy to hold and emphatically teach contained within it an implicit recognition of population pressures and rapidly developing industrial systems impelling a need for expanding trade into "new" territories. These expediencies he presented as "justification" for European expansion across the world. And the National rivalries were such that if the main expansion into what was then seen as "open territories" hadn't been a British effort, then it would've been that of the other European Powers.

The main rivals for this expansionist role being Spain; France; Holland; Belgium; Italy; Russia; Portugal; Germany, et al. Therefore, it seemed it was just a question of who amongst these rivals appeared to be the most worthy to take on the "mission". To our teacher and the majority of British people, the obvious answer would be: "the British".

This reply would be given in the context of a period wherein such ambitions became the aim of every power able to "extend" itself. This (those giving the "obvious" reply would know) had been the case ever since time began - as the evidence of all the once existing ancient Empires testified. They also knew America had extended its dominion to its west and south, then out into the Pacific to the Hawaiian Islands and even into former Spanish areas as far as the Philippines.

Czarist Russia had pushed eastwards as far as Alaska and even to California. In addition, it had extended south to and over the Caucasus and then south-east to the edges of Afghanistan, with a hovering ambition towards India. Everyone who could do it did it, it seems. Britain, being a major player in this great push between rival powers, would be seen (in terms of our teacher's perception) as the greatest player of all (for whatever reason). Therefore, Britain's effort would appear to be a cause for justifiable pride (for whatever reason he accepted as being justifiable).

Circumstances shaping our present perceptions seem to impel apology for the perceived "mistakes" of the past - chief amongst these being colonisation and its resulting Empire. However, and as implied: this impulse disregards the fact that these mistakes weren't seen as mistakes by the vast majority of people at that time but were seen as the natural order of things. Similarly, the Western Powers now see it as the natural order of things - and, indeed, a duty - to spread a particular political system throughout the world. This done by various means of economic and even military persuasion for the believed - and no doubt sincerely believed - benefit of the world in general.

Our kindly and enthusiastic teacher would've expressed great sympathy towards the last-stated point of view; but would also set this benefit in the context of his believed civilising mission of the British Empire and its associated spread of prosperity through trade.

So, apologies for the mistakes of the past appear, it seems, as futile as some future period's apology for the mistakes of our present; which is - perhaps - like a middle-age person apologising for the mistakes they made as a teenager. This disregards the fact that the knowledge and dispositions then held by the teenage-self would be vastly different from those held by the matured, apologising, person - a person belonging to a later "age" with its own perceptions, experiences and hindsight.

It therefore seems obvious that if the person of our example returned to the state of their teenage-self - with the level of knowledge and all its conditions exactly as they existed at that stage - they would behave exactly as they did at that stage. So, the mistakes weren't mistakes but represent the way things were shaped by the prevailing knowledge and circumstances at that time. It is therefore futile and even unfair - and may even be deemed as arrogant - to judge the past without possessing all its attributes and excluding from our awareness all the perceptions given to us by a later position in history.

Our present position's judgement of the Jubilee Party might deem those patriotic expressions emerging in the apparently jingoistic songs and pride of possession as false "compensations" for the deprivations of that time. Moreover, the same judgement might suggest that people will accept being given less than the best if persuaded to feel they are part of the "best" - and this was the motive behind the political trick mentioned earlier. But whatever the "correct" view may be, the fact remains that although great divisions existed in the nation, in an economic and class sense, there seemed to be none in the patriotic sense - as the nation-wide enthusiasm for the Empire Exhibition and the Jubilee appears to indicate. The nation seemed to be "as one" on this issue; and this, I believe, gave to the nation those qualities that a strong and unified personality confers upon the individual.

These qualities usually take the form of an unshakeable self-confidence that believes it can face any difficulty with a firm conviction of eventually triumphing over that difficulty. At the personal level, displays of these attributes could appear to those with a more modest mien as supercilious; yet we can admire the resoluteness associated with this unshakeable self-confidence - especially in times of dire trouble. Manifesting as it did during the Jubilee celebrations, this quality appeared to serve the Nation well just a few short years later; when, in a period of its direst difficulties, it came to the fore.

For instance: shortly after the retreat from Dunkirk in the May of 1940, when by all objective and apparently sensible assessments the Nation seemed to have very little chance of survival (to the extent that an "unofficial" report from the American Embassy predicted a surrender in less than three weeks) no mass panic ensued. In fact, from my experience of those around me, the possibilities of defeat were hardly ever voiced.

I remember at that particular time listening along with other members of the family to William Joyce - then known as "Lord Haw Haw" (a name invented by Jonah Barrington of the Daily Express after Joyce's first broadcast from Germany, on September 18th 1939). Haw Haw declared that the people of Britain would soon be brought to their knees under the onslaught of the mighty Luftwaffe. To this, our Dad remarked:

"The silly old S.O.D. We're already on our knees. But wait 'till we get back up!"

Nobody within or outside of the family circle would've challenged this seemingly foolhardy and unjustifiable confidence expressed soon after the Dunkirk retreat, and apparently shared by virtually everyone around. Those from elsewhere would - as they did - deem this aberration could only arise from a complete absence of any sense of reality. They wouldn't believe this apparent loss of connection with the real world could be an attitude the majority of sensible Britons would hold - as the mentioned American Embassy document seemed to imply. The massive preparations along the Channel Coast, under the code name "Operation Sealion", whose purpose besides actual invasion was (according to General Jodl, the German Chief of Operational Staff) to "substantially intimidate", took into account the expectation that all sensible Britons would soon acquire "rationality".

Records of that period also indicated that the German Minister of Propaganda, Dr Goebbels, had growing concerns that both the military victory in France and the following threat of imminent invasion seemed to have failed to induce what he considered one of the most essential ingredients in the success of any invasion: panic in the population of Britain. He also became concerned that the broadcasts of William Joyce, far from generating the fear and despair they were designed to achieve, were becoming a source of amusement - as the name "Lord Haw Haw" cheerfully implied.

In fact, the gentleman's broadcasts produced a regular following of eager listeners in the way "Soaps" do in the present age; and - like these - became the source of much conversation.

A typical example of this came in the form of an exchange between two of our neighbours, which - as far as I can remember - went something like this:

Lady neighbour in a state of excited concern commenting to a gentleman neighbour:

"Hey! What do you think of Lord Haw Haw? He said the Prince of Wales has been bombed. That's the pub my sister-in-law goes to!"

Gentleman neighbour - slightly amused:

"He didn't mean the pub, he meant the battleship."

Lady neighbour - indignantly:

"Well! Why didn't he say so! 'Causing all this confusion!"

Needless to say, this conversation became a source of local amusement to embellish Lord Haw Haw's regular offerings.

However and returning to the more serious matters. Immediately after Dunkirk and in accordance with expectations of a coming sense of reality implied by the previously mentioned American document, Hitler believed surrender inevitable and waited impatiently for its announcement. When this failed to materialise, he, in his resulting fury - and as intimated by Lord Haw Haw - flung his Luftwaffe into the fray to flatten what he called: "this ludicrous intractability". But as we now know, his effort failed to eliminate the trait he found frustrating.

His error in the first instance and lack of success in the second is factual history. But consider the affect on subsequent world events if the Jubilee Party's attitude hadn't existed; and, instead of that "arrogant" belief in invincibility, the Nation became crippled with the feelings of defeat most outside observers expected to occur.

Imagine Britain collapsing under the weight of a post-Dunkirk hopelessness and seeking a negotiated capitulation, as did France. This would have opened up all of North Africa, the Mediterranean and the Middle East to Hitler's occupation - offering immediate access to the vast reservoirs of Middle Eastern Oil. Thus - with all his forces being released from facing Britain and waging the North African campaign - imagine an attack on Russia taking place a full year before it did and in the height of a favourable summer, with a far less able Russia Army - as indicated by its difficulty in the Russo-Finnish conflict of 1939-40.

Imagine the invasion of Russia backed by the full might of Hitler's military forces diverted from other concerns and invigorated by the triumph of a recent massive victory over Britain. What is more, this attack could've been on two fronts: one across the European frontiers and the other through the Caucasian Mountains, via the Middle East, into an area which, as we know, is also "oil rich".

Additionally, and as we also now know, it's an area that contained the possibility of its indigenous people being eager to ally themselves with those whom they'd most likely - and, perhaps, readily - believe were freeing them from the Soviet yoke. Within this possibility, Hitler may've obtained his expected victory over the Soviets within a year.

Also at that time, the mood in America was one of uncertainty. Those of German origin had some sympathy with Germany but those of Jewish origin had very little. The powerful sentiment of isolationism then existing, with its mood inclined to turn away from European troubles, would hardly suffer much unhappiness from seeing Hitler directing his attentions towards the East: an action satisfying those with deep anti-Communists leanings. Standing aside and allowing things to take their course would seem "sensible".

Under this protection from interference offered by American uncertainties, and with the highly possible quick defeat of the Soviet Union and the acquisition of its resources, the development of Hitler's rocketry could have taken a great leap forward in power and range. This would've been enormously assisted by the German facilities in the West being untouched by British bombing and the technological resources of an occupied Britain supplementing Hitler's own.

In this frightening scenario I believe American could've found itself hard pushed to resist what may've been a possible attack from two fronts - the Atlantic and the Pacific. This attack being given added impact from the territorial connecting of German and Japanese forces brought about by the occupation of Soviet territories.

Of course, America may've negotiated a settlement with the proviso of "staying in its own backyard" and commanding its own area of the world - a possibility suiting the substantial number of isolationist in that country at the time. However, even if America had reacted much sooner, and with hostility from a fear of Germany's rapid expansion after the collapse of Britain, to launch anything like a feasible offensive against Germany would be an impossibility. With Russia defeated and the full weight of the German forces ready and waiting, invasions from more remote places would've had less than the proverbial snowball's chance in hell of success. An invasion of mainland Europe required a crucially resolute and unoccupied Britain to give it any practicality.

In this situation, I believe (and it is, of course, only my belief) America may've sought the suggested accommodation; and the Third Reich, if not lasting for Hitler's thousand years, would, at least, have lasted for a very long time. Therefore, whatever we may think about conditions in our later period, it's highly likely they would've been far less to our satisfaction if the spirit represented by the event of May 1935 hadn't existed. So, if these conjectures are correct, three cheers for the Jubilee Party.

However, and irrespective of what may be fanciful and erroneous speculations on my part, the enthusiasm invested in decorating the streets, four short years away from Hitler's onslaught, indicated a deeply felt confident, and - yes - an unyielding patriotism allowing the mentioned songs to be sung with pride and conviction.

Anyway, we kids thought they were jolly good songs. Worries about their truth or falsity; rightfulness; morality; propriety; justification and other philosophical and ethical considerations, or whether their sentiments could play any part in a desperately needed "will to resist" in a possible conflict that might occur a few short years away, didn't disturb us in the least. Our immediate concern lay in the Jubilee Party's success - and that's all that mattered.

Being children, we possessed our own convictions. On that day the sun shone warm, just as we knew it would. We knew with our own absolute and unshakeable certainty that nothing could frustrate all the preparations we'd seen taking place - and certainly not that all important final result, the Jubilee Party, when there'd be "cake for tea".

Those houses able to bring out their sturdy tables into the street did so. These they covered with white calico on which were arrayed plates of cakes; sausage rolls; chocolates; sticky buns and lemonade, and lots of other foods grown-ups seem to like but which us kids hardly noticed - having eyes only for the "tasties" mentioned.

The celebration began with the launching of ourselves into the sensible business of eating. Whilst we did this, those adults partaking of liquids conferring a mistaken belief in the possession of a melodious singing voice rendered the mentioned patriotic songs in an all-join-in session. However, we didn't object to their frivolity - just as long as they retained enough wit to hand out cake and pour out lemonade as fast as we made these disappear.

Next day, news spread around the district that a street along Rochdale Road had won the "best decorated" prize. We all trooped off to have a look. I remember crowds congregating at the end of the street; but, being small, I managed to wriggle to the front to see what spectacular attraction commanded their attention.

My gaze became riveted by a cul-de-sac wherein every house-wall was painted red; and all the front doors painted blue; and all the window-sills painted white; and masses and masses of red white and blue buntings suspended across the street - from every upstairs window! And the flags of Saint George; Saint Andrew; the red Welsh Dragon - everywhere - even on the chimney-stacks!

And - wonders of all wonders: the slate-roofs of the end houses facing up the street painted as a massive Union Flag!

You don't believe me? Well! Take a look...

JUBILEE '35

They held a party in the streets:
buns and cakes, and special treats.
Each house brought its table out —
the ones with legs they knew were stout.
They lined them up in one long row;
and covered the tops with calico.
They painted roofs: red, white, and blue —
and doors, and walls; and windows, too.
The kids ate 'til they had pop eyes.
    The cul-de-sac won
    the Jubilee Prize.

30
As a Matter of Interest:
King George V.

The offered photograph is a copy of one taken some months before the depicted King George V died, in the January of 1936.

It shows the King with his wife, Queen Mary, along with their granddaughter who became the present Queen Elizabeth the Second.

The photo appeared in a newspaper then known as the 'News Chronicle' and was one amongst many presented in a supplement issued on December 11th 1936. This concerned the new King - known as George VI - who was, of course, the son of the two shown in the photo and also the father of Elizabeth.

However, this narrative is mainly about the man the photo presents. He came into the world at 1:30 a.m. on the 3rd June 1865; and thereby became the second son of Edward, Prince of Wales (subsequently Edward VII) and Princess Alexandra of Denmark - thus becoming a grandson of Queen Victoria.

At the time of his birth, the American Civil War had just ended and Dr David Livingstone - famed for his African explorations - had recently returned from the region in which he had been allegedly lost.

The British-born Henry Morton Stanley - then working for the 'New York Herald' - had "found" Livingstone who, on his return to Britain, began publishing details about his meanderings through Africa. These were eagerly read by an admiring public along with Stanley's book: 'How I Found Livingstone'.

Also in the year of his birth, Lord Palmerston of "Gunboat" fame died - as did Mrs Elizabeth Gaskell who, through her novels, disclosed the problems afflicting the poor in the industrial North of England.

A family controversy arose soon after the future King's birth because Queen Victoria had a "thing" about names. She had a strong aversion towards the name "George" - probably due to the unfortunate disability exhibited by her grandfather, George III. Nevertheless, she very much liked the name Albert (her recently deceased husband's name) and didn't mind Frederick (a popular name amongst the Hanoverian royalty).

However, the Prince of Wales - sticking firmly to his own and his wife's first choice, but making a concession to the Queen - had the new-born Christened on the 7th July 1865 in Saint George's Chapel, Windsor, to receive the names: George, Frederick, Ernest, Albert.

George happened to be the second son, but his elder brother (Albert, Victor - Duke of Clarence and Avondale) died in 1892 of influenza and George thereby became next in line to the throne. Not only this, he married, one year later, on the 6th July 1893, Albert's intended bride: Princess Mary of Teck (Teck being a small German Kingdom at that time).

It seems Queen Victoria had a great keenness for having Mary brought into the family; and, when Mary found herself without the expected prospect of marriage, Victoria exhibited her desire by soliciting various members of the family to arranged as many meetings as they could between George and Mary.

One such meeting took place at the home of George's sister - Princess Louise - in the May of 1893. Louise suggested George should take Mary into the secluded garden to look at the frogs in the pond. It seems this peep at the amphibians had the desired affect, and they were married within three months of this inspection - much to the delight of Queen Victoria.

On the death of George's father (King Edward VII) in the late evening of the 6th May 1910 - as Halley's Comet streaked the night sky - George became King almost within a few weeks of his forty-fifth birthday and his wife therefore became Queen Mary.

His father, the deceased King Edward, was, it seems, a popular monarch; this being demonstrated by the fact that - despite the severe thunderstorms raging overhead - more than 250,000 people formed long queues so that they could file past where he lay "in state", for three days, in Westminster Hall.

A year later, on the 22nd June 1911, the new King George's position became "officially" declared by a Coronation at Westminster Abbey. 50,000 troops lined the processional route, commanded by Lord Kitchener of the First World War poster fame that stated: "Your Country Needs You".

The procession made its way under a sky of fleeting clouds laden with threats of drenching showers. Nevertheless, this didn't deterred the tightly packed crowds gathered along the way; who, in those days, loved the "pomp and circumstances" offered by such occasions and would not, in the least, question or feel embarrassed about its elaborate display - or, it seems, be put-off by the weather.

As previously stated: George's father (King Edward VII) had established a firm popularity during his reign and George strived to establish his own particular "connection with the people" by asserting his Englishness.

In one such affirmation directed towards the writer H. G. Wells - a staunch republican, who accused the King of being the head of an "alien and uninspiring court" - the King remarked:

"I may be uninspiring, but I'm damned if I'm an alien."

The Queen backed this stance by declaring herself: "English from top to toe," and renounced speaking the language of her native province.

In the 1914-18 war, the King again affirmed his allegiances by renouncing Germanic association and taking on the title of "Windsor" - thus instituting the dynasty as it is today. This did much to confer public approval amidst wartime tensions, since the name Windsor seemed quintessentially English. Saxe-Coburg-Gotha (their original title) lacked an "English ring" and tended to "disturb" people.

Present sentiments, mindful of race, may be inclined to suggest a taint of "racism" in the King's attitude. However, his action in other fields emphatically denied this. For instance: he insisted that clubs and public places in India should be the province of all races. Moreover, he instructed that visiting Indian Maharajahs and their wives should, at palace luncheons, be placed in the "honourable" position on the Queen's right-hand side when visiting England. (He may've got his enthusiasm for India from his grandmother, Queen Victoria?)

Another way he "pleased" the crowds was by making as many visits as possible to areas all over Britain. Lancashire, for instance, witnessed this in the July of 1934 when he embarked on a royal tour around the County, which included a special visit to Manchester.

During the forty-eight hours spent in the city, he officially opened the Manchester Central Library in the presence of massive crowds lining the route and pressing around the building in order to get a glimpse of his presence. Thus he became very popular in the Manchester area, and the city's enthusiasm for the Jubilee of the following year reflected that popularity.

The King also used this method of being widely seen in the nation's capital, resulting in the same popularity that he generated in

Manchester. His success in achieving this popularity was implied in The Daily Telegraph's issue of May 7th 1935, related to the Jubilee festivities in London. This particular report stated:

Vast crowds surrounded Buckingham Palace all day and until the early hours of the morning. At 9:15 p.m., in response to frequent cries of "We want the King", their Majesties appeared on the balcony for the third time since their return to the Palace, to be acclaimed by a crowd of between 150,000 and 200,000. The King commanded the floodlights to be turned on and for five minutes stood with the Queen, waving to the throng.

The crowd cheered again and again and repeatedly sang: "For He's a Jolly Good Fellow". Shortly before ten, his Majesty pressed a button in the Palace. At once, the great bonfires burst into flames - and a chain of 2,000 beacons blazed out on every hilltop in Britain.

Enormous crowds turned the West-end of London into a carnival city. The revels in the street continued until dawn and in some places, later. It was the merriest London night since the Armistice.

In addition to being widely seen in public, the King became widely heard over the wireless. For instance: in 1923, John Reith, the general manager of the newly formed BBC, invited the King to do a national broadcast.

This invitation carried with it the first model of the very latest wireless-set, as a gift - this proffered on behalf of the BBC (as an encouragement?). Soon after the invite, the King opened the previously mentioned British Empire Wembley Exhibition, in the April of 1924, thereby taking the opportunity to submit himself to the increasing persuasions to broadcast. As a result, his voice became heard for the first time over the new media and therefore by a public whose extent was never before thought possible - in this case, millions of eager listeners.

Many broadcasts followed over the next eight years, especially on ceremonial occasions. In 1932, he instituted the Christmas Day message presented at 3:00 p.m. This, as we know, traditionally continues up to the present time, with the present monarch.

Rudyard Kipling, in his capacity of being one of the foremost and immensely popular poets at that time, wrote some of the words contained in the first broadcast. Its opening stated:

I speak now from my home and from my heart to you all; to men and women so cut off by the snows, the desert, or the sea, that only voices out of the air can reach them...

In the light of all these efforts to become the "people's king", we can readily see why the Party we witnessed contained so much enthusiasm for the person whose Silver Jubilee it was - and for which he expressed his gratitude over the wireless that day to everyone attending the celebrations.

The King died on the 20th of January 1936; and, in the four days during which he laid where his father had laid in Westminster Hall, some twenty-six years previously, 809,182 people were counted as having walked silently past his resting-place to pay their respects.

The Daily Mail's publication of Tuesday, January 28th 1936, graphically expressed this scene when it stated in its Memorial Supplement:

It was a wonderful and awe-inspiring manifestation of the love and reverence felt for King George by men, women and children. Their sadness was marked by a silence intensely profound. Mile upon mile the pilgrimage stretched through the streets. Hour after hour it crept past the catafalque with no sound beyond the sibilance of moving feet...

Thus, the jubilation of 1935 changed to the silent sorrow of 1936.

It was as if this truly heralded the end of an era.

This we can contemplate in the narratives to follow...

31
What Will the Neighbours Think?

~~~~~~~~~~~~~~~~~~~~~~~~~~~~~~~~~~~

An aspect of the old neighbourly communities that may seem totally bizarre to the present-day mind is contained in the phrase: "What will the neighbours think?" Most people now shudder at the though of the watchful neighbours this phrase implies. It resurrects the dreaded image of "twitching curtains" and busybody gossiping.

However, before we react to this image in the way our present perceptions may incline us to do, we need to recognise that the present period seems quite comfortable with the ubiquitous scanning lenses of Closed Circuit Television. Any anxiety we may feel about these is, it seems, diminished by the belief that they have a "policing function". We therefore feel content in believing that only those transgressing against the instrument's role of monitoring the good behaviour that the law expects of us need fear its "watching" function.

Perhaps another reason we feel comfortable about such devices is that we believe them to be impersonal. This appears to make them acceptable within our present period's aversion towards "personal" interference. By contrast, the feeling that a twitching curtain requires a person behind it - to make it twitch - gives us a sense of unease. However, we seem content to ignore the fact that many CCTV systems have a watchful person constantly directing their attention to the display-screen; and if there isn't one watching, in the immediacy, there can be one soon afterwards to view what's been recorded.

All this indicates a substantial shift of perception that's taken place over the periods we're considering, related to what is believed to be acceptable watching. For instance: the time that "lived with" what twitching curtains implied expressed great horror about the type of system that we now accept as part of everyday life.

This we find potently expressed in the 1949 publication of George Orwell's futuristic novel, 'Nineteen Eighty-four'. In this, it was the impersonal, ubiquitous and hidden nature of the "watching" that the period of "twitching curtains" found so chilling. That period would no doubt suggest that our present period has put something like the impersonal watching-system into daily use - without us feeling any "chill".

We also accept various degrees of Neighbourhood Watch, now consider as a "sensible arrangement" for any neighbourhood to have.

However, its watching is not so much concerned with those belonging to the neighbourhood but with those external to it. But as we saw during our visits: the people in the neighbourly communities of our interest rarely concerned themselves with "outsiders", because they'd see these as having little affect on the continuing stability of their community. Therefore, the watchful neighbours in the old communities were more concerned about the moral behaviour of those living amongst them, because this - they'd feel - had immediate affect upon their neighbourhood.

What mischief strangers might commit would, and should, they'd rightly believe, come under the watchful eye of their official "neighbourhood watch" represented by the bobby-on-the-beat.

Again and as previously implied: present-day dispositions would react in horror towards the idea of neighbours "policing" the morality of neighbours. However, we've seen many expressions of moral indignation emerge in present-day situations; where, for instance, people of certain communities have forcible reacted towards those they didn't want as neighbours. They were, we can assume, "policing" their neighbourhood to ensure that only those they believed were conforming to "acceptable standards" would be worthy of remaining amongst them.

From this, the conclusion seems to be that it isn't so much the idea of watching that disturbs people, but the way it is done and who does it. It may therefore prove interesting to examine the watching tolerated by the old communities within what the people of that time considered "acceptable standards" of behaviour.

Again, this means going back to previous periods in history, which inevitably involves a trail with many twists and turns. However, the main path of the route to tread is clearly indicated because its signpost is marked by a conspicuous Victorian belief. This held that morality must stem from a source over and above the individual to be truly "authoritative". The general acceptability of this expectation is encapsulated in Viscount Morley's observation presented in his book 'The Life of Gladstone', which declared:

In every field of thought and life he [Gladstone] started from the principle of authority; it fitted in with his reverential instincts, his temperament, above all, his education.

Running alongside this expectation was the belief that guilt and its associated shame should be the reaction of a "normal" individual when transgressing against the morality decreed by the higher authority - be it religious or secular. As previously suggested: the immediate custodians of this morality in the Victorian-influenced communities of our visits were the people constantly encountered in the course of everyday life; and in those compact and still very much Victorian communities, these would be the neighbours.

Our present perceptions would find this tyranny of neighbourly judgmentalism as comically absurd. Moreover, the idea of submitting to a morality because of its authoritative status would be seen as a chronic "deferentialism" (to coin a word). The fact that present-day perceptions are inclined that way illustrates the comment made in L.P. Hartley's novel 'The Go-between', set in Edwardian times; wherein his often quoted first line declares:

The past is a foreign country. They do things differently there.

As far as that part of the past revealed by our visits is concerned, we saw this to be substantially true. However, one of the most powerful and enduring regulators of behaviour - in all periods - is a constant sensitivity about other people's opinions. Moreover, the capacity to feel unease when sensing the disapproval of those whose appraisals we value is an important mechanism in what students of society call "social control". Thus, there's always a strong inclination to avoid the "pain" of disapproval. This, along with the capacity to feel shame if transgressing against accepted opinions, was the self-imposed mechanism behind the anxiety about "what will the neighbours think".

Although applications of social control of whatever type is an essential in any orderly society - and therefore needs to be a common and enduring theme connecting every period - the difficulty L.P. Hartley's novel implies resides in the thought-process peculiar to each period. Therefore, unless we gain insight into the mind-set of the past, the "control" it exercised is bound to appear foreign.

Again and as it happens: the convenient start of the period whose thoughts we need to delve coincides with Alexis de Tocqueville making his visit to Manchester, in the July of 1835 - just two years or so before Queen Victoria came to the throne. No conjectures were made during his first introduction as to the "why" of his visit. However, one reason arose, it seems, from the removal of Charles X from the French throne in 1830, impelling that person to flee to England for refuge.

This event made Tocqueville doubt the stability of French society and impelled him to follow the King's tracks - to see the type of country willing to provide protection.

At this stage, you might say:

"Whoa! We're straying far too far from the setting we're supposed to be considering. And what has a French visitor in 1835 got to do with the neighbours and their thinking - let alone bringing a king into the picture to create additional confusions?"

Well, it tends to be a truism that if a person's past is known, then their behaviour and beliefs can make more sense. This principle is one which, I believe, applies to communities, societies and even nations. So, in trying to understand the watchfulness of neighbours in the communities of our visits, the insight needed might reside in the preceding Victorian period. And this brings us back to the where we were before the assumed objection.

As previously implied: Tocqueville's visit stemmed from his anxieties about the stability of French society. This impelled a desire to explore the social and political backgrounds of what he thought was the comparative stability offered by the newly emerging democracies taking shape in Britain and also in the America that he'd previously visited. However, in crossing the Channel, he found himself in a country deep in the process of what, for him, were the massive and unexpected changes he witnessed in Manchester.

Judging by his reaction, it seemed he saw in this new "revolution" the stirrings of the same anxiety he had about France - a fear of social instability. This fear he detected in many prominent members of the English aristocracy that had befriended him. Although he, himself, eventually became optimistic about England's chances of avoiding the civil war suffered by his native land, he had, nevertheless, previously held the opinion that:

England seems to me in a critical state in that certain events, which it is possible to predict, can throw her into a state of violent revolution.

The cause and nature of the fears held by many in the English upper echelon are well documented, in as many history books on that period as one could care to find, so we needn't go into great detail. Sufficient to say that prominent in the English mind were the disorders the French Revolution of 1789 engendered, whose repercussions were still reverberating with various degrees of intensity when Tocqueville arrived in Britain.

The English anxieties were exacerbated at the time of the original French disturbances by the many supportive sympathies voiced on this side of the Channel. The poet Wordsworth, for instance, expressed his own sentiments and those of his associates when he stated in the part of his Prelude related to the French Revolution:

But 'twas a time when Europe was rejoiced, France standing on the top of golden hours, and human nature seeming born again.

In the important political realm, Charles James Fox, a prominent member of the Whig Party, also welcomed this happening and openly declared his enthusiasm in Parliament. Additionally, and soon after the fall of the Bastille on the 14th of July 1789, he emphatically expressed his feelings in a letter to his associate, Richard Fitzpatrick:

How much the greatest event it is that ever happened in the world! And how much the best!

Although all these sympathetic and potentially revolutionary voices were, at first, ignored by the main body of the British Establishment (who, in the beginning, saw the French disturbances as diverting a main European adversary away from these shores) nevertheless, the declaration of war against Britain by France, in 1793, along with the French invasion of Holland - with its apparent aspirations to spread revolutionary fervour abroad by military conquests - forced Britain to "sit up and take notice", so to speak. The activities resulting from this "taking notice" we've seen glamorously and fictitiously portrayed in the 'Sharpe' series on TV.

Less than glamorous and certainly far from fictitious to the people of that time was Napoleon assembling an army comprising 150,000 men at the port of Dunkirk (the same number as the German assembled 136 years later) for an intended invasion of Britain. The "concrete" substantiation of this anxiety we see in the seventy-four Martello Towers, constructed in great haste in 1804 along England's south coast - some of which are now used for the happier purpose of popping in for a cup of tea and having a good view along the seashore, when holidaying.

It's easy to imagine that cups of tea and a relaxed view along the coast were far from the minds of those constructing the defences. Foremost in their minds was the real prospect of an immanent invasion, which the previously mentioned sympathisers in this country potentially supported.

However, much to the relief of those fearful of British revolutionary aspirations, the "Terrors" against the enemies of the French Republic (as cruel in their execution as the more recently documented Bolshevik and Stalinist persecutions) caused, in itself, a drastic decline in the original sympathetic voices.

Admiral Nelson sunk any possibilities of invasion by destroying the French fleet at Trafalgar in the October of 1805. Then the Duke of Wellington finally stamped out the revolutionary torch at the Battle at Waterloo, in the June of 1815.

Nevertheless, some heat remained and anxieties about a possible spread of revolutionary aspirations still smouldered. This anxiety became heated by the traumatic event at Saint Peter's Square, in Manchester, on the 16th August 1819 - when a meeting of 60,000 mainly working-class people was suppressed with an intense nervous fear on the part of the Authorities. This outburst of the Establishment's anxiety eventually became known as the 'Peterloo" Massacre' - involving 15 people killed and 420 seriously injured.

As a reaction to this, Percy Shelley, in his poem the 'Masque of Anarchy', tried to whip up revolutionary fervour against those he believed responsible, by declaring:

> *I met Murder on the way –*
> *He had a mask like Castlereagh...*
> *Rise like lions after slumber*
> *In unvanquishable number,*
> *Shake your chains to earth like dew*
> *Which in sleep had fallen on you –*
> *Ye are many – they are few.*

Despite the awful repression at Peterloo (a name derived from the merging of the words "Peter" and "Waterloo") unrest continued in various forms during the following decades. For instance and again in Manchester: when Stephenson's Rocket arrived at the newly constructed Liverpool Road Station, at 2:35 in the afternoon of Wednesday, 15th September 1830 - after its journey from Liverpool - a gathering of hand-loom weavers assembled in the adjacent Ordsall Lane met the train. Their gathering arose from an incipient fear related to loss of employment caused by the type of mechanisation the train represented.

Whilst waiting for the train to arrive, they "decorated" the station with French Tricolours as an expression of their discontent. On the arrival of the train, they hissed at and jeered the Duke of Wellington - Prime Minister at that time, and erstwhile victor over Napoleon at Waterloo - as he sat in one of the train's carriages.

Such was the intensity of protest and the size of crowd that the journalist, witnessing what they hoped would be a triumphal end to a journey of historical proportion, feared the onset of mass revolution. This they anxiously noted in their reports along with the threatening symbol of the displayed Tricolour.

Alongside the displaced workers' anger were the rumblings of the Chartist Movement, with its demonstrations demanding extensive political concessions and social and industrial changes - with threats of violent unrest if such weren't soon forthcoming.

So the anxieties emerging before Tocqueville's visit still persisted after he arrived. Interwoven with all this was the belief on the part of the established "Authority" that, although the French Revolution seemed to arise essentially from political pressures, its ensuing cruelties were the consequences of an increase in personal immorality. These, the establishment held, were generated by atheistic attitudes.

Those affirming this supposition pointed to the trends found in many pre-Revolutionary writings and especially that of the prominent and widely influential French philosopher, Voltaire, who, in his pronouncements on religion, stated:

Every man of sense - every good man - ought to hold the Christian sect in horror...

Whether Voltaire was - at the time - justified in his pronouncement or not is another matter; but what does matter for our purpose is not the truth or falsity of Voltaire's statement but the fact that his statement appeared to many on this side of the Channel as leading to a breakdown of traditional beliefs - and therefore of social order. This perceived immoral spectre, evoked by the French disturbances, continued to haunt the English mind. An influential English historian and biographer of that time, James Anthony Froude, expressed the Victorians' faith in religion's role in banishing that spectre when he declared:

...an established religion...is the sanction of moral obligation; it gives an authority to the commandments, creates a fear of doing wrong and a sense of responsibility for doing it.

So, the cry of "Liberty", loudly proclaimed in the French Revolution, far from being heard as the cry of a victorious and glorious human nature being born again, became in many English minds synonymous with the cry of "Licence". This being an easy correlation for those holding firmly to the Biblical concept of Original Sin and the morality a "higher authority" decreed necessary to control that affliction.

Those with a cynical disposition might suggest that all these fears and their justifying beliefs were, in reality, the concerns of the ruling class about a threatened loss of property and privilege. Moreover, they might also say that the use of a religious underpinning could be - as Karl Marx later proposed around the time of 1850 - a devious concoction to "sedate" the discontented masses into an acceptance of the existing status quo, favourable to the ruling class.

Whether this cynicism is justified or not, and whether or not a revolution similar to that in France would've been a good thing for this country - to sweep away the "old repressive order" - which some people then and even some people now think was needed - is a matter of political taste. But if such a revolution had occurred, the historic road would not be the one we're now attempting to follow. Also, it's an odds-on bet that many Britons would've found themselves marching in Napoleon's army, helping to extend his European Empire - this forming a close alliances with the erstwhile American Colonies from which, perhaps, many nominated Governors of Britain, friendly to France, would arrive to replace the disposed aristocracy.

In this scenario, it's obvious that we wouldn't be talking about a Victorian Period. And the concerns those in Heelis Street had about "what will the neighbours think" may've been expressed in some version of French - that is, of course, if that street existed for us to eventually comment upon those who lived in it.

However, and as we know: the path we're following had no "Napoleonic deviation" (fortunately or unfortunately - depending on one's political stance). By the time the Victorian period became established, anxieties had moved away from the possibilities of external invasion and began to centre on the contingency of internal disruptions, arising from that previously mentioned moral decline the Victorians believed fermented the French Revolution.

Yet a concern about morality hover in almost every age one may care to examine. For instance, the late playwright, Dennis Potter, indicated unease about the underlying possibilities in a TV discussion, when he suggested "anyone being offered licence would take it". He appeared to imply that if any person happened to be offered the power to do exactly what they wanted, free from hindrance or consequences, they would find the offer "attractive". Whether or not Dennis Potter was right or wrong in his estimation of the nature of human nature is, again, another matter. But the desire to do what we want without adverse consequences, which he insinuated exists in all of humankind, is probably the dream of every child - and, no doubt, the spur goading every dictator's ambitions throughout history.

Humankind without any adherence to moral imperatives to temper and control its "greed and passions" can present quite a frightening prospect - as the Terrors of the French Revolution seemed to imply to those who'd viewed its ravages from this side of the Channel.

Additionally, the early Victorians would have in mind the lesson of Peterloo and the warning the philosopher Edmund Burke (1729-1797) offered in his statement:

The use of force alone is but temporary. It may subdue for a moment, but it does not remove the necessity of subduing again: and a nation is not governed which is perpetually to be conquered.

Burke's caveat referred to the American Colonies' rebellion in 1775 but no doubt carried a weighty warning related to the type of reactions subsequent disturbance could elicit.

Alongside Burke's warning about reactions to national disturbances, the Victorians became mindful of the fact that individual acts of lawlessness and immorality were not just an isolated problem confined to the individuals concerned, but acts that could, cumulatively, affect society and therefore the nation in general.

This realisation turned Victorian minds towards emphasising the previously quoted James Anthony Froude's faith in religion's role in creating the "individual conscience" believed necessary for an orderly society. The success of an Evangelistic Movement - preaching the "worthy" instruction to "improve one's life and give obedience to the Laws of God", thereby adhering to the old moralities - was welcomed by the Victorian upper echelons as assisting this orderly development.

Alongside this came the increasing prosperity generated by expanding industries. These economic and religious persuasions began to divert revolutionary minds away from social disruption and turned them towards the more cautious view of gradual reform.

Another "saving grace", if we can call it that - and one seeming to justify Tocqueville's perceptions about the newly emerging democracies - was that the ruling class (unlike that in France) seemed wisely willing to make political concessions before tensions became too tense. In contrast to his gloomy view of the industrial scene, he formed a brighter one of the political vista. He observed the "openness" of the English aristocracy in the changing commercial climate and concluded:

The English aristocracy can therefore never arouse those violent hatreds felt by the middle and lower classes against the nobility in France where the nobility is an exclusive caste, which while monopolising all privileges and hurting everybody's feelings, offers no hope of entering its ranks. The English aristocracy has a hand in everything; it is open to everyone...

Even the fierce old Duke of Wellington accepted the necessity of reducing the social barriers, along with its implications. When asked would the aristocracy eventually lose its property and privileges, he resignedly but cynically remarked:

Yes; but we shall not have a commotion, we shall not have blood, but we shall be plundered by the Rule of Law.

No doubt he said this with the warning of Edmund Burke and his reception at Liverpool Road Station in mind.

These powerful political concerns generated various responses to the "mistake" of Peterloo and the continuing rumblings of the Chartists Movement. They appeared in the Reform Bill of 1832 followed by the 1867 and 1887 enactments - resulting in the gradual transference of power from the aristocracy to the people. This highroad towards order was further secured by Sir Robert Peel's instigation of the London Police Force in 1829, whose system spread throughout the country by 1856. Its modus operandi was that of enforcing law and order equally and impartially and without the centralised, armed, and sometimes repressive, police force known in other countries - which seemed to the early Victorians as being prone to "political mischief".

But even with all these measure, the path to stability remained perilous. Old habits of discontent didn't die out and the reasons for its uneasy expression still hovered. The rough and uncertain road that the Victorians hoped they were paving with the solid flagstones of institutional and political reform still contained the less easily-paved over potholes of that other anxiety: moral decline.

Containing as this does some of humankind's most powerful and potentially disruptive passions, it seemed less readily directed or even dealt with by force or parliamentary acts. This difficulty seem even more intractable with the dramatic increase in prostitution - a trend the more cynically inclined suggested (maybe correctly) wasn't helped by the extremely low wages for long and arduous working hours offered to females in the industrial cities.

For instance, at the start of the Victorian Era, various authorities set up to administer the Poor Laws estimated more than 50,000 prostitutes in England and Wales with at least 8,000 of these operating in London. In addition, something like 40,000 yearly births outside of "wedlock" imposed a charge upon a Poor Law system already overburdened by the vast displacements of people caused by economic pressures.

All these social disruptions the early Victorians were forced to face. This they did with only a rudimentary knowledge about the cause and cure of diseases spread by prostitution and the disorders produced by poor sanitation in the "thrown together" and rapidly expanding industrialised cities. In addition, they had the problem of a rapidly expanding population. That of England and Wales rose from 9 to 18 million in the years from 1801 to 1851. The population of Manchester, for example - estimated at 22,000 during the latter part of the 1700s - increased to 235,000 by 1830. These social problems make those of our present age appear, by comparison, quite minor.

In this setting, the early Victorians struggled with their perennial problem concerning law and order and moral decline. The answer to the first we saw in their various political reforms. The answer to the second increasingly appeared to reside in the safeguards offered by a properly constituted family embraced by religious ethics.

Their fears about failing to ensure the family's firm foundations are succinctly observed on page 85 of Professor Thompson's book 'The Rise of Respectable Society' - published in 1988 by Fontana Press:

Many early Victorians supposed they were witnessing a 'crisis of family' that threatened, unless successfully tackled and resolved, to undermine the entire fabric of society and to sweep the nation into turbulent, uncharted, and perilous times of chaos and anarchy.

The Victorians believed that the family represented a microcosmic society from which a "natural order" would spread throughout the wider society. They began to trust that "from good homes grew good nations" and trusted that the children within these homes would be tutored to be dutiful and disciplined, so that (to use another Victorian concept) "the nation could grow from the nursery".

Through these emerging religious and social sentiments (probably assisted by Victoria's marriage to her cousin, Albert, in the February of 1840 and her subsequent and obvious idolisation of her husband) the picture of home and family-life began to assume its Victorian vision. This they saw as a union at whose head the authoritative figure of the father stood and at whose heart the firm but gently controlling figure of the mother resided - this no doubt reflecting the position, in sentiment, then existing in the Royal Household.

The Victorians therefore began to see the institution of the family - publicly declared within secular law and bonded by the solemn act of a religious marriage - as reflecting the commitment under religion and law of a well ordered society. They saw it as offering the stability wherein the emotional needs of the two "joined together" could be fully and safely satisfied, and as the proper setting in which the resulting children would become "industrious, god-fearing and law-abiding". The prescription for this domestic order was offered by the 18th Century English Jurist, Sir William Blackstone, who, in his 'Commentaries on the Laws of England', 1775, stated:

> *The main end and design of marriage [is] to ascertain and fix upon some certain person, to whom the care, the protection, the maintenance and the education of the children should belong.*

Due to the long established economic and biological nature of things, and the Victorians' historical predisposition towards patriarchy, this "certain person" became emphatically the male, whose duties and responsibilities were seen as those declared by Blackstone. The social benefit of this arrangement, with its implied division of domestic roles, became affirmed and extended by Edmund Burke's comment (made at the same time) that it represented:

> *...the contract which renovates the world.*

In addition, Victorian religiosity saw this "secure arrangement" as an optimum means of controlling the Original Sin engendered by Adam's disobedience against God, resulting in expulsion from the Garden of Eden with its consequential loss of "innocence". This loss of original "purity" became entangled in the sexual act that followed the expulsion, as the King James Version of the Bible (Genesis, Chapter 4) implies:

> *And Adam knew Eve his wife, and she conceived...*

Coupled (no pun intended) with this "knowing", and emblazoned across the Victorian mind, would be Saint Paul's "call to morality" in his First Epistle to the Corinthians; and more especially the part about marriage, as expressed in his declaration:

> *...to avoid fornication, let every man have his own wife, and let every woman have her own husband.*

He then stated why this should be so and declared the dreadful consequence of ignoring the "why":

> *But if they cannot contain, let them marry: for it is better to marry than to burn.*

By "contain" he obviously meant, "maintain a state of abstinence". The Victorians therefore saw sexuality as a necessary but dangerous condition, whose expression only marriage could "safely" allow.

In our secularised period, many would find these declarations as an amusing indication of Victorian preposterousness. However, the Victorians took it all very seriously, not only because Saint Paul's declaration would be considered as "authoritative holy writ" but also because what Saint Paul deemed as the act of fornication created many of the previously mentioned social problems.

Various emotional pressures therefore focused on keeping the male and female - and especially the homemaking female - in their "safe" family setting by the weight of social conformity. Those not having entered its protective haven were encouraged to do so as soon as their feelings impelled.

You may now rightly be thinking: "Everyone knows what happened in that restrictive time called the Victorian period - with its impositions, confusions and difficult to defend dual standards - so when are we going to get to the point of hearing about the neighbours?"

Well, the neighbours will soon return to the scene, to reveal what they do think. Also, it's all too true that the Victorians have a bad press - particularly when related to the assumed hypocrisy that lived alongside their morality. So much so that the antipathy their period evokes is now so entrenched that an accusation of having Victorian Values is one of the most damning invectives - especially in the political realm.

However, in order to appreciate what we now see as "Victorian peculiarities" it might be useful to attempt placing ourselves in their stage of history. In doing so, we need to appreciate the fact that - before a developing science allowed the latter half of the twentieth century to see things from a vastly different perspective - the Victorian period was one in which the usual consequence of even the "family-safe" union was for the woman to enter into a serial pregnancy. Therefore, to the Victorians, it would seem part of a natural ordinance for the woman to be domestically confined and for the man (freed by nature from the physical bonds of giving birth) to be the "provider and protector". To repeat Tennyson's previously quoted affirmation:

Man for the field and woman for the hearth.

It would've been remarkable if - within the context of their experience and considering their uncertain knowledge concerning birth control - the early Victorians had arrived at a conclusion other than the one that they did. In this respect, their prescriptions for the family weren't élitist, anti-feminist, chauvinist, or whatever "ist" our later periods may be inclined to ascribe to Victorian values, in this and many other considerations. The only "ist" that seems appropriate would be "common-sensist" (to coin a phrase).

As happens in every age: attitudes are formed by "opinion leaders" - as we would now called them. In the time we're considering, these came mainly in the form of royalty; statesmen; religious leaders; writers and philosophers. To be a successful shaper of thoughts these notables had to voice the concerns and anxieties of people and offer apparent solutions - as is the case in any period.

A typical example of Victorian advice directed towards the unmarried, and the possible social problems which could arise from that status, appeared in a popular and widely circulated magazine of that time - The Westminster Review. It asserted the behaviour necessary to avoid sexual impropriety by declaring:

And what, in these days, can preserve chastity, save some relic of chivalrous devotion? Are we not all aware that a young man can have no safeguard against sensuality and low intrigue, like an early, virtuous and passionate attachment?

In this counselling for those with "worries", the word "passionate" would mean "honest and ardently sincere" rather than the sexual bias a later age conferred upon the word.

Another widely circulated magazine of that time, with a section equivalent to the present day Agony Aunt, echoed similar advice to that offered in the Westminster Revue, by stating:

Lovers should not go further than a chaste kiss before marriage, but conduct themselves with perfect propriety, purity and chastity. If a man's love be pure, he cannot commit an impure act or indulge even in wicked thought or desire towards the woman he loves.

These "recommendations" would be met with astonishment within our present perspective - especially from the perspective of gender equality finally emerging in the latter half of the 1900s. The typical lad and lass of our time would laugh the Victorian agony aunt's advice completely off the page. They would - indeed - think it came not only from a foreign land but also from a downright peculiar one. And the suggestion that we should stifle "desires", which the media constantly reminds us all that we should freely enjoy - to the point of making us anxious that we might not be doing so - would be thought of as "unhealthy repression" and an infringement of our "personal liberties". But the responsible Victorian lad and lass would've taken both sets of advice very seriously; for, as previously suggested, the results of not abiding by such advice could be dire for all involved.

No Welfare State existed to provide for individual difficulties and to offer services without judgement or financial consequences upon the "victim". Such a system would hardly be ideologically possible within the Victorian state of knowledge and its insistence on individual responsibility and self-reliance. Samuel Smiles's best-selling book 'Self-Help' (1859) epitomised this ethos in its opening words:

Heaven helps those who help themselves… The spirit of self-help is the root of all genuine growth in the individual…it constitutes the true source of national vigour and strength.

The burden of responsibility for individual circumstances therefore rested upon the individual. The condemnations applied to those who "strayed" beyond advised moral safeguards would be directly related to this belief and the absence of our taken-for-granted protections.

Thus, what we've now come to think of as the harsh moralistic Victorian attitudes held their sway. The belief that fidelity was the supreme virtue and infidelity in sexual behaviour the "blackest of sins" determined propriety. This belief became constantly reaffirmed by a public opinion absorbing the published advice we've read, the social trends we've traced, and the morality portrayed by many Victorian novels. This anxiety associated with "intimate matters" and their possible dangers if "uncontrolled" cut deep into the Victorian psyche to the extent that its trauma continued long enough to influence the thinking and the type of films we saw in the nineteen-thirties.

Related to this felt need to control "dangerous behaviour", Henry Hobhouse, the American ecologist - in his book 'Forces Of Change' - commented upon the vast shift in attitudes the onset of sexually transmitted diseases had created. He observed these were the first that could be directly related to human action and from this arose the horror regarding promiscuity. He also observed:

The middle classes [in Victorian England] developed a strong sense of sexual ethics which would one day be called "Victorian", sometimes an adjective of contempt. This contempt could only be expressed by those who ignored the fact that syphilis raged throughout Victorian England - except amongst those who were prissily careful.

In the late 1850s, most of the major London hospitals had over fifty percent of their patients suffering from various forms of sexually transmitted diseases.

Another aspect of promiscuity the "prissily careful" feared was the gangs of abandoned waifs and strays portrayed in Henry Mayhew's 1851 surveys, entitled London Labour and the London Poor, whose conditions had a based-on-fact portrayal in Charles Dickens' Oliver Twist, written in 1838.

As previously implied, we need to wipe out of our minds the protections and the social supports we now enjoy and, without the sustaining comfort these provide, drift back into Victorian times to really understand its anxieties. In doing so, we might be able to see what we now believe to be Victorian evasions; prudery; suppression; prissiness; hypocrisy; false-idealism - call it what we will - emerged amongst enormously complex social problems. In addition, we might now be able to see why people at that time emphatically insisted upon "family virtues", which our archetypal Victorian poet, Alfred Lord Tennyson , avowed would produce:

Household happiness, gracious children, debtless competence, golden mean.

In all ages, ideals are not easily maintained - and this applies to Tennyson's avowal. Our present period is inclined to be suspicious about what dark thoughts and deeds may have transpired behind the respectable lace curtains of Victorian parlours, with the much venerated motto "Home, Sweet Home" displayed on their walls. We tend to judge much of what did go on - within and without the home - as hypocritical; especially in the context of the previously mentioned double standard concerning men and women.

We become even more suspicious of this double standard when recognising its absolutely ludicrous and unjust embodiment in the male-biased Contagious Diseases Act of 1864; whose implications held the belief that the male use of a prostitute was "natural" although the prostitute allowing it was "wicked".

The social reformer, Josephine Elizabeth Butler, made a courageous attack on this chicanery. Her vigorous campaigning in 1886 resulted in its repeal and in raising the age of "sexual consent" from 13 to 16; thereby ameliorated one of the major social problems concerning exploitation of children. It also produced a proper recognition that all aspects of morality could - and should - be the responsibility of both men and women, equally.

However, the status of women in the home represented a different "morality"; and this forms the next part of the trail we need to follow; at whose end we'll hear what the neighbours think.

Despite the obvious value-distortions revealed by Josephine Butler's campaign, the Victorians still clung to the belief that the responsibility for the all-important moral and emotional stability of the domestic setting essentially resided in the female. Lapses, or possible lapses, of the central figure of the family - the "gentle and virtuous" wife and mother - were seen to be the main threat to "domestic harmony". Whilst the person occupying that crucial role remained steadfastly "pure", male lapses would be felt as transient in their affect if the more strongly virtuous female showed a lenient understanding.

But, again, before we give way to the outburst of astonishment our present position in time may incline us towards (along with the assumption that the above-stated proposition must obviously represent a male's point of view, and a rampantly chauvinistic one at that) the concepts just offered were affirmed in a highly popular novel written by George Eliot (pseudonym of Mary Ann Evans - who also acted as editor for the Westminster Review whose "moral pleadings" we previously read).

The fact that she was writing from a woman's mind - and one seen in those times as possessing a high capacity for independent thought - may give an indication of how acceptable this home-making responsibility ascribed to the female had become. For instance: in her novel, 'Silas Marner', written in 1861, one of her main characters, Godfrey Cass (whose "bad habits" are attributed to "growing up in a home without a mother") expresses his desire to marry Nancy Lammeter - the girl of his affection. This he wished to do because - to quote the appropriate line in the novel:

She would make home lovely to him and leave the ear open to the voice of the good angel; inviting to industry, sobriety, and peace.

It goes without saying that our period would give an impatient and, perhaps, an angry dismissal to this idea of the virtuous female upon whom the male depends for the maintenance of his virtuous behaviour - and could therefore implicitly hold the woman responsible for any of his lapses. However, its wide acceptance in the Victorian era (implied in George Eliot's phrase: "the good angel") engendered what we now tend to see as the quaint (or even demeaning?) respects and courtesies the Victorian and post-Victorian societies obliged the male to direct towards the good angel's embodiment.

The idea of a comfortable home with the female figure providing a refining and virtuous influence became so entrenched in the Victorian mind that magazines specifically directed towards home and family matters were constantly published. They held as much popularity and were just as eagerly read as the many magazines dealing with personal problems and concerns that the present period offers. For instance, the magazine 'The Family Friend' could, in 1862, readily suggest:

A wife's duty is to make the home as comfortable as possible so that her husband may always look forward with pleasure to the time when he reaches home.

This sentiment (no doubt then offered without fear of contradiction) implies the old and now amusing "pipe and slippers" image of family life. To the Victorians, this image would fit easily within their moral framework just as slippers were supposed to fit comfortably on the feet of the "breadwinner", who returns home.

The desire to cloister the woman in her perceived-as-essential domestic place - and thereby isolate her from the believed corruption of the world - unfortunately went to obsessive extremes. It reached a reluctance to see females taking part in the "coarseness" of political life. This required the protests of the suffragettes and the demonstrated ability of women to face the harshness of the First World War to eventually open the restrictive door, and let her out into the wider world - so to speak.

Also, the anxieties about keeping women in her "natural place" went as far as laws ensuring her "matrimonial servitude" by taking away property rights and therefore independent viability. Astonishing to our present-day mind, it even went as far as prohibiting the wife redress for infidelity on the part of her husband - forcing upon her the role of the "understanding good angel". Or to use a popular concept of our time: exhorting the good angel to be "non-judgemental".

However, as we've seen from previous incidents: anxieties in the face of fears those anxieties represent can cause all sorts of injustices - and, possibly, many of them unintended? Prime Minister Gladstone - who presided over the repeal of the previously mentioned Contagious Disease Act - admitted this potential social-blindness when he later declared in one of his pamphlets, written near the end of his life:

It has been my misfortune all my life, not to see a question of principle until it is at the door...

Nevertheless, injustices prove difficult to sustain, even in the face of Victorian fears. Attempts to introduce a degree of equity emerged in the 1870 Act that allowed women property rights and then the 1878 Act permitting the courts to grant separation and maintenance orders against husbands committing persistent wrongdoings.

Yet, and as we've seen: many highly intelligent and "liberated" females of that time, including the aforementioned George Eliot, persisted in focusing on the female as being primarily responsible for ensuring initial control of moral situations, and therefore shouldering the burden of possible consequences if they failed to do so.

If nothing else, our long and winding road of Victorian thought affirms the point previously made: there's a considerable line of events involved in shaping an age and its attitudes.

However, we've reached a place along that road where we can witness, in actuality, the affects of the attitudes we saw taking shape in the Victorian moral landscape. This relates to a situation concerning Nancy (whom we met in one of our first visits to the nineteen-twenties) and her child "conceived out of wedlock", and what the neighbours thought about her circumstances.

During the conversations with my mother about her early life, and when the incident of her school-friend, Nancy, was mentioned, I asked why all the condemnation seemed to focus on the girl in question, to the exclusion of the man involved? My mother then told me of the time her mother - my Grandmother - gave "guidance", during what we'd now call my mother's early teenage years. She was told to be well aware that "it was for the man to try, and for the woman to deny." She told me this "rule" was one given to her mother, in her time, and represented an attitude generally accepted as "common-sense".

Another guidance she received along with the one mentioned was: "those who suffer the most from any act must take the most care".

The implications of both these rules - and therefore the likely judgement of that time on the part of the neighbours - would be this: if the woman hadn't insisted enough to "deny", it would be assumed she had behaved - at the best - foolishly and - at the worst - wickedly, and must therefore be primarily to blame and take full responsibility for her act. Gladly, my mother disregarded this prescription in her attitude towards her friend.

Nevertheless, the consequences of Nancy not adhering to its ordinance were sadly illustrated by her situation. In being abandoned by the man in question, Nancy was "left holding the baby". And the reason given by the man to his friends for not facing up to his responsibility was he "believed" Nancy couldn't be "any good", otherwise she wouldn't have "accepted" his advances.

Again, an astonished present-day mind may be inclined to protest that the past was, indeed, a foreign country in which people did things not only differently but also perversely. But (in accordance with our aim of trying to understand the past, and thereby attempting to understand what we would now call "reasoning bordering on the callously cruel", to the point of it being accepted as reasonable by many people of that time) we must recognise the following fact. Ever since time began, the male of our species always had the option to do exactly what the aforementioned man did; whereas the woman almost invariably had to face the possibility of being left with the "evidence" - as in Nancy's case.

Until medical science freed the female from this old inevitability, the focus of attention invariably fell upon the person left with the unmistakable "burden" of what had taken place. The male "carried" no evidence of his "adventures". Therefore, before science devised means for testing male involvement, the female had very little chance of avoiding sole responsibility and the judgements that went with it.

Whether this be fair or unfair; just or unjust; kind or cruel is a matter to be taken up with Nature; Evolution; God - or whatever, or whoever, we believe shaped things the way they were and the way they happen to be. But whatever it was, or is, that formed the physical nature of male and female, it made it far easier for the male to go on his way without carrying with him any evidence of his part in the "act" - if it served his purpose to do so.

Accepting these physical facts, we may be able to grasp the reason why the old morality's blunt logic ascribed to the one who would suffer the most the greater responsibility for avoiding that suffering. This more especially when denying the male any premarital and therefore, for her, a potentially perilous submission (even if enjoyed) would be seen, in a time without "protections", as what any sensible female should do. This, my sensible old grandmother implicitly stressed in the context of the rules she gave to her daughter.

Perhaps we can now appreciate why the Victorian magazines put so much stress on male chivalry and sense of duty? It seemed the only available way of coercing the male into behaving "responsibly" if the female "lapsed" and "foolishly" allowed him to "take possible advantage" of that lapse.

We can also appreciate that not many daughters in the present-time would receive this and its implications without a great deal of amusement, and, possibly, a large amount of indignation. Nevertheless, they fitted the circumstances of the time in which my mother received, what was for that time, sound advice; and poor Nancy's situation would've dispelled any doubts she might've entertained about the validity of the advice given.

But getting back to the force of neighbour's opinions. It seems the expectations about neighbour's judgements contributed its pressure to ensure such predicaments were kept comparatively rare. For instance - and if you don't mind being bombarded with statistics: the illegitimate birth-rate for the years between 1900 and 1939 averaged 43 births for every 1,000 in the population. Figures on the same basis for the 1990s indicate an average of 310 per 1,000. Considering that birth control methods and their availability was virtually none existent in the early nineteen-hundreds, compared with the situation in latter half of the century - and accepting that the pressure of human passions remains constant throughout the ages - the figures seem to show the reverse of what one would expect.

However, to be comparable, we must also take into account a difficult-to-determine proportion of the high number of minimal risk, and perceived as legitimate, abortions becoming increasingly acceptable as a form of birth control for the "unmarried" in the latter half of the twentieth-century. The ease of this is showed by one well-known clinic - offering a "ten minute termination" - recording over 7,000 clients in one year, for that service. The recent overall figure for England and Wales, for all clinics, is something in the order of over 180,000 per annum.

In the time of Nancy's situation, clinical terminations would've been accessible only to a comparatively small section of the population, colloquially known as "the upper class with connections". The working class girl's option would be to go through with the pregnancy or face the horror and the enormous risk of a "back street solution" - which only the extremely desperate would face.

Of course, to be in tune with our later period's thinking, wherein the word "illegitimate" has very little meaning, we'd need to use a term something like: "births and/or conceptions considered to have taken place outside a traditional marriage situation". Even so, the seven-fold increase over the early 1900s figures shown by the 1990s figure (which excludes the latter period's high rate of relevant abortions) indicates a very different force of opinion and a different set of attitudes influencing behaviour.

All this indicates that formal pleadings may have some affect on individual actions, but when these pleadings are supported by widespread and consistent social disapproval, the combination seems to influence even the most strongly passionate inclinations.

This suggests that the most widely used method of birth control generally practised by the unmarried in the period before 1939 seemed to be the most reliable of all methods - i.e. abstinence - and the severe censure shown towards poor Nancy was probably even more severe because her "lapse" was unusual.

Additionally, Nancy's position would represent a defiance of public opinion, because the pressure before the birth of the child, from family and neighbours, would be to confer legitimacy to the child by what our later age would humorously refer to as a "shotgun wedding". The impossibility of this solution in Nancy's circumstances made her situation seem even more incautious "for getting involved with a man like that, who would not face up to his responsibilities" - as the neighbours would no doubt say.

It seems the suspected man removed himself from the discomfort of neighbours' suspicion and its associated insinuations by leaving the district - thereby "escaping" to a place where he wasn't known.

Although the neighbourhood involved may've gained the removal of a person they considered unacceptable, Nancy's situation remained as it was before. In such circumstances, the last resort for a person in her position would be to give up the baby for adoption, as a way of freeing herself from the continuing stigma represented by the baby. But the attachment she had for her infant seemed to disallow that way out. However and as we saw when we met Nancy in one of our previous visits: she eventually found a husband and thereby gained the "protection and respectability" this situation conferred.

So, leaving Nancy in what gladly appears to be the happier circumstances she finally achieved, let's now focus upon the wider conclusion that the long and winding though-trail we've been following seems to indicate. Which is: the anxieties about social stability experienced by Victorian society cut deep, emotional channels. Within these, the mainstream of social control for matters not amenable to the pressures and persuasions represented by formal law became centred on the approbation and condemnation of the agents in a position to exercise such. These - in the Victorian and post-Victorian communities - were mainly the neighbours.

Although the origins of the Victorian fears about social stability hardly existed in the minds of those who constituted neighbours in the communities of our interest, nevertheless, the people within them were substantially shaped by the powerful emotional attitudes arising from the Victorian concerns. These, as we've seen, converged upon order and morality.

Towards the end of the Victorian period and into that of our interest, the words "Order" and "Morality" became virtually synonymous and eventually blended into one word: "Respectability". This implied "conforming to conventionally accepted standards of moral behaviour" and thereby "meriting respect or esteem by virtue of that behaviour" - as the dictionary definition suggests. Therefore, presenting the appearance of respectability, not only in those aspects of moral behaviour receiving the cutting edge of Victorian and post Victorian condemnation, but also in all aspects of behaviour seen as respectable to those in the immediacy - and therefore in a position to judge such behaviour - was something one must do.

Victorian respectability spread its expectations to embrace respect for person and property (the special concern for the latter causing much annoyance to Karl Marx). However, respect and the protection it gives to both were seen - in addition to moral propriety - as an essential in maintaining an orderly society.

So, receiving the approbation that abiding by all aspects of respectability would confer became a source of pride; and avoiding the condemnations (voiced or otherwise expressed in the form of a disapproving silence) any failure to meet respectability's demands could incur was always a persisting anxiety. Thus, this way of regulating behaviour constituted a powerful aspect of the Victorian and then the post-Victorian communities.

If, within the context of present-day thinking, we find ourselves being disdainful about this conformity-producing mechanism, we must recognise a point previously made: the tendency bringing it into existence is found in all of us.

In our present period (wherein scientific sounding phrases tend to express ordinary concepts) the sociological term for the influence of those whose opinions are valued, and therefore have power to direct behaviour, is encapsulated in a more grandiose sounding phrase: "virtuous peer pressure".

The agencies imposing standards are therefore less direct and less easily seen than "the neighbours" of the old communities. They are now embodied in agencies such as "opinion leaders" and "purveyors of fashionable trends". Or, more influentially subtle: the felt authoritative opinions of the powerful purveyors of "correct" ideas and fashions generally disseminated by the media - which must be "taken up" if a person wishes to be considered correct by those whose appraisals that person values.

If our later period is not so much concerned with "what will the neighbours think", it carries the concern of what those who seem to matter think. Or even what is imagined those who matter - but are not, in reality, known but are felt to be known - could think? Thus, we are all the inheritors; the enactors; the victims - describe it as we may - of our own nature and how historical pressures impinge upon us in any particular period.

The trail we've followed shows that the social controls which once operated in the old neighbourly communities have now, for good or ill, disappeared and have been replaced by something less direct; more abstruse; and - possibly - less effective?

This is because we live in different times; with different influences; and different neighbours - who think differently...

32
In Tune with the Times

~~~~~~~~~~~~~~~~~~~~~~~~~~~~~~~~~~~~

By the time the communities in the decades between the two World Wars developed in the way our visits revealed, the great emotional storms that generated the more intense Victorian attitudes had subsided. The gravity of the Victorian demeanour, with its well known "stiff upper lip", had become somewhat eased by the Edwardian loosening of the straight-laced moral corsets and by the aftermath of the First World War, which demanded: "We've been through hell, so let's now enjoy ourselves."

So, the stiff upper lip - although still highly prized when having to face difficulties or onerous obligations one might prefer to avoid - became more capable of stretching into a wide grin, which could easily lead to a good laugh. This expressed itself in the wild enthusiasm for the new music, exemplified by the visit to England in 1919 of a band known as 'The Original Dixieland Jazz Band' (or the O.D.J.B. as it came to be called). Its completely novel and astonishingly "jazzy" music seemed to fit the mood of the period - looking as it was for a good dollop of fun to counteract the memories of those previous, horrific, four years.

The music had something like the impact of our later time's rock'n'roll - also received from across the Atlantic after the Second World War, similarly producing a desire to throw off all the old conventions and restraints "in tune" with the tempo of the times.

This music's jazzy beat lent itself to a dances-craze emerging in the 1920s, expressed in energetic forms such as the 'Black Bottom', the 'Charleston' and the 'Shimmy Shake' - performed by an enthusiastic following called the "Flappers".

It's claimed that the term "Flapper" originated from what was then considered "daring" and unconventional females inclined to ride on motorbike pillion seats. This part of the seat had the name "flapper" because it could be lifted to expose the petrol tank's filler. The term extended its scope to describe the actions of the same daring, motorbike riding, females whose "wild" dances appeared to the older generation - brought up within the controlled elegance of the Victorian waltz - as if its performers were "flapping about outrageously".

All its energy eventually calmed down a bit (but not all that much) to express itself in lively tunes exemplified by the one called 'Happy

Feet' - snappily played by the then famous Paul Whiteman and his Orchestra and issued on record in the February of 1930. And if you ever get a chance to listen to it, you'll probably start dancing.

The rebellion this new music seemed to represent confined itself mainly to the dance floor and also the wearing of "indecently" short skirts and dresses. It never became the deeper and more widespread challenge to convention as did the later rock'n'roll enthusiasm. Its manifestations were predominately expressed by the young of the so-called leisured upper classes, with the time to be that way. The working classes, to which my mother belonged, were, as always, fully occupied with day to day problems. Nevertheless, similarly wishing for a little bit more cheerfulness in their lives, they also embraced the new music - particularly when it softened into its less exuberant expression known as "sweet swing".

The most popular British dance bands produced vast numbers of ten-inch 78-r.p.m. shellac gramophone records in the latest style. Their live performances became widely transmitted by the recently formed BBC, to emerge in many households by way of the newly acquired wireless sets - such as the one you saw in our house. This increasingly popular music no doubt came to the eager ears of our district mainly through the auspices of Henry Hall's Dance Band, broadcasting from Manchester's Midland Hotel. His sessions ended with his own composition, 'Here's to the Next Time', that eventually became his signature tune.

Because of weak signals and crude receiving equipment compared with present-day technology, regionally located transmitters were needed throughout the country. The regions became classified as 'London and the Southeast'; 'the West'; 'the Midlands'; 'the North'; 'Scottish'; 'Northern Ireland' - these producing programmes related to regional taste. The communities of our visit would "tune in" to the Northern Region for most of their listening; but anything considered national had its hearing throughout the country by way of relays using the regional transmitters.

Returning to Henry Hall's broadcasts: he eventually formed the New BBC Dance Orchestra that went on the air for the first time in 1932 - broadcasting nationally from London. He presented a forty-five minute session starting at 5:15 p.m. each evening, for five nights per week. This coincided with the time when many children would be listening, so he responded by playing their favourite pieces.

Another of his popular session went by the name of 'Henry Hall's Guest Night'. This began on 17th March 1934, resulting in a weekly

Thursday night broadcast starting at 8:30 p.m. and continuing for over a decade. He'd commence every programme with the words spoken in his modest, hesitating voice: "This is Henry Hall speaking, and tonight is my guest night". It became a popular phrase to the extent that a large audience would tune in just to hear him say the words.

However, listening to his programme in its entirety became a "must". It offered many additional attractions along with its popular music. These came in the form of various top entertainers appearing from time to time in every session; such as Flanagan and Allen, George Formby and Gracie Fields - to mention but a few.

My favourite was Leslie Sarony. Him, I particularly remember, because he sang what might be called a "daft little ditty" with the title of 'Tweet Tweet'. Its first verse went:

> *I lift up my finger and I say tweet, tweet,*
> *Shush, shush, now, now, come, come!*
> *I don't need to linger when I say tweet, tweet,*
> *Shush, shush, now, now, come, come.*
> *When the baby screams and shatters my dreams,*
> *Do I start to sing or hum?*
> *No!*
> *I lift up my finger and I say tweet, tweet,*
> *Shush, shush, now, now, come, come.*

This song may fail to appeal to those suffering from an overdose of sophistication but it appealed to me as child (and still does - although I wouldn't admit it). However, music of this and every other type has always been important to people, even if only for relaxation or eliciting a particular mood (or for having a little titter when listening to 'Tweet Tweet'). But let's consider something more serious than Tweet Tweet.

We've seen, at length, how people we met during our visits reacted to social and economic circumstances, but now it's time to consider what the folks of that time were *really* like in terms of temperament?

Listening to the music they enjoyed is a good way of getting to know their "mood". So if, one evening, we happened to visit our house, spilling out of our wireless's Bakelite case we would - in all probability - hear the previously mentioned Henry Hall and his Orchestra. We could thereby listen to the jazzy sounds of 'Happy Days are here Again' - composed in 1930 but a persisting favourite throughout that decade. Also 'The Wedding of the Painted Doll' - emerging in 1928 but surging again in popularity in the Thirties. Again from his orchestra, we'd no doubt hear the popular 'The Music goes Round and Round' and 'Around the Marble Arch' - these representing the numerous cheerful and jazzy tunes played at each session.

We might also hear ones loved by millions of kids; such as 'Teddy Bears Picnic' and 'Hush, Hush, Hush, Here comes the Bogie Man' or 'Who's Afraid of the Big Bad Wolf'. The first mentioned two, sung by Val Rosing, proved popular to adults and children alike - as did the last one when sung by whoever happened to sing it.

As a matter of interest: the Teddy Bear rendition sold over a million records, which represented an enormous amount for that time. This tune had its first composition in 1908 - but without words. The version emerging from Henry Hall's Band had music rearranged by him and words supplied by an associate named Jimmy Kennedy. As a matter of interest: the BBC eventually used this arrangement as a "test piece" because of the tune's wide ranging notes, varying from the high of the xylophone down to the deep of the bass-saxophone.

We'd also hear a great variety of music from many other popular bands. For instance: Jack Payne; Joe Loss; Bert Ambrose; Ray Noble; Jack Hylton; Roy Fox; Harry Roy, etc, etc. They'd play tunes such as the amusing 'An Elephant Never Forgets' - enjoyed in 1933 by kids and adults alike; the cheerfully jazzy: 'We'll all go Riding on a Rainbow'; also the exceedingly happy 'Whose Been Polishing the Sun' - 1934; and the very romantic 'Everything's in Rhythm With My Heart' - 1935.

In that last mentioned year, we'd hear: 'All the Kings Horses and the Kings Men' - originally composed in 1931, but enthusiastically and jazzily repeated by Jack Hylton's band for the Jubilee in 1935.

The vocals associated with all the songs of that time were sung clearly and distinctly so that their words could easily be learnt and remembered. They'd readily emerge amongst those who felt like having a good sing to themselves or with family and friends in the local pub, if cash allowed.

A favourite frequently pouring out of the Burton House Pub (and particularly after the "chara" outings of the kind we witnessed in one of our visits) was the sentimental 'Nellie Dean'. Gertie Gitana - the musical-hall singer - made this an all time hit at the turn of the century, but it stayed at the "top of the pops" even into the nineteen-thirties. Also, you'd hear the popular 'Lily of Laguna' - first made famous in 1898 by the music-hall singer Eugene Stratton.

These were just a few out of the persisting "oldies" constantly supplemented by the many hundreds of new compositions arising each year. Those emerging in the Thirties mainly represented the style we previously called "Sweet Swing". If you ever get a chance to listen to its expressions, you'd soon recognise that the people enjoying its music could only have done so if they possessed a "cheerfully romantic" disposition and a strong and whimsical sense of humour - as did my mother and father and also most of the people I knew in our street. This, as I remember, is what the folks of that generation seemed to be like. They were generally happy people in spite of the not very happy conditions many of them constantly had to face.

It may be said that the folks of that time needed - like the earlier Flappers - cheerful music in order to "dance away" what our present circumstances might believe were horrific years? But people only respond to cheerful things if they possess an innately cheerful nature - or, at least, the easy inclination to give that disposition its expression.

Those only aware of the economically deplorable conditions of that period might wonder how the sentiments represented by the popular music were given even a tentative expression in those financially arduous circumstances. They may even incline towards believing that folks of those times must've been lunatic to listen to songs such as "Happy days are here again", without the high degree of cynicism one would expect their circumstances to make them "sensibly" display.

However, and as constantly pointed out: judgements about the past must be done with some understanding of the past and its people; and this understanding must take cognisance of the fact that the people of that time generally behaved "in tune" with the music they enjoyed.

This proposition may seem, to some, as representing nothing more than an unexamined enthusiasm for a particular time and its people; and also a sentimental trap easily fallen into by those inclined to fall. However, it may come as a surprise (to some) that the British people were once acclaimed for their "polite and cheerful pleasantness".

Again, this statement may appear as another unexamined enthusiasm - this especially to a period in which widespread misbehaviour creates constant anxiety. So - for support - let's call upon the testimony of independent witnesses who were on the scene and observing a time when "pleasant politeness" seemed to be the expectation.

We can, for instance, call upon the testimony of the American philosopher, George Santayana, who - after a long stay in this country - wrote in his 'Soliloquies in England' (published in 1922):

The typical Englishman is disciplined, skillful and calm...well dressed without show and pleasure-loving without loudness...the ideal comrade in a tight place...

Also, the Czechoslovakian, Karel Capek, wrote in his essays 'Letters from England' (1924):

Wherever on this planet ideals of personal freedom and dignity apply, of tolerance, of respect for the individual and inviolable human rights, there you will find the cultural inheritance of England, which is the home of civilised people. If you were a little boy, you would know that you could trust them [the English] more than yourself and you would be freer and held in more respect than anywhere in the world; a policeman would puff out his cheeks to make you laugh, an old gentleman would play ball with you and a white-haired lady would lay down her four-hundred-page novel to look prettily at you with her bluish-grey and still young eyes...

In addition, we can call upon the testimonies of two well-travelled witnesses who knew the country from the "inside" and could therefore compare its attributes with other countries. For instance:

George Orwell wrote in his 1941 essay 'The Lion and the Unicorn':

The gentleness of the English civilization is perhaps its most marked characteristic. You notice it the instance you set foot on English soil.

Professor Geoffrey Gorer, the psychologist and anthropologist, wrote on page 13 of his book, 'Exploring English Character' (1955):

...in public life today the English are certainly amongst the most peaceful, gentle, courteous and orderly populations that the civilized world has ever seen... football crowds are as orderly as church meetings...

These comments represent impressions acquired by academics and political journalists who'd spent their lifetime observing human behaviour. Unfortunately, such accolades might now be difficult to find?

Regarding football crowds: during the first cup-final at Wembley, April 28th 1923, one policeman, George Scorey, riding a well-behaved white horse (called "Billy") managed to quickly restore order amongst an over-packed crowd of 130,000 spectators excitedly spilling out from the stands onto the pitch.

Those having a sceptical disposition might suggest that the lone policeman on his white horse and the mentioned observers happened to meet and be faced with a completely unrepresentative sample of exceedingly polite and well-behaved people. Also the observers were - some might say - "overstating the case" due to a possible sentimental attachment to the land of their visit; and they may've developed a more balanced view by travelling more extensively throughout the country? Yet all of them did travel widely and their observations are implicitly supported by that period's exceedingly low crime figures.

Music makes the mood. So, what went wrong? Is it our music? Or is it our mood?

But to avoid what might appear to some as a trite and over-simplistic conclusion about music and its affect upon temperament, we can experience a day wherein this quietness of character had its expression; a day that may be difficult to comprehend from our present fast lane of life.

In the Thirties and its previous decades, Sunday saw the closing down of every shop and virtually all services except for essential utilities. Folks usually retained a set of clothes especially for Sunday. They'd don their "Sunday best" to attend church services (if inclined that way) and/or visit relations for "tea", or stay at home to relax (except, of course, for the usually hard-working "housewife" who prepared the Sunday dinner). People fortunate enough to have a Municipal Park within reasonable distance took the opportunity to walk amongst its greenery.

On Sunday afternoons, a local brass band invariably occupied the park's bandstand, to play light classics of a cheerful and restful variety. These could include selections from Gilbert and Sullivan; music from operettas such as 'Lilac Time'; overtures from 'The Merry Wives of Windsor'; various waltzes by Johann Strauss; the preludes to Wagner's Lohengrin and suchlike - or whatever seemed suitable to a mood of relaxation. But when wintertime excluded such out-door enjoyments, I liked being at home and sitting near the blazing fire whilst waiting for teatime. The wireless could be tuned-in to the BBC Northern Orchestra's programme of popular tunes or a Palm Court Orchestra concert from Eastbourne's Grand Hotel, playing light classics.

There might be a presentation of songs sung by famous singers. Peter Dawson, for instance, was a particular Sunday teatime favourite - singing songs such as 'On the Road to Mandalay' and 'Floral Dance', amongst many others. Or there might be music from a stage-show to suit the Sunday mood. I particularly liked 'In a Persian Market' and especially one of its songs called 'Myself When Young' - sung with the deep, rich voice of Lawrence Tibbett.

I suppose the title appealed to me because I happened to be very young at the time. I discovered some years later (when very much less young) that its words were based on verses from Omar Khayyam's Rubaiyat. The first lines of the song went:

> *Myself when young did eagerly frequent*
> *Doctor and Saint, and heard great argument:*

But evermore,
Came out by that same door wherein I went.

I also realised this verse expressed a quest for absolute truth and understanding - resulting in the inevitable frustration.

However, as far as our quest is concerned, we may be able to claim that an introduction to the music enjoyed by the people we met during our visits has provided some understanding of their musical tastes; and - with it - an impression of their temperament.

Having acquired this, we may be able to claim we were - for a while - "in tune with the times"…

33
A Question of Coal in the Backyard

~~~~~~~~~~~~~~~~~~~~~~~~~~~~~~~~~~~

Continuing the theme raised in the previous narrative, one of the most startling contrasts between the first and second half of the twentieth-century is in the degree of crime each half experienced.

Levels of crime remained consistently low between 1900 to 1939. It began to rise somewhat during the social disruptions of the 1939-45 war then declined immediately afterwards to near pre-war levels. The end of the 1950s saw the start of a sharp increase, persisting ever since.

The question is: Why?

Perhaps part of the answer resides in the apparent ineffectuality of what we now call "dysfunctional communities". These apparently fail in cultivating the necessary habits of law and order amongst several of their residents. If this be so, the neighbourly communities that existed in the period of our visits may be worth examining in greater depth, in order to find possible reasons for their lower level of what we now call anti-social behaviour.

We could, for instance, consider what appeared to be the essential ingredient contained in that sense of neighbourliness exhibited in the community we visited. This, I believe, we'd find in two simple words: "Our street". It's a phrase that seems to have hardly any parallel in our present period, wherein people generally see themselves as living in a location which "just happens" to be in the same postal convenience as those also living in the same setting. In this collection of houses, it isn't at all unusual for the inhabitants to remain completely unaware of the names of those living as near to them as next-door-but-one and, sometimes, those living next-door - as recent surveys indicate.

This might seem an oversimplification to those suspicious of what could appear as too narrow a view. Objectors may suggest that a wider perspective could indicate there's as much neighbourliness now as there was in the past. People being people - they'd claim - will form relationships and behave very much the same as they always have.

This may be true. Human desires and dispositions have a tendency to remain constant - or, at least, have that potential; and if we were to examine enough situations in the present setting, no doubt some will be found to support the assumed objection. However, those who'd experienced a street wherein everyone knew everyone else would perceive things somewhat differently. For instance: Heelis Street had a total of twenty-five houses. Even now, after all these years, my sister can name every family who lived in those houses along with all of their members; and not only that, also name many families and the members thereof who lived in adjacent streets.

This awareness wasn't at all unusual for those living in the type of setting we experienced in our walk. Although just a child at that time - and with interests mainly confined to families providing "playmates" - I held a similar perception. I can easily recall well over half the families in our street and the names of their members. In fact, this awareness represented the normality. If one was bold enough to enquire around housing estates representing present-day communities, the same situation might not readily be found. Therefore, to suggest that this detachment of neighbour from neighbour is a feature of our present period mightn't be the overstatement it appears at first sight.

Its affirmation is found particularly in the worse examples of High Rise Dwellings that sprang up so profusely in the early 1960s. In these, people can live for many years without knowing those who dwell above and below them - occasionally meeting their neighbours as "strangers on the stairs".

By contrast and to me as a child (and I believe to virtually all of those who shared the same settings) "our street" had the same connotation as "our house". Our street was therefore an extension of our house, as it was for all the other houses forming our street. The street "belonged" to all of us who live in that street. It was impossible for anyone in that street to be "detached" from it. The street was the centre and the heart of its dwellings. It was the place where everybody met, and talked, and played.

Perhaps the fact that the present style of life rarely provides this sense of belonging generates the nostalgia frequently expressed by people who knew that time. It may also be the reason why so many people of the present time seem to yearn for village life. They probably feel these comparatively small and compact communities, whose dimensions can be readily and "humanly" grasped, may offer what they, perhaps, instinctively sense their general way of living lacks.

Yet even these settings can produce an isolation which, in many ways, is worse than that experienced in the towns. We see dormitory villages whose inhabitants commute to the towns, each day, for employment the village can no longer provide. We have villages without a village school or a real commitment to that traditional centre of village life: the Church - which did, at least, provide a place where people could "gather together".

Those inclined to distrust what may seem as memory's capacity for sentimental distortion could suggests that the myopic vision it engenders creates an illusion of a Golden Age, that never really existed. They may suggest the "glow" from this illusion prevent those suffering its distortions from seeing the complete picture in its own true light. Again this may be true, but our return to the past lit no pleasant glow to soften its sharp edges. We witnessed, sometimes in harsh detail, some of its awfulness as well as some of its worthiness.

We readily saw no period, still less that of our visits, has ever provided the complete solution for all of humanities ills and woes. Even the balm of the all embracing neighbourly communities couldn't cure every social ill. Although a child at the time, I became well aware of those who the community's embrace failed to save from despair, or hold back from trouble and misfortune - or even wrongdoing.

As previously implied: day to day tensions between neighbours could often arise; sometimes stretching the community's "in-built" capacity for moderation and restraint and demanding the efforts and careful mediation of other neighbours to ease. This they did under the pressing need to "live together" in a situation offering very little possibilities for privacy or withdrawal.

By contrast, that previously mentioned detachment of neighbour from neighbour our present period constructs removes the necessity of having a particular concern about the attitudes and activities of those around us. We need not, any more, be over-anxious about maintaining their goodwill. This offers the advantage of conducting our affairs without being over-mindful of people having no claim upon us - other than the mere "accident" of a shared location.

In addition, the ability of our later age to banish much of the ills and woes we saw existing in the past, and to provide widely available care unimaginable to previous times, has bestowed its own freedoms. One of these is the freedom from the desperate need for and dependence upon the mentioned goodwill of neighbours and the charitable institutions we witnessed in our visits.

Poverty - if it does occur in our Welfare Age - is not so much an existential fact created by the conditions of its period, but more the result of personal or social maladministration. And even where poverty is deemed to exist, it's assessed on a standard far above what a previous age would judge as being in that category.

All these benefits our later age confers have contributed to an enormous increase in life expectancy. This is dramatically illustrated when we consider the average span at the beginning of the century of our visits, for what was then called a working-class person, was around fifty-five years. It's now beginning to exceed seventy-five - and is producing an "embarrassment" for those responsible for financing pensions.

This longer life-span is reflected in vastly improved health and physique. For instance: the average height for a working-class male in the year of my mother's birth (1902) was five feet six inches and that of a female: five feet two inches. The corresponding figures for 1991 (the year of her death) was five feet nine inches and five feet five inches, respectively.

In addition, the present period has the capacity to provide a readily obtainable level of affluence way beyond the wildest dreams of those in the old communities. I remember my mother chiding a somewhat disgruntled member of our family - one having no memory of the period we visited. She said: "If I could've had the things you have, now, to help me with my housework - when I was a young woman - I would've thought I was in paradise!"

So, it seems, the benefits of the munificent age first emerging in the 1950s became fully appreciated by a person who'd spent a large part of her life in a less kindlier period - as far as housework was concerned. In addition to this "easing" of domestic chores, there are innumerable gains in comfort and leisure enjoyed to the point of being accepted as a normality and therefore difficult to imagine being without. Again the question arises: in the face of the obvious fact that our later period is far more fortunately endowed, why does it have a higher level of crime? Moreover, why do some people feel nostalgic about a time which, in a multitude of ways, was so deprived?

Perhaps an answer to these important questions may reside in the fact that - regardless of the numerous and undeniable benefits the post-war age increasingly came to enjoy - the often mentioned equation has produced its effect. In gaining these benefits, others have been progressively lost (and one of these - possibly - being the capacity for real appreciation). However, the most crucial loss is represented by the withering away of that sense of community which appears to be the cause of many present-day "ills". The main ill, it seems, is the often complained-about decline in respect for people and property.

Again, those wary of what might be seen as sentimental distortions may say: "Nonsense! Previous times had no more respect for people and property than there is now, and can therefore tell nothing about our present situation!"

Well, be that as it may or as it may not be. Arguments about this could go on and on and on. All I can do is offer a few experiences out of many, which could, perhaps, indicate a different perspective.

Remember Mr. Ingram, the "Burial Club" collector we met during one of our visits? At the time of his collecting he was well into his sixties and therefore without the "protection" of youth. Nevertheless, he'd walk around the gas-lit streets, at night, in the process of his collecting, carrying a bag of coinage in an area whose inhabitants were sometimes - if not for most times - desperately short of money. He'd do this without any sense of danger and without anyone even entertaining the idea that he could be in danger. The suggestion that he could be "mugged" - to use our present period's term - would've raised incredulous eyebrows.

Also, households could keep coal in their backyards and leave their backyard door unlocked, in streets where maintaining an adequate supply was a constant anxiety, with a certainty they'd find the coal still there in the morning - undisturbed.

Again, those inclined to be wary of the mentioned capacity for sentimental selectivity (and, in this case, centring on an insignificant little pile of coal) may also suggest that the reason for this apparent honesty does not relate to any fundamental difference in the attitudes of people - then and now. Those finding themselves in - for instance - the desperation of having no means to warm themselves would "naturally" have this condition attended to by caring neighbours, in whatever period, so no need would exist to take what would naturally be offered - on the asking?

This is, of course, generally true. Caring and kindly neighbours can always be found. However, an essential in any neighbourliness is the "awareness" each person has about those around them. In the communities we're considering, an immediate awareness of and a concern for each neighbour's welfare existed as a matter of course.

In Heelis Street, for instance, an informal monitoring involved observing if the window-blinds of any elderly persons living alone were raise in the morning at an expected time. If this proved not to be the case, the first observing neighbour took it upon himself or herself to knock on the door to find out if the person of their concern happened to be all right. This constant and informal practice applied to all the streets around - and would be found in all similar districts.

So, in this and many other respects, in a setting wherein everyone knew everyone else along with their day-to-day circumstances, it became almost impossible for anyone to be "isolated". By contrast, our present-day communities generally assume such concerns are the province of a formal, and therefore impersonal, social worker having very little knowledge about the person concerned, other than their "entitlements". This makes it possible for many people to be overlooked - especially the uncommunicative ones.

However, getting back to the question of coal left in the backyard and its unlocked door. What on first consideration could be thought a triviality hardly worth mentioning seems to go to the very heart of the matter raised earlier: the one about respect for people and property. Within the action of leaving the door unlocked is a multitude of implications. The essential one being an implicit trust people feel towards those around them; and for this trust to endure, it must be supported by the constant affirmation of it not being violated. By this, each neighbour acquires respect for each other and therefore for each other's property.

An important aspect of this trust would reside in the desire to avoid appearing untrustworthy in the eyes of a community whose goodwill one constantly needs. In this, even thoughts of being "found out" in taking advantage of an unlocked door could cause feelings of shame sufficient to inhibit transgressions.

Such feelings and their capacity to constrain behaviour became - for various reasons we can explore later - unfashionable in our present period, which began to see shame, in particular, as a negative emotion. Perhaps this is why there's so much nervousness about laying down rules of morality that might resurrect the sense of shame needed to make them effective? This reluctance would hardly occur to those of the old communities, wherein feelings of shame if failing to abide by moral commitments were a general expectation.

However, back to our little pile of coal. In order for this apparent triviality to have any relevance in the wider scheme of things, it must be shown that the persisting Victorian attitudes with their associated respects and moralities that we've assumed kept people and property safe were not just a local peculiarity, confined to the small area of our visit. In this context, we could, perhaps, consider Professor Geoffrey Gorer's previously mentioned remark about orderly and well-behaved crowds attending football matches and see if the orderliness it implied related to a general disposition.

The crowds he observed required no wire-mesh or steel barriers to keep unruly spectators off the pitch or to separate rival supporters from each other. In most instances, there'd be no more than two or three representatives of the law in attendance - this because of it being accepted that the crowd would be "orderly" of its own accord. Why - those of the communities we've visited would ask - should it be otherwise? Also, when the trams and buses brought the spectators to and from the grounds, it was likewise expected they'd be free from damaged seats or even one mark of graffiti. Again, it would be asked: why should it be otherwise?

Another possible factor influencing this orderliness may reside in the fact that spectators of that time perceived sport as mainly a relaxing entertainment. Their behaviour would, therefore, tend to be in accordance with that perception; this because the centre of their lives would be, first and foremost, their home, their work and their neighbourhood, whose combination gave them all the sense of belonging they needed.

Although giving enthusiastic support to their chosen team, the game and the teams involved would be peripheral to their main identity. The mood during the game and as the crowds emerged after the game would therefore be mainly associated with relaxation appropriate to an enjoyable afternoon. No hostility would be present. Perhaps this is why it required only one policeman riding a white horse to quickly restore order amongst an over-packed crowd of 130,000 spectators spilling onto the pitch at the Wembley football cup final, in 1923.

Many spectators in our later age appear to lack the same sentiment. Supporters seem to see their hopes and expectations heavily invested in the fortunes of "their side" in whose collective support they may feel a sense of belonging and a communal identity, not readily found elsewhere. This may induce the highly charged, emotional reactions often emerging in the face of defeat - or even in the face of victory?

At this stage, it might prove useful to speculate on why this sense of belonging (this longing to belong) seems so important in peoples' lives, and why it appears to have such a widespread and disruptive affect if it fails to find its proper "home". Also we could ask why people feel a sense of incompleteness in its absence and therefore seek to find it in all sorts of unlikely activities - such as the one just mentioned.

A "need to belong" may, perhaps, stem from the aeons of tribal society in which humankind existed before towns and cities gave their protection, where banding together became essential to the survival of our species in a world dangerously hostile to the isolated individual. If this be so, the impulse to band together under one unifying identity would offer a powerful benefit - both practically and psychologically - and would therefore be deeply embedded in our nature. Thus, we see an impulse towards gregariousness and the need, even now, in the age of towns and cities, to seek a common identity with those who might offer such?

This intense sense of belonging is found, it seems, in banding together to support a football team. It also appears that this "instinctive benefit" makes the individual feel far greater than they actually are if identifying with something above themselves. Perhaps this is why one of the most anxiety producing imposition is to isolation a person from social contact by "sending them to Coventry" - to use an old phrase. It may also suggest why this sense of belonging sometimes demands constant and emphatic affirmation - especially when its source is so tenuously uncertain as supporting a football team? As an indication of this, a football supporter - recently interviewed on TV about an outbreak of disruption in which he took part - offered the following comment:

If you see some of your own supporters being attacked by the other side's, it's like seeing members of your own family being attacked; so you've got to get involved.

So, it seems, this important and much sought-after sense of identity and its feeling of commitment to something held in common takes various and complex expressions. When we attended the Jubilee Party, we saw it firmly embedded in a strong sense of neighbourhood arched by a unifying National Pride.

However, returning to our seemingly trivial pile of coal: those who'd leave it untouched would possess the same disposition as the football crowds and those enjoying the Jubilee Party. Nearly all of them would feel a deep sense of belonging to a community that many of them expected to live within for most, if not all, of their lives. Therefore, doing anything giving cause for their community's disapproval would generate the unease previously suggested.

Once again, those suspicious of what may seem like an attempt to ascribe simple assumptions to complex behaviour may suggest that a sense of identity possesses far more complications than where a person just happens to live. However, there seems nothing amiss in the simple assumption that it's people's attitudes that directs people's behaviour; and that these attitudes first take shape in a person's family and become constantly affirmed by the community from which that family derives its values. The people of the area in which our previously-met Mr Ingram safely collected his pennies; and the people who'd leave our little pile of coal untouched; and the people who formed a large part of the orderly football crowds were mainly a product of the type of communities we visited. Philosophers, Statisticians, Sociologist, Criminologists, Professors of Morality and Politicians - and we - can no doubt draw appropriate conclusions from this.

Nevertheless, let's cast our evidential net far wider than the confines of coal in a backyard and seek the testimony of some statistics. For instance: in 1931, the census for England and Wales recorded a population of 39,952,000. Unemployment hovered around an average of 21 per cent and the number of reported robberies with violence (what we'd now call "muggings") for the whole of that area, for that year, showed a total of 217. (Yes, 217 - a figure that our present-day experiences makes unbelievable.)

Taking 1991, for instance, the population of the same area had risen to 49,890,000. Unemployment stood generally at eight per cent and the number of reported robberies of a similar kind for that year was close on 72,000 cases. Allowing for the difference in levels of population and possible changing criteria for recording crime, there's one hell of a difference in that particular rate of offence? Again, allowing for the changing factors, my primitive mathematics indicate this offence was near enough 280 times more likely to occur in 1991 than in the earlier period mentioned - and this figure shows no subsequent reduction.

Doubts sometimes cast upon using such figures for comparative purposes focus on this: people in the nineteen-thirties, and especially in the type of communities we visited, had hardly anything worth "nicking", and this explains the comparatively low incidents of theft?

Well, what Mr Ingram carried in the form of collected coinage represented a small fortune to many living in the area at that time. Moreover, a bucket-full of coal had probably more value to those without warmth than a video holds in terms of real need to the people of today. So, if we accept the statistics on the basis of need, we've got to ask ourselves why the enormous difference between then and now?

To repeat the essential point: it's no-one else but people who commit these acts and the statistical examples offered seem to indicate that people are now more inclined to commit such offences - for whatever reason - than they were in the period of our visits. And this in a setting that would appear to those in the communities we visited as offering an unbelievable increase in affluence - and therefore what should be a far more contented way of life?

In fact, affluence appears to play such an important part in people's lives and their reason for living that relevant studies suggest a sudden decrease in its circumstances could be a major factor in the number of suicides. If this is so, let's consider the following actualities.

To suggest that the nineteen-thirties represented a more satisfying period in terms of affluence, compared with the present time, goes against the facts. Even a superficial glance soon indicates that the standards now considered basic are what a great many people in that earlier period would describe as being "unbelievably well-off". In those circumstances, and at the height of the 1930-32 economic depression, the peak suicide rate for England and Wales was - as near as can be ascertained - 148 per 100,000 of population. If, for instance, we take the figures for 1991 for comparative purposes - and this presents problems due to changing methods of reporting - the rate, as near as can be ascertained, stood at 172 per 100,000 of population.

Again, those wary of statistics - and especially ones subjected to the mentioned methods of reporting - might suggest these figures indicate nothing of any real relevance about the periods being compared. This caveat may be worth noting, because someone once observed that statistics are generally used in the same way as a drunken man uses a lamppost: more for support than illumination.

But if we examine what the changing methods of reporting involved, this may provide both support and illumination; especially since the resulting changes make the recent figures lower than they would be if the 1930s' system of recording was used. For instance: recent figures record suicide *only* if "positive" evidence exists for its assumption - such as a suicide note or the existence of a medically recorded depressive state of mind preceding the act. In the 1930s, both "positive" and "suspected" cases were included.

However, leaving aside speculations about what should and should not be included - and taking the statistics as they are - a further and more telling picture emerges if we take into account the background to each set of figures. If we accept the previously quoted unemployment rates for the same area for both periods (i.e. an average of 21 per cent for 1931-32 and 8 per cent for 1991-92) one would expect the 1931-32 rate of "economic despair" to be nearly three times that of its later period.

Yet, as we've seen, the figures indicate the reverse bias. And this in the context of the meagre and almost punitive financial support for the unemployed in the nineteen-thirties, compared with what people of those times would've seen as the "amazing generosity" afforded to those similarly placed in nineteen-nineties and thereafter.

Another factor seen as crucial in that "final act" is the availability of the means for its enactment. Taking into account that nearly every home in the 1930s had an immediate facility in the form of a gas oven -

which could supply a lethal amount of gas in an extremely short time - the period's lower figure is, again, not in accordance with what one would expect from the availability of means. In fact, a jocularity often heard to "lighten" the situation during the economically desperate nineteen-thirties was: "I'd commit suicide if I had a penny for the gas!" (As you no doubt noticed: most houses in the areas of our visit had a gas-meter - thus the need for the mentioned coin.)

But joking apart, and again considering the act in question: an important factor believed to be instrumental in preventing the final desperation is the ready availability of support (what our later age calls "Counselling") and/or medical aid an individual in a depressive state can call upon. In the time of our visits, no such organisations as the Samaritans and other formal support-groups - now readily available at the end of the widely accessible telephone - existed. Also, the immediate access to medical practitioners with their supply of anti-depressant drugs (such as they were in those times) was, for the vast majority of people, completely absent - especially in the case of those affected by unemployment. So, the apparently lower figures for that time is again not quite what one would expect a severely economically depressed period to show. Therefore the question again insists: why the comparatively lower number of incidents?

An answer may reside in the fact that those in a state of despair in the type of neighbourly community we visited received other forms of support, existing mainly as an informal aspect of that community. Because it existed in this "natural" form, it's not easily quantifiable. Nevertheless, it could have made an important contribution towards lowering the number of incidents, at a time economically horrendous. As you no doubt gathered from our visits: this kind of support - always readily available on the doorstep, so to speak - may've been all the more effective because of it being given by people who cared, or at least had knowledge about those to whom they offered "support". This involved people sharing the same experiences and circumstances and therefore possessing a deeper appreciation of each other's problems.

The social intimacy implied by "we're all in the same boat" and experiencing the same "currents and storms" is probably an essential in generating the nostalgia those having known the old communities tend to feel. It also seems to explain the apparent contradiction expressed by people claiming that they felt the 1939-45 wartime-period as a happy time. Unbelievable as this may seem, it appears to have support from the fact that the suicide rates for that period showed a marked decline.

This "happy-time" sentiment no doubt arose from the type of experience expressed in 'Voices from the Twentieth Century' - the compilation published in 2002 by the Imperial War Museum. A contributor (Elizabeth Quayle) made the following observation about sheltering in the London Underground during the air raids known as the Blitz:

At night on the underground, only the eighteen inches or maybe two feet near the rail was left, and all the rest were rows of people with their belongings, cats and dogs and children. They were as good-tempered as it was possible to be. Looking back on it, everyone was much more friendly - you would have thought nothing of leaving your bags or your suitcase there; nobody would have taken anything.

The part of the comment about eighteen inches or so near the rail refers to the space left between the people and the edge of the platform - this to allow a walkway for communication; and the latter part of her comment exemplifies the omnipresent mutual trust the safety of our little pile of coal implies?

However, let's now examine the statistical "hard facts" related to the safety of people's belongings, and, by implication, also that of our little pile of coal.

The 1930's recorded figures for general theft in England and Wales indicate an average of 110,159 incidents per year. For the 1990s (a period experiencing comparatively substantial affluence) the figures for the same category of crime show an average approaching 2,000,000 incident per year. Again, my primitive mathematics indicates these incidents as being around 290 per 100,000 of population in each year of the 1930s and around 3,845 per 100,000 for the 1990's. To put it simply: the rate for the 1990s is over thirteen times that of the 1930s.

Again the question: why the astonishing difference running counter to what one would expect from the circumstances generating these figures? It appears to confound the common sense assumption that the greater the poverty the greater the thefts, and the less the poverty the less the thefts. So, if poverty is not the prime influence on the figures mentioned, some other factor must be involved?

Perhaps an answer might be found in the notion we've suggested previously: if a community provides models and expectations of behaviour of a certain kind, intentionally or unintentionally, from whatever basis, so, then, will be the products of that community. Again to press the point: where else do we in the beginning learn behaviour except from those around us? And, as our enquiry on play seemed to suggest: in the beginning, children do not need to be taught to be bad (if we take this to mean self-centred and undisciplined) they need to be taught to be good (if we take this to mean self-controlled and considerate of others). So, if we accept the statistics offered as valid, something in those old communities must've operated in a very different direction from what now appears to be the case.

As a possible indicator of this direction, we could, perhaps, call upon the words of another eminent person - the poet, Alexander Pope - who said: "Just as the twig is bent, so the tree inclines." Obviously, many factors must be involved in this inclining process, but one possible contribution worth considering appears to be contained in those two previously mentioned words: "Our Street". We saw, for instance, how the post-war building enthusiasm could isolation neighbour from neighbour. By contrast, we saw how the nature of the streets in the old communities was such that the inhabitants of each house had to constantly use the space thus formed for their comings and goings. By this, everybody in the street acquired - and had to acquire - the first and basic requisite of any viable neighbourly community: that of all its members knowing each other.

Moreover, because the car had not yet demanded priority of space, most of the streets were virtually free from traffic. This made such streets the naturally preferred play-centre, especially amongst the younger children. Since all the houses viewed directly onto the street, and since most adults desire orderliness - for their own comfort if nothing else - adult eyes always happened to be there to unobtrusively monitor children's behaviour. Moreover, because most adults in the street were "shaped" by a similar setting they therefore shared the same set of beliefs about what constituted proper conduct. This offered the possibility for any adult to be a natural agent in a united and consistent but informal disciplining process.

Again, this raises the issue of watchful neighbours operating their informal policing process. However, in those communities, this process was one supported by a continuity of values from family, to street, to school, and back again. Within this, the widely accepted rule regarding children's behaviour was: children must never insolently challenge adult's admonitions and adults - in making admonitions - must always be fair. This fairness had to include recognition of the "natural" mischief to which children may be prone when impulsively probing the boundaries of acceptable behaviour - as they always will.

In fact, fairness seems to be an essential part in children's ready acceptance of authority, even of the strictest kind. During a recent BBC radio discussion about "acceptable" disciple, an issue arose concerning physical punishment and whether or not it should be part of that acceptability. A contributor mentioned a body of research indicating that people who'd experienced physical punishment rarely remember "being smacked" except for those incidents they considered to be unfair. This revelation both surprised and pleased me, because it happened to fit in with my own experience relating to a schoolteacher who mistakenly imposed upon me physical punishment for an act in which I had no part (honestly!). Even after all these years of simmering resentfulness, I cannot help remembering that incident with a certain "smarting irritation". Similar events involving (deserved?) punishment left no such impression; and - I'm delighted to reveal - has produced no other quirks in my character (or - at least - I can't detect any!).

However, and in all seriousness, and getting back to the mentioned system of fairness. In the case of adults, the pressures maintaining a willing acceptance of and conformity with the rules concerning this informal disciplining process resided in the expediency that a person thought to be consistently unreasonable would soon evoke disapproval from all the other adults in the street. In that close-knit community, most adults sought to avoid this unpleasantness and its possible loss of important goodwill.

The previously mentioned radio discussion - and even the need for it to take place - implies that the simple adult/child discipline of the old communities would present a problems in our authority-challenging ethos. Attempting definitions of and creating agreement about behavioural boundaries could raise much dissent, especially since children are now permitted and are - indeed - expected to have more "voice" in what these should be.

Yet our visit to the play-world indicated that the worse thing a child can receive during the process of what we might call "correcting" is contradictions about values and methods - which, it seems, the firm consensus possessed by the old communities largely avoided. The crucial importance of avoiding confusions, when presenting the world and its expectations to those trying to make "sense" of the one they've not long since entered, shouldn't cause surprise, since it must hold true in any learning situation.

This may seem obvious to the point of being trite. Nevertheless, one of the greatest difficulties the young in our present period seem to suffer is the confusion of views and the countervailing views they have, somehow, to accommodate. They're constantly bombarded with views and more views, and the contradiction of views. Certainties come and go with each fashion, and with each "Guru" of fashion. The value of every value is questioned so that there are very few values to be valued. Each belief is supposed to be on a par with any other belief so that no-one can, any longer, be certain about any belief. All beliefs become equally "true" - or just as equally "false"?

The resulting confusions arising from such "relativism" should be what one would expect. In any game or activity, the clearer the rules the more orderly the play. The same principle must therefore apply to communities whose rules are supposed to create the predictable and orderly expectations necessary for orderly and predictable interactions. Our later period, with its stress on self-referencing, may say: "That's all very well; but what if the price to be paid for this orderly society is conformity to a set of conditions people might find irksome and repressive. In this case, the so called orderly communities wouldn't be a happy and relaxed situation but an inward-looking imposition, where neighbours become something like George Orwell's constantly watching big brother."

Although our present emphasis on privacy would support this protest, we should, by now, be wary of any judgement any period may make about a previous period, without, at least, some understanding of that previous period. As our visits seem to indicate, the people in those old communities may've seen what we would now perceive as intrusive impositions in a very different light. For instance, when we play a game we tend to see its rules as a condition allowing free and orderly activity, and not as a restraint. Such rules are therefore willingly accepted and social rules may be seen in the same way.

An example of this is in the way people addressed each other in the time of our visits. For instance: convention insisted teachers were always "Sir" or "Miss"; and, to children, all adults were always "Mr" or "Mrs" - except where they'd be "Mother" or "Father" or "Mam" or "Dad". Friends were addressed by their first name and very close friends had an affectionate nickname. Those not in the "friend" categories would be addressed by title or surname.

Such conventions, rather than restricting interaction, may've helped to free them up. This social utility is entrenched in the widely followed convention of using names specific to gender. If, for instance, we're told a person's name is "James", we can - or should - reliably assume that person is masculine, just as we consider the name "Jemima" carries the assumption of being feminine. This way of implicitly indicating gender is so generally accepted its usefulness is hardly given a though - until its "rule" is confounded.

For instance: if, in a business situation, a Salesman is informed he's to entertain a "James Bloggs". The Salesman - and we - might reasonably assume a particular name-implication. If, say, the Salesman is given a commitment to provide an evening's entertainment along with overnight accommodation, preparations would - in all probability - take a particular line based on assumptions related to the name. Having made arrangements in accordance with his belief, the Salesman may feel a sense of discomposure if the arriving "James" proved to be of a gender opposite to his expectation.

This simple and obvious example, to the point of seeming banal, indicates how naming conventions can provide many in-built expectations, explanations and descriptions; and may explain why this convention persists for so long in so many societies. In the context of the old communities and its naming formalities, children and everyone else in that setting could readily discern relationships and its interplay along with the networks of affections, respects, authorities and courtesies - in their degree and in their place. By this, people probably felt such conventions possessed a great deal of utility. Moreover, by declaring the title by which a person would prefer to be addressed, that person could indicate in a direct and simple way the relationship they'd like to expect, vis-à-vis the addressee.

Our later period's desire to remove what it deemed to be rigid formalities and the barriers these were believed to create has made the ways of addressing people so relaxed they've almost ceased to provide any specific indication of most relationships. For instance: children are expected to readily address adults as Tom, Dick or Harry, or Tracy, Debbie or Hilda - or whatever their first name happens to be - irrespective of their position in society or their relationship to the children involved. This "rule" is an expectation regardless of who happens to be involved - be it teacher, casual acquaintance, parent, neighbour, or even Prime Minister. And, for all of us - whether adult or child - first names are now obligatory, even on first meeting.

This takes us back to the argument about values: if all values are of equal value, none are, really, of any particular value. In the case of names: if we call everybody by first name on first meeting, what do we reserve for our friends - what "name-value" do we give them? To children, adults are children, children are adults - or, according to the naming convention, so it may seem; because no difference is implied by the mode of naming. In this setting - and to the always intensely observing child - there's no way of predicting or reliably assuming the relationship of one person with another when hearing the style of address.

As a further "for instance": in the spirit of giving all relationships an equal status, the male-female relationship that the pre-1939 ethos assumed must be "husband and wife" - and refer to it accordingly under the assumption it could not "properly" be otherwise - has lost its certainty. No surety can readily be deduced about such unions. Therefore, those involved can only be safely referred to as "partners" - whatever the degree of affection, permanency or commitment their relationship may possess.

Within this informality, an outsider cannot readily tell what the relationship really is. Are they partners for a game of darts? A game of cards? Are they business partners? Are they partners in crime? Are they partners in a passionate and illicit love affair? Are they partners in bringing up children? Are they partners at a dancing school? At a bridge club? At tennis? Are they husband and wife? What sort of "partners" are they?

The child, who is always trying to match the words heard to the behaviour perceived, enters a world where the verbal indicators of relationships hardly exists - or, at least, they're so blurred to be almost indiscernible. Children may, then, perhaps, begin to feel that all relationships are, after all, "casual", since the words describing them are - likewise - casual.

The point of all this belabouring the point is again to suggest that the verbal and behavioural boundaries the old communities willing accepted and maintained arose from the practical reasons indicated. Just as children appear to feel more certain and secure when boundaries are clearly defined, and are thereby predictable, so it may be for all of us - in whatever situation.

As noted before, certainty about rules appears to be an important aspect in allowing people to live together. Under that inevitable rule of gaining and losing, the price we may pay for our greater "freedom" from rules could be we lose the predictability which helped keep the old neighbourly communities as cohesive as they seemed. If this is so, freedom when pushed to excess may, in removing predictability, leave us as individuals with our own particular values and beliefs or with nothing at all. In this situation, there's nothing left for those so placed but to devise their own rules, whatever they perceive these should be.

In the extreme (where it becomes no longer certain what should be properly said, or what should be properly done, and how it should be said or done) the child and the emerging young person may search desperately for agencies which seem to present the guidelines and certainties they seek. Or, later, and in the end, if no anchoring certainties are to be found anywhere, and no guidelines are found to follow, they may retreat from the anxiety this creates into an escapist world induced by narcotics; or into a constant round of meaningless entertainment; or iconoclastic out-groups - or even worse: rebellious destruction.

The relevance of all this to our enquiry is to suggest that no community can be properly formed on such basis - only fragmentation of communities, in countercultures and subcultures; and at the edges of these, alienated individuals, not sure of anything any more. So however repressive the restraints arising from the old rules and conventions may appear to be from our later perspective, it seems they did help sustain the grounds for the orderly situation we saw existing in the - still very much Victorian - nineteen-thirties.

As indicated previously, the latter part of the Victorian period witnessed a reduction in crime by as much as fifty per cent. The results of this trend were maintained in the eventual "climate of respectability" inherited and fostered by the communities we visited.

In fact, this early trend towards a low crime rate is indicated by the experience during the Crystal Palace Great Exhibition of 1851. The Authorities responsible for its supervision expressed concerns about the maintenance of law and order amongst the vast crowds expected to attend. However, their anxieties proved groundless. The Exhibition recorded 6,063,986 visitors in its 140 days of opening. The offences charged during that period constituted no more than twenty-five cases: ten for petty larceny, nine for picking pockets and six for attempting that particular offence.

Queen Victoria wandered amongst the crowd without protection during her many visits. This "orderliness" permitted the newspapers at that time to acclaim the Exhibition as "a pageant of domestic peace".

Another important factor adding its influence to the low crime-rate seemed to be what we now call an attitude of "zero tolerance" towards crime. This had its formal beginnings in the Victorian period and continued into the nineteen-thirties (a "solution" which, it seems, is being resurrected in the face of the present day's escalating problems).

In the period we visited, this mode of policing had no other name except that of "normal policing". Very little leniency existed within its normality, but the local bobby-on-the-beat would, in his community policing, soften its severity by occasionally turning the proverbial "blind eye" to innocent and minor transgressions. We saw this in the case of my sister and her friends in their flower selling activity and the toleration towards kids using the street lampposts to support a swing.

Yet this tolerance only existed at the very narrow margins of transgressions. Disruptive, disorderly or offensive behaviour received a quick reaction with appropriate punishment hard on its heels; even if this, in the case of children, meant the "on the spot and judged to be deserved" quick clip behind the ear by the policeman involved - an action that would horrify present perspectives. However, this immediate application of the law operated under the common-sense basis that a transgression quickly followed by the shock of punishment - authoritatively delivered by the bobby-on-the-beat detecting the act - could have more potency regarding the impressionable young than any form of punishment inflicted long after the event.

In the case of the implicit rules governing adult/child admonitions mentioned previously, such applications would be administered under the consideration that the "pain" inflicted upon the transgressor must be seen to be justified and mainly - and no more than - that needed to wound mischievous pride. A further extension of this "wounding" was the consequential shame and humiliation when the community to which the wrongdoer belonged became aware of the misdeed.

By contrast, this immediate street-censure would now place the "offending" policeman in serious trouble. Nevertheless, in that apparently strange period when such censure seemed appropriate, it rarely needed to be applied - because of the knowledge it could always be applied. Also, the vast majority of offender's parents would support the action and even be grateful for its application. This they would do in the belief of it being deserved and it being preferred to a court hearing. In addition, they'd feel it could deter any future mischief.

Their support would also arise in the context of the "correction" being administered by a person (the bobby-on-the-beat) with a good knowledge of the parents and children concerned. He would therefore be bound to act under the imperative of keeping the respect of the community in which he constantly did his rounds.

Under this agenda, actions now commonly perpetrated and receiving hardly any attention (such as riding a bike on the pavement; obstructing the pavement; riding a bike without proper lighting; defacing or damaging public property; kicking a ball in the street to constitute annoyance or danger to people or traffic; or damage to property; and even using "offensive" language in public; and so on) would receive the due weight of the law. In this context, Professor J. Harris in his book 'Private Lives, Public Spirit' (1993) observed:

If the legal standards in vogue in the decades before the Second World War were applied now, most of our youth would be in jail.

Of course, no society would want most of its youth to be in jail; but most of the youth of that time weren't in jail because they behaved in a way to avoid its "shame".

It seems the judiciary of that era fully entertained the spirit of zero tolerance. Sir Ernest Wild exemplified this, in 1931, when presiding as magistrate at the trial of a person named John Claridge. The accused - caught in the act of burgling a house - had sustained injury to his arm during a struggle whilst committing the act. This caused him a permanent disability.

In the process of sentencing, the magistrate stated:

"If Claridge lost the use of his arm it was his own fault. If people burgle a house, they must expect to be injured."

When asked by the defence solicitor to consider the offender's incapacity when sentencing, Sir Ernest said to the defendant:

"I do not think it matters in the least if you had broken your neck. No-one would have the slightest sympathy with you."

John Claridge was duly sentenced to eighteen months in prison with hard labour. The Magistrate indicated this "light sentence" was offered because no person, except the offender, received physically injury in the struggle. He stated that the "leniency" shown was because the offender made no profit from the offence. It was not due to any legitimacy residing in the plea of mitigation attempted by the defence.

It could easily be imagined that no magistrate would get away with such an "unsympathetic" attitude in the present social climate. Nevertheless, our new thinking - albeit without the shame element - seems to be echoing some of the old thinking in its belief that more immediate and punitive applications of the law to minor crime (zero tolerance) could substantially reduce major crime.

This "strictness" appears to have statistical support. For instance: the daily average of prison detainees was 11,346 for the year 1931 and 55,537 for the year 1991. Relating these figures to the proportion of population, the 1930's figures represent, near enough, 28 people in jail per 100,000 of population. In the case of the 1990s, its figure represents nigh on 108 people per 100,000 - indicating nearly four times the increase in incarceration above that of the 1930s figure.

Assuming similarity in offences: if we relate the findings to the 1990s tenfold increase in crime in general, compared with the 1930s, it seems to indicate our later period shows far more leniency in its sentencing compared with the 1930s. This by having only four times the number of people in prison whilst having ten times the crime rate?

Professor A.H. Halsey in his 'Twentieth-Century British Social Trends' (published in 2000) indicates:

Had it not been for policies which successfully diverted many offenders from stringent criminal processes and custodial penalties, the prison population would have been very much larger.

"Diverted from stringent criminal processes" refers to the use of Community Service, introduced in 1987. This obviously reduced custodial sentencing - as Professor Halsey implies. Based on the figures previously given and assuming the 1930s' policy being applied and the crimes generally comparable, the prison population for the 1990s would need to have been 138,842 and not the apparently lenient figure of 55,537 (that's if my uncertain mathematics are correct).

This less punitive attitude appears to be reflected in the change of name from "Police Force" to "Police Service" - a change made in the belief that it would take away the severe image which the word "Force" suggests. The period of our visits may, however, claim that the word Force was the appropriate one to use; since the police are not providing a service to a group which never seeks attention but desperately and constantly try to avoid any attention forced upon it.

The earlier period could also claim that the change of name indicates a shift to a more lenient stance, and the word "service" reflects that shift. Moreover, it could also claim that it represents our later period's uncertainty about how to deal with crime in a climate that demands "understanding" (offering a service to?) the wrongdoer yet at the same time needing to limit the wrongdoing.

Whether or not the old system was right in its use of the word Force, and whether or not the values and philosophies the use of that word implies were correct, the application of its law did, it seems, assist in controlling the number of offences that period experienced. This may give support to the seemingly common-sense disposition to "nip things in the bud"; and the earlier and more tender the bud, the easier it is to nip - which appeared to be the intention behind that quick clip on the ear accepted by the old communities.

It seems, then, that delving into why the old communities had less anti-social behaviour than those of the present time has produced the following conclusion:

A low-crime community is a consensual community that has an uncompromising attitude towards wrongdoing and possess a disposition to "nip misbehaviour in the bud" and "bend its young twigs" towards a proper inclination. To do this, its people must have common agreement about what constitutes "acceptable behaviour" and the "corrections" appropriate to any impropriety.

More importantly, it must be able to inculcate feelings of shame sufficient to inhibit any misdemeanour a member might be inclined to commit against that community.

Finally, the community must have a setting that allows its people to readily get to know each other and thereby generate feelings of neighbourliness. From this, the people should feel that they belong to the community and thereby value its goodwill.

We saw all these attributes in the community we visited. With this in mind, we can return to the time wherein we left our little pile of coal; and, perhaps, do so with sufficient confidence to feel that we'll find it undisturbed...

34
The End of a Time?

~~~~~~~~~~~~~~~~~~~~~~~~~~~~~~~~~~

Certain commentators with an interest in the social, economic and political climate of the pre-1939 years consider it inexplicable that the disorders Sir Oswald Mosley and the Communist Party General Secretary, Harry Pollitt, sought to ferment did not occur.

Photos of the rain-sodden lines of the October 1936 Jarrow Marchers, carrying a bedraggled banner and led by their mouth-organ band, should, one would expect, portray men who were "ripe for revolution" considering the economic situation forcing them to protest.

However, the commentators' perplexity would suffer even further confusion from the fact that the men appear disciplined and orderly, and displayed no other banner than that declaring who they were.

The commentators would be even more exasperated by the fact that those men of Jarrow - when marching by way of the Mall to present their petition to the House of Commons - lustily cheered the passing King (then Edward VIII) as he rode by in a sumptuous carriage. So, in the context of this assumed perplexity the commentators suffered, it might prove interesting to examine the reasons why what they thought should "logically" occur did not occur.

Perhaps one of the causes of the suggested commentators' confusion is that they hadn't taken into account how far the habit of law and order and its associated attitudes towards constituted authorities had entered the disposition of that age.

For instance: after making their march of something like 300 miles in atrocious weather, and after "paying respect" to the passing King Edward, and then presenting a petition to their parliamentary representatives, the marchers - funded by a group of sympathisers - took a train back to Jarrow. Shortly afterwards, a police report concluded:

The march through the Metropolitan District seemed well organised and the men well disciplined. The general public was sympathetic and generous and the demonstration kept free from political propaganda. During the marchers' stay in London, conduct was exemplary and no incident occurred necessitating police action.

From the perspective of our later period and that of the suggested commentators, their action, or lack of it, might be see as mindlessly subservient; this considering especially the "respect" they displayed towards someone riding past their ragged and rain-soaked line in a sumptuous carriage. But before finally judging the Jarrow Marchers, let's hear another police statement made four years earlier, in 1932, at the height of the Depression - during what was then called the most serious industrial protests experienced in London:

Only a small number of injuries occurred and the total cost of damage from the disturbances was about £220 - a part of this being one shop window accidentally broken, which cost £120 to replace.

So, this habit of lawfulness (or subservience, as another perspective might have it?) persisted even under circumstances in which the previously mentioned commentators might deem energetic protests rightful to enact.

However, let's consider a reported incident presented in a newspaper of that time, when the economic depression was at its height, which could further perplex the commentators.

As an act of protest, a group of approximately one hundred shabbily dressed men entered the fashionable Grill Room of London's high-class Ritz Hotel at the hour when that establishment catered for those well able to afford its teatime luxuries, served amongst all the usual fineries. They took whatever places were available and asked to be served tea, whereupon the management -

feeling that they shouldn't be there and suspecting they hadn't the means to pay for the service - called the police.

Upon their arrival, the men withdrew in an orderly manner and without protest.

Other newspapers carried articles contrasting the plight of these unemployed men with that of the usual Ritz frequenters. This incited a volume of letters supporting the men's "symbolic act", as a popular newspaper at that time reported:

The numerous letters we received indicate a wave of sympathy from every section of the community.

Before then, what our imagined commentators thought should happen nearly did happen. This especially during the tense nine day General Strike in the May of 1926, when the 1917 Bolshevik Revolution's reverberations were still echoing loudly enough to make the Authorities fearful of a similar disruption in this country.

When the situation neared that possibility, preference for the "rule of law" rather than revolution seemed to determine its outcome. The leaders of the strike began to fear its success even more than its failure. Their anxieties led to the strike's unconditional calling off, even when the strikers' will to continue seemed unshakeable. This they did in the belief that:

If the dispute continued, the more revolutionary militants in the regions would gain control and possibly provoke disorders not easily contained.

Yet, immediately before this calling off, a police report stated:

During the strike, no physical casualties occurred and out of the three and a half million strikers, only a reported handful was arrested for violent actions.

This indicates that the majority of strikers possessed an attitude similar to that displayed by the Jarrow marchers ten years later.

Manchester did experience an outbreak of violence at the beginning of the 1926 strike, when resentment became directed towards the "voluntary strike-breakers". One such incident took place in Stevenson Square, not far from Smithfield Market, when a group of strikers attempted to stop cars and coaches by setting fire to a motor-lorry in Market Street, whereupon the group dispersed when the police arrived. However, the report for the duration of the strike was "Manchester appeared to be generally quiet".

The "amiable" relationship apparently existing between police and strikers no doubt assisted this type of restraint. For instance: at the height of the strike, a football match took place in Plymouth between the two groups. The strikers won 2-1 and were loudly cheered by the police and their supporters.

Although these incidents between strikers and representatives of the law may be considered as minor in the greater scheme of things, nevertheless they seem to expresses a major principle about the "habit of lawfulness" and its concomitant accord between police and public. In Professor Geoffrey Gorer's 'Exploring English Character', this is exemplified by a comment made by a working class lad from Wolverhampton, during one of its interviews:

We're led to believe that Britain has the best police force in the world. This I believe is due to the fact that Britishers do, and have to, respect the law who gives us a true sense of freedom and security.

This implied mutual respect existing between police and public was no doubt built on foundations laid by Sir Robert Peel.

Included amongst his nine points directing policing methods were:

The ability of the police to perform their duties is dependent upon public approval of police actions.

Police must secure the willing co-operation of the public in voluntary observance of the law to be able to secure and maintain the respect of the public.

Police, at all times, should maintain a relationship with the public that gives reality to the historic tradition that the police are the public and the public are the police; the police being only members of the public who are paid to give full-time attention to duties which are incumbent on every citizen in the interests of community welfare and existence.

His aim was to make the police "approachable"; and this constituted a reason for them being unarmed. The result finally coalesced in the image presented by the "Dixon of Dock Green" TV series, which showed a person helpful to the public but harsh towards wrongdoers. It also engendered popular songs such as "If you want to know the time, ask a policeman" and the music-hall jollity called "The Laughing Policeman". This once, very noticeable, amiability the bobby-on-the-beat projected was admirably portrayed in the comments made by the Czechoslovakian, Karel Capek, in his essays 'Letters from England' - mention in a previous narrative.

However, back to the strike: whether or not it was right and proper to call off the strike before it had chance to work itself out - to whatever consequences it may've generated - is a matter of political taste. But one thing the calling-off appears to indicate is the fear of home-based disorder - planted in the English mind during the French

Revolution and the years following - seemed to stir again in 1926, not long after the Russian Revolution.

Minds seeded by Victorian anxieties about disorder produced the attitude that the strike leaders exemplified - this allowing peaceful action rather than political disruption to grow. It seems the hard grounds of law and order the Victorians had to plough yielded its intended flowering. This flourished even in a time when Stanley Baldwin - the Prime Minister during the time of the General Strike - stated:

Conditions in Britain came closer to civil war than they had for nearly three hundred years.

An outbreak of strikes in the summer of 1911 did cause serious disturbances reminiscence of the early Victorian political unrest. It required the calling out of army units to support the police in establishing control of a situation involving the destruction of railway equipment. This reached a peak necessitating reading out the Riot Act, to those involved. A crowd of strikers continued the destruction immediately after the reading, and attempts to quell their excesses led to many injuries on both sides. Perhaps the comparative moderation in the later strikes of 1926 was influenced by the "lesson" of the 1911 disturbance, causing old anxieties about disorder and a possible uncontrollable situation to reappear on all sides.

However, let's return to the Jarrow March. It appears that it achieved no direct and immediate political benefits for the men concerned, but it did achieve the status of folk legend. Those who marched obeyed the rules and did not act disruptively. By this and their reported "lawful dignity", they generated enormous admiration and public sympathy which added its moral weight to their protests - this in the same way as did the incident we saw at the Ritz Hotel.

Our later period might suggest that the displays of public admiration and shows of sympathy were all very well, but it didn't get the marchers any jobs - and the ones demonstrating at the Ritz didn't even get a cup of tea! Well, history does, indeed, indicate this to be true. But history also indicates their actions eventually achieved something more profound. It seems the demonstrators' way of behaving had a great deal to do with moving the national mind towards the "must" of a Welfare State; which, as we know, emerged immediately after the 1939-45 war - just a decade later than the Jarrow March.

No doubt many of the men involved in the Jarrow demonstration and the other mentioned incidents fought in the 1939-45 conflict in order to maintain the "freedom" of their country (one being the right to go on strike). Thus their efforts saw the establishment of what our later age enjoys and appears to be unable to do without; and whose implementation those men, even in their wildest dreams, couldn't imagine as a possibility at the time of their demonstrations.

However and as previously noted: in generating positives, it seems we unavoidably generate negatives. The Welfare State is now - in the manner of all human institutions - showing signs of unintended and adverse consequences. Aneurin Bevan's dream of NHS diminishing costs as the nation's health improved has now become the nightmare of ever increasing monetary demands and unforeseen ailments. Moreover, the laudable idea of universal welfare seems to be diluting the sense of individual responsibility. The help and support that neighbours once readily offered in the old communities, which fostered and maintained the social cohesion of their neighbourhood, is now the responsibility of an impersonal welfare system. This seems to be a main element in making the old supportive communities no longer necessary.

As suggested previously: the decline in neighbourly communities is considered to be a substantial factor in the increasing crime rates; and the following statistics implicitly support this connection.

In 1938 - a few years before the social disruptions caused by the 1939-45 war - the total number of indictable offences for serious crimes known to the police stood at 283,200. Just thirty years later, In 1968, the figure had risen to 1,207,354 - representing something like a 76 per cent increase in crime for less than a 13 per cent increase in population. Again these figures seem to indicate a once comparatively orderly and cohesive society suffering a severe dislocation - this to the extent of making the pre-war period appear so unreal and remote that the words "once upon a time" would seem appropriate.

But returning to the previously mentioned demonstrations. Those who knew that time towards the end of its time would see the restraint the demonstrators exhibited as in no way surprising. The men involved were of the same generation as my mother and the Tea-lady we met at the beginning of these narratives. They were typical of their time and were people who'd accept a situation as it was and worked within the law to do what they could about it. In this, they'd make whatever adaptations they thought necessary and show enterprise and initiative within whatever circumstances they had to face.

As in the case of my mother - in her, perhaps, comparatively insignificant but in many ways just as acute circumstances - those two hundred or so Jarrow Marchers weren't apathetic. Apathetic men don't embark on a three hundred mile march and apathetic women aren't inclined to search desperately for any job they can find to ensure the survival of their family - as we saw many of those in Heelis Street did.

These people were by nature cheerful in whatever circumstances came along, and were therefore not easily defeated. We saw this confirmed by the optimism they displayed during the uncertain part of the war, when the apparent disaster of Dunkirk had to be "looked in the face". We also saw how they derived entertainment from the propaganda Lord Haw Haw thought was bound to make them "fearful and depressed". Furthermore, the Tea-lady we met readily displayed a cheerful humour - even after her house had been reduced to rubble.

A Gallup Poll conducted in the most desperate time of May 1940 remarkably portrayed the qualities mentioned. This showed only three per cent of the British people believed that they might lose the war; and by the end of that year, those believing in the possibility of defeat had dropped to a proportion so small it could hardly be measured.

Many outsiders perceived the result as unbelievable and suspected the accuracy of the Poll. However, an American reporter, Virginia Cowles, witnessed with astonishment the attitude of the British people soon after the fall of France, followed almost immediately by the apparent disaster of the Dunkirk evacuation. She declared with astonishment:

For the first time I understood what the maxim meant: "England never knows when she is beaten."... I was flabbergasted. I not only understood the maxim; I understood why Britain never had been beaten.

Those fully aware of the people of that time will not be surprised by their historically induced capacity to "cheerfully resist". We saw its mood implicitly expressed at the Jubilee Party.

So, in view of the perplexity various observers seemed to have expressed when experiencing this temperament - in wartime and in the economic circumstances preceding - let's return to examining what attitude of mind sustained such people in circumstances that were less than cheerful.

Improbable as it may seem, one of its main ingredients was a sense of contentment - which, despite all the deprivations of that time, actually existed. Research found this in regions other than that of our main interest. For instance: the Pilgrim Trust - a research organisation active during the period of the 1926 General Strike - commented upon the remarkable absence of grievance within many of the communities experiencing the worst levels of unemployment.

The research concluded that the Durham miners, for example - who remained on strike for six months after the ending of the more widespread strike - seemed to possess a determination to:

...make the best of things; taking their references from those within their own community and only a small minority failed to make this adjustment.

Some years earlier, that careful observer of economic scenes - John Maynard Keynes - in his essays 'The Economic Consequences of the Peace' (1919) - noted:

The greater part of the population, it is true, worked hard and lived at a low standard of comfort, yet were, to all appearances, reasonably content with this lot.

As we observed during our earlier visits to the old communities: one of the factors assisting this "contentment" was the absence of a ubiquitous media submitting the outside world to the constant gaze of every household, and thereby raising myriad expectations amongst its viewers. People would, therefore, make comparisons only within the immediate experiences of their neighbourhood - as the miners did.

Different places of brief and limited contact had a quality of "not relating" to one's own circumstances, as we saw when visiting those other, far away, houses where my mother did her cleaning job. The community of our main interest - and the essentially similar setting represented by that of the Durham miners - formed such a powerful part of a person's self as to make other areas of the world appear so remote from their own centre of existence that they hardly registered as having any significance.

Comparisons can only be made in the context of what is relevant to one's position and within perceived changes that make one's position appear less satisfying. Yet despite its changes, the world as it then was seemed unchanging. For instance: the pattern of life my parents and their parents experienced and the values and beliefs they - when children - acquired were very much the same as those I experienced and acquired as a child. Moreover, many of the games and rhymes know to each generation and the way that they were played and sung were essentially the same - all this implicitly transmitting a sense of "comfortable" continuity. Along this uninterrupted road, it wasn't difficult to feel content and "at home" in one's community.

As far as the children were concerned, they found it easy to understand and give deference to the long established values and experiences each generation had acquired and passed on to the next. That remarkable but unsettling social manifestation - bringing into being newly invented words such as "teenager" - had not yet emerged;

and the ambiguities, challenges, tensions, and contradictions a separate culture could create did not, nor could not, exist.

Before its emergence, those waiting to become adults saw the long continuum of experiences and forms of entertainment established by adult standards as being unquestionably supreme. Before and up to that drastic, society-changing, 1939-45 war, there's hardly a sign of any group other than adults having control or influence on the course of events. To history, other groups hardly had presence - and, even if acknowledged, were considered nonentities as far as influence was concerned.

In this setting we - the children of that time - were too absorbed in the freedom that being nonentities allowed. We knew we belonged to a generation, which, like all previous generations, lived in a world as it always seemed to have been. And whilst we, ourselves, were waiting to become adults - with all the responsibility and authority that would incur and bestow upon us - we saw ourselves in the way all children of that time saw themselves: seeing our role as demanding conformity to the adult world as it then existed. To question its legitimacy would've been - to us - like challenging the whole of creation.

Future historians will, perhaps, make comparisons with this and the disposition of teenage culture emerging in the early nineteen-sixties, and growing thereafter under the gigantic commercial pressures generating its emergence. They will, perhaps, consider how this formed and imposed its own set of values - many running counter to the traditionally entrenched adult standards.

The imagined historians might also examine how its emergence created a culture within which the natural rebelliousness of youth (once bridled and directed by the restraints of long established customs and conventions) demanded freedom of "rein" to an extent that their predecessors would find unimaginable. But whatever may or may not be concluded, we, the kids of the Thirties - living as we were in the last decade before the great change - had no reason to do otherwise than to accept without question those long, unbroken traditions. We saw ourselves as being in no way different from the way children had always been and had always been committed to be.

This may've proved advantageous in many ways - especially when compared with the situation arising thereafter. In our acceptance, we were left to our own devices: free to be unrestricted children and young persons, investing our time in whatever pursuit we found to absorb our interest, until that important, eventual, happening when the number of years permitted our entry into the adult world.

In the meantime, we were careful not to give offence to the requirements of the established conventions. If we did (and there were times when we tried - as all generations of children and young people do - to "kick over the traces") then the whole of the united and correcting world of adulthood would descend upon us with all its weight; and all its might; and all its unquestionable authority.

This apparent conformity supported by an implicit coercion would be felt as unbearable in our present period. However, its "weight" wasn't felt by most people of that time - young or old - unless they, for some reason, became conscious of it as an imposition. The majority - young or old - found it comfortable to bear because they felt the network of deference and respect it represented were necessary for an orderly society.

The "respect" the Jarrow Marchers paid the king as he rode by in his coach implied this attitude. To the marchers, and to most people at that time, the king represented, consciously or unconsciously, the symbol of a traditional stability, as did the police to the previously mentioned working-class lad from Wolverhampton. This network of deference would also include all those holding roles conferring authority and its associated respect in their own ambiences - such as schoolteachers; railway guards; bus-conductors; postmen; park-attendants and even road-sweepers. All these figures were - consciously or unconsciously - seen as representing a long-established order going back in time. Therefore, their assigned roles were perceived as an aspect of an orderly society's maintenance, and the authority ascribed to such roles stemmed from that "service".

However, back to the children. In that financially restrictive period, adults could also command respect and authority by way of economic circumstances; since children and even the adolescents (teenagers) of that time, were almost completely dependent on the adult world for monetary benefits. Our street contained about fifteen or so children of the "play in the street age" and nearly as many of those we now call teenagers. If all their collective pockets were emptied at any particular time, the amount of cash produced would, more than likely, be insufficient to buy a pair of bootlaces.

Cash benefits came mainly from the meagre surplus adults could spare; and that benefit - if forthcoming - largely depended upon the good behaviour of the recipient and the corresponding goodwill this behaviour might engender.

Besides this, much of the educational system we previously glimpsed had a structure directed towards sustaining a respect for established authority, both formal and informal. This emerged in all aspects of schooling - overtly or covertly. For instance: the natural desire of children to fidget and move around was constantly disciplined by the restricting, regimentally placed, rows of desks and the teacher's position on a raised dais. This setting offered no escape from an "authoritative gaze" demanding immediate attention.

The old Victorian discipline of laborious rote learning held sway, with its repetitive arithmetic tables and recited historic dates - all of which had to be remembered to avoid the "sanctions" applied to those unable to recite what "had" to be remembered. Thus, the school process was one of instilling the "must" of obedience and the "duty" of learning (however irksome these might be) as required by an authority with the long established status to demand acceptance of its dictates. To suggest a lesson might be boring would've evoked incredulity, along with an unsympathetic retort such as:

"What has boring to do with schooling? You learn what you are told to learn. Liking has nothing to do with lessons!"

Our present period would see this insistence that children should submit to what they found unpleasant as improper. However, an echo of "doing what you must do - like it or not" emerged in the conversations with my mother; extending its implications into the wider, adult, world. Whilst discussing her friend, Nancy, I repeatedly remarked that she must've felt very unhappy in her circumstances. I think my mother eventually found what appeared to her as the usual exhibition of my naivety a bit irksome. After one such remark, she replied - with some surprise mixed with impatience showing in her eyes:

"What's happiness got to do with it? She had a duty and obligation to her child. And that's the way she saw it, and that's the way it was."

The last, dying, declaration of duty and obligation having a claim on conduct, over and above that of personal desires, emerged in the film, 'Brief Encounter' - set in the nineteen-thirties and issued in 1945. After this, the world was to change so much as to make the actors' careful pronunciation and grammatical correctness seem stilted and quaint; and the behaviour of the portrayed people seen as the manifestations of severely repressed personalities.

Particularly inexplicable to our later period would be the portrayed shame, guilt and feelings of humiliation arising from the depicted liaison between the male (Alec) and female (Laura) - these emotions containing such depth that they frustrated the "consummation" of the passion felt by the two involved.

Almost beyond the realms of our later time's credibility would be a scene in which Laura portrays guilt about neglecting her "wifely duties" when faced with the possibility of being late home, and thereby not ensuring the evening meal being properly prepared for her husband. This conflict (bordering upon what our later period might judge as a peculiar and inexplicable type of hypocrisy) indicated the powerful struggle in the minds of the two torn between "obligation" and "passion": a conflict which the film deemed must finally be won by obligation - as the ethos of that period demanded.

But more inexplicable would be the politeness exhibited by Alec towards Laura's cheerfully-chatting female friend who (obviously believing there couldn't be anything "improper" in the couple being in each other's company) had, by chance, intruded upon their final and agonising minutes together in a railway-station buffet. Alec's politeness would seem even more inexplicable because of the friend's declare intention of catching the same train bringing about Laura's departure - thereby taking away the last brief moments Laura and Alec would ever have to make their farewell.

An earlier scene, portraying Laura sitting alone on a park bench in the dark of a late-evening whilst trying to come to terms with her emotions, and then the policeman arriving on the scene being more concerned for her possible state of health rather than for her "safety", would, to the period we now know, appear unreal. But the fact that it would be perfectly acceptable to the viewers of that period declares the drastically different times the two eras represent.

I happened to discuss this scene with my sister. She remarked it wasn't surprising because, in the mid-thirties - when in her early, what we would now call, "teens" - she often walked home from a late film with a girl of the same age, along gas-lit streets and alleyways, without anyone being in the least concerned. My sister's ready acceptance of the mentioned scene's "realism", based on her own experience, supports the previously raised comments concerning the taken for granted and naturally expected law and order of that time.

But, as constantly reiterated in these narratives, people are essentially a product of their time and the learning experiences each period's communities offer its initiates. At the time of the film's setting and the times preceding, an in-built aspect of early learning directed itself towards teaching the dispositions the film implicitly portrayed and my mother's remark about her friend's "obligation" encapsulated. These dispositions demanded the applying of any reluctant nose to any irksome grindstone - whether that grindstone took the form of work, duty, obligation or any other commitment. Moreover, this applying had to be done - if not with complete willingness - with at least a substantial degree of acceptance.

Duty and obligation came, it seems, first and foremost. Individual preferences came - it seems - secondary.

The educational system therefore had appropriateness to the world as it was then. Much of the work and circumstances many children would eventually meet in life could be as irksome in its requirements as the symbolic "cleaning out the drains". It was a life demanding that all its requirements and unpleasant aspects must be faced and done, willingly or unwillingly and like it or not, if the far more irksome consequences of not doing so are to be avoided.

Only those brought up under what we would now see as an inadmissible regime could, perhaps, uncomplainingly and with a remarkable degree of endurance, "accept" the horrendous trenches of the First World War - and emerge with morale substantially intact?

This supposition about endurance is less absurd than it might seem. Recent studies indicate that what might be called "emotionally controlled" people appear to have a higher tolerance of pain and discomfort than those less inclined towards that disposition. It concluded:

The more emotionally controlled subjects displayed a higher tolerance of pain under physical test, and would report discomfort when these tests reached greater intensity than that experienced by the less emotionally controlled.

The study also indicated that the endurance of pain and its discomforts is very much governed by the attitude towards it: whether pain is considered as something to be ignored or as something to be deplored; or perceives as something to be endured or something to be immediately cured? If this is true, it could "explain" why the stiff-upper-lip appeared to be so highly valued by the Victorians in their Dickensian 'Hard Times' and similarly valued by subsequent periods still influenced by Victorian sentiments and also enduring their own hard times.

This attitude of mind may explain why my poor old grandmother endured what must've been crippling discomfort whilst scrubbing the floors of a hospital - as we witnessed in one of our earlier visits.

It may be that her endurance stemmed mainly from what we previously noted: the inability to pay for medical relief forced it upon her out of necessity. Moreover, she'd have concerns about declaring a disability that would place upon those near and dear to her a duty of care - when they, themselves, were already burdened by many difficulties.

The fact that she did endure showed a capacity to tolerate a situation which, I believe, very few people of our later period would accept - or believe they should accept? However, her capacity to "live with" such painful discomfort stemmed from the circumstances of her time, because her endurance wasn't at all unusual for that time - as the men of the trenches proved.

As previously implied: this "learning to control" emerged early in life as an aspect of an educational system that our later period might perceive to be stiflingly and therefore not conducive to individual creativity. Nevertheless, this perception doesn't quite fit the fact that the children subjected to its system seemed highly inventive in their play - as the games we saw during our visits indicated. As we then witnessed: the words "I'm bored" or "there's nothing to do" never seemed to enter their vocabulary. They invariably found multitudes of things to occupy their time - which would always seem, to them, insufficient to cater for the many exciting activities they could find to fill it.

It therefore seems that any assumptions about education must include more than what takes place in the classroom. It is a continuing process mainly acquired through constantly affirmed attitudes, expectations and beliefs and the quality of people children find around them and what their culture implicitly "tells" them they should be? Within this extended learning process, the classroom, perhaps, has just one particular part to play; and when classroom experience enmeshes with the other, external, processes in the wider community, it may have a different shaping affect than the one we imagined it would or should produce.

Nevertheless, whatever combinations of learning and circumstances intermingled in that time, they seemed to produce people who were widely adaptive, inventive and forthright. This we know they proved to be in the face of the supreme tests of national survival imposed upon them by wars and the crippling economic conditions in between.

The discipline and conformity embedded in the old education system along with the insularity of that time may've been part of the complexities inducing the socially cohesive qualities the old communities seemed to possess. And, perhaps, only in their setting could the previously mentioned "authority of roles" be maintained and respected.

Yet, to us - the children of that time - those self-contained and apparently inward-looking neighbourly communities represented an immensely safe and "freedom-rich" playground. They offered far less restrictions and far more room for children to be children than any child of our later period could possibly imagine. What more could we hope or wish for - or even want?

However, besides the community of our visit, there were others with their own characteristics and way of life. One mostly resembling that of our visit would be found in London's East End, where the Tea-lady we met lived. The one she knew would have similar "village-community" housing arrangements, economic circumstances and experiences. On the wider scene, there were those that J.B. Priestley commented upon when he mentioned his "Four Englands".

Although Priestley's other Englands contained communities vastly different in their life-style and circumstances to the one we came to know, nevertheless they no doubt enjoyed a Jubilee Party expressing values, sentiments and beliefs essentially the same as those we experienced at the party we attended.

This unanimity seems to be supported by Professor Gorer's survey, completed in the latter part of the 1940s, where, on page 303 and as part of his conclusion, he states:

The upper middle and lower working classes, the mother-centred North-West and the father-centred North-East and North depart to a somewhat marked extent from the habits and attitudes of the rest of the country; but in the main the English are a truly unified people, more unified, I would hazard, today than at any previous period in their history.

Professor Gorer's implied concordance would, more than likely, stem from those communities that offered the sense of belonging we observed in our visits. Attached to its various forms would be the essential word "our". It could be "our village"; "our district"; "our valley"; "our street"; and - over and above this sentiment of sharing and possessing - there'd be the concept of "our country", as Professor Gorer's statement suggests.

The surges of spontaneous generosity that the Jarrow men experienced along the route of their long march arose from this feeling, causing many people to see the marchers as "our people". The men of Jarrow would implicitly sense this when given free tea, corned beef and boiled potatoes at a farm near Bedford and at the many other places where they received similar generosities.

However, to end with the original question about the Jarrow Marchers and the perplexity experienced by the suggested commentators.

It appears that the marchers' behaviour arose from a habit of lawfulness produced by a law-abiding community. This habit grew from controls internalised, which thereby became an aspect of their nature. Their march was, therefore, "self-controlled" and needed no outside impositions.

To me, the time of that march and the final period of our visits represented the last decade of a historically induced and firmly entrenched consensus about life and about life's meaning. Our later period may, perhaps, question some of its values; and - as our visits and enquiries indicate - many of these could easily be seen as questionable. But each age tends to define its own values as "right and proper" within the context of its own time; and each age must be judged on that basis.

Many complexities caused the attitudes and attributes of the time we visited to emerge - as all our delving showed. These qualities were sometimes formed by accident and sometimes by design. It may be that the old communities were the final flowering produced from the grounds we saw the Victorians striving to cultivate, in which chance and intention put a unique mix of ingredients that they hoped would allow the seeds of stability to perennially grow.

In the next narrative, we can attempt to answer another question. What caused the passing away of the old communities?

35
No Step to Sit On

~~~~~~~~~~~~~~~~~~~~~~~~~~~~~~~~~~~~

Everything comes to an end: empires; communities; and even the eternity of childhood. By the time of the 1935 Silver Jubilee, the forces that would bring about monumental changes - ranging from the ending of long established Empires down to the break-up of the old neighbourly communities - were beginning to form. Nobody - except, perhaps, for a few visionaries - seemed to realise the vast transformations that would take place; and certainly not us kids, immersed as we were in the all-absorbing world of childhood.

Nevertheless, the forces of change were already on the march, so to speak. Not long after the Jubilee, Mussolini's armies invaded Abyssinia (now known as Ethiopia) in the autumn of 1935. All we knew or cared about this event we light-heartedly expressed by way of a song in vogue at the time - which we thought great fun to sing as we skipped, uncaringly, along the street:

> *Will you come to Abyssinia,*
> *Will you come?*
> *Bring your own ammunition,*
> *And a gun.*
> *Mussolini will be there,*
> *Shooting bullets in the air.*
> *Will you come to Abyssinia,*
> *Will you come!*

This "ditty" must have been a local invention (I've never heard tell of it elsewhere) and sung to the tune of a popular song of that time: "Roll along covered wagon, roll along". Also, it contained only one verse. However, its perky rhythm and rhyme captivated our musical quirks; so much so that all its implications were lost to our awareness - even if we sought the complications such awareness could bring about.

Nevertheless, awareness or not, Mussolini's success in occupying Abyssinia, was, it seems, the spur to Hitler's occupation of the "demilitarised" territory of the Rhineland in the March of 1936 and thereby the formation of an accord between Hitler and Mussolini - resulting in the Axis Pact in October of that year. "The dark clouds of war were already on the horizon" (to use a phrase whose origin I'm unable to trace). And as we now know, the wanton and destructive forces to form new "Empires" - possibly far more repressive than any the world had ever seen - would be, within a few short years, let loose.

As we also know: the resulting vast and calamitous conflict to thwart these attempts would leave within its wake a profound moral taint associated with Empires. A taint so pervasive in its effect on the world's will and conscience as to make the relinquishing of all the old established domains - including those whose possession was a source of great pride at the time of the Jubilee - inevitable.

Just a few short years after that blissfully unaware party of 1935, the approaching "clouds" were, it seems, beginning to cast their long, dark shadows upon the general mood of the country. Because of this, the Coronation of King George VI in the May of 1937, although popular, didn't appear to generate the same degree of hopeful excitement as did the Jubilee (or so it seems to me). But this may've been due to the continuing gloom cast over the country by the death of the much respected King George V in the January of 1936; to be followed by the abdication of Edward VIII in the December of that year.

The uncertain future all these disturbances appeared to augur would be felt in a far more direct way by the inner-city communities formed within the third quarter of the Victorian era. Their age, along with the crowding together of row upon row of compacted houses, which present standards would deem as providing no more than basic living conditions, became a major concern of the 1935-36 Housing Acts.

The old communities had, it seems, become tired and outdated - as the Housing Acts implied. Their tightly packed streets, lacking the facilities judged proper to the Acts, became a target for "demolition". In this, the houses in and around Heelis Street - built in the 1870s - came within the Acts' intentions. Such was the desire to clean away the old bricks and mortar that the Acts' first phase included something like 1,300,000 houses, nationally.

However, 1938 saw the first stumbling steps leading to inevitable conflict taking place at Munich, in the form of an Agreement signed on the 29th of September of that year. These stumbles became a lurch when Germany occupied all of Czechoslovakia in the March of 1939 and then a plunge six months later with the invasion of Poland, on the 1st of September. Thus, the world lunged into the war that caused the first and second half of the century to split apart.

Although the initial phases of the Housing Acts began prior to the war, the turning of national attention towards rising hostilities made the demolition of houses assume a low priority. Nevertheless, in the ensuing conflict, the Luftwaffe arrived to augmented the process with a different intent - indiscriminately damaging or destroying something like 5,000,000 houses during the 1940-45 period; one of which belonging to the Tea-lady we met at the beginning of these narratives.

The crucial events of this conflict - ranging from the downturn of Dunkirk through to the glorious uplift of the Battle of Britain and then to the war's end, heralded by the Normandy invasion - are etched in history and therefore are widely known. So, for our purpose, no further comments are needed. Our main consideration is what happened after the war.

Unlike the First World War's hard slog to advance a few hundred yards at a time, from trench to trench, the war that followed thrust its participants into a world of fast movement, quick communications and rapidly changing scenes. In this, many of the men and women from the old, inward looking, self-referencing communities experienced startlingly different ways of living from those they had known. The comparisons they were able to make with the possibilities they saw and the way they had lived added to the country's developing mood for radical change. In this, the static world of restrictive traditions and entrenched privileges had to go.

Although venerated for his wartime role, Winston Churchill seemed to personify the old order and therefore he, along with what the voters believed he represented, had to go. The mood was one of "high hopes and great expectations". The Labour Party captured this mood with its 1945 manifesto, declaring "Let us face the Future". This short and simple invitation became a "winner". It appeared to offer a future worth all the recent fighting - and a future that could put the moribund past well and truly into the past.

The country read the promises of great things to come with understandable joy and enthusiasm, containing as they did an almost unbelievable catalogue of benefits. This new vision derived its zealous sense of direction from three philosophical signposts. The first being the laudable plea expressed by John Lilburne in the Levellers' socialistic Manifesto of 1647:

The poorest He that is in England hath a life to live as the Greatest He.

Then the attractive prescription offered by Edmund Burke, as long ago as 1795:

If we command our wealth, we shall be rich and free; if our wealth commands us, we shall be poor indeed.

In addition, it seemed to take note of the observation made by John Stuart Mill (1806-1873) in his series of 'Dissertations and Discussions':

When society requires to be rebuilt, there is no use attempting to rebuild it on the old plan.

The measures to ensure the spirit of equal opportunities, the sharing of wealth and the rebuilding for a new beginning unconnected to the past - as prescribed by the men of ancient times - emerged in various Acts. All major industries were nationalised along with the Nation's bank. The National Assistance Act abolished the last vestiges of the old Poor Law; the National Insurance Act offered social security for all; the National Health Service Act gave universal medical and hospital attention, free at the point of use; the Industrial Insurance Act protected and insured against injuries at work; the Agricultural Act offered large subsidies to reduce the cost of food - and so on.

All these measures would, it was emphatically believed, bring about a nation with sustained health, greater contentment and an even lower crime-rate than ever before. The voters expressed their approval of such gratifying things to come in the July of 1945. This they did by replacing Winston Churchill's administration with Clement Attlee's Government - giving it the largest majority of the century.

The new vision also incorporated a grander scheme for re-housing those who would be displaced by "clearances" - as presented in the Housing Act of 1946. Its intentions envisaged providing space and airiness that the timeworn inner-city communities lacked.

An aspect of its objectives appeared in the High Rise blocks, reaching to the sky from wide and extensive grass covered spaces. Not only did they seem a quick and comparatively easy method of solving the post-war housing shortages but also the Housing Ministry - committed as it was to providing massive housing subsidies - saw the standardisation that high-rise building represented as a way of keeping down costs. In addition, the New Towns Act - also of 1946 - added its low-cost horizontal spread by using easily obtainable farmland. On these wide-open green fields, rapid and unobstructed building could take place.

However, as urgently necessary the provision of new housing had become, and as desirable space and airiness appeared to be, many of its results produced conditions less conducive to neighbourliness. This seemed unimportant as low-cost communications and increasing possession of personal transportation allowed easy and ready contact with friends and relations living elsewhere. In these new circumstances, neighbours began to lose significance - especially when expanding State-welfare increasingly marginalised the support they once provided during difficult times.

The constant neighbourly interactions and day-to-day chats that the less spacious living arrangements once offered seemed no longer of any consequence; and the urban planners - concerned as they were about maintaining their new vision - considered the old arrangements that allowed such associations to take place represented a disadvantage.

The science of sociology defines a neighbourhood as:

An area in which people can develop face-to-face relationships.

Our visits showed how the row upon row of housing allowed the social intimacy crucial to that definition to take place. In the new arrangements, neighbourliness was left for chance to cultivate. However, it isn't a process that flourishes of its own accord. It requires the right grounds for it to take root.

Yet, as suggested many times during these narratives: there seems to be an inescapable rule of life - mostly overlooked and even if recognised is generally ignored in the "push towards progress". This rule is embedded in the constant, universal play of positives and negatives: in creating a positive, we invariable generate a negative. Or, to put it more directly: in gaining something, we lose something.

The positive-something that the post-war period and therefore its subsequent periods appear to have lost (or overlooked?) is the prescription for neighbourly conditions. In that first reaction against the Dickensian image of smoke and slums (and zinc-plated baths hung in little backyards) planning intentions excluded anything resembling those Victorian "villages" that took root in the inner cities. To paraphrase a timeworn cliché: it seems that the happy baby was thrown out with the ostensibly stained bath water. Although the thrown-out baby whimpered for attention, the new vision turned to other post-war considerations; one being to blur those homogenous communities that appeared to perpetuate the separation of social classes.

In the resulting post-war political climate, the inward looking nature of the old enclaves was believed to produce the restrictive horizons that sustained social and political quiescence. Moreover, "being content with one's lot" that the old communities seemed to engender was thought to sustain the uncomplainingly accepted of inequality - a believed infliction that the post-war world wished (rightly?) to banish.

Thus, those crowded streets, whose inhabitants shared the same life-styles, attitudes, problems, values and beliefs, were seen as having few virtues. Any worth they may've possessed appeared too abstruse to delineated, therefore no attempt was made to study what these happened to be or if they should retain a place in the envisioned future.

Yet, the future produces its own prescriptions - these written by a pen that nothing except the unpredictable controls.

At the beginning of the end of my childhood, when I found my community was about to be no more, I had no thoughts of all the philosophical implications attachable to the place in which I'd seemingly lived forever, or of the social changes bringing about its end - even if I was remotely capable of such thoughts.

There was a cat I used to stroke on my way home from school, which sat in the sun, on a step, at the corner of our street. I wondered what would happen to it?

Our Dad said it was more than likely it would return home - to the street it knew...

~ Mrs McKenzie's Cat ~

Number eight has gone; and fourteen, too –
to those new houses, near Belle Vue.
The rest will soon be on their way:
The last one out, by Friday.
They say it's near the fields and trees.
The new Estate fills all their needs.
They'll all have gardens – and a shed.
Electric lights in the streets – they said.
Old Mrs. Mckenzie will take her cat.
Some say it's bound to wander back.
But when demolishing is done,
it'll have no step –
to sit on.

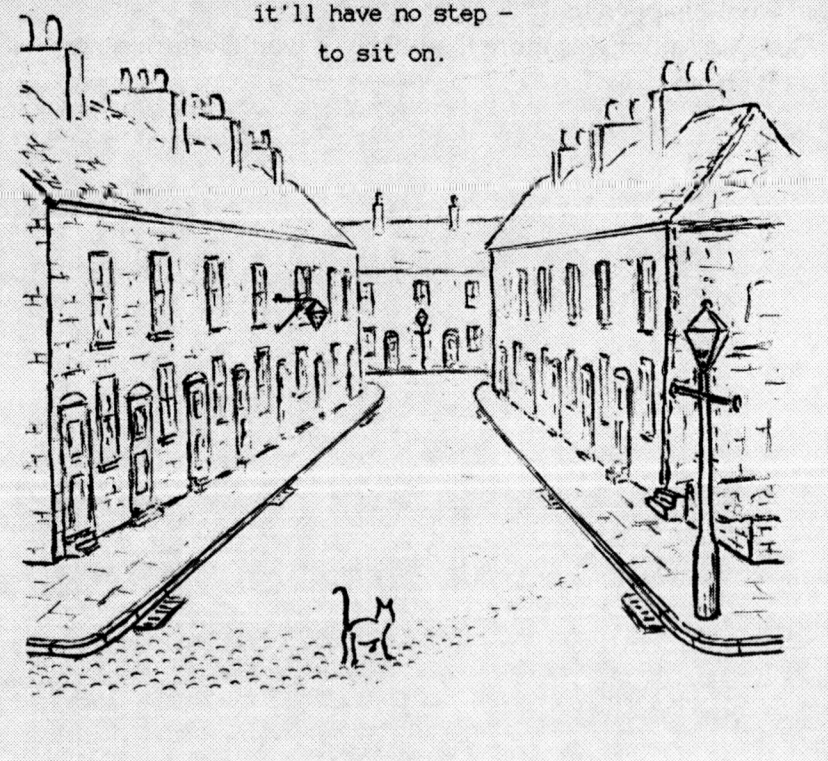

36
Epilogue

~~~~~~~~~~~~~~~~~~~~~~~~~~~~~~~~~~~~~

Some time ago, I returned to the area where Heelis Street once stood.

My visit happened by chance and before thoughts of writing what I hope you've now read occurred. It also happened to be the first visit since living there, as a child, well over half a century ago.

I remembered the area as an immense world; yet, to my astonishment, I found the highly populated labyrinth of streets as it existed in my mind occupied, in reality, a space not much more than a couple of football pitches.

Only four streets retained their original names: Burton; Almond; Dalton and Davy (the latter known in our visits as the "bruw"). The access to these from Rochdale Road was - and still is - by way of what we knew in our visits as Buckley Street. This had been given a name-change and was now Bucknell Street.

At the junction of Rochdale Road and the erstwhile Buckley Street, a high-rise block (named Bucknell Court) covered the space that once contained the building where the stray owl perched and where the Rex Cinema and its adjacent Bronze Street and Rhoda Street used to be.

Opposite this high-rise, and across the tarmac covering the old cobbles of the former Buckley Street, is the area we knew as the Flags; but the expanse of paving on which the kids played whip-and-top had gone and was now a grassy triangle containing a few small trees, trying to adjust to recent planting.

A pub - built in the modern style and bearing the name of Robert Tinker - stood not far from what would've been the edge of the Flags and the end of what used to be Birtle Street. The pub's name implicitly gave testimony to the creator of Vauxhall Gardens, which existed long before Heelis Street and its surrounds were built.

Although the pub occupied a position some distance away from the actual area that the Gardens once covered, its name seemed appropriate to my mood of trying to recall things gone. However, its proximity to the long-since-disappeared Flags made me feel that a title more fitting to my recollections would be "The Whip and Top".

Thoughts of games once enjoyed on the old expanse of paving made me pause for a while. I wanted to see if any children would come to play on the grassed-over area and, if they did come, what games they might play.

But none came.

However, whilst standing there, I noticed the only recognisable features remaining from the time when the Flags existed were the railway wall on its far side and (surprise) the original three, cast-iron, stumpy bollards that the kids once leapfrogged over. These still occupied the entrance of the short pathway leading to Rochdale Road.

In addition, the yard situated at the base of the railway wall and to the right of the stumps - which we knew as Burke's Coal-yard - was still there but had become an enclosure for storing building materials.

I then walked the short distance to the upper end of what is still called Davy Street - which I judged extended across the old line of what was once Worth Street. Here, a high-rise block named Dalton Court covers the space where Agnes's grocery shop - in Davy Street - and Emily Archer's fish and chip shop - in Worth Street - used to be.

On the opposite side of Davy Street from the high-rise, a terrace row of two-storey maisonettes, facing up the slope towards Rochdale Road, occupied the area that we knew as Worth Street. Backing on to this, and starting from the bottom of the bruw where the old Burton House Pub once stood, was a row of three-storey maisonettes. These faced down the slope and fronted a length that had retained the name of Burton Street.

From a spot half way down the slope of this immensely changed bruw, I judged the space that was once Heelis Street now laid buried beneath the rear gardens contained between the two rows of maisonettes. I then glanced along the wire-fenced gardens, to see where our house might have been - without, in this age of "unease", making my action appear too suspicious. A small clump of blue delphinium grew in what could've been the position of our front door.

I then walk the remainder of the bruw to the place we called the Fount. Its area had been filled to make it level with Burton Street; and the slope of sparse grass and outcrops of clay where I once played had disappeared under a mound covered with a scattering of gorse.

It was then that I became more aware of the vague perplexity I felt soon after entering the area, and when standing at the place I once knew as the Flags. Trying to match the Flags and now the Fount with what my memory held and what I was seeing told me its real cause. It arose not so much from the vanished features, or from the realisation of how small the whole area really was, compared with the immensity my memory contained, or from the other changes making a place I had intimately known seem so strange.

It was because of the silence: there were no sounds of children playing; no shouts; no laughter; no clatter of running feet.

I then realised the spirit of the place I knew all that time ago lived in the sound of children's voices; the singing of rhymes; the hubbub of play - which, for me, had kept its memory alive all these years. And if I stayed too long in this place - now seeming so unfamiliar to the point of denying the way I remembered it to be - I felt all the images and sounds I could easily recall would be lost.

It seemed the only means I had for returning to that once lived time was by way of memory; and what I was seeing could overlay the memories so that they too would be buried - as Heelis Street lies buried beneath the gardens and the Fount beneath its gorse.

I felt I must leave this place where once I played and what used to be my home - but which now I did not know.

I turned and walked away; wanting to keep alive in my memory the streets full of people; and life; and laughter; and the sound of children playing...

Once upon a once lived time
(perhaps of toil - perhaps of grime)
Of kettle, coal,
And rooms, gas-lit;
Of doorsteps
Where pet cats would sit
- And cobbled streets -
- And slate-clad roofs -
(And sounds of trams, and horses' hoofs).
The people lived in terrace rows:
Back-to-back,
With sash-windows.
No credit cards; no bright TV.
No Hi-Fi sounds; no fast Mini.
No trips to Spain;
No package tours.
Just streets,
With kids,
And open doors.

Once upon a once lived time,
Children sang and danced to rhyme...

~ ~ ~

37
To Complete the Picture

~~~~~~~~~~~~~~~~~~~~~~~~~~~~~~~~~~~~~~

Some of the previous narratives delved into what appeared to be the most important events shaping the values and beliefs held in the nineteen-century's first half, along with the political mood that emerged immediately after the 1939-45 war.

To complete the picture, tracing the possible reasons why the second half become so astonishingly different from the first now seems an appropriate thing to do.

The relevant narratives speculated about the medical, scientific and technological advances, creating possibilities of different life-styles, and how changing patterns of peoples' circumstances influenced the way they perceived life and each other. In addition, speculations were made about how attitudes held in any particular period are substantially shaped by historical events. Other narratives suggested how the pre-1939 world was one extensively influenced by Victorian Values. Therefore, our final purpose may be served by examining why many of these seemed to be firmly rejected and then replaced by those the present period appears committed to hold.

A useful path to follow is the one indicated by Alan Brinkley's statement, quoted in the Prologue to all these narratives.

As a reminder:

Where once society organised itself around a cluster of powerful and widely shared values, many of them emphasising restraint, self-discipline and personal responsibility, it is now dominated by a new and more permissive ethos that emphasises personal fulfilment, desire and identity.

If we accept this statement as substantially true, then the main signpost to follow will be the one pointing to events and influences that produced the implied shift of attitudes.

A start can be made with the shaking of the Victorian foundations caused by Charles Darwin's evolutionary theories, offered in 1859. His propositions created wide, conceptual cracks in the beliefs about the nature of human nature and the religious revelations that underpinned many Victorian and post-Victorian perceptions.

Another foundation-disturbing event occurred in 1875, with the prosecution of that remarkable woman, Annie Besant, for the "immorality" of publishing a pamphlet on birth control - this being produced under the euphemistic title of 'The Fruits of Philosophy' to make it appear more acceptable.

Fortunately, Charles Bradlaugh - an influential Liberal Member of Parliament at that time - championed her cause and averted a prison sentence. However, her trial brought to the fore the ambivalence and nervous confusion the Victorians had about such matter. For instance, they considered large numbers of children desirable in order to fill the mills of the expanding economy and satisfy the military needs of a growing Empire, but were also fearful about large numbers of "uncontrolled" children promiscuous activities produced.

The Victorians saw the biblical "be fruitful and multiply" as an injunction related to the marriage bed and not to the production of undesirable fruits represented by waifs and strays. They feared that one of the main inhibitions confining the sexual act to the believed safe bonds of marriage - and thereby avoiding the possible spread of debilitating and virtually incurable diseases - would be removed by Annie Besant's injudiciousness. Birth control, they though, could open the door to transient and hazardously unrestrained relationships on the part of the unmarried - and even the married - if the possibility of a resulting child was diminished; or - more "dangerously" - eliminated. Therefore, the fear of promiscuity remained foremost in Victorian minds and this kept the door firmly shut on the knowledge Annie Besant wished to release.

However, keeping the door closed against individual control over such matters proved difficult. The door was finally flung wide opened by Marie Stopes establishing Britain's first instructional birth control clinic, in March 1921, at Holloway Road, London. This, and its slow but sure extensions to various parts of the country, began offering to all those who wished (married or unmarried) an increasing knowledge and availability of contraceptives and a greater reliability of means and methods - and, eventually, easy abortions. Hence, our subsequent time could finally "shrug off" the chains of morality it believed the Victorians had (prudishly?) locked around themselves.

With the unshackling of these "chains", and with the banishing of all the old anxieties that the advent of penicillin and other modern drugs allowed (before the coming of AIDS?) our later period no longer had, or even thought necessary to have, the old Victorian fears and the associated beliefs these fostered. So, our later decades began to reject what seemed to be the bizarre notions held by earlier times about sexuality constituting a constant danger, whose instincts should be restricted and controlled for the sake of personal and social stability.

Also, the idea that chastity outside of marriage and even fidelity within its bonds should be insisted upon with the harshness that the Victorians and those still holding their attitudes thought "fitting" seemed even more "unfitting" to our time. With the freedom the increasing knowledge about diseases and their cures conferred, our later age found it could avoid or even ignore the old moral insistences that the Victorians and those in the direct line of their influence believed protected society.

In addition, the psychoanalytic concepts formulated by Sigmund Freud at the beginning of the 1900s directed subsequent periods to believe human emotions are not easily contained by repression, exhortation and condemnation - and especially those having deep passions. Thus, our later age, increasingly influenced by what appeared to be liberating, scientifically supported, bodies of thought became inclined to abandon emotional mechanisms used by preceding times as a means of social control - now that we could afford to do so.

All the above-mentioned considerations involve issues whose influences can readily be appreciated. However, issues not so readily appreciated, but having a substantial affect on any society's basic beliefs, need to be included in order to complete the full scene. Such beliefs usually concern the nature of human nature and underpin many of a society's laws and expectations. So - as bizarre as it may seem to appreciate the origin of our present beliefs we need to go back to the biblical beginning; and even more bizarrely, we need to consider the incident concerning a fig leaf.

In the "believing" European mind, this biblical episode raised questions about whether or not humankind is inherently good or bad. It also raised the important question of whether or not the human mind has inborn predisposition or if it comes as a tabula rasa - the blank slate suggested by John Locke in his 'Essays Concerning Human Understanding' published in 1690. This "attractive" blank slate concept developed an early and widespread acceptance at "highly intellectual" levels. For instance, in 1707 the influential educationalist, James Talbott, wrote a book of instructions directed at charity schoolmasters. He included amongst its extensive advice the "reminder":

The minds of infants resemble blank paper or smooth wax…capable of any impression.

This reiterated John Locke's perception of a ready-made and pristine material upon which society can write its prescriptions. In this case, James Talbott's instruction implied prescribing with the intention of doing good (whatever that "good" was considered to be, at that time).

As we saw when looking at the French Revolution, all these issues about human nature raged backwards and forwards for hundreds of years in Europe and continued well into Victorian times, amongst the Victorians themselves. A dominant theme in all this controversy concerned the Biblical loss of primordial innocence. The Book of Genesis describes its affect upon Adam and Eve, thus:

And the eyes of them both were opened, and they knew they were naked; and they sewed fig leaves together and made themselves aprons.

Additionally:

Unto Adam also and to his wife did the Lord God make coats of skins and clothed them.

You might now be asking how this relates to our present period; especially since our secular age regards Genesis as a myth. Moreover, you might be asking what has nakedness to do with the issue - even if its condition increases the sale of magazines and makes for popular viewing on TV, when portrayed.

Well, the point is this: the Biblical account had a deep affect upon the Victorian mind, which perceived nakedness as directly related to the shame Adam and Eve suffered in their act of disobedience against God. Because of this, it was seen as a condition needing to be "covered up" - as God demonstrated by the act described in Genesis. Hence the Victorian Missionaries' eagerness to "clothe the natives" and the much enjoyed by us - but unverified - story of table legs being draped with concealing coverings in Victorian parlours.

However, sufficient for our purpose is the fact that Victorians came down on the side of believing that humankind was inherently inclined towards bad, due to the "Original Sin" described in Genesis. From this, they held to the belief that the human mind came with the capacity to know the difference between good and evil and the freewill to chose between the two - as Adam demonstrated in his act of disobedience. It wasn't a blank slate but more of a scroll with prewritten prescriptions. Therefore, Victorian religiosity affirmed a view of man as a fallen creature with base passions, who needed a properly guided freewill supported by the grace of outside agencies to achieve a "higher state".

This is a view our present time would emphatically reject. So, to understand the present view, we need to explore what it was that eroded the Victorian belief of innate iniquity and replaced it with the more generous concepts of human nature that our present period generally holds.

We can start with the proposition that people - naturally and understandably - like to think they are, by nature, inherently nice and not nasty. This inclination constantly surfaced as a counter-measure to the not so flattering Victorian view, which no doubt engendered uncomfortable feelings of guilt. The contrary notion focused on the situation before the act of disobedience and therefore saw nakedness as a symbol represented the original condition of innocence, which could be reinstated by cultivating the simplicity and lack of shame its condition implied. So - in the context of this cultivating - imagine the Renaissance mind being confronted with people who actually went around naked and felt perfectly innocent about this and exhibited no trace of shame.

To get an idea of how this impacted upon minds believing in the original "purity", we can call upon Pietro Martire d'Anhiera who wrote a report regarding the peoples Columbus encountered in 1492, in what became known as the "New World". Here is an extract of a relevant part as it was then expressed:

They seem to lyve in the goulden worlde of which owlde truthe speake so much; wherin men lyved simplye and innocentlye without inforcement of lawes, without quarrelling Iudges and libelles, contente onely to satisfie nature, without further vexation for knowledge of thinges to come.

The English writer Thomas Traherne (c. 1636-74) later and eagerly picked up this theme (along with a dose of guilt) when he declared:

For verily there is no savage nation under the cope of Heaven, that is more absurdly barbarous than the Christian world. They that go naked and drink water and live upon roots are like Adam, or Angels, in comparison to us.

So the civilised world - with its laws, judges and impositions that divorced society from its original and "natural" condition of innocent simplicity - was one of "corruption". Therefore, its redemption appeared to reside in attempting to emulate the moral simplicity of the "Noble Savage" that Pietro Martire d'Anhiera's description implied.

The term, Noble Savage, was coined by the English poet, John Dryden (1631-1700), in his poem 'The Conquest of Granada' - which graphically recaptured the theme of a Biblical innocence in these lines:

> *I am as free as nature first made man,*
> *Ere the base laws of servitude began,*
> *When wild in woods the noble savage ran.*

By now, you may be thinking that this business about a noble savage running wild in a wood has no relevance to our present time.

And we have enough knowledge in the present time to indicate that humankind can be just as nice, nasty, noble or ignoble no matter what its state of dress. So all this argument about innocence is completely naïve and can be dismissed - without further though.

Well, it may seem that way. However, the point of it all is to set the stage upon which the learned and very-important-to-our-time Swiss-French gentleman Jean-Jacques Rousseau (1712-1778) can present his ideas.

He arrived in the world twelve years after Dryden's death and took up the concept of a primordial innocence implied by Dryden's poem. He denounced civilised society as a corruption that had debased the original nobility humankind once possessed. More importantly, Rousseau did what had not been effectively done before. He indicated an intellectual and secular path to follow in order to free people from the religious guilt and societal demands that he declared perpetuated debasement. By following this path, the original purity - both personal and societal - could be restored.

This may provoke a further frustrated:

"What is the use of all this water under the proverbial bridge! And what the heck has the ideas of a person born in 1712 got to do with the attitudes of now? And how can going all that way back in time to hear ancient and possibly irrelevant voices be anything more than just an exercise in curiosity: leading to irritation?"

Well! If we examine some of the things the person in question said, we might think he's still around - or, at least, his ghost is smiling and muttering approvingly over our shoulders. His thoughts about the nature of humankind and the purpose of society presented in his 'Du Contrat Social' of 1762 echoed persuasively down the ages and carried its philosophical voice well into our time. The publication's main preoccupation centred on concepts of individual freedom - a theme now loudly insisting its "rightness" in our present way of thinking. The first line in chapter one of Book One of his 'Social Contract' starts with the dramatic and famous declaration:

Man was born free, and everywhere he is in chains.

Alternatively, if you want to read it in the original French as it was much lauded and shouted out by the crowds during their Revolution of 1789:

L'homme est né libre, et partout il est dans les fers.

As some of the previous narratives indicated: the Victorians felt very suspicious about all the enthusiasm displayed in the disturbance across the channel. Edmund Burke - the British political writer and

Whig Politician of that time - expressed this in his 'Reflections on the Revolution in France and Other Writings' (published in 1790-91) which asked whether or not the Revolution's sentiments had merged with:

...morality and religion; with solidity and prosperity; with peace and order; with civil and social manners...without them, liberty is not a benefit that lasts, and is not likely to continue.

Burke's words solidly laid the foundation of the Victorian ideal regarding a civil society and its wariness of revolutionary disorders. However, all the implications of a civil society were the very thing Rousseau saw as repressive and destructive. His theme of breaking the bonds of a corrupt society again surfaced as a revolutionary intent in 1848, in that all too familiar echo of Rousseau's original declaration offered by the Communist Manifesto compiled by Marx and Engels:

The Workers have nothing to lose but their chains.

Discounting this political slant, more subtly direct and immediately relevant to our later age was Rousseau's writings on education expounded in his book, 'Émile', published in 1762. In this, the most striking phrase for our particular purpose emerged in his chapter one:

Everything is good when it leaves the Creator's hands; everything degenerates in the hands of man.

The implication embedded in this is that purity represents the original condition, whose corruption can be avoided if the "hands" are "cleansed". The way towards this purification constantly surfaced in the theme of 'Émile', which suggested that all instructions should proceed by appealing to the child's innate curiosity and unspoilt natural intelligence rather than imposing the cut-and-dried notions entrenched in an inherently corrupt society. He implied evil arises not from original sin but from the moral and intellectual distortion society imposes upon the child - this through all the inevitable errors and deceits society generates and fosters.

He proposed that men and woman in their "natural state" - free from the corruption of what he identified as "artificial elements" - are both happy and good. These artificial elements Rousseau saw entangled in the customs and traditions each society maintains, and the adults so affected perpetuate such distortions by imposing them upon each new generation.

This theme found a powerfully modern expression in the highly influential writings of the psychiatrist, R.D. Laing, and particularly in his 'The Divided Self' and 'The Politics of Experience' published in the 1960s. Both of these echoed Rousseau by implying that since the family represents the main agent for maintaining society's customs and traditions, it is - ipso facto - the agent for perpetuating disorders.

Laing further extended this concept into the modern psychiatric realm by stressing the role society and that agent of society (the family) has in fostering conditions such as schizophrenic disorders and severe psychosocial inhibitions. His boldly declared proposition generated a large following, to the extent that many groups influenced by his beliefs sought other - what they believe might be - less restrictive social arrangements.

The view of the traditional family representing a "dangerous condition" became an intellectually respectable view to hold. Philip Larkin (1922-1985) took up this theme in his poem 'This be the Verse'; which alarmingly declared:

They fuck you up, your mum and dad…They fill you with the faults they had and add some extra, just for you.

This "suspicion" of the domestic setting gained increasing support from the feminist rejection of the immemorial division of the male and female roles that the Victorians thought was the natural and the most harmonious way of underpinning family stability - and therefore that of society. Although the old Victorian prescription of the family being the bulwark against possible tides of social disruption is echoed, from time to time, by various religious and political leaders - as a solution to our present period's concerns - the old prescription seems to lack power to pursued and even brings forth a degree of antipathy. This no doubt because it goes against the prime principle of individual choice and the freedom to exercise choice our later period sees as paramount - as implied in Alan Brinkley's previously mentioned statement.

Therefore, in an age allowing substantial freedom to choose, the idea of a "binding contract" that the old institution of matrimony represented no longer appealed to an increasing number of people. What the Victorians saw as the essential bond holding society together is now increasingly seen as a possible transient condition reflecting individual choices and individual accommodations between equals.

Thus, in the period where freedom of choice is considered the essential freedom, the focus is on individual "wants" rather than "collective shoulds". This sharp change of emphasis struck at the core of those Victorian sentiments holding such commitment in the communities we visited; so much so that the first half of the nineteenth-century appears to its later period as increasingly difficult to understand.

However, getting back to Rousseau's philosophies: unlike R.D. Laing, Rousseau offered no seemingly objective support for his beliefs - because he never put them to the test. The five children he produced by way of an apparently naïve and illiterate servant-girl (which offered the potential to "tests out" his learning theories on ready made and newly formed "natural material") he immediately deposited in a foundling-hospital soon after birth.

From this rather abrupt method of unburdening himself from family cares, and his capacity to present views arising mostly from feelings rather than from facts, it might be imagined that the person in question had predominately feckless traits and his views should be discounted? However, despite these apparently less than responsible attitudes exhibited in this and other aspects of his affairs, he would've failed to attracted the audience he did if his "case" hadn't been cleverly presented and composed to be in tune with the mood of his time.

As a matter of interest: Richard Lovell Edgeworth (an inventor and a member of the prestigious Lunar Society) strongly influence by 'Émile', submitted his son, in 1765, to the educational theories expounded in the book. His "disturbing" conclusion was:

I found myself entangled in difficulties regarding my child's mind and temper. It was difficult to urge him to do anything that did not suit his fancy.

Nevertheless, and despite what seemed to be an experiential caveat regarding Rousseau's educational theory - and despite his mentioned peculiarities - he emerged as a dramatically original thinker. He acquired many eager followers in "highly intellectual places" - this no doubt because his theme implicitly expressed a valid protest about the rigidity existing in many aspects of society at that time.

Also, his insistence on "going back to nature" in order to "re-discover" nature, and that product of nature we call human nature, became the main inspiration for what is now termed the Romantic Movement in art and literature. This turned the traditional view away from the entrenched repetitions of the Classic Greek and Roman styles and towards a new and more imaginative perspective.

We find this influence in the poems of Wordsworth and those of his associates, expressing their "love of nature and its mystical grandeur" (the first "friends of the earth"?) a sentiment also seen in the broad, colourful and imaginative landscapes presented by Turner and Constable - whose reproductions we see on the walls of many "semis".

But getting back to the question of human nature: it seems one of its enduring dispositions reside in its impulse to accept ideas not necessarily because they have the support of demonstrable facts but because they possess strong emotional appeal. In this, Rousseau's proposal had great appeal to a great many people; centring as they did on the liberation of the individual whose original purity suffers distortions because of society's "corruption", and not because of any innate disposition.

Perhaps the attractive subtlety embedded in this proposal is: if we are all originally pure, we cannot, really, be held fully responsible for our subsequent lapses; since, according to Rousseau, the responsibility for these must be ascribed to faults inherent in society.

So, in the light of this seemingly letting us all off the proverbial "hook", so to speak, the big question springing immediately to the fore is: why were the Victorians inclined to cling desperately to a concept of human nature carrying with it the harsh responsibilities implied by an unfettered freewill? Why did they not choose Rousseau's rather attractive leniency that appealed to so many "great minds" at that time and - by its rejection - choose to become so unsympathetic to "individual weak will"?

Well, apart from their belief that the moral and political licence that occurred in France (which Rousseau's writings apparently supported) seemed an infection which could bring about the collapse of English society, the deep anxiety the Victorians held about maintaining established religious, political and moral concepts they thought essential to any orderly society made them react against anything antithetical. Although the latter part of the Victorian age tended to be one of rising enquiries generating religious doubts, the greater body of Victorians remained essentially "firm in their faith" and hostile to what they considered "ungodly". Within this, they clung to the orderly Calvinistic prescription of faith, hard work, self-denial and an insistence on individual responsibility for individual actions.

To the Victorians, the surging tide of religion flowing through their early and mid periods appeared to constitute a force that could wash away what they perceived as an inimical atheism. This surge of religious feelings also carried a comforting and compensatory hope of "rewards in a realm to come" along with the believed unification with their "dear departed" - which even a quick walk through the old Victorian cemeteries, with their elaborate monuments and earnest declarations, will attest as being sincere in their expectations.

It also directed the body of Victorian views towards the desirable "doing of good works" in this (less important?) life that they believed only provided a preparation for the significant one to come - in which they would be judged and be appropriately rewarded (or not?).

Wealth had to be justified by philanthropic work. Many charitable institutions such as the one that we saw in Charter Street arose from this impulse. It also brought forth numerous social reforms and the extension of literacy - the latter, at first, directed towards bible reading.

The general usefulness of literacy then showed itself in the workers' ability to understand factory instructions - which indicated its utility at every level of society. This engendered the establishment of free lending libraries instigated by the 1850 Public Libraries Act (the first one appearing in Manchester in 1852) and the extension of free education necessary for an expanding industrial society.

However, despite the increasing education and scientific enquiry that the Victorians eagerly fostered, the original view of life and of death had such powerful coloration it never fully faded in the glare of rising doubt - as we saw in the period of our visits. These sentiments persisted until the opposing intellectual and scientific changes and massive social disruptions accelerated by the Second World War reduced this view to the pale shadow that it now appears to be. But this view, when possessing its full body, explains a phrase common to the Victorian period and also to the time we visited, which maintained: "We're not put on this earth just to enjoy ourselves."

The shift of emphasis from an "obligatory should" to an "individual want" is indicated by the fact that the mentioned phrase is often heard and/or implied in our later period, but with the deletion of the word "not". (What a difference a word makes?)

Also - and to accord with the secular trend and its suspicion of religiosity emerging in our later age - we should remove any traces of a biblical sense by taking out the word "put". This further emphasises the tremendous ideological gap between the time in which the old compensations and reasons for living held sway and the time when they seem no longer credible. Other compensations have now taken their place - as the dedicated devotion to shopping on the day of the old "Sunday Worship" seems to declare.

Along with the fading of the Victorian view came a desire to avoid what was seen to be the greatest of all its faults: that of insisting on moral standards of a height difficult to reach. Our later period believed this had an in-built propensity for hypocrisy on the part of those who failed to reach that height yet nevertheless insisted it should be reached. The "honest" solution appeared to reside in reducing moral demands to a level less difficult to attain; and, in this, moving the centre of morality away from societal demands - applicable to all - to an individual frame of reference.

This focus on self-reference returns us to Rousseau's concepts of innate virtue corrupted by societal impositions. Important to our present period is that its principle penetrated the crucial realms of education to push aside what was thought to be "the rigidity of traditional learning". Its push gained powerful impetus from the writings of the American philosopher and educationalist, John Dewey, who began the main core of his "child-centred" thesis in the period 1900-1922. His theme finally took hold soon after the 1939-45 war and happened to harmonise with the widely published Doctor Benjamin Spock's beliefs about childcare, emerging in the late 1950s.

Spock deplored the rigidity found in the traditional way of bringing up children and stressed the importance of diminishing its impositions - a sentiment echoing Rousseau's principle of allowing the "natural" child to develop. Hence, the view in both child rearing and education became child centred; seeing the child needing to escape from the domination of parent and teacher in order to decide upon, and thereby live, an uninhibited life of its own. This idea emerged in the educational practices of the Montessori method (1912) and the experimental school of A. S. Neill - the latter taking root in 1921. Both these methods emphasised spontaneity and freedom from restraint.

The new models of education focused on Dewey's declaration that the value of immaturity is that it "frees the young from dwelling in an outmoded past". The rigidity of the previous education system - with its rote learning, embedded respect for custom and tradition and the strict discipline the old communities felt entirely appropriate to impose - was perceived as an undesirable aspect of that past.

Abolition of the old regimented rows of desks became a central feature of the new mode of education. The open classroom, thought to encourage free and spontaneous experimentation, became the in-thing. Within this, children were encouraged to follow their own inclinations and self-selected projects with the minimum of instructions and impositions. The teacher, far from being an imposer of knowledge (as we saw the system of education in the communities of our visits demanded) became a "facilitator". Their role was to assist pupils in a "knowledge discovering" endeavour, wherein - as one influential teacher-training tract suggested:

Teachers will be enthusiasts and not examiners anxious to create a moral hierarchy of approved books, knowledge and behaviour.

The essentials of this process (i.e. children seeking without external impositions those activities stimulating their interest and innate creativity) we saw occurring informally, spontaneously and unnoticed in the extensive play that constantly took place in the communities we visited. Therefore, the application of its principle was far from new. Around the streets and those open spaces we saw industry had accidentally left for the children to use, this process wasn't recognised as one of any particular distinction. It had the simple name of "children's play".

However, and back to the influences shaping post-war society. In the wider arena, the impulse to escape the restrictive past vigorously "flowered" in the Hippie Movement. This sprang primarily from the college campuses and educational establishments in the early Sixties, whose essential theme was to "drop out" of the traditional way of life. The politically inspired student's riots in Paris and those emerging in other locations sprang from the same source - all directed towards overthrowing the old order and wiping the slate "clean" of all its previous markings.

R. D. Laing's thesis - that a disturbed mental state should be valued as a potential for a cathartic and transforming experience - surfaced in the Hippie centres in the form of using drugs. According to Laing, the societal distress conventional society imposed could be transformed by taking a "shamanistic trip" aided by a perceptive Guru. The traveller would return from that journey with important insights and become an enlightened and much wiser person - consequently reaching a state of "liberation" (to employ a buzzword of that time). The use of the drug LSD (lysergic acid diethylamide) became the main means of inducing this mental disorientation, which would open the way to the believed personality changes.

This "liberating" affect of LSD became the core-creed preached by the American psychologist, Timothy Leary, in his book 'The Politics of Ecstasy'. His "turn on, tune in and drop out" became the hippie mantra as did "pass the acid-test" that he demanded of his disciples. The novelist Ken Kesey - who, in 1962, wrote the novel 'One Flew Over the Cuckoo's Nest' - also took up Leary's theme and abandoned writing to become a high priest of the hippie movement, thereby preaching the "spirit" of the ideas we've traced.

The belief that drug usage could open the mind and allow natural creativity to escape its societal limitations became substantially entrenched in the late 1960s. Many iconic artists and entertainers took it up, believing that it could enhance their talent. Whether or not this implicit approval from people in "high" places was the prime cause of making drug-use acceptable to the wider society is open to debate. Nevertheless, statistics published in 1934 by the League of Nations recorded less than 300 addicts for the whole of Britain. In the 1950s, the habit was still confined to a restricted number. However, in the year 2000 a British Crime Survey recorded 16,000 people in the 16-24 age-group using cocaine; and estimated nearly 1,000,000 in that particular group taking or experimenting with other types of illicit drugs.

More recently, research indicated that over a third of schoolchildren experimented with drugs ranging from cannabis to heroin. At one time - and in that different time containing those 300 addicts - the greatest concern about children's illicit activities involved taking a surreptitious drag on a fag behind the bicycle sheds.

However, the political philosopher Herbert Marcuse (1898-1979) asserted that any social harmony the past might've achieved was mainly by way of authoritarian oppression and suppression. In his book 'One Dimensional Man', published in 1964, his combination of Marxism and Freudianism envisaged a non-repressive society with non-alienated labour and free and open sexuality - this to produce a society with happiness-enhancing qualities. His "vision" excited the emerging counterculture, as did its various formulas for ensuring the demise of the old social order - one of which was exploiting any tolerance and sensitivities in order to erode resistance against change.

The previously mentioned Paris Riots of May 5th 1968, organised by a student, Danny Cohen-Bendit (who went by the name of "Danny the Red") were "inspired" by Marcuse's prescription. However, Danny's attempts to effect its intentions were less than subtle and therefore without success. (He is now - at the time of writing - a reasonably quiescent member of the European Parliament.)

Although Marcuse is no longer on the scene, his ideas live on to influence the present time. Much of the radical opposition towards "Global Capitalism" and the subtle process that we now call "Political Correctness" (that makes use of certain social sensitivities to change old concepts and assert new ones) echoes the Marcuse formula.

The antipathy towards the perceived corruption of the past was, as we've seen, expressed by many influential voices to eventually shape the perceptions of the present time. Previous times were increasingly seen as representing a catalogue of "mistakes", committed by people glaringly different in their attitudes and orientations to what we now perceive ourselves to be. The mixture of error and enlightenment the past contained could no longer be seen as a series of lessons from which we might learn or as offering incidents that can be reasons for pride and emulation, as previous times sensed history to be.

Instead, the new sense of disassociation inclines many towards excluding from awareness those events that seem incompatible with the way they feel events should've taken place. Events allowed to stay acutely in awareness seem to be the ones impelling an apology; and, having satisfied this need, are then held as examples of an erroneous past. This seems to influence the present method of teaching history in a way a previous age would find quite startling.

In that age which would've been truly startled by the present perspective, the chronology of history was seen as a long, unbroken, eternal thread connecting the past with the present and therefore one to hold firmly as it extends towards the future. Prime Minister Stanley Baldwin implied this in a speech he made to a gathering on Saint George's Day, in 1924, when he said:

The sound of England is in the tinkle of the anvil in a country smithy, the corncrake on a dewy morning, the sound of a scythe against a whetstone, and the sight of a plough-team coming over the brow of a hill. A sight seen in England since England was a Land and may be seen again in England long after the Empire has gone. For centuries, the one eternal sight of England.

George Orwell felt something similar when he commented in his essay 'The Lion and the Unicorn' published in the February of 1941:

Yes, there is something distinctive and recognisable in English civilisation...it is continuous, it stretches into the future and the past...

Prime Minister John Major, in a speech he made on the eve of Saint George's Day, in 1993, held to the same theme when he said:

Fifty years from now Britain will still be the country of long shadows on county cricket grounds...Shakespeare still read in school. Britain will survive unamendable in all essentials.

Baldwin's declaration had a satisfied reception. Orwell's sentiment was generally taken as self-evident. Major's attempt failed to raise any enthusiasm. In fact, it raised some "titters".

This inclination to push an embarrassing past into a past that could then be disassociated from the present gained rationalisation from the authoritarianism perceived to have instigated the horrors of the Second World War. Its happening created an emotional scar on the psyche of the immediate post-war period to something like the depth inflicted by the French Revolution on the early Victorians. But in contrast to the people of that earlier time (who were all too ready to admit the terror of the French Revolution as being an aspect of human nature stemming from "original sin", which needed to be controlled) the post 1945 age became fearful to even consider the terror of its own experience could be, in any way, a real aspect of the species to which it belonged. Instead, it hoped such inclinations represented an aberration caused by the distortions embedded in certain social conditions and - echoing Rousseau - inclined towards the belief that all manifestations of evil are somehow related to such conditions.

So, if it wasn't the nature of people that produced the 1939-45 happenings, it must've been the nature of society. The ideas and beliefs of those who asserted this solace were therefore adopted as appropriate, to be reflected in many of the social policies and ideas of justice the present period supports. The reaction against the perceived "socially-flawed" period believed to have induced the horrors of 1939-45 and the anxieties it caused, led to substantial legislation emphasising individual rights and the protection of minorities. From this, various authoritative Commissions, Boards, Committees and Organisations arose in order to ensure the application of these Rights and their supportive Laws in practice.

By contrast, we saw how a strongly felt connections with and respect for the past constituted an important aspect of the socially stabilising neighbourly communities. Alongside it all had to be a willing acceptance of established rules and obligations, even to the extent of subordinating individual wishes and desires. The harmony prevailing in such communities was possible only with these attributes dominating.

The degree of conformity such social homogeneity represented would seem oppressive to the present way of thinking and therefore difficult to construct and sustain. How effective the aims and attitudes the present period values will prove to be has to await the judgement of time; just as the judgement of time has seen fit to pronounce upon those the Victorians and post-Victorians held.

Yet each age tends to believe its view of the world is as the world should properly be viewed; and that its own reactions arising from this viewing are indisputably well placed in their affects and consequences. Each age remains convinced in the rightness of its views until things go wrong and changing circumstances make what once appeared right, appear right no longer - as invariably happens. All periods experience the possibility of unpredictable and unintended consequences, as admirably implied by Robbie Burns in his poem 'To a Mouse': *The best laid schemes o' mice an' men gang aft a-gley.*

But leaving aside Burn's observation of the poor wee mouse's unfortunate experience in its ploughed-up field, there's a more pertinent caveat for our present time in a very ancient insight offered by the Greek philosopher, Plato (427-347 BC), about the road we now seem impelled to take:

All forms of government destroy themselves by carrying their basic principles to excess. Democracies become too free in politics, in morals, even in literature and in art until, at last, even the dogs in our homes rise up on their hind legs and demand rights. Disorder grows to such a point that a society will then abandon all its liberties to anyone who can restore order.

The past, if we care to acknowledge it, contains much advice and many insights. However, each age is committed to form its own attitudes about where it came from and where it should be going and where it looks for insights. Our visits to the past indicated that - even with a clear vision of where a particular period wishes to go - the way ahead will become full of unexpected twists, turns, diversion and changing views. Along this road, the travellers of each age can only adapt to each twist and turn as they appear, and hope the road's direction is favourable to their needs.

The finality of our conclusions must reside in the fact that history and life is a one-way track that allows no turning back. It's as if the road we travel falls away as we progress. We cannot therefore construct identical conditions to those we've left behind, since the materials each period has at hand are always different from those of previous times.

Yet, our present period can justifiably claim it is the first in history wherein concerns for freedom and individual choice have assumed such prominence. In this, we seek to build communities based on a multiplicity of attitudes and beliefs that we hope will be held together by an over-arching tolerance, supported by legal prescriptions.

In the BBC's first Reith Lecture, 26th December 1948, the philosopher and mathematician, Bertrand Russell, implied the difficulties it might create. His first words raised the question:

How can we combine that degree of individual initiative which is necessary for progress with the degree of social cohesion that is necessary for survival?

Although the present period has lost the certainties and sustaining belief previous times may've possessed, it has the advantage of being knowledgeable to an extent thought impossible before a powerful technology created world-wide communications and easy access to extensive information. Furthermore, it has the experience of a long and varied past to call upon. It should therefore be able to envisage the direction it needs to take. However, the many uncertainties besetting its progression appear to indicate it has yet to find the right road.

Yet our wandering along the road of time shows that in trying to comprehend the past we then begin to see why we are the way we are and where we are - and, possibly, know the way we ought to be going?

Perhaps, even in understanding this, we may have gone a little way towards answering the various questions raised in the course of these narratives...

>Omnia mutantur nos et mutamur in illis.
>Felix qui potuit rerum cognoscere causas.

Lightning Source UK Ltd.
Milton Keynes UK
UKOW04f2239290713

214580UK00006B/799/A